Grant me, O Lord, to greet the coming day in peace. Help me in all things to rely upon thy holy will. In every hour of the day, reveal thy will to me. Bless my dealings with all who surround me. In unforeseen events, let me not forget that all are sent by thee. Teach me to act firmly & wisely, without embittering or embarrassing others. In all my deeds & words, guide my thoughts & feelings. Direct my will; teach me to pray; pray thou thyself in me.

(Metropolitan Philaret of Moscow)

The prayer of Metropolitan Philaret of Moscow, one of Rowan William's favourites, here written in his own hand

Rowan's Rule

The Biography of the Archbishop

RUPERT SHORTT

HODDER

Publishers Note

Minor amends have been made to the text between publication
of the hardback and this paperback edition

First published in Great Britain in 2008 by Hodder & Stoughton
An Hachette Livre UK company

First published in paperback in 2009

1

A CIP catalogue record for this title is available from the British Library

ISBN 978 0340 95433 1

re_____n
sustain_____cted
to c_____in.

For Glyn Paflin

Contents

Preface

In 2002, I wrote a slim book, *Rowan Williams: An Introduction*, and likened it to a sketch. Six years on, the rationale for publishing a full portrait of my subject is twofold. In the first place, his time at Lambeth has coincided with an era of acute turbulence in the Anglican Communion. The Archbishop's response to the storm already forms a tale with many chapters. A second ground relates to shifting content. The main emphasis of my first volume was theological, rather than biographical. Numerous details of Dr Williams's doings before his translation to Canterbury – let alone since – remain unreported until now.

Rowan's Rule is thus a more traditionally structured Life than its precursor. I have sought to give due attention to abstract matters (much of the second and all of the fourth chapters deal with the Archbishop's ideas), but the accent is on accessibility. Readers seeking a more technical discussion may wish to consult *God's Advocates* (2005). Based on transcripts of conversations that I had with distinguished Christian thinkers over a ten-month period, this book includes a long chapter devoted specifically to Rowan Williams, as well as several other sections – on philosophical theology, Trinitarian doctrine, Radical Orthodoxy, and ethics – with a bearing on his very broad mental landscape.

A second caveat seems appropriate. As well as not being an

academic compendium, *Rowan's Rule* does not pretend to be a history of recent Anglicanism either. Those hoping for an exhaustive review of contemporary church politics (not a huge number of people, I suspect) will be disappointed. The general picture is sure to be addressed by others at a later date. Meanwhile, the Archbishop's story merits a chronicle of its own.

For the chance to write it, I am grateful above all to Rowan Williams himself, who saw me regularly (including once during his sabbatical in Washington, DC) as my researches developed. Both he and his wife, Jane Williams, have been unfailingly helpful. For agreeing to be interviewed, I thank the following friends and colleagues of the Archbishop, here listed misleadingly in a neutral order: Donald Allchin, John Armson, Peter Atkinson, Anna Baldwin, Alan Billings, John Binns, Ronnie Bowlby, Tim Brown, Michael Burgess, Fred Burnham, Gregory Cameron, Luke Capel, the late Henry Chadwick, Priscilla Chadwick, Sarah Coakley, Robin Cormack, Jim Cotter, Colin Coward, Barbara Dancy, D. P. Davies, Adrian Dorber, Tim Ellis, Barry Evans, Henry Evans, Richard Fenwick, David Ford, Giles Fraser, Gerald Gabb, Ann Gawthrop, Mick Gawthrop, Brian Golding, Tudor Griffiths, Frank Griswold, John Habgood, Glyndwr Hackett, Richard Harries, Simon Holden CR, Nick Holtam, George Hounsell, Owen Hughes, Douglas Hurd, Graham James, Frank Jenkins, Christopher Jones, Huw Jones, Peter Jones, Kenneth Kearon, John Kennedy, Nicholas Lash, John Lewis, Tim Livesey, Pam Lunn, Marilyn McCord Adams, Alison Milbank, John Milbank, Barry Morgan, Peter Morgan, Janet Morley, Ernest Nicholson, Oliver O'Donovan, Tony Pierce, Martin Reynolds, Nancy Richards, John Riches, Chris Rowland, Mark Santer, John Saward, John Saxbee, Peter Sedgwick, Thomas Seville CR, Ken Sharpe, Jane Shaw, Martin

Short, Colin Slee, Timothy Smiley, Chris Smith, Ronald Spears, John Sweet, Stephen Sykes, Mary Tanner, Richard Tarran, Huw Thomas, Patrick Thomas, Angela Tilby, John Walters, Brian Watchorn, Benedicta Ward SLG, Kallistos Ware, Derek Watson, Albert Weale, Lionel Wickham, Cynwil Williams, Robert Willis, Peter Woodman and Tom Wright.

For advice, practical help and other forms of assistance, I thank, Catrin Alun, Pat Ashworth, Stephen Bates, Lucy Beckett, Andrew Brown, Hugo Brunner, Sam Copeland, Peter Cuming, Ruth Gledhill, Jonathan Goodall, David Halpern, Diana Healey, Arnold Hunt, Rónán McDonald, Alister McGrath, Dan Matthews, Josine Meijer, Abeydin Moosuddee, the late Christopher Morgan, Simon Oliver, José Prado, Timothy Radcliffe OP, Renato Rosa, James Rosenthal, Andrew Shanks, Alison Shell, Tom Shortt, Pippa Turner, Rosa María Valverde, Sarah Walker and Hugh Wybrew. I am also most grateful to the staff of Hodder in the UK and Eerdmans in the US – especially Judith Longman, Cecilia Moore, Claire Portal and John Pott – for their kindness and efficiency, and to the Society of Authors, which supported me with a generous grant.

Four people gave me the regular benefit of their wisdom while I was writing: John Walters, Rowan Williams's oldest friend and a priest of rare quality; the journalist John Whale, who died shortly before the manuscript was completed, but commented on the Introduction with characteristic incisiveness; and the sociologists David and Bernice Martin. My debt to them is immense.

Rupert Shortt
London, September 2008

Love is not a victory march

Leonard Cohen, 'Hallelujah'

Introduction

One day in early 2003, Michael Harper, a bearded convert from Anglicanism to the Eastern Orthodox fold, was approached by a stranger in London and asked if he was the new Archbishop of Canterbury. Harper quickly set his questioner straight. By coincidence he ran into the real Archbishop later on the same day, and recounted what had happened. Rowan Williams, then on the verge of his enthronement, grinned and suggested that the two men exchange places.

He has always spoken many a true word in jest. The job of archbishop, like that of pope, is one that holders of these offices are not supposed to seek. Pious sentiment and reality coincide in Rowan's case. He has never been a natural leader or operator, and almost became a monk in his youth. The Welsh friend who described him as 'a recluse with a massive social conscience' was too pungent, but the comment contains more than a grain of truth. Besides, the Church was becoming a much more volatile place by the time Rowan appeared in the frame for Canterbury. The challenge of averting deep splits in the Anglican Communion would have been intractable, whoever was at the helm. As the crisis became ever graver, many people thought that a major intellectual talent had been squandered in forlorn bids to reconcile factions on either side of the gay debate, and all the other arguments – over biblical authority or church government or the limits of diversity – for which disagreement about same-sex relationships is a proxy. And behind the public face, sympathetic observers saw a sensitive human being enduring a prolonged form of torture. Those with access to his study could not fail to notice a large nail, captioned with the INRI abbreviation, mounted on a wall beside his armchair.

During the bad times he can still take refuge in irony, as well as mirth. Asked once for his opinion of a strident fellow cleric, the Archbishop replied by expressing envy for people who view the world in black and white. The remark was really a put-down of those who live in small mental rooms, and never venture outside them. It was also an oblique reference to what he considers to be his core task – the difficult, costly but vital attempt to keep doors open in the household of faith.

Has he been right to spend so much effort in promoting dialogue, or should he have led from the front, even at the price of disunity? On his appointment, opinion about him was split along familiar liberal–conservative lines because of his pro-gay leanings. Later, the debate about him would centre on his tactics and ecclesiology rather than on sexual morality as such, with the result that some of his erstwhile supporters and opponents swapped sides.

One verdict on Rowan's tenure at Canterbury therefore tells of dynamic hopes deflated. No recent primate, on this view, had enjoyed such a fair wind of hope and expectation at the outset. An unpleasant and at times sulphurous campaign was waged against his appointment by hardline conservative Evangelicals, but to many others this seemed like further confirmation of his calibre. In any case, even a large portion of his critics granted that he was an exceptional human being: humble, holy and prodigiously intelligent. His fans added that he would be a great liberating force. At least one well-placed figure described him with reference to Lamb's tag about Coleridge: 'the neighbourhood of such a man is as exciting as the presence of fifty ordinary persons'. Prose, then, would give way to poetry in the conduct of Anglican affairs, and the Church would re-engage the imagination of secular culture – not least through having a leader with sane views about sex.

There were solid grounds for the tall-sounding claims. Intellectually, Rowan is the most distinguished occupant of Augustine's chair since St Anselm (c1033–1109), who framed the ontological argument for God's existence. His profile is unusually high, extending across the Roman Catholic and Eastern Orthodox folds. He is a fine linguist, an accomplished poet, and has a rare talent for preaching to the unconverted, as well as those inside the religious loop. One source of the optimism about a fresh approach to sexuality lay in a lecture, 'The Body's Grace', that he gave for the Lesbian and Gay Christian Movement in 1989.[1] Until that time, traditionalists and reformers had broadly agreed over what the Bible says about physical love: they had simply parted company over whether or not it should be accepted. Rowan recast a sterile debate by arguing that the Bible condemns corrupt forms of same-sex desire, but does not reckon with stable, monogamous partnerships. Church teaching could therefore be revised in accordance with Scripture's underlying message about the link between sex and commitment rather than in defiance of it. At once progressive and anchored in tradition, this conclusion was characteristic of the Williams style – a product of the big theological tent he had erected during the 1980s and 90s.

3

Then, doubters say, the poles of this structure began to wobble. A few months after moving to Lambeth in late 2002, Rowan gave his backing to the nomination of Jeffrey John, a priest in a celibate gay relationship, as Bishop of Reading. By later changing his mind over this appointment, the Archbishop colluded in a decision based on pragmatism, not principle. Liberal disappointment turned to anger as he then blessed a process that produced the 2004 Windsor Report, aimed at stopping parts of the Anglican Communion from acting on their own initiative in disputed areas; and plans for a Covenant, through which provinces might opt in or out in the manner of a formal confession. Supporters of the status quo insisted that the historic appeal of Anglicanism rested in its tolerance. Like the proverbial Australian farm, it is (or was) a Church with few fences but many wells. Theological elasticity over issues of secondary importance had applied at a structural level. The old system where national Churches were autonomous reflected deep cultural differences and a belief that relations should depend on trust and friendship, not on institutional arrangements or enforceable rules. If the Windsor Report had been implemented a generation or two earlier, its opponents argued, then other contentious developments such as the ordination of women would never have been allowed either.

Yet conservatives felt vindicated on similar grounds. The Communion would have faced a crisis over homosexuality whether Rowan had stood by Jeffrey John or not, because the consecration of Gene Robinson (another gay man with a partner) as Bishop of New Hampshire went ahead in late 2003 despite international pleas for the Episcopal Church in the United States to desist. This was the moment at which many traditionalists concluded that the Anglican Churches' provincial autonomy as previously understood was no longer viable. Unity had already been stretched to breaking point over women bishops; now the sexuality question was proving unendurably divisive. 'What had once been like a gentlemanly game of tennis that needed no umpire had . . . become more like a scrappy game of football calling out for the restraint of a referee,' one commentator wrote.[2] The Communion needed to streamline its structures and talk with a clear voice – which is what several of its ecumenical partners, especially in Rome, had been crying out for all along.

In this light, Rowan's stance appears a good deal more justifiable – far-sighted, even. Christians have always differed on whether the pursuit of one cause or another can ever be important enough to break ranks over. Rome's reply, very roughly, has been 'No'. Catholicism thus understood is a conversation, extending backwards and forwards in time. The luxury of sectarianism – of rejecting whatever in the conversation is incompatible with current attitudes – is not an option. The other end of the Christian spectrum is occupied by spiritual descendants of the Puritans – those who feel their certainty about the will of God entitles them to march to their own drumbeat, tarrying for none. Rowan occupies the tougher terrain between these two positions. He is clear that being an Anglican is by definition to believe that gospel imperatives sometimes require unilateral action to break the Church's visible unity. Even when freer to speak his mind, though, he had had a Catholic, as well as a gay-friendly, cast of mind. (He did not support same-sex couples out of a hazy instinct to be 'inclusive', but because he thought the standard case against gay relationships was less robust than often imagined.) While accepting that tradition might not have the last word, then, he felt certain that gay Christians would never win the argument unless they engaged with history.

His many remaining supporters made two further points. First, that conservatives do not come from the same stable: not all are bigots like Archbishop Peter Akinola of Nigeria, who has compared gay people unfavourably with animals.[3] There are thoughtful Evangelicals prepared to countenance a change in church teaching, but not before a full-blown discernment process. Second, that it is wrong to restrict your definition of political dexterity to hardline management. There are other diplomatic skills that manifest themselves in listening. 'Rowan Williams has enacted the collegial spirit to an extraordinary degree,' one Evangelical theologian told me. 'The kind of person given to putting his foot down would only have messed things up.'

So Rowan's apparent weakness has been a strength, even if those with a less nuanced outlook don't appreciate the value of lowliness or of behind-the-scenes work to lower the temperature of debate. This is the second main verdict on his record. A recent historical parallel can also be enlisted in the case for his defence. While much has been made of the differences between Rowan and his predecessor as Archbishop of Canterbury, far less is said about the similarities with his predecessor but one. A tribute to Robert Runcie by the historian David L. Edwards is instructive in this context:

> The crack that he had nailed his colours to the fence was relished and repeated by those to the right or left of his position, and he hated it; but it was not an entirely inaccurate account of where he sat. The mistake made by his critics was that they did not acknowledge that with his complex temperament and the role

changes of his life it was impossible for him to join more than a few crusades: normally he sat where he could see both sides of any argument and try to persuade the two parties to talk over the fence. And his critics also failed to see that, with so many battles going on, a less consensual and therefore less 'indecisive' arch-bishop would have been unable to do the main job in the 1980s. In this job Runcie's performance was more creative than was admitted either by his critics or by himself.[4]

Rowan has expressed almost identical views about the man faced with leading the Church of England through another blustery period. Researching this book, I found a review he wrote in 1992 of *Archbishop*, Jonathan Mantle's biography of Robert Runcie. Tellingly entitled 'Appointed to lead in an age of political thugs', the notice likened Dr Runcie to the allegedly lily-livered Pope Paul VI:

> Such figures are destined neither for charismatic triumph, nor for the overtly noble and tragic role of the straightforward martyr: they carry the unresolved tensions of their communities in their own persons, and so guarantee that uncomfortable truths are not buried. There are worse ways of leading churches – given some of Saint Paul's remarks about the contradictions of being an apostle.[5]

Ultimately, the same kind of approach did not prevent a battle royal two decades on from Robert Runcie's time in office – although the menace Rowan has faced (ecclesiastical rather than secular political thuggery) is a good deal more severe. This is why disaffected liberals remain downcast. The Archbishop's argument and his supporters', that dialogue is itself a form of truth-telling, prompts a familiar counter-charge – that truth is not served by the denial of justice to gay people in a setting where the discernment process has already been going on long enough. If fairness can be achieved only by a parting of the ways, then this is a price worth paying, especially in circumstances where clashes of outlook between some liberals and conservatives are so deeply rooted.

There are lengthy essays to be written about whether current disputes herald even deeper problems for Anglicanism by dint of its cloudy ecclesiology, or whether the Communion's woes are more the consequence of an admirable willingness to face awkward questions. (Amid all the strife of the past few years, Anglicans should draw some comfort from having at least debated a question that other Churches are still too reluctant to confront.) But this is the story of an individual, not of an institution, even though the two are inevitably intertwined in some ways. For one thing, the church rows of the past few years correspond to several other dualities in Rowan's own makeup to a striking degree. He once told his friend Albert Weale (a Cambridge contemporary, now Professor of Government at Essex University) that he thought his greatest sin was pride. Weale grants that this remark was puzzling on the face of it: 'He has a lot to be proud about, yet with all these talents, I would never describe him as a proud person.' Rather, Weale suggests, there is a conflict within him 'that one sometimes sees in very able people'. On the one hand, Rowan has often been turned to for guidance and leadership; on the other, he sees a core part of the Christian message as service to others. In Weale's words:

> He profoundly believes that the soul is central and the intellect not. I do not know how far Rowan's interest in Russian

> Orthodoxy reflects an interest in the idea of the holy idiot, but he once said to me that this idea was important in his thinking. For someone of very high abilities who has a sincere commitment to the idea of the equality of all human souls, there is bound to be a tension . . . I see this as a real problem for a man who is committed to the importance of the still small voice of reason and who is himself reasonable in a very unreasonable world.

A psychologist might want to supplement these remarks with observations about Rowan's status as an only child, and the effect on his personality (even if successfully grappled with) of having been viewed as little short of a genius from an early age. Weale's insights, however, are of greater importance in my view. The enemy, the unreconciled, always has first claim for Rowan: he understands that Christianity is not just about loving your friends. God loves Peter Akinola and Ian Paisley, as well as *bien pensant* liberals. But discipleship *partly* consists in loving your friends. The deeper question hinted at by Weale is whether Rowan's principles themselves – especially the notion that you advance by self-denial – are really conducive to fairness in his conduct of church business. Everyone has their blind spot, it seems. 'Rowan assumes he knows what liberals think, that he represents their view, so doesn't feel he needs to surround himself with them,' a senior bishop told me. 'Sometime ago, I went to a day conference at Lambeth on the future of the Church. No one to the theological Left of me was present. Almost all the rest were Evangelicals and other traditionalists.'

The paradoxical corollary of these factors will now be evident. If the 'other' to which you yield is better drilled and more vociferous, then self-emptying – always easier for white male heterosexuals, as feminist and gay Christians often point out – may well look like capitulation to bullying. The Church of England is increasingly influenced by the Evangelical wing, partly through its size (a fact that any archbishop of Canterbury would need to reckon with) but also because of its campaigning zeal. 'I'm reminded of the way the Militant Tendency almost hijacked the Labour Party during the 1980s,' says the incumbent of a large London parish. 'Rowan needs to beware. Although Evangelicals are better organised, and may beat on his door more frequently than other groups, their views are not necessarily more representative of the Church at large.'

So the accusation that Rowan is vulnerable to the buffetings of others, for all his sophistication, needs taking seriously. Angela Tilby, an old friend of the Archbishop, makes the point with candour: 'I now don't think we would have women priests in the Church of England if Rowan had been at Canterbury during the 1990s. His natural conservatism, combined with the way he always bends over backwards to accommodate opponents, would have stopped him from giving a lead on the matter.'

His record as Bishop of Monmouth also tends to lend substance to this criticism. In some ways it was very mixed. He was admired as a devoted and inspiring pastor, excellent on parish visits, in one-to-one settings, in schools. But his managerial skills were weaker, and in the view of several senior sources in the diocese, he made a number of unwise appointments. Tellingly, the root of his perceived misjudgements lay in his instinct to side with the underdog. 'This caused him to be manipulated by some very unsavoury characters,' one of his former colleagues told me. 'He gave the benefit of the doubt to a number of people who went on to cause chaos.' Another senior cleric rephrased this view more positively: 'Like God, the

Archbishop believes that no one is unredeemable. And like God, he tries to ensure that no one is unredeemed!'

So has Rowan's rule seen a display of uncontrolled forbearance and mercy at the expense of grit and discrimination? To some, certainly, the revelation about his difficulties in Monmouth fuels questions about his suitability for the highest office. The gentle Archbishop himself had pointedly told his diocesan synod on the eve of his move from Wales that he felt like St Augustine preparing to evangelise the 'savage' English. For a twenty-first-century occupant of Lambeth Palace, the ordeal would include merciless press scrutiny: of his sometimes tortuous prose, his well-meaning but not always astute pronouncements on economic policy or sharia law, and even of the (absurd as well as false) rumour that he had attended orgies as a student in Oxford during the 1970s.

It is true that his life was in some respects rather sheltered before his move from Wales, and that he has shown an abiding reluctance to leave his political comfort zone, somewhere to the Left of Old Labour. But the charge of naivety can sometimes reveal more about the accuser than the accused. Christianity is about far more than the art of the possible, and anyone who takes the gospel seriously will know how pragmatism can easily shade into smugness. Rowan is among the last people who could ever be accused of self-satisfaction. If Wordsworth was right that 'that best portion of a good man's life' is 'His little, nameless, unremembered acts / Of kindness and of love', then a large part of the Archbishop's career must perforce remain unrecorded. The news sometimes seeps out, of course. Many know that he was near the World Trade Center on 11 September 2001; far fewer are aware of his brush with death, or of the bravery and calmness he showed in supporting those who assumed that they would die with him. We shall return to this still largely untold story later on.

* * *

I hope that my rationale for clearing the ground at some length in this Introduction will now be evident. I have no wish to lead the reader by the nose, still less to pre-empt my conclusions – merely to explain at the outset why the Archbishop is a multi-layered figure who defies simplistic labels. In outlining some of the main verdicts on him I also hope to have conveyed my familiarity with different points of view, and willingness to report them as fair-mindedly as possible.

A further set of observations seem to me crucial, given that much of the discussion so far has involved church politics. It is unfortunately necessary to point out that theological squabbles about sex are either irrelevant or off-putting to the huge numbers of people with no religious ties, and that the preacher's first responsibility is to talk about what C. S. Lewis called 'mere Christianity'. Rowan Williams would be among the first to draw us back to the deeper matters behind church disputes, and elucidate them with skill.

Some may be surprised to learn that the theological armoury is currently well stocked. Attendance at worship continues to decline in the West, and parts of Britain, especially, are post-Christian. But all the mainstream denominations worldwide are growing. Furthermore, the two decades before the turn of the millennium saw a recovery of nerve in Christian thought (a trend much associated with Rowan himself), and growing opportunities for spreading the gospel in new ways.

To the Archbishop's detractors, even his account of core doctrine is lost in a fog of equivocation. But while it is true that some of his work is under-edited and unduly mystifying, the complaint is unjust. He can encompass very complicated subjects in simple language, but his books and sermons are also grown-up affairs. In the words of Richard Harries, formerly Bishop of Oxford, 'his mind is such that he can't think a sentence without at the same time thinking every possible qualification and nuance'.[6]

Can an evidently intricate picture be described straightforwardly? One signpost comes from Rowan's poetry, which displays the difficulty George Steiner has called 'tactical': the sort that slows reading and attempts to 'deepen our apprehension by goading to new life the supine energies of word and grammar'. The best summary of Rowan's approach has been given by Oliver O'Donovan, a leading Evangelical theologian, who sees his former colleague as a very unconventional apologist. Most varieties of apologetics emphasise how Christianity supplies the missing pieces to the puzzle of existence. For at least some of the time, Rowan is with Kierkegaard in wanting to make Christianity difficult – reversing the strategy of the apologist who wants to purge religion of its bewildering aspects – but then making a missionary opportunity out of the resulting sense of dislocation.

As O'Donovan puts it, Rowan uses his hearers' perplexity

to appeal to an experience of the world that is more broken and less ordered than we usually like to acknowledge. He seizes on awkward and unassimilable fragments that will open the way to the mysterious, those that defy smoothing out, just as faith itself does . . . Rowan can be quite difficult for the proverbial 'plain man'. Paradox and unexpected reversal [are] the essence of a Williams train of thought; the Kingdom of God is always slipping its hand surreptitiously into the doubter's back pocket and replacing the wallet and credit cards with a better-funded set. His engagements with ethics and politics tend to be night-time raiding parties, less interested in knowing how they work than in finding out where they break down, and not with any idea of repairing them, either . . . I have learned something from the apologetics of fracture, perhaps under Rowan's influence. But I don't want to stay my eye on that cracked glass, but through it pass and then the heaven espy.[7]

Rowan the heaven espies too, of course, though to him it may be a little more distant: in theological language, his thinking is more cross-shaped, O'Donovan's more resurrection-shaped. *Tokens of Trust*,[8] the Archbishop's introduction to Christian belief, is one of the clearest, as well as the best, short books on the subject in English. This volume will be discussed in a later chapter, because it distils a large body of more technical material. As a sample of the Archbishop's style, though, one might quote the definition of the Almighty he gave to the broadcaster Melvyn Bragg:

God is first and foremost that depth around all things and beyond all things into which, when I pray, I try to sink. But God is also the activity that comes to me out of that depth, tells me I'm loved, that opens up a future for me, that offers transformations I can't imagine. Very much a mystery but also very much a presence. Very much a person.

For a Christian, there is no better short answer to Bragg's question.

What is more, Rowan's range makes him a better diagnostician than most of the spiritual disease for which Christianity offers a cure. Rejecting the atheist fundamentalism of Ludovic Kennedy (a precursor of Richard Dawkins), Robert Runcie once wrote that 'in the rituals and artistry of faith, one might argue that it is the religious who are the liberators now – keeping open the door to the transcendent lest we be cut off in a self-contained colony of existence'. This sort of remark strikes a chord for the believer. Sceptics tend to remain sceptical. Though very able and urbane, Runcie did not pretend that his teaching rose above the level of *haute vulgarisation*. George Carey's contribution to intellectual debate was trifling. Alone among recent archbishops of Canterbury, Rowan Williams is an original thinker. Before his appearance on the national stage, it was often commentators of uncertain religious allegiance who produced more persuasive accounts of why anything still matters in postmodernity's hollow hall of mirrors. Take a very important reflection[9] by Roger Scruton, better known as a political controversialist than as an accomplished professional philosopher. It casts a sidelight on Rowan's own world view, and gives clues to his singular importance as Archbishop. Scruton begins by noting that there are certain truths about the human condition that are hard to formulate and hard to live up to, and which we therefore have a motive to deny. It may require moral discipline if we are to accept these truths and also to live by them. For instance, he writes,

> there is the truth that we are self-conscious beings, and that this distinguishes us from the rest of the animal kingdom. There is the truth that we are free, accountable and objects of judgement in our own eyes and in the eyes of others. There is the truth that we are motivated not only by desire and appetite, but by a conception of the good. There is the truth that we are not just

objects in the world of objects, but also subjects, who relate to each other reciprocally . . . To the person with religious belief – whether Christian or Muslim, whether monotheist or polytheist, whether a believer in the afterlife or not – those truths are obvious, and their consequences immediately apparent. Religious people may not express the truths as I have done, since I am adopting a secular idiom. Nor will they normally be aware of the philosophical reasoning that would defend those truths against modernist and postmodernist doubt. Nevertheless that is how they see the world. For them the 'human form divine', as Blake described it, is set apart from the rest of nature. Our form bears . . . the marks of its peculiar destiny; it is capable of sanctity and liable to desecration; and in everything it is judged by a standard not of this world. That way of seeing people enshrines the fundamental truth of our condition, as creatures suspended between the empirical and the transcendental, between being and judgement. *But it deploys concepts that are given to us through religion, and to be obtained only with the greatest effort without it* [my italics].[10]

Whatever the exact status of Scruton's beliefs, he supplies a critically important foundation on which to challenge the multitudes who dismiss faith as mumbo-jumbo. Rowan's role in giving a Christian shape to the metaphysical insights outlined by Scruton is pivotal. Another glimpse of the Archbishop as apologist can be seen in his address at an Alpha course supper:[11]

By listening to what Jesus says, and by watching what he does, people's whole sense of their world changes . . . Reading [the New Testament] is like watching people feeling their way into the new landscape and seeing the light in it. Bit by bit people put together a jigsaw and you end up with that really strange and mind-bending notion that God . . . lives in Jesus in an absolutely unique way . . .

But how do we know it's true? Christians have never been able to come up with a simple answer to that. It's a bit like saying, 'How do you know that your husband or wife is lovable?' . . . There's something about the 'knowing' that is involved with your whole personality changing. But of course Christians have always tried to make some sense of it, and to put it into some kind of intellectual shape. Among the things they've said would be things like:

'Does it never occur to you as rather strange that a random, unintelligent process of evolution should have thrown up beings capable of understanding the process of evolution? Has it never occurred to you as a bit odd that a blind universal system, working in its own regular but undirected ways, should produce the questioning, agonising, imagining, loving people that you are?'

Nobody can prove to you that human beings are not the result of blind chance and undirected process, but from time to time it's worth stopping and asking that question. *Doesn't it strike you as a bit odd?* I sometimes feel I'd like to ask that question of Richard Dawkins, a man who has devoted huge amounts of energy and tremendous intellectual sophistication into proving that there is no structure or meaning to the process which he so elegantly, intelligently and brilliantly outlines.

The other thing Christians say is, 'It's not just about mind, it's about love.' 'Mind' on its own – powerful intelligence – is never creative just by itself. Think of human relationships, think of artists – even scientists – at work. It's not intelligence alone – it's absorption, commitment, love, and the leak of imagination that goes with real love. Only love can make something completely different and rejoice in its difference. God is not just intelligence, but loving intelligence – and you can't pull them apart for a second . . . Our existence as intelligent creatures – loving, risking, questioning – somehow fits with the idea that God is a God of loving intelligence, who loves what's different . . . There is no single, knock-down argument for the truth of all this. If there was, we probably wouldn't need Alpha courses, or indeed anything else. Everybody would just sign up without asking any questions.

There is a leap of faith involved – or what I'd rather call a 'leap of the imagination' – that sudden sense of, 'Yup – it all makes sense, I see how it fits.' And the claim Christians make is that when you see how it fits, everything changes.

These words qualify rather than contradict O'Donovan's perspective. The Williams style can reassure, as well as unsettle. Whether it – or, indeed, any other serious form of Christianity – appeals to our car bumper-stickerish culture is another matter. The Fleet Street veteran Andrew Brown makes the point in characteristically bracing language: 'Newspaper readers, like everyone else, have only a faint preference for the truth. They have a strong preference for excitement, drama, and stories with which they can identify. Editors who are good at their profession understand this. (Morally bad ones pander to it as well.)' One brief illustration confirms this point. In 2006, the Archbishop paid a week-long visit to Rome, where he had a productive meeting with Pope Benedict XVI and gave two meaty, well-received lectures. (An unsung benefit of the Williams primacy is that Anglicans are now talking more deeply with Catholics, and getting on better with the Orthodox.) Much of the press paid little attention to a good-news story – that is, *not* a good story – focusing instead on the Archbishop of York's support for a British Airways employee's right to wear a crucifix at work. Then came the predictable barbs about the allegedly clearer Christian witness coming from Bishopthorpe than from Lambeth . . .

*   *   *

Now, perhaps, we have reached an adequate vantage point from which to begin considering Rowan Williams in the round, for his approach to church leadership is deeply coloured by his earlier calling as a theologian. The sundry elements from which his various profiles are composed have been summed up insightfully by Richard Harries, with reference to the Archbishop's book *Christ on Trial*:[12]

> Rowan reflects on the silence of Christ, as recorded by Mark's Gospel. Jesus simply refused to answer the questions put to him about who he was and Rowan writes: 'What is said will take on the colour of the world's insanity; it will be another bid for the world's power, another identification with the unaccountable tyrannies that decide how things shall be. Jesus described in the words of this world would be a competitor for space in it, part of its untruth.' Rowan will know, better than most of us, that anything he says will be part of the world's untruth and the more he conforms to the expectations of the headline culture, the more untruth there will be in it.[13]

Harries – the author of some of Rowan's problems by proposing Jeffrey John's candidacy as a bishop in the first place – once told him that 'God has given you all the gifts, and as your punishment, he has made you Archbishop of Canterbury'.[14] Some of the evidence suggests that Rowan did not know how lacerating the punishment would be. But he did not accept the job with his eyes closed. Elsewhere in the review of *Archbishop* quoted above, the then Professor Williams wrote that the period of Robert Runcie's primacy 'was one in which the good points were about as unfashionable as they could be, and the not-so-good ones constituted massive vulnerabilities'.

These words, too, were prophetic in unintentional ways. Whether Rowan Williams's own vulnerabilities, massive or otherwise, are rightly seen as even deeper strengths can only be judged over a longer – perhaps very much longer – time frame. But interim verdicts are not out of place. There is already a long trail of evidence to follow.

PART I

I

Semper Sursum

As a primary school pupil in Cardiff during the 1950s, Rowan Williams hung his school crest – motto: *Semper sursum*, 'Ever Upward' – beside his bed. He always knew that these words had little to do with secular fortunes. But they could nevertheless be applied to his career, as well as to his spiritual advancement. Grand estimates about a young person's talents often invite scepticism. The destiny of a meteor is to explode. In Rowan's case, though, exalted prophecies became hallowed by time. Students at Oxford and Cambridge during the 1980s regularly spoke of him as a future Archbishop of Canterbury; his oldest friends knew that the forecast had already been echoing for twenty years. The devout boy at Dynevor Grammar School in Swansea between 1961 and 1968 seemed sure to get ordained, and his devotion to the Church suggested a pastoral role more stretching than the narrower beat of academia.

So his formation allowed of few eventualities other than senior ecclesiastical office. His lineage is harder to interpret. The Williams home had a modest feel: Rowan's childhood, like those of Robert Runcie and George Carey, was not stamped with the privileges available to most recent occupants of Lambeth Palace. He was not even baptised an Anglican. His mother, Delphine, came from a Congregationalist clan, the Morgans, who had moved from north Carmarthenshire to the Swansea valley in the 1810s. His father, Aneurin, the son and nephew of miners, was originally a Presbyterian. Yet both sides of the family were steeped in piety, and included notable chapelgoers within living memory. We can learn unexpected things about Rowan by looking upriver from the confluence marked by his parents' marriage.

The genealogical background has been traced by Cynwil Williams in his Welsh-language biography, *Yr Archesgob Rowan Williams*.[1] Delphine was the great-granddaughter of Morgan Morgan, one of a stream of smallholders and shepherds drawn into the Swansea valley at the start of the nineteenth century. Most were prompted by a combination of hardship – life was comfortless in the highlands between Epynt and the Brecon Beacons – and hope of work in the recently established coal, iron and lime mines south of the Black Mountain. Morgan Morgan's route took him from Llanddeusant in Carmarthenshire, along the River Gïedd and through a ravine into the Cwmgiedd area, then known as the Lord's Valley, because of its devout culture. Several villages abut one another here, including Gurnos, where Rowan was born, and Ystradgynlais, a larger community where Delphine had grown up. Swansea lies about ten miles to the south-west.

Morgan Morgan found a wife, Elizabeth Griffiths, and fathered fifteen children by her before his death in a colliery accident in November 1856. Elizabeth had two equally fertile sisters – Mary, who also had fifteen offspring, and Ann, who produced sixteen. The three were hailed as sources of a 'great vein' which has stimulated interest from contemporary local historians such as John H. Morgan and David Richards. The Swansea valley resembled many other parts of Wales in being a hotbed of religious enthusiasm during the Victorian era and subsequently. Generations of Morgans and their relatives rubbed shoulders with figures including Thomas Levi, editor of *Trysorfa'r Plant* ('The Children's Treasury') for half a century, and a pioneer of ministry to the young. As girls, Elizabeth and her sisters worshipped at Bryn-y-Groes, a farmhouse in which local Methodists had congregated before the opening of a larger building, Yorath Chapel, in 1804. By the end of the nineteenth century, Yorath had also become too small for its burgeoning congregation and a chapel called Tabernacl – where Rowan would be christened – was built to accommodate the overflow.

Delphine's distinguished forebears included the Revd William Leyshon Griffiths (Gwilym ap Lleision in Welsh), a member of the Bryn-y-Groes fellowship. He is memorialised in a stained-glass window at Yorath Chapel as 'a faithful minister, a wise counsellor, a true friend, a capable teacher of cynganeddion' (a pattern of alliteration in Welsh poetry with many complex rules). William Griffiths in turn took pride in being a descendant of Lleison Tomas, the last Abbot of Neath Abbey, eight miles from Ystradgynlais, and dissolved at the Reformation. Cynwil Williams sees a thread linking Rowan Williams with William Leyshon Griffiths and Lleision Tomas: 'Over the centuries, from the Middle Ages to the present day, here are three members of the family keeping the faith and supporting the best of Wales's culture.'[2]

Most telling of all, perhaps, is a belief Rowan imbibed with his mother's milk – that he might be descended from William Williams, Pantycelyn (1717–91), Wales's greatest hymn-writer and a leader of the eighteenth-century Methodist revival. This sprang from a decision of Morgan Morgan's son William (b. 1845) to return, in the manner of the Old Testament patriarchs, to his father's country in search of a wife. The journey brought him to Cil-y-Cwm, where Presbyterians had built a renowned chapel called Ty Newydd (New House), in which many of Pantycelyn's descendants worshipped. Here he met and married Elizabeth Jones, before going back to his first home. From the evidence of local family trees, it is reasonable to infer that the traditions Rowan had heard about are reliable.

William Morgan sold books. His appetite for reading was inherited by his children, including Annie, Lemuel (Lem) and Morgan. Annie, mother of Delphine, married a bookbinder named James Morris, and settled in Gurnos. They could count on getting extra supplies of food from Lem, who ran a farm called Pengorof, and for childcare from Annie's sisters. Morgan became a wealthy landowner. Tabernacl still receives a share of the rental income from buildings once owned by him.

The farmhands at Penygorof included Goronwy Williams, brother of Aneurin, who had refused to work in the local mines. The first meeting between Rowan's parents came about because of Goronwy's job. The Williams brothers had five other siblings: Eluned, Rachel, Ceridwen, William and Douglas. Their father, George, lived in Ystradgynlais, and worked successively as a fireman at a local colliery and a milkman in the town. A fervent devotee of Welsh, he banned the speaking of English in his home. This sometimes hotheaded patriarch was from Sardis, a village ten miles to the west. But he and others had shown their independence of mind by leaving home and building a small chapel called Brynawel, north-east of Ystradgynlais. Only his sons got married. His three daughters lived frugally in their home area; Eluned, a cleaner, and Rachel suffered long periods of infirmity.

Rowan's father fared better. His prospects had been raised by his education at Maesydderwen Grammar School, and National

Service in the RAF. After demobilisation, he began working as an engineer for the Ministry of Defence, and would later be responsible for designing lighting systems in public buildings. An array of friends have spoken of him as a mild, thoughtful man, similar in temperament to Rowan. Delphine, known as Del, was more outgoing – a 'compulsive' hostess, as her son recalls – despite severe health problems of her own. It is well known that Rowan almost died from meningitis in infancy, and that his physical weakness as a child led him to spend much time alone. Del had a heavier cross to bear. Polio as a child left her with a lifelong limp, which caused ever-growing difficulties as she grew older. Rowan describes the affliction as follows:

> She had a lot of perennial discomfort with her left leg. Occasionally it was actively painful. There was always, I remember it so well, the awful business of getting used to a new pair of shoes. She had to have shoes specially made, because the one leg was so much shorter than the other, and the left shoe had to be built up. She found someone in Northamptonshire who made shoes very effectively, which suited her well, but then he died. After that it was more and more difficult for her. I recall the pain she went through in breaking in another pair of shoes from another shoemaker who hadn't quite understood the problem.

Born in 1919, a year before her future husband, Del was brought up by her Auntie Polly, a spinster who gave her the extra attention she could not have received from her parents. In further recognition of her delicacy, she was sent to school at the Ursuline convent in Swansea during the 1920s (a very unusual move at the time, especially given the extent of anti-Catholic sentiment in her family). Before meeting Aneurin, she worked as a clerk for the South Wales Electricity Board in Swansea; her cousin Sidney, academically the brightest member of the family, became a Latin and history master in Mountain Ash, near Cardiff. Rowan recalls reading several books won as school prizes by his mother, and sums up the differences between Del's and Aneurin's families:

> It was clear that my father's family were very much closer to a basic ground level of life in Ystradgynlais at the time, with their connection with mining, and several of them working in the local factories, especially the clock and watch factory in Ysta-levera. One uncle [William Williams] must have stopped being a miner when I was a boy. It was the time when the pits were beginning to close: this was a culture that was shutting down. But it was much clearer that my father's family were anchored in that. My mother's family had slightly wider horizons, and, of course, the farming connections.

Aneurin and Delphine were married at St Cynog's, Ystradgyn-lais, around midsummer of 1948, and spent the first years of their life together in Annie Morris's house. Rowan Douglas – his middle name seemed a natural choice, being common to both sides of the family – was born on 14 June 1950. The contrast between the two sides of the family can also be seen in their differing attitudes to the Welsh language. George Williams's contempt for English was not shared by the Morrises and Morgans; on the contrary, Del and other members of her generation tended to see the speaking of Welsh as an incon-venient mark of provincialism. 'I don't think it was an anti-bilingualism on principle,' Rowan believes: 'it was just that feeling, strengthened by the war, which of course took many people out of their normal frames of reference, that Welsh stood for an older, narrower way of life.'

Aneurin and Del therefore communicated in English most of the time, only shifting into Welsh when they didn't want Rowan to understand – a move that naturally stirred his appetite to learn the language. He remembers that his mother's sisters occasionally talked to each other in Welsh, and that they always spoke Welsh to their mother. In due course, they resorted to English more and more; even in his father's family, Rowan detected a steady weakening of commitment to speaking Welsh all the time. On visits to Sidney and his wife Janet, conversation could be bewilderingly bilingual because Del and Aneurin moved in and out of Welsh within a single paragraph. Rowan remembers Janet, especially, as someone who was quite capable of beginning a sentence in Welsh and ending it in English, and who didn't seem conscious which language she was speaking for much of the time. Another consideration for Del was Rowan's fragility. Anything that was not going to make his life easier would be bad, and she reckoned that two languages were unnecessarily stressful.

The trauma that would consume the family in February 1952 was witnessed by Nancy Richards, one of Del's oldest friends. When meningitis was diagnosed, Rowan was taken to the Morriston hospital in Swansea. His parents knew that he might die at any time; having visited him every day, they usually stopped to see Mrs Richards and her husband on their way home at bedtime. Del described how Rowan's lumbar area had been punctured to release some of his spinal fluid and ease the pressure on his brain. This procedure was acutely painful. The infant screamed in terror every time he saw the woman doctor who performed it. Several weeks passed before he was felt to be out of danger; then began the convalescence that would affect him for a very long time.

The boy's early years were thus unmarked by the rough and tumble of a more conventional family life. For a while this made his father's cousin Gwenda think of Rowan as a spoilt brat, but relations were soon patched up. Aneurin moved the family to Cardiff in 1953 when he was offered promotion to a post in middle management. The choice of Rowan's first school was governed (as in his mother's case) by thoughts about his health. He was deaf in his left ear – a permanent affliction – and suffered a limp for several years. Del chose Lamorna, a fee-paying primary in the suburb of Whitchurch which was also attended by several of Rowan's cousins. The long periods at home gave him unrestricted time to read, and his evident talents were promoted by Uncle Sidney, who talked to him in detail about subjects of shared interest, and gave him what he describes as 'very unusual and imaginative' presents – generally books that he would not have chosen for himself. Among these was a Latin grammar that he received at the age of ten. While other children might have looked on this as a mixed blessing, Rowan was delighted.

The picture of his milieu that emerges – tight-knit, rooted in the world of the hearth, infused with a spirit of decency – is reasonably familiar, especially to anyone acquainted with a classic of social history such as Richard Hoggart's *The Uses of Literacy*. Rowan's later writings on culture reflect the influences of a group including Hoggart, Raymond Williams and E. P. Thompson: he shares the gravitas of these earlier figures, along with their disdain for the homogenising effects of television soaps and other forms of mass entertainment. But Hoggart's scholarship boy, one of his most memorable composite portraits, is a working-class figure pitchforked from his original setting by intellect, yet denied satisfaction in his new life by social uncertainty. Rowan was socially mobile as well as environmentally rooted, and therefore almost always at ease in different sorts of company. This says much, not only about his personal traits but also about the opportunities that he seized from the start. Hoggart, moreover, was much more interested in culture than religion, and too ready to take church decline for granted. The seriousness with which Rowan viewed his faith as a child was less unusual than it would have seemed even a decade or so later. His experience bears out the view of a sociologist such as David Martin, who rejects a single-track model of secularisation.[3]

In Cardiff, the Williamses worshipped in the Presbyterian congregation at Park End Chapel, and Rowan went to a well-attended Sunday school there. The minister, Geraint Nantlais Williams, was the respected son of Nantlais Williams, an even more renowned cleric. Geraint preached and taught in English, and many of his sermons are embedded in Rowan's memory, even though he was under ten when he heard them. He later encapsulated his early formation in the interview with Melvyn Bragg already cited:

The Presbyterian Church of Wales was a very great institution in its heyday and more like the established Church than the Church of England sometimes . . . we had a minister who preached with enormous fervour and intelligence, and even as a boy I liked listening. I thought, 'This is exciting.' A big world [was opened by] the hymns we sang, the lessons we learnt in Sunday school . . . all of which combined to make me feel, Yes, there's reality here. And I think a lot of my mental world still is deeply shaped by not only Welsh Presbyterianism, but aspects of Welsh revivalism, too.[4]

In 1961, the family was transferred back to Swansea through Aneurin's job, and settled at Norton Road in the Mumbles, on the western end of the bay. One day Rowan ventured into the local Anglican church, All Saints', Oystermouth, a fifteenth-century hillside landmark much enlarged in Victorian times, with a commanding view out to sea. Impressed by the experience, he asked his parents to take him back there. Within a short time their change of allegiance was almost complete. All Saints' provided the classic, moderately high-church diet known as Prayer Book Catholicism. Preaching and musical standards were high; incense would make its appearance on major feast days. This fare was far richer than that of Park End Chapel. John Walters, Rowan's oldest friend, later quipped that the Williamses were like the Russian envoys in medieval Constantinople who felt transported to heaven by the splendours of Byzantine worship and quickly decided that Christianity should become the new faith of the Slavs.

Rowan's espousal of Anglicanism and his parents' willingness to fall in behind him still seem surprising. Del and Aneurin had been observant Nonconformists, and their son, as we have seen, was already a mature and committed product of this tradition before leaving primary school. The shift was certainly based on more than the appeal of elaborate worship. Historical considerations were of greater importance. For centuries before disestablishment in 1921, the Anglican presence in Wales had been viewed in quasi-colonial terms as a foreign import. During the twentieth century, far more effort was made to promote the Church in Wales's claim to be the country's historic Christian body. This mood gathered pace under the influence of Glyn Simon (Bishop of Llandaff, 1957–71; Archbishop of Wales, 1968–71), who embraced the Welsh language with the enthusiasm of a latecomer, and remains associated with the growth in confidence felt by Anglicans during the 1950s and 60s. Under the tutelage of his Uncle Sidney, Rowan became enthralled by Wales's national heroes and the legends surrounding them; by Hengerdd (the earliest Welsh-language poetry); by the lives of saints such as David and Peulin, and the achievements of medieval Welsh monasticism. The schoolboy thus felt chapel life to be shadowed by a more venerable Christian tradition, and his friends are right to speak of his arrival at All Saints' as a kind of rebirth.

The Church in Wales offered a richer diet than Nonconformity in other ways, too. By the 1960s, many Methodist and Presbyterian clergy could have been fairly accused of reducing their spiritual inheritance to a set of simple and invariably puritanical messages. Anglicanism, by contrast, had been passing through an impressive phase. The 1940s saw a flowering of talent in the Church of England not matched subsequently: T. S. Eliot, C. S. Lewis, William Temple, Dorothy Sayers, the liturgist Gregory Dix, the philosopher–theologian Austin Farrer and the artist John Piper were all at or close to the peak of their powers. As he entered adolescence, Rowan felt a rising urge to breathe the same air as these and other luminaries.

His impulses were harnessed by a formative influence on his own doorstep. All Saints' was run by a very good vicar, James Edmund Crowden Hughes (known as Eddie), who would be Rowan's foremost mentor until he met the great Anglo-Catholic lay theologian Donald MacKinnon at Cambridge. Hughes had come to faith through Anglican sacramentalism, and wrote poetry for much of his life. Service in the army had given him a taste for disciplined routine. Huw Thomas, who was his curate for three years from 1965, told me that he thought Hughes might have become a monk if he had not got married. Like his immediate predecessors, George Wilkinson (later Archdeacon of Brecon) and Harold Williams, he stayed in the post for several decades. On occasion his Spartan attitudes led to moments of chilliness: some people, including fellow clergymen, could feel a little intimidated in his presence. But he was an essentially generous man, particularly with those who seemed to be on his wavelength.

Ecumenism, a movement then on the upward path, struck him as theological fudge. When a parishioner became engaged to a local Methodist, the vicar refused to give her communion. Roman Catholicism – at least as practised in the neighbouring parish of Our Lady Star of the Sea – Hughes considered a species of peasant religion. As a teenager, Rowan spent many hours at the vicarage discussing theology and history. His confidence in Anglicanism was enlarged by the rich trail of intellectual breadcrumbs that the vicar provided.

Differences in ecclesiology, then, were not a trifling matter. But there were also continuities between Park End Chapel and All Saints'. Rowan continued to feel gratitude to Geraint Nantlais Williams for teaching him that life's big questions – whence, whither and why? – were answered by the *magnum mysterium* of Christianity. From Hughes he absorbed two things in particular: that the only truly fulfilling life rests on a conception of earnest altruistic endeavour; and that secular reason is not reasonable enough, because it fails to reckon with the fuller context of meaning that religion supplies. The form of the faith he ingested was orthodox and Augustinian, both a refuge and a challenge. Two brief quotations give a flavour of this heritage. One is Coleridge's description of Christian faith as 'the substantiating principle of all true wisdom, the satisfactory solution of all the contradictions of human nature, of the whole riddle of the world. This alone belongs to and speaks intelligibly to all alike, the learned and the ignorant, if but the heart listens.'[5] Another is a line (from Sermon 163) of St Augustine himself, Rowan's single greatest influence, and the greatest of all Christian thinkers in his view: '*Deambulat autem in nobis praesentia maiestatis, si latitudinem invenerit caritas*' (Yet the presence of his glory walks among us, if love finds room).

Rowan was fifteen when he met Huw Thomas, and had lately experienced a form of spiritual breakthrough. He had learnt that religion is 'not just about words, but it's about developing a sense of a relationship with something, someone, who's enough like a person to be able to talk to in these terms, and yet, enough not like a person for you to need to be very careful about what you are saying'.[6] The fifth-former struck the curate as full of the milk of human kindness, and he stood out further for his very unusual combination of brilliance and modesty. 'We looked on him as an equal,' Thomas recalls. 'He seemed older than his peers, but in a way that did not alienate them.' This status – confirmed by his becoming deputy head boy – may have been easier to achieve then than now. In some ways, teenagers grew into adults more quickly before the 1970s, especially if they were hard-working and bookish. The early 1960s was still a time when 'to be young was a social encumbrance', as Ian McEwen has written in his novel set in that era, *On Chesil Beach*. The special achievement of Rowan, a more than usually complicated boy, was to seem uncomplicated. He had little time for the banausic outpourings of much rock and pop, but still went to parties of a polite sort. Bob Dylan or Simon and

Garfunkel would naturally feature on the musical menu, but as the newly appointed Archbishop revealed when he appeared on Radio 4's *Desert Island Discs* in 2002, Swansea teenagers in the 1960s also sang hymns such as 'Calon Lân' (A Pure Heart) during their knees-ups. Rowan also had a party trick. For a time, at least, he could wrap one of his legs around his neck.

Bryn Davies, a teacher of Welsh at Dynevor, spoke for many in describing the student as 'a quiet, shy boy, but extremely brilliant', for whom a bright future was predicted, 'even though he loved seclusion'.[7] George Hounsell, who taught Rowan Latin for A level, lauds him as the most gifted pupil he ever knew. 'His work was faultless. Sometimes I went out of my way to find mistakes in his translations, but couldn't do so. He was always friendly, other students liked him, and he was never superior. He read a good deal off the syllabus. One of my colleagues who taught English literature pointed to Rowan one day and said to me: "There goes a boy who knows more about my subject than I do."'

By the time Rowan started at Dynevor, his awkward gait had largely righted itself. But he remained rather languid. John Walters, a native Welsh speaker, soon became his closest companion. In part the friendship reflected Rowan's growing awareness of his national identity, as well as his fascination with the 'dark backward and abysm of time'. His sense of history was pricked further by the bus ride to school each morning. Swansea retained some fine Victorian buildings, but its glory had been tarnished by bombing and the hammer of greedy, short-sighted developers. The natural setting, including the bay, with its views across to Devon, was more memorable. A walk up the hill to All Saints' also afforded stirring vistas of the valley and the Gower Peninsula.

The past was present to Rowan's new friend as well. Above all, John was a kindred spirit: warm, loyal, devoted to classical music, equally uninterested in bats or balls, and also contemplating ordination. He is now vicar of Pontarddulais on the outskirts of Swansea. When Rowan's appointment to Canterbury was announced, John relived their early days together in an article for the Welsh-language magazine *Y Llan*:

> We would meet regularly for a period of an hour and a half a week. We hated sports and athletics, both of us wore glasses, were shy and quite plump; by the third year, the Headmaster realised that there was no point trying to convince us of the advantages of keeping fit! Despite that, he insisted that both of us went to the playing fields. The school was in the city centre, and the playing fields a ten minute journey on a public bus . . . Our exercise would be walking and walking round and round the perimeter of the two rugby pitches, three football pitches, two hockey pitches . . . and an athletics track. 'Where's your kit boy?' 'Excused, sir!' 'Permanent note, sir!'; 'Start walking then!' and in the walking and the stepping around 148 other boys who were hard at it trying to be the second Dewi Bebb, John Charles or Ivor Allchurch, Rowan and I would share comments about the Church and the Chapel; Augustine and Calvin; Bach and Mozart; Shakespeare and Wordsworth and, thank heavens, Aneirin, Taliesin and Gwenallt.[8]

The photographic record of Rowan's childhood and youth appears sparse. But words matter more in his case, and there is plenty of written evidence about his hobbies and interests as a teenager, especially as he edited the Dynevor school magazine for a period. He first made his mark with historical essays showing a sharply etched historical awareness, yoked to a disciplined prose style. One, entitled 'King Arthur – Myth or Man?', is characteristic. It was written not long before his fourteenth birthday:

We have probably all heard of King Arthur at some time. The name conjures up visions of castles turrets, fair damsels (usually in distress) and heavily armoured knights. A popular picture, perhaps, but not a true one. There seems to be little doubt as to the existence of an historical Arthur, but he is very different from the Arthur of Malory or Tennyson.

The earliest mention of him is in the 8th century *History of Britain* by a Welsh monk named Nennius. In this chronicle, he appears simply as a successful military leader of the Britons against the invading Saxons. He is the victor of twelve battles, one at Glein, four at Dubglas, one at Bassas, one in the forest of Celidon, one at the 'City of the Legion', one at castle Guinnion, one at Tryvyrwyd, one at Mount Agned and the last at Mount Badon. All these names are obsolete, so we do not know the exact sites of the battlefields. However, it is thought that Glein, Dubglas and Bassas were in Lincolnshire, Celidon in Southern Scotland, the next two in South Wales (Caerleon and Caerwent?), Tryvyrwyd in the south of England (Chichester?), Agned near Edinburgh and Badon somewhere near Swindon. Eleven of the battles are mentioned only by Nennius, but Badon is named in all the early documents.

Unfortunately, Nennius is not always reliable. His *History* is mostly based on legend. We are, however, fortunate enough to possess a contemporary record of the invasion – '*De Excidis et Conquestru Britonum*' (concerning the downfall and conquest of the Britons) by another Welsh monk named Gildas. He has been called, with good reason, the British Jeremiah for his gloomy prophecies about his countrymen and the inevitable fate in store as punishment for their wickedness. He refers to Arthur by his name of 'the Bear' (Bear in Welsh is '*arth*') and states that one of the British kings was at one time his charioteer. He looks back to Arthur's days as a golden age 'When kings, public magistrates, priests and private people all did their duty'. Why he never mentions Arthur by name is a mystery, but one manuscript hints at a personal quarrel between them. He fixes the date of the battle of Mount Badon between 510 and 520, which agrees with the date in the Mediaeval *Annals of Wales* where it is given as 516. Indeed, most evidence points to a British rally about this time.

One more thing we know of Arthur; he was a very devout Christian. Nennius claims that he won the battle of castle Guinnion because he carried with him the image of our Lady, and the *Annals of Wales* state that on Mount Badon he bore the standard of the Cross.

Thus we can reconstruct a picture of Arthur as the brave leader of a united Christian Britain against the Saxon invader. But his successors were weak and slowly the Saxons overran almost all of Britain; Arthur became a treasured memory amongst the Britons of North and West, and that memory has never died.

Dates:

First Saxon settlement – 449 AD.

Arthur becomes leader of Britons – 510 (approx.).

Battle of Mount Badon – 516.

Battle of Camlann and death of Arthur – 538.

Battle of Deorham (Saxon victory over Western Britain) – 577.

Three years later, Rowan showed still greater confidence in disentangling myth from actuality in an essay on St David and his sixth-century milieu:

> David was baptised, it is said, by Aelfyw, Bishop of Mynwy (West Wales; the modern Roman Catholic diocese of Menevia), and was educated at Vetus Rubus, or Henfynyw, in Cardiganshire; legend has it that, when he was in class, a dove with a golden beak would come and 'play at his lips . . . teaching him to sing God's praises'. Later, after being ordained priest, he . . . then embarked on a preaching tour, founding some twelve monasteries, including that which now bears his name, St David's, and here he settled as abbot . . .
>
> The story merges gradually into legend; according to Rhigh-farch, and others, David and his colleagues . . . travelled to Jerusalem, where the Patriarch consecrated them as Bishops . . . After returning from the Holy Land, David and most other prominent Welsh Clerics attended a Synod at Brefi (Llanddewi in Cardiganshire) . . . Unreliable sources say that the Synod appointed David as Archbishop of Wales, a bit of mediaeval propaganda on behalf of the See of St David's during the struggle to secure its independence from Canterbury.

We can infer from these and other writings that Rowan was unusually churchy as a teenager, but his teachers maintain that he was not religiose. Poetry ranked uppermost among his other interests. At that time one rite of passage for an aspiring intellectual living in Swansea was a Dylan Thomas Phase. Unusually, however, it was Thomas as a religious poet who first grasped Rowan's imagination, because of an essay the schoolboy read by a maverick critic, Aneirin Talfan Davies.

Like others, Rowan then began to produce sub-Dylan material, but soon gave up. 'You come to realize,' he later wrote, 'that part of Dylan's skill is to conceal a lot of quite tough connections and carefully worked movements under the fireworkish tricks of the musical surface, and that the surface is embarrassingly vacuous without the tight underlay. I retain mixed feelings about him, but can't be immune.'[9] Talfan Davies engaged Rowan's interest by making a connection between the substance and symbolism of faith – a theme with which the schoolboy poet was already much engaged. 'I saw something of how words – like the Word itself of himself – transform by moving experience from one context to another, how metaphor and transubstantiation connect; how the breakage and silence in language embodies some sorts of gift and meaning.'[10]

These are the rounded observations of an adult; again, it is the school magazine that most clearly charts the spread of his abilities. We have some charming early lyrics about Annwn (the other world of ancient Welsh legend) and the Valkyries. Even as a thirteen-year-old, Rowan was acquainted with the *Ring* cycle – which is perhaps why he felt brashly confident of having outgrown Wagner by the time he entered the sixth form. (As it happens, his mind has not changed on this subject.) He saw sublimities unlimited in the music of Mozart and, above all, of Bach, but felt less regard for Beethoven. His dislike of the Romantic canon owes something to scepticism about the importance of pure feeling and the 'authenticity' of experience.

Among the first of Rowan's maturer poems is 'The Age of Faith', published in December 1965:

The candle flickers thinly in the draught,
And light seeps faintly from high, narrow windows
As stained-glass saints look down with wide and timeless eyes.
The little congregation – women, men and children –
Kneel; enough for them to hear the murmur of the Latin,
To see the priest's embroidered, jewelled vestment,
And coloured, gold-laced tunics of the deacons.
And, above all, to see the little, round, white wafer
The priest holds up; to them it is God's Body, God to earth
Descending, God who died for them upon the rood.
This was the age of faith, the age of relics, shrines,
Of churches and cathedrals, built to God's glory alone;
When God was very close, the Maiden Mother closer;
When England was Our Lady's Dower, and men in truth loved
 God,
And faith humbly accepted Mystery, and recognised
That God was all in all and man was nought.

This was the age which we dismiss as barbarous:
An age of ignorance, credulity and superstition.
Thus, in our age, when God has been abandoned,
And Man become God, we pass judgement on an age
Of Faith: how then shall we be judged?

Structure is subordinated to the message in this poem, with uneven results. Form and content were soon united more effectively; it was the vision underlying 'The Age of Faith' that remained constant.

He also became a capable pasticheur, translating a number of poems from Welsh. His 1967 rendering of Thomas Gwyn Jones's 'Ystrad Fflur' stands out, both from Rowan's other translations and from the efforts of his peers. Ystrad Fflur was a Cistercian abbey in west Wales where 'Dafydd' – Dafydd ap Gwilym, arguably the country's greatest medieval poet – lies buried:

> On trees in Ystrad Fflur, the leaves
> Are murm'ring in the breeze;
> There, sepulchred, twelve abbots lie –
> No sound disturbs their ease.
>
> And there, beneath the mournful ewe,
> Lies Dafydd, sweet of rhyme,
> And many chieftains (sharp their swords!)
> Beyond the cares of time.
>
> In summer-time, the awakened tree
> Adorns its boughs with leaves;
> But man sleeps on: his handiwork
> Decay's slow touch receives.
>
> I see Death's sad oblivion,
> Faith's ruined monuments –
> But when I walk in Ystrad Fflur
> Hushed are my heart's laments.

Later the same year he wrote a poem of his own, 'To the Name and Honour of George Herbert'. Fittingly, pious thoughts are expressed with a large number of monosyllables.

> What sweeter troubadour had God than he?
> Who, with a touch

As light and soft as Easter lilies' scent,
    Could paint, from such
A curious palette as the English tongue
(His brush a quill – a feather from an angel's wing
Brushing his arm), a soul whose love was Christ alone,
Whose tears watered this seed of love to flower, full-grown
Into the brightness of the Son of God, his King;
    One, who, among
Men's greatest praises, highest earthly fame,
    Fixed his intent
On one who was content to bear men's shame –
Minstrel of Heaven's court, entreat for me.

The third main strand in Rowan's written output as a teenager was political. Anti-Vietnam War protests were at their height. In March 1967, he issued a rallying cry at the climax of a 2,000-word article, 'What the UN Means to Me'. That the organisation has sometimes been ineffectual is no reason to give up on it, he warned:

in the past, human greed and ambition have all too often made peace impossible, and so it is today. The future is in our hands, the hands of youth; it lies with us to make the UN an effective force in the world of tomorrow, and thus it is our duty to learn about the UN, and how it affects us and our lives; indifference is still, tragically, all too common. The very fact of the existence of the UN shows that there is a worldwide desire for peace; the United Nations Organisation has a vast potential, and the only hope for peace in our day is for this potential to be realised and made a fact; that will be the task of today's youth, citizens of tomorrow's world.

His faith, too, brought him out into the world. This entailed social work (he regularly visited patients in Swansea hospitals, for example, and helped run a radio request service for them), as well as layers of Christian fellowship. Huw Thomas ran a Sunday evening youth club at All Saints', but Rowan quickly graduated from this to a high-powered discussion group run by Tony Pierce, then a curate at St Mary's, Swansea, and later the diocesan bishop. In the summer of 1968, just after Rowan had done A levels, Pierce took him and other young people to the ecumenical community at Taizé in Burgundy. The group stopped en route to see the great cathedrals at Chartres and Bourges.

When not studying, the schoolboy devoted much time to the stage, playing Dogberry as a cod-Italianate figure in a production of *Much Ado About Nothing*, and drawing unqualified praise for his performance as the Stage Manager, a Chorus-like figure, in Thornton Wilder's *Our Town*. 'I have purposely left mentioning Rowan Williams as the stage manager until now,' a reviewer wrote towards the end of his notice.

I do not think everybody appreciates the importance of this part in the play. The timing has to be faultless; the gestures have to be rigidly disciplined, the tone has to be appropriate, varying from Prologue, to Chorus, to angry old lady, to Minister of the Church, to the voice of Fate itself, and finally to genial Epilogue bidding us all 'have a good rest too', thus soothing us after the emotional strain of the final scene, and seeming to assure us that 'All is best'. All this Rowan Williams did with command, dignity and sincerity. His performance inspired confidence from the very first, and this confidence was not misplaced.

His teachers expected him to go to one of the ancient universities, and he put his name down for Cambridge. The application involved a rare stumble. He aimed high by opting for St John's College, but the Dean (senior chaplain), Stephen Sykes, was away on sabbatical. Instead, Rowan was interviewed by another cleric, Andrew McIntosh, who turned him down. Then rescue came in the form of an offer of a place at Christ's College. On Rowan's appointment to Canterbury thirty-four years later, McIntosh, an expert in Semitic languages, acknowledged his earlier mistake by sending Rowan a postcard in Hebrew. It quoted words from Psalm 118:22 – 'The stone which the builders rejected has become the head of the corner.'

* * *

Cambridge was probably England's most formidable seat of learning in the 1960s. High-minded as well as high-powered, it had an ethos still in some ways very different from Oxford's. The intervening decades have seen a blunting (though not the eradication) of older Roundhead–Cavalier differences. Cambridge, long the more affluent town, is now one of the largest centres of high-tech light industry in the world outside Silicon Valley. But when Rowan went up it was still a quiet, rather isolated place. Hush usually reigned around the university and beyond after 11 p.m.

He remained sociable, as well as studious. The theology faculty was small in those days: about a dozen students were recruited each year in total. But new faces, especially those thinking of ordination, had more scope than most for applying learning to life. The university abounded in faith-based societies such as the Student Christian Movement (SCM), and there was much scope for voluntary work under church auspices. The faculty's small size also made it conducive to fellowship. Under-graduates congregated at the Divinity School, a cavernous Gothic Revival building opposite St John's, for lectures. A good number of Rowan's contemporaries became friends of his, and several, such as Angela Tilby and David Ford, are well-known faces in the Church.

Christ's itself was congenial. Only one student gained admission to do theology each year, yet talent was not in short supply. Two of Rowan's closest contemporaries, Christopher Rowland and John Day, would later hold chairs in biblical studies at Oxford. The chaplain was Derek Watson, a well-liked figure who went on to be Dean of Salisbury. Rowan quickly volunteered to sing in the chapel choir; this meant that he was usually in church four times on a Sunday. Having sung at Matins in college, he went to Mass at Little St Mary's, Cambridge's best-known Anglo-Catholic parish, and later attended the evening sermon at the University Church (usually a weighty address from a well-known visiting speaker). Finally, he would join the group singing the late-evening office of Compline back at Christ's. Rowan himself would in due course try his hand at conducting. Decent performances of Rubbra's Mass and Fauré's Requiem took place under his baton in 1969 and 1970. Drama remained his other favourite hobby; sport continued to repel him.

He was troubled by the condition of homeless people and sometimes had tramps up to his room for a chat and a Welsh cake, supplies of which were sent by his parents, who had recently moved back to Cardiff. Occasionally he would allow down-and-outs to stay the night – in heroic defiance of college rules – if they had no other refuge. Sunday afternoons were spent helping out at a home for children with cerebral palsy in Meldreth, a village near by. Here Rowan got to know Michael Burgess, two years ahead of him and also destined for priestly training at Mirfield, the theological college in industrial West Yorkshire. Burgess's recollections of their friendship are still green:

> Rowan was a delightful personality, without any side. He said he might become a Roman Catholic monk, and I wasn't surprised. He introduced me to the work of Ronald Knox [the Anglican-turned-Catholic cleric], and Rowan himself reminded me of Knox, with his mixture of humour and deep faith. He showed me Evelyn Waugh's biography of Knox with its examples of 'Wimbournes', where pictures and captions are misaligned. Rowan also got me reading the philosophy of Eric Mascall and Charles Williams. We talked a bit about politics. He was very hostile to Enoch Powell and the anti-immigration 'Rivers of Blood' speech. He said Powell was trying to rationalize a view that was fundamentally irrational. And we sang together. He taught me pennillion [a Welsh system of improvised harmony]: I provided the bass and Rowan sang the top line.

Rowan's sense of humour comes across in several pieces of light verse he wrote in 1968–9. One lampoons a self-satisfied prelate:

> I'd like to be a bishop, and among the bishops stand,
> With gilded mitre on my head and crozier in my hand,
> And linen sleeves (with chaste decorum gathered at the wrist),
> And ring – which strict correctness requires should be kissed.
> Such dignity and holiness would from my features shine
> That no rebellious dean would ever fail to toe the line.
> With canons to the right of me, and canons to the left,
> Sweet moderation I'd display, of bigotry bereft.

My pastoral affection would embrace all schools of thought –
Except such sharp fanatics of the more extremist sort:
As Evangelicals – and Modernists – and Anglos too,
Whose narrow-minded prejudices simply will not do.
In short, my measured tolerance and careful charity
Would be as great as any in the dear old C of E.

Another impish poem was inspired by the number of theology
dons – John Sweet, Henry Hart, William Frend, Ninian Smart,
John Sturdy and John Riches – whose surnames were either
nouns or adjectives, or – in Don Cupitt's case – sounded like
other words:

Ah Sweet: Since Cupitt's arrow pierc'd my Hart,
Thou (more than Frend!) alone can heal the Smart.
With Sturdy courage do I now design
To make the Riches of thy beauty mine.

(He presumably tried but failed to shoehorn in a reference to one
of his favourite teachers, the New Testament scholar Charlie
Moule, pronounced 'mole'.) And a limerick pulls the leg of
Mark Santer, Rowan's future principal at Westcott House.

The Dean of Clare College named Santer
Was much given to frivolous banter:
From a sanctified Host
He made hot buttered toast,
Which he fed to the ducks on the Granta.

George Hounsell's feelings about Rowan at Dynevor were
shared by his new friends. He mastered his course work at a

gallop, and imparted premonitions of future greatness. 'We all knew early on that he was something quite special,' according to Pam Lunn, then a maths student at New Hall and now on the staff of Woodbrooke, the Quaker college in Birmingham. She met Rowan at a monthly SCM supper, known as an *agape* meal, and soon saw his maturity and spiritual depth. 'He was an intellectual heavyweight from the start. There was even a rumour that by the time he reached the halfway mark in one of his courses, he was starting to footnote his own work.' This story may be apocryphal; other equally stupefying tales are not. One of the most entertaining comes from Barbara Dancy, a mature student at Girton, who took a lead in organising student get-togethers over coffee and biscuits. One day she asked Rowan if she could borrow his notes from a lecture she had missed. 'Yes,' came the amused reply. 'But you might have a bit of trouble, because I wrote them in Latin.'

A similar reaction to that of Pam Lunn was felt by Janet Morley, who went on to work for Christian Aid and the Methodist Church. 'Though very academic, he wasn't a geek,' she comments.

Early on I had a conversation about the sacraments with him and thought, 'This is the real deal. This man will probably end up Archbishop of Canterbury.' There could be quite a lot of academic hedging in his conversation, but it was balanced by a talent for hitting the nail on the head with the right word. He'd read everything, and yet was still interested in what I felt. Few other men viewed women as intellectual equals. I remember contrasting Rowan with a lot of the ex-public schoolboys at Cambridge who were superficially impressive, though their learning was only skin-deep.

The critic Clive James has observed that men fall in love through their eyes, and women through their ears. If this is broadly true, then Rowan's enormous popularity with female students is not hard to fathom. His wardrobe was plain (its staples were dark clothes under a duffle coat), but he already had a mansion of a voice – deep-toned and resonant. This, together with his charm, gave him 'a sizeable Girtonian fan club', in the words of Sarah Coakley, a couple of years his junior and a future professor of theology at Harvard and Cambridge.

Two of the fan club's leading members were Angela Tilby and the poet Eleanor Nesbitt, who went on to a career in education. Angela was not smitten straight away. 'My initial impression was that Rowan was a funny little Welshman with a heavy five o'clock shadow. I didn't know whether he was a Gollum-like nerd, or an immensely likeable and interesting person. His star quality emerged over time.' The object of all this emotion was often coy with his female admirers; shyness was probably boosted by popularity. He acquired an additional following on the stage. Though not part of the in-crowd that dominated the Cambridge University Dramatic Society (some of whom saw themselves as West End stars in the making), he took part in offbeat productions such as *Le mystère d'Adam*, a twelfth-century French mystery play staged at St Edward's Church in 1970. The director, Anna Baldwin (née Barber), gave Rowan the role of God, and the cast had fun pushing to one side a pulpit once used by Bishop Latimer. 'Rowan's voice was right for the part,' she comments, 'and I could see how mature he was for his age. I tried to get closer to him by going to some theological lectures he was attending, but didn't succeed. I was attractive and had my fair share of admirers, but Rowan seemed unattainable.'

So he was friendly but not very physical with girls. There was no enigma here. He was a nicely brought-up boy. But as the recollections of Michael Burgess reveal, Rowan's reticence is partly explained by the fact that he was thinking of a monastic vocation, as well as the priesthood. If he had a second decisive point in his spiritual formation – a moment when he really began to feel 'taken over' by God, as he later described it[11] – it was round about the age of twenty. The appeal of the religious life was strengthened by visits to Quarr, the Catholic Benedictine abbey on the Isle of Wight. At Downside or Ampleforth, many of the monks are also schoolmasters, but Quarr has a Continental rule of life. The timetable consists of manual labour, study and all the traditional offices sung in Latin. Yet he was not set on one course alone. His attitude to celibacy sometimes see-sawed in response to his feelings about close women friends. He also had to deal with rivalry between his admirers. In his third year he had a romantic friendship with Eleanor Nesbitt, whom he had supported through a period of acute depression. Angela Tilby admits to having been overcome with jealousy. 'I was cross and told him not to get involved with Eleanor,' she says. 'I also thought, "If you are going to go out with any of us, it ought to be me."'

Among the few other students in Rowan's intellectual league was Albert Weale at Clare College. His observations reveal in more detail how Rowan dealt with conflict:

At the time, his Welshness was important to him. I still pronounce 'Caerphilly' 'Cayerphilly' rather than 'Carephilly' after Rowan once corrected me, just as I still say the name 'Dylan' as 'Dullen' for the same reasons. He could be a very amusing conversationalist, and I remember him once excoriating the acting not only in *How Green Was My Valley* but in other Hollywood productions as well. One of the things his Welsh background might have given him is a distrust of the cosy complacency of the members of the establishment. There could be quite a lot of complacency around Cambridge, even among the undergraduates, in those days . . .

He was a person for whom the ideal of service was important, but this did not make him coyly meek or someone who could not correct people when necessary. On one occasion, I had a row with another undergraduate as a result of an incident on a train. I am someone who tends to think of himself in the right on most occasions, and I managed to get myself in a lather of righteous indignation about the matter and I would not speak to the other person. (To be fair to myself, he would not speak to me either.) Rowan had a polite but firm word with me about whether my behaviour was consistent with the principles I espoused. On another occasion, we talked about the subject of miracles. I took a modernist line on the subject, and called in aid a passage in the New Testament that seemed to me to be a plainly absurd account of how some miracles of Jesus were accomplished. Rowan very firmly pointed out to me that whatever the passage might mean, it could not possibly bear the absurd interpretation I was placing on it. He was right.

I might have given the impression here that Rowan could be censorious, but this is far from the truth. Indeed, in many ways he seemed to manage combining firm moral and religious convictions with a profound human warmth and understanding of the frailties of others . . . I was a modernist in the strong sense. Through *Honest to God* and other influences I came to read Paul Tillich, Rudolf Bultmann and Dietrich Bonhoeffer. I still find the modernist programme of whether one can reformulate traditional Christian theology in a vocabulary that is consistent with a disenchanted conception of the world an interesting one. I do not think that Rowan was ever attracted by modernism in this sense.

Each of these comments is exact, and the last, especially, needs looking at in more detail. It reveals that while Rowan undoubtedly fitted in at Cambridge, many of his attitudes to religion were out of kilter with the times. Anglican theology was then on the intellectual back foot far more than during the 1990s or since. The roots of this can be traced back to the Enlightenment, and the limits on human knowledge laid down by secular reason. The process had not only been accelerated by science: theology was still coming to terms with contemporaries of Darwin who had pioneered the historical study of the Bible. As a historical record, the New Testament appeared so murky under the critics' scrutiny that the creed itself was thrown into doubt. Liberal Protestantism had duly recast basic Christian beliefs in an attenuated form – what Weale means by 'theology consistent with a disenchanted conception of the world' – while the Roman Catholic Church had at first turned its back on the debate through blanket condemnations of modernity.

In Continental Europe, the tide turned after the First World War. Karl Barth, the century's most notable Protestant theologian, launched a one-man crusade to insist that theology has its own coherence and can stand on its own feet. His gargantuan project was elaborated in the multi-volume *Church Dogmatics*. In essence, one of its principal arguments is that Christians get their name for God from God's own revelation of his Trinitarian being, not from their own notions. In the Catholic world, other giants such as Henri de Lubac and Hans Urs von Balthasar pioneered the so-called *nouvelle théologie*, which provided answers to the secularist challenge through a recovery of ancient Christian thought, long concealed by neo-Thomism, the officially approved theology.

By contrast, Cambridge and other English universities were relatively untouched by these developments. The world Rowan stepped into in 1968 was still caught in the headlights of liberalism, often hostile to Barth without really grasping the scale of his achievement, and, with a few significant exceptions, almost wholly ignorant of the intellectual currents that had nourished the Catholic world before and during the Second Vatican Council. This mindset was not only encapsulated by *Honest to God*,[12] the best selling theological work in British history, but also by other influential books from the early 1960s such as *Soundings*,[13] a collection of essays by Cambridge theologians including Harry Williams, Alec Vidler and Hugh Montefiore.

There were significant differences as well as similarities between these figures. If challenged, though, most would have agreed on two propositions: that theology should be based on reason and critically interpreted experience, not on external authority; and that the Church of England needed jolting out of its post-war complacency. They were clear that trite formulae needed replacing with fresh ideas about central planks of belief – especially the doctrine of the incarnation – but many of their philosophical assumptions remained undeclared.

No sensitive observer could dismiss the impulse to remint ancient teachings in fresh language; and liberal theology raised important questions of substance, as well as style. Before the Enlightenment, gospel claims about Jesus (his miracles and divine status, for example) had been legitimated in ways often judged indefensible in a scientific age. The implications of this awareness for orthodox belief might be profound – and profoundly unsettling. Rowan was happy to acknowledge the creditable aims underlying much liberal theology, and the profit derived by many who read works like *Honest to God*, which popularised the ideas of then fashionable existentialist theologians. His doubts about the enterprise flared up early, however. In part, this was connected with his remarkably secure faith. Sarah Coakley remembers him as someone 'who inhabited a traditional world far more readily', at a time when she was facing all manner of doubts. Weale is right to imply that Rowan's conception of the world never really ceased to be enchanted in the first place, either at Cambridge or subsequently. He would have agreed with the great insight placed by G. K. Chesterton into the mouth of his character Basil Grant, judge-turned-flâneur: 'Truth must of necessity be stranger than fiction, for fiction is the creation of the human mind, and therefore is congenial to it.' Without sticking his head in the sand, Rowan would have maintained that the creed is for singing, not only for reciting. He might have added that what is too subtle to be said can be sung. And not just what is too subtle, but what is too deeply felt, or too revealing, or too mysterious: these things can also be sung and *only* be sung. As he puts it himself,

> if I say I've never found the creed difficult, I think that gives the wrong impression, but it does seem to me that the kind of difficulty that it represents is not the 'Is this true or isn't this true?' or 'That sounds silly' kind of difficulty, much more 'If this is true it needs a lot of hard work to understand it' – you know, the kind of difficulty that you face when you're trying to read

Frege's *Foundations of Arithmetic* or something like that: the idea there must be something so important here if it's so difficult to get hold of. That, on the one hand, combined, I suppose, with a rather celebratory sense of the creed which has always been very important. I don't think it's entirely accidental or irrelevant to this . . . that I learned the creed by singing it. I don't imagine I'd ever encountered the Nicene Creed before I learned to sing it to Merbecke in All Saints', Oystermouth, and that means it becomes part of the idiom of worship, and you inhabit it in that way, not any other way, which is why, when I came to look at it critically or historically, I couldn't just turn off the music or the context . . .[14]

His head was as committed as his heart in all this, because he also judged revisionist arguments to be defective on intellectual grounds. The Christ of much liberalism is a moral mentor rather than God incarnate; and Rowan saw deep problems with this model on both textual and conceptual grounds. It was unclear how an inspired teacher could be the saviour of humanity, and doubtful in any case whether such a picture was genuinely biblical. As he later summed up the matter when Bishop of Monmouth,

however much of the acid of criticism you drip on to the gospel texts, it remains clear that Jesus claims to be rewriting the rule book and redefining what it means to belong to God's people. He is acting like the God who chose Israel in the first place. In the Old Testament, God had chosen his cluster of slaves to be a people; and Jesus, in choosing his fishermen, tax collectors and prostitutes, repeats and re-embodies this moment of choice: he claims a creative liberty for himself that belongs strictly to God.[15]

So he never seriously doubted that the Synoptic Gospels (Matthew, Mark and Luke) provide a historically reliable record of Jesus' mission. This, of course, is a necessary but not sufficient ground for Christian belief. But he drew a vital theological corollary besides: that if the Church is the vessel of divine revelation, then the Bible cannot be an assortment of texts from remote antiquity alone. To orthodox Christians it is a sacred text, which means that its reach extends beyond the human matrix. Admittedly, this cannot be proved by historical enquiry. Rather, the conviction arises 'from a reading context that assumes a continuity between the world of the text and the world of the reader, and also assumes that reader and text are responding to a gift, an address or a summons not derived from the totality of the empirical environment'.[16]

I have tried to investigate liberal–conservative disagreement at a more technical level elsewhere;[17] for our purposes, the unease Rowan felt can be summed up in one of his pithiest aphorisms: 'If we are not self-created, we are answerable to a truth we don't produce.' The heart of his counter-challenge to what was then the theological establishment springs from the doctrines of creation and revelation. Is religious talk really reckoning with a world we did not make, and an initiative that is not ours? These questions derive from the French thinker Paul Ricoeur, among others. The way you answer them is likely to shape your whole perspective on Christianity. They will also influence your view of what does or does not count as reasonable. And to Rowan, the achievement of the Catholic theologians de Lubac and von Balthasar was probably even more significant than Barth's in the long run, because they subverted the sharp distinction between nature and grace on which the *Church Dogmatics* is based. Conventional opinion had it that conservatives rated revelation above reason, and liberals, reason above revelation. More penetrating Catholic voices, especially those associated with the *nouvelle théologie*, replied that there is no such thing as 'ungraced' nature, and therefore that reason and revelation are complementary elements in Christian discourse. Rowan was feeling his way towards this conclusion as an undergraduate, and it is hard to exaggerate its importance to him.

The theological profile he chiselled at Cambridge stood him in good stead with many Evangelicals later on, because a number of future leaders in this tradition were thinking along similar lines. The experience of Tom Wright, for example, who was then reading classics and theology at Oxford, provides an instructive comparison. Wright often felt patronised by liberals, and frustrated by the (illiberal) notion that full-bodied belief was for simpletons. 'There was a sort of sense of frustration,' he told me,

> and in the universities and in the churches as well, that the theologians were letting us down, and saying 'Well, we can't believe this, we can't believe that' . . . the Bultmannian paradigm was still ruling in the New Testament world, so that it was just assumed that only somebody hopelessly naive and ignorant and behind the times would think that the Gospels actually referred to Jesus. Everybody *knew* that this was Matthew's construct and this was John's pet theology or whatever, and the idea that it went back to Jesus – well, if you believed that, you tended to be greeted with a sneer: 'Oh well, you're taking the Bible a bit too seriously, never mind you'll soon grow out of it.'

For Wright and others, the answer lay in outmanoeuvring their opponents through the quality of their scholarship:

> We had a sense that if you did your homework, if you burrowed down to the historical grassroots, whether it was Qumran or the finer points of historical interpretation or whatever, then you might gain respect by the sheer learning that you could amass, as long as you then knew how to deploy it. So I think that was the challenge. Could we out-think, out-research the sceptical forebears under whom we were studying? Could we actually go away and do the hard slog sufficiently to convince them that we had to be taken seriously, while always being open to the possibility that when we did that we might find things that knocked us sideways?[18]

The New Testament was never Rowan's prime area of expertise, though he later co-led a seminar with Wright in Oxford dealing with the historical warrant for doctrinal claims about Christ. And like all Cambridge students of his generation, he had to study the Gospels in detail. Unsurprisingly, the experience was a mixed blessing. Source criticism, in which scholars took texts with a rich finish and dissected them into their putatively original and independent chunks, was a typical example of the style Rowan disliked. To him and others who questioned the point of this approach, it seemed to be based less on a real understanding of the text, and more on such matters as word frequencies or distributions, and perceptions of inconsistencies between passages read in a literal-minded way. Whether or not this description is entirely fair, it reflects a strongly held view. Rowan expressed his contempt for the technique by composing a source-critical version of *Winnie the Pooh* for *The Garden of*

Eden, the theology faculty magazine he edited for a time with Angela Tilby. Richly ironic, it is still an entertaining read.

So the novice theologian was genuinely counter-cultural, because he rebelled against rebellion. He evidently never felt that Christian belief was something to be apologised for. If one were to cite an opinion that really inspired him, it would have been the best-known soundbite of St John of Damascus (*c*655–*c*750): 'the original is one who returns to the origins'. But he didn't reach this vantage point in isolation. Despite the influence of liberalism at Cambridge, there was a major figure on the scene – Donald MacKinnon, Norris-Hulse Professor of Divinity – whose commitment to orthodoxy was also underwritten, not threatened, by the depth of his thought. Moreover, he was a tortured eccentric with few social graces and no talent for expressing himself clearly ('Donald would even tell you the time of day with the angst of Auschwitz', as one former colleague puts it). What he said went over the heads of his students in many cases: some of the people interviewed for this book admit to spending more time mimicking him than following his arguments about Kant or Hegel.

Rowan did understand the message, and felt deeply swayed by it. He soon hailed MacKinnon as his greatest teacher. Unlike liberal theologians who were cowed by philosophy without always understanding it, MacKinnon was steeped in all the main currents of secular Western thought. His ambition, in brief, was to out-think modernity by undermining a Kantian picture of the world. Kant's model was famously challenged by Iris Murdoch (herself much influenced by MacKinnon) in her essay 'The Sovereignty of Good over Other Concepts':

How recognizable, how familiar to us, is the man so beautifully portrayed in the *Grundlegung* [Kant's *Groundwork for the Metaphysics of Morals*], who confronted even with Christ turns away to consider the judgement of his own conscience and to hear the voice of his own reason. Stripped of the exiguous metaphysical background which Kant was prepared to allow him, this man is with us still, free, independent, lonely, powerful, rational, responsible, brave, the hero of so many novels and books of moral philosophy. The *raison d'être* of this attractive but misleading creature is not far to seek . . . He is the ideal citizen of the liberal state, a warning held up to tyrants. He has the virtue which the age requires and admires, courage. It is not such a very long step from Kant to Nietzsche, and from Nietzsche to existentialism and the Anglo-Saxon ethical doctrines which in some ways closely resemble it. In fact Kant's man had already received a glorious incarnation nearly a century earlier in the work of Milton: his proper name is Lucifer.[19]

Though not a conventional believer, Murdoch had a good deal in common with Christianity in emphasising that there is a moral grain to reality – that morality is discovered, not invented. From MacKinnon's more orthodox standpoint, the Enlightenment had proved an especially mixed blessing. Kant's man, for example, is pride personified. Knowing nothing of sin and atonement, he has few resources for dealing with tragedy, and no real need of God. MacKinnon saw crucial lessons flowing from a due reckoning with the reality of evil: that humanity 'come of age' cannot do without the transcendent; that tragedy calls out for redemption; that the cross is the decisive means by which God both absorbs and transforms evil; and that any theology worth the name must be rooted in an ethic of compassion and love.

From MacKinnon, Rowan learnt his aversion to facile certainty (both liberal and conservative) in religion, and a further lesson he would often repeat, at least before he became a bishop: 'Never think you can resolve a disputed question just by arguing that "The Bible *says* . . .".'

It will be apparent that some of the leitmotifs in Rowan's work come from MacKinnon, including his sensitivity to the dark side of human nature, and his deepening sense that the data of our experience pose the questions to which Christianity supplies decisive but never unchallenging answers. Rowan felt that his teacher towered over everyone else in the Cambridge Divinity School, and displayed the genuine radicalism that most of his colleagues lacked. MacKinnon returned the compliment, in due course coming to regard Rowan as his intellectual heir. Given the older man's intensity, the status was probably a burden at times, as well as a privilege. But the two remained friends until MacKinnon's death in 1994.

His intellectual inheritance was large (it ranged from a defence of the bodily resurrection to Christian–Marxist dialogue), and his top pupil took some years to soak it up fully. The process cannot be seen as positive in every respect. Rowan's prose style tended to grow in complexity, becoming more like that of his guru, as he rose up the academic ladder. Part of the trouble was naturally connected with subject matter, since both men were seeking to ford some very fast-flowing intellectual waters. As time went on, though, Rowan recovered his earlier lucidity. His undergraduate essays and exam papers were models of concision. He would not have scored top marks – a First in Part One of the theological Tripos in 1969, and a starred First two years later – if he had not been clear as well as clever. Much of the cleverness resided in the clarity. A recollection of Professor Ernest

63

Nicholson, who marked Rowan's Old Testament papers, is typical of a broadly held view. It was then fashionable for scholars to dismiss the Exodus narrative (especially the idea that Moses came out of Egypt) as myth. In his Finals scripts, Rowan sabotaged this theory with a simple but devastating observation: that 'Moses' is an Egyptian, not a Hebrew name, and shares the same root as 'Ramesis'. The claim that Moses had no connection with Egypt therefore looks unsustainable. 'Rowan's essays were absolutely brilliant, and I learnt a good deal from them,' Nicholson says. 'They could have been published there and then in a learned journal. The range of his skills – he came top in his year in Hebrew, for example – was also very noteworthy.' Stephen Sykes, later Bishop of Ely, had a similar reaction to his student's term-time work. 'I was hearing things for the first time from an undergraduate. What is more, Rowan was drawing his own conclusions from the primary texts.'

This breadth 'also meant that we all thought he'd do research in the subject we'd taught him', according to John Sweet, a New Testament lecturer at the time. But to be acquainted with textual study was one thing, to find fulfilment in it another. Having left the Calvinistic Methodists for the 'larger room' supplied by Anglicanism, Rowan was once again seeking more space in which to hone his vocation. After securing a place to do a doctorate at Oxford, he turned his back on every branch of theology he had studied so far, and elected to steep himself in the very different thought world of Russian Orthodoxy.

2

Tradition and the Individual Talent

While Rowan had excelled at Cambridge, then, sizeable parts of the syllabus there were unpalatable to him. Studying the Bible as pure history could sometimes seem like analysing a Beethoven quartet in terms of the decibels in its constituent bars. More broadly, he believed that knowledge in theology should be self-involving – the opposite of dry detachment. At Oxford he could follow his own lights. Eastern Orthodoxy in general, and Russian culture in particular, were longstanding sources of fascination to him. As a teenager he had read the great Russian novels, attended Orthodox services in Swansea, wallowed in Slavic music, watched Eisenstein's films. He had become strongly aware 'of an alien cultural presence on the other side of Europe which had a hinterland of imagery both odd and seductive', as he later remarked. From music and literature he moved inexorably towards Russian religious philosophy and some of its key terms, including *sobornost*, an untranslatable word meaning something like togetherness. Above all, it refers to the unity of many persons within the organic fellowship of the Church. The theory, at least, is that members preserve their freedom and integrity, while sharing the corporate life of the whole. Orthodox apologists see a 'Trinitarian analogy' in the ordering of their Church, over against Catholicism's emphasis on juridical authority and the individualistic tendencies of Protestantism. In the earthier language of Theo Hobson, a theologian and journalist: 'To Anglo-Catholics in the 1960s, Orthodoxy had something of the appeal of rock'n'roll: it was exotic, authentic, exactly the shot in the arm that Western theology needed. And blest was it in that dawn to be an ecumenist, for there was a slightly utopian belief in the possibility of reunion – largely an effect of the Second Vatican Council . . .'[1]

But a rosy picture was framed by dark tendrils. Towards the end of Rowan's first spell in Oxford, his friend Hilary Watson, a young woman who was evidently in love with him, took her own life. A tragedy for her, this was probably his bleakest moment before he himself narrowly escaped death near the World Trade Center on 11 September 2001. Hilary, known as Lori, was a talented but needy student in poor health, who had sought and received extensive support from Rowan. He made offers of help in a spirit of charity. But he was also an amateur in the art of counselling, and was on the receiving end of eroticised projection. These aspects of the relationship became fully clear to him only after Lori's death. It was a heavy burden to carry, and illuminates a friend's recollection that 'he was acutely aware of the fragility within himself at this time'. It struck him that he had better acquire the distance-creating skills of the professional pastor or therapist, in case a similar situation arose in future. He acted on the lesson with diligence. By the time he became chaplain of Westcott House, Cambridge, several years later, Rowan was showing a strong non-specialist understanding of mental illness in discussions with experts at Fulbourn, the local psychiatric hospital.

Oxford, of course, had many benefits, including lively social and ecclesiastical scenes, but it never matched Cambridge in Rowan's estimate for general warmth. His first college, Christ

Church, was probably ill chosen. He applied because it was where his doctoral supervisor, Donald Allchin, had studied in the 1950s. Its reputation as a place where rampaging aristocrats bayed for broken glass was chimerical – or at least outdated by the 1970s. Yet Rowan felt sufficiently ill at ease to move within a year to Wadham, a smaller college with a more liberal reputation. Its prevailing ethos had long been secular. That the Governing Body awarded a hotly contested senior scholarship to an apprentice theologian was a clear mark of his calibre.

Despite feeling that he was less in his element than at Christ's, he quickly became president of the Origen Society (a forum for theological debate), and made a bigger impression, both as singer and actor, than during his Cambridge days. He attended daily Mass at St Mary Magdalen's, and was a regular at Pusey House (a chaplaincy in the Anglo-Catholic tradition) on a Sunday morning. Peter Atkinson, a future Westcott student who met Rowan at Oxford, recalls a familiar combination of industry, charisma and piety:

> He was learning Russian for his doctorate. When I first called on him, he was learning the part of Thomas More for a college production of *A Man for All Seasons*. He was singing the bass solo in some college concert or other. Naturally, he was the cleverest person among my student friends. He recommended me books on prayer. He wanted to become a monk.

In retrospect, Atkinson sees certain parallels between Rowan and More – 'two devout men of razor-sharp intellect seeking to thread their way through a maze with integrity'.

The monkish impulses were reflected in Rowan's appearance, which was growing more distinctive and conservative. His clothes (including the trademark duffle coat) remained unostentatious. The beard, grown over the summer of 1971, became a permanent fixture. Not everyone approved of it. 'I think it made him seem more than ever like a *staretz*, or Russian holy man,' says Sarah Coakley, 'and it made me wonder whether he wasn't assuming the persona of someone twenty years older. When I went to visit, it was obvious that he had quickly become surrounded by a circle of people who were absolutely fascinated by him.'

His conservatism was more than sartorial, despite his left-wing credentials. He did not change his mind about homosexuality until reading the 1979 Gloucester report, a church-sponsored document on the subject, and opposed the ordination of women until his mid-twenties. Nor was tub-thumping his scene. Though happy to take part in CND demonstrations, he ignored the sit-ins at the Examination Schools in 1974, held to support the setting up of a central students' union. He occasionally attended services at St John's, Tony Blair's college, and the two would have been in the same congregation there more than once. The future Prime Minister had become a practising Anglican under the influence of Peter Thompson, an Australian graduate student, though Blair's grasp of Christianity would remain unnuanced for some time.[2] Had they met and talked, it is probable that Rowan would have looked askance at Blair's coltish enthusiasm. When their paths finally crossed more regularly in 2002 and 2003, just before and after the invasion of Iraq, the Archbishop's verdict was characteristically wry: 'Tony Blair is very strong on God, but very weak on irony.' Thompson is nevertheless a longstanding fan of both men. He was among several influential figures advising Downing Street behind the scenes that the Archbishop of Wales was the best man to succeed George Carey.

Rowan did not only look like a monk in mufti at Oxford. He was also genuinely attracted to the religious life. Fairacres, tucked away below the Iffley Road and home to the Sisters of the Love of God, became especially important to him. Its rule is based on that of the enclosed Carmelites, and the community included several fine spiritual directors and writers, including the superior, Mother Mary Clare. Donald Allchin ministered as resident chaplain at the time. Benedicta Ward, a junior member of the community, was also working on a doctorate; she and Rowan became close friends. 'Both his appearance and his lodgings in Holywell Street were scruffy, and I think he fed himself rather badly,' she says.

> But I liked him straight away and we had a lot of fun. He belonged to a nucleus of his chapel choir known as the Wadham Singers, which toured the country. He was very good as Thomas More. I especially remember the moment in the play where Rich has been offered a bishopric in Wales as a ploy, and Rowan's enunciation of a line such as 'For the world one might give one's soul, Rich, but for *Wales*?'

Their circle included Hélène La Rue, later a curator at the Pitt Rivers Museum, and future scholars such as Brian Golding, a historian, and Norman Vance, a literary critic. They all met regularly for a walk at local beauty spots such as Binsey, a village across Port Meadow to the west of the city, which has a holy well that provided the inspiration for Lewis Carroll's treacle well in *Alice*. The friends sat beside the Thames reading *Winnie the Pooh* – Rowan was Owl – and other children's classics. In college he joined a group of mummers (players traditionally specialising in folk drama, especially at Christmas), and wrote for the stage, as well as performing. One of his works was a half-hour playlet, loosely based on *Beowulf*, in honour of Brian Golding. Entitled *Little Brian and the Bodley Worm*, it was performed in 1973 in aid of the homeless.

The group went on holiday together – to see the York Mystery plays during the long vacation in 1973, then on a youth-hostelling tour of Brittany the following year to look at some of the celebrated representations of Calvary there. Rowan also helped out at several summer camps in the south of England, where disadvantaged children from south London were given a taste of country life. And the Wadham Singers performed across Britain. One of their tours took them to Llandaff Cathedral; Rowan sang the bass solo in Britten's *Rejoice in the Lamb*. And while obviously rooted in the Catholic tradition, he impressed others by the spread of his sympathies. 'I am a traditional Evangelical,' Golding told me. 'I went to OICCU [the mainly conservative Oxford Inter-Collegiate Christian Union] and the college chapel. Rowan never displayed either personal or institutional antipathies. For several years I visited him in Cardiff for a few days after Christmas. His parents were delightful people, and immensely proud of him, of course.'

*　　*　　*

So he had an active social life, and although there was no one who influenced him as Donald MacKinnon had done, he was befriended by the Dean of Christ Church, Henry Chadwick, and profited from the company of traditionalists such as Geoffrey Rowell of Keble, Andrew Louth of Worcester and, above all, John Saward, who was chaplain of Lincoln during the 1970s before becoming a Roman Catholic in 1979. The student was at least the dons' equal: journals such as *Sobornost* and the *Eastern Churches' Review* at this time give further proof of his range and confidence. Examples include his magisterial articles on the Holy Spirit,[3] on the Greek thinker Christos Yannaras[4] and on the vision behind the art of Eric Gill.[5]

Whence, then, the fragility behind the fireworks? The simple answer sounds pious, but is no less true for that. Like all self-aware Christians, Rowan saw discipleship as a costly struggle, often involving self-delusion and many wrong turns. A potent influence on him in this period were the novels of Iris Murdoch. As we have seen, her ideas have a Christian outline, even if not a full Christian shape, and are in some ways a match for those of Donald MacKinnon. Wadham ran an essay society in which members would read papers to each other after dinner. Rowan once made Murdoch his subject at one of these gatherings. The text of the talk is unavailable, but it is not difficult to identify his main points. Several were reprised in a reflection he wrote a decade on, entitled 'Art: Taking Time and Making Sense'.[6] Murdoch maintained that art is not the assertion of the artist's will over his or her material. It entails something more like submission to the reality or vision being brought to life. So good artists are virtuous, or at least possess some important virtues (even if they fall short in other spheres of life), because the forging of art 'is an image of how human beings can use *time* and the things that live in time (bodies, sounds, stories, textures) to make *sense* – that is, to make a world that can be shared by other beings with mind and feeling'. The good artist is not treating the things that live in time 'as the background for the drama of a greedy self, time for acquisition, time for the success and the consolidation of security – and nor is the virtuous fictional character'.[7]

Some of the most apparently high-minded people in Murdoch's books (James Tayper Pace in *The Bell*, for example) are among the most spiritually jejune, because they haven't stripped away what the novelist once termed the 'anxious, avaricious tentacles of self'. Conversely, the characters derided by others for their lack of sophistication are likely to be holy fools: naive in the world's eyes, but in reality close to the good – or to God.

In different ways MacKinnon and Murdoch point to principles of the highest importance in understanding Rowan's mental landscape. They hinge on a distinction between the saint and the hero. The saint's lineage extends back to Christ; the hero's to Kant and, ultimately (following the genealogy sketched in Chapter 1), to Lucifer. Samuel Wells, a moral theologian much influenced by Rowan, summarises succinctly these two competing models of living:

> The hero is in many ways still the model we look up to in contemporary society . . . We all feel it's our job in our generation to make the story come out right, which means stories are told with heroes at the centre of them . . . for if the hero failed, all would be lost. By contrast, a saint can fail in a way that the hero can't, because the failure of a saint reveals the forgiveness and the new possibilities made in God, and the saint is just a small character in a story that's always fundamentally about God. So the saint's story is a very different story from the hero's story, and I think that distinction between saint and hero can portray the difference between philosophical ethics and theological ethics . . . [8]

Scarcely anyone displays only 'saintly' or 'heroic' attributes, though. Good people want to be heroes at least some of the time, and there is no reason to think that Rowan was entirely free from a universal urge. Eleanor Nesbitt, who found him 'scintillating' at Cambridge, speaks of a 'great white light' coming out of him, and points to the danger in implicit halo talk: 'perhaps there was bound to be trouble in his life at some point, because he was so magnetic. Some critics said that he trifled with other people's emotions. I just don't think he realised what an aura he gave off.' Furthermore, once installed on a pedestal, he might have been hard-pressed to kick it away. 'Perhaps he didn't do enough to undo the projections he received,' Sarah Coakley comments. 'On the other hand, once received, it was very hard to purge them.'

This forms some of the background to the disaster of Lori's death in April 1975, and the unjust criticism later made of Rowan at the inquest. The two met through a counselling network. She was four years older than him, had read theology at Birmingham, and was in Oxford studying applied social work at St Anne's College after an unhappy spell in the Iona community. According to Dr Eleanor Jackson, one of her closest friends, Lori's low spirits were greatly intensified by a combination of chronic asthma and emphysema. She had made at least two unsuccessful attempts to kill herself.

Lori also knew Pam Lunn, and telephoned her in Leicester, where Pam was teaching, at 12.30 a.m. on the night of the suicide. Pam Lunn felt surprised by the call, but chatted for a few minutes, not wishing to sound unfriendly, before eventually asking Lori why she was ringing so late. The reply was evasive, and included the words, 'I want you to tell Rowan that it's not his fault.' Then Lori put the phone down. Having been woken up, Pam still felt groggy. But before returning to bed, she tried to call Lori back (the line was busy), and attempted without success to reach a mutual friend. After several hours of fitful sleep she awoke at 7 a.m., only then realising that the situation might be irretrievable. The inquest revealed that Lori had spoken to a Catholic priest, Father Tom Rock, after ringing Pam, which explained why the telephone had been engaged, and then consumed a lethal mixture of whisky and sleeping tablets. One of her final acts was to turn on an electric blanket. This stopped her body from going cold in the night, and meant that the pathologist was unable to pinpoint the moment of death.

Pam, Fr Rock and Rowan – probably the last person to see Lori alive – were summoned to appear before the coroner. Rock announced that he could not break the seal of the confessional, and refused to take part. Evidently irritated by this setback, the coroner asked Rowan a series of questions implying that he had set himself up as a source of spiritual counsel without due training. 'He was deeply uncomfortable about this,' Pam Lunn explains. 'The coroner asked him if he had any idea whether Lori's suicide could have been anticipated, and Rowan answered sharply with a counter-question: "Do you think I'd have left her on her own if I'd suspected what might happen?"' Pam was asked why she hadn't called the police in the small hours, and replied that she felt this question reflected the wisdom of hindsight. In particular, it did not occur to her until the following morning that her geographical distance from Oxford had been a factor in Lori's choice of whom to call. It meant that she would have been unable to go to her friend in person. 'The inquest was plainly immensely upsetting for Rowan,' she told me:

> The coroner's line of questioning was probably insensitive. But one problem he did identify was that Rowan had a manifest spirituality, and people flocked to him, even though he had no training, all of which was 'unprofessional' because this wasn't a 'professional' situation. Unfortunately, Rowan's humility was such that he

probably didn't see himself as a counsellor in the formal sense. At that time he seemed to be wholly unaware of the transference, to use a psychoanalytic term, that was occurring in mixed pastoral/friendship relationships, such as with Lori. This refers to a process whereby the therapist comes to represent significant others, most often parental, to the client. The expert can deal with this, because they have mechanisms for establishing professional boundaries. In situations involving students at universities, there tended not to be proper boundaries, and fantasies could have free rein. Rowan didn't understand the full extent of what was going on.

Other friends, including Albert Weale, point to a difference in attitudes towards psychological problems during the 1970s compared with subsequently. 'We should not underestimate the influence of films such as *One Flew Over the Cuckoo's Nest*, and books like Thomas Szasz's *The Myth of Mental Illness*,' he suggests. When asked now about the ordeal, Rowan replies simply that Lori's death remains a source of pain to him. He believed that some members of her family blamed him for her death at the time – 'and, I think, still do. That hurts.'

Though it is certainly mistaken to associate monasticism as such with mournfulness, it seems equally clear that Rowan's interest in joining a religious community at this period was linked to his periods of dejection. His undergraduate visits to Downside had resulted in a friendship with Dom Illtyd Trethowan (1906–93), an Augustinian thinker whose then unfashionable views Rowan found very appealing. But the abbey's social atmosphere was somewhat frosty, and he would not have wanted to teach in the adjoining public school.

For a contrasting sample of community life, he went to the Carthusians at Parkminster in West Sussex. Unsurpassed in strictness, the order's way of life is in some ways sharply at odds with the usual monastic pattern, because the brethren are hermits and live in individual enclosures. They even worship and eat in solitude, and only speak to each other during a long walk once a week. For much of their history they have had a special liturgy of their own, traditionally chanted in very slow, rhythmic Latin. Rowan attended the Prior's Eucharist: even a low Mass took about fifty-five minutes.

His special admiration for the Benedictines of Quarr was cemented during his early twenties. He also found a touchstone of authentic witness in one monk especially, Joseph Warrilow, who became his spiritual director. Harry Williams, the Cambridge theologian who joined the Mirfield community during the 1970s after a severe breakdown a decade previously, held that monks are often less, rather than more, spiritual than others. His claim sprang from the lesson that holiness, like happiness, generally comes as a by-product of other activities. The conscious (often self-conscious) spiritual search can be full of trap doors, which is why Joe Warrilow's virtues can be thin on the ground in abbeys and other places dedicated to prayer. Warrilow's own guilelessness was probably innate. (This was my own impression during a visit to Quarr during the 1980s.) Other people acquire an innocence at the far side of worldly experience, for example after abusing alcohol or drugs. Rowan's wrestlings were of a different order. His challenge was to apply his learning to life, which involved tracing clean spiritual lines amid mental complexity. This led him in the end to opt for the commoner path to fulfilment through marriage and fatherhood.

It could thus be argued that his success had as much to do with renouncing renunciation as with asceticism. But did he really stand on the threshold of becoming a monk at this time? The prospect was certainly a worry to his mother, whose view of what constituted a proper career did not embrace the religious life. (Even on the day Rowan was consecrated a bishop, Del was heard to quip that with a brain like his, he would have done better to pursue a high-flying legal career.) And his prayer life was nothing if not deeply serious. Peter Sedgwick, who shared a room with him during an academic conference in the late 1970s, notes that Rowan rose soon after 5 a.m. to pray for at least two hours before breakfast. A query may still be raised about his intentions, though, because he was not also worshipping regularly at a Roman Catholic church in Oxford, or receiving instruction for a possible change of allegiance. John Saward became very close to Rowan in 1971–2, and then, having served a brief curacy in Warrington, when he returned to Oxford in 1974 as chaplain of Lincoln College. 'I think it's curious to ask, first, about the shape of your own vocation, and only then to consider which Church you should belong to,' he comments. 'It's putting the cart before the horse.'

One answer is that Rowan already considered himself to be a Catholic Christian, especially as the ecumenical tide was then reaching its highest point. For an Anglican considering the religious life, it was natural to weigh up the options available to a Catholic, because of their greater variety. But after the first avenue was ruled out by his resolution to seek a wife, the second became far less likely because he could not accept papal infallibility. 'I believed that vocations to the religious life are usually very specific,' he explains, 'so I thought I should meditate on the general in the light of experiencing a particular community. I would have had to deal with the infallibility question at some point, though in fact it tended to be my Catholic friends who said, "We don't believe this either – just keep your fingers crossed." '

The Orthodox option was considered, but dismissed more briskly. As Rowan put it to his friend Sara Maitland, the novelist, he couldn't spend the rest of his life 'in intellectual and ethnic fancy dress'. The apologia for Anglicanism he gave soon after his appointment to Canterbury sums up convictions that he had held unwaveringly from the mid-1970s onwards, at least until talk of a covenant arose in 2005:

> For me, Anglicanism is a Church that has tried to find its unity less in a single structural pattern, or even a confession of faith, than in a pattern of preaching and ministering the sacramental action. The acts are what unifies it – the sacraments and the threefold ministry, and preaching the word . . . If you are looking for a Christian identity that is dependent neither on a pyramidal view of authority nor on highly specific confessional statements, there's a lot to be said for Anglicanism.[9]

This is not to say that the appeal of Orthodoxy was only skin-deep. Donald Allchin told his student as early as 1972 that he had nothing left to teach him; so Rowan completed the thesis under his own steam. Entitled 'The Theology of Vladimir Nikolaevich Lossky: An Exposition and Critique', it was very well received by the examiners, Kallistos Ware (doyen among Anglican recruits to Greek Orthodoxy) and E. L. Mascall.

Lossky (1903–58) left revolutionary Russia as a young man, spending most of his career in France. His achievement is sometimes described as analogous to that of Karl Barth, because he was concerned (at least on the surface) to recall Orthodox theology to its primary data: Scripture and the historical experience of the Church. He was thus suspicious of attempts by some nineteenth- and twentieth-century Russian thinkers to bring about a rapprochement between theology and philosophy. In particular, he criticised Sergei Bulgakov (1871–1944) – the first object of Rowan's research, before he settled on Lossky – for a purportedly excessive dependence on Hegel.

One of Rowan's principal achievements was to establish the relative novelty of Lossky's own thought. Far from being entirely rooted in the 'unsullied' soil of primitive Christianity, as he claimed, Lossky owed a major debt both to modernity and to Catholicism, which made some of his anti-Western jibes look silly. The thesis was not a debunking exercise, however. Lossky's synthesis is presented as having been more original than he himself would have cared to admit. At the same time, due attention is paid to the areas where Lossky's veneration for the Fathers can be taken wholly at face value. The respect clearly shared by Rowan for the intellectual achievement of early Christianity is significant. In the 1960s and 70s, it was not uncommon for liberal scholars to view patristic theology with the same condescension as a contemporary astronomer might display for an instrument used by Galileo. The thesis emphasises how the Fathers steered a middle course between intellectualism and agnosticism through an insistence both on God's absolute incomprehensibility in himself, and his accessibility to humanity. Here as elsewhere, the Trinitarian mystery acquires greater focus. God is transcendent; but he transcends his transcendence, expressing his unknowable 'essence' in his 'energies' – that is, his manifestation in the world.[10]

Enthralled by the Eastern Churches in his own youth, Donald Allchin had also thought of leaving the Church of England, but was advised instead 'to be Orthodox in an Anglican form'. We can get a more vivid picture of what this entailed by looking at contrasting interpretations of a familiar Gospel episode such as the Transfiguration, rather than tracing Rowan's evolution in technical detail. As a sixth-former he had read Dennis Nineham's Pelican Commentary on Mark's Gospel, a classic essay in liberal Protestant exegesis. Among other things, we are told that the Lord's exaltation with Moses and Elijah expresses early Christian belief that the Law and the Prophets testified to Christ, and that the voice from the cloud in Mark 9:7 singles Jesus out as a prophet of the last days. 'But Jesus is more than that,' Nineham adds. 'He is actually God's own Son – indeed, his only Son – the one to whom alone men now should give ear . . . The voice which makes this pronouncement is described as coming *out of the cloud* which had overshadowed the scene, and for St Mark that will have meant that it was the voice of God himself . . .'[11]

Nineham deliberately eschews devotional language in favour of a 'neutral' style. In the view of traditionalists, he risks overlooking the Gospels' status as deeply pietistic works. For a sample of a very different approach – a move, in Rowan's view, from monochrome to Technicolor – consider the following gloss on the Transfiguration from the pen of David Bentley Hart, a leading Orthodox theologian:

> The light that radiates from the figure of Christ is the eternal glory of His godhead shining through – and entirely pervading – His flesh. It is the visible beauty of the glory that entered the world to tabernacle among us in the person of the eternal Son: the same glory that passed through the history of Israel, that transfigured the face of Moses, that dwelt in the Temple in Jerusalem, that rested upon the Mercy Seat of the Ark of Covenant, that overshadowed Mary when the angel of God appeared to her, and that has at various times throughout the history of the Church revealed itself to and in the saints.[12]

Typically for a commentator from the Byzantine tradition, Hart concentrates on the power of iconography to re-present an episode in Christ's life: Orthodox Christians believe that whoever gazes prayerfully at an icon of the Transfiguration should see themselves 'taken up into the incarnate God, and refashioned after the ancient beauty of the divine image'.[13] Some will see a false comparison here, because Nineham and Hart are performing different sorts of task. Two inferences are germane for our purposes, however: that Rowan felt far greater sympathy for the style represented by Hart, but that he didn't think it necessary to leave the Church of England in order to appropriate it.

*   *   *

Orthodoxy charged his political batteries as well. He has always wanted economics to be informed, or even governed, by theological principle – with mixed results. On the positive side, *sobornost*, 'personalism' and cognate terms gave him an integrated vision rooted in Christian assurance about a unity to human experience – the belief that every river runs into the same sea. Bulgakov is especially associated with faith in an all-embracing creative principle that foments unity and makes equal sense in artistic and economic terms. As Rowan puts it:

> He proposed understanding business, commerce and, in fact, much of daily life in the context of creativity. In his book *The Philosophy of Economy* (1912), he said there was no such thing as economic man, *homo economicus*, which was to say, no set of economic answers that could tell us how society ought to be run. The context was Russia's first twentieth-century attempt to modernise by borrowing economic ideas from the West, and already Bulgakov was arguing, against certain German eco-

nomists, that pure economics wouldn't work in Russia. You can see a reflection of Bulgakov in the contemporary idea that pure economics is a fiction; that you need to factor in externals like trust to get a true picture. The Cambridge economist Partha Dasgupta strikes me as writing in a Bulgakovian spirit.[14]

The real question here concerns the nature of the social world to which Bulgakov was responding. If that is not engaged, then talk of personalism at the political level can seem like pseudo-mystical babble. Rowan would not disagree with the assertion that Orthodox theologians have as much to absorb from Protestants and Catholics as vice versa, but he downplays the even larger lessons that the Christian East (and other parts of the world) can learn from the West about political economy. The main reasons for this are readily identified. He has always concentrated his self-critical impulses on his own culture, as well as on himself. It is not his style to claim the high ground (at least not in public), and to tell others they are wrong – even when the evidence points that way.

But the chief explanation for his sympathy with Bulgakov lies in his already established political profile. Socialism was integral to the world view of many Welsh Nonconformists, who tended to stress that Christianity is all about comforting the afflicted and afflicting the comfortable, and that modern liberal society lacks the bonds of friendship underlying communitarian-based political systems. To Rowan, the Left was more likely to stand for such virtues as civic-mindedness, frugality and a critical attitude to the prevailing culture. The Right appeared less interested in many of the concerns dearest to his heart: nuclear disarmament, Third World development, and urban deprivation closer to home. To his critics, his mistake lies in assuming that those who care most about a given problem must therefore have the right prescription for dealing with it. That raw capitalism tends to increase the extremes of luxury and want is certainly true. This is why the welfare state is a force for good, and government action sometimes necessary to break up monopolies in the interests of competition. But this does not undermine claims that the social market, for all its faults, is still the least worst mechanism for bringing prosperity to the greatest number. We shall return to politics in a later chapter, but it is worth noting in the meantime that despite the many problems associated with globalisation, poverty fell more steeply around the turn of the millennium than at any other time in modern history, mainly because India and China, where most of the world's poor live, jettisoned their command economies during the 1980s.

Things often appeared very different in the 1970s, of course. The Left was clearly far more of a force to be reckoned with than today. Marxism was still intellectually chic. Rowan's friends included Ken Leech, rector of St Matthew's, Bethnal Green, in east London. By 1974, Leech had become so alarmed by a perceived political lethargy among high-church Anglicans that he made a public bid to stop the rot. 'Sickly pietism and a right-wing stance in social and political issues' represented 'a serious betrayal of the social tradition of Anglo-Catholicism', he warned, and this 'might spell the death-knell of the movement as such'.[15] Behind this comment lay a twofold concern: that Anglican Catholics had learnt neither from the social gospel expressed in the 1930s by renowned priests such as Conrad Noel, nor from the *aggiornamento* (modernisation) ushered in by the Second Vatican Council.

Leech's remarks struck a chord, and resulted in the setting up of a network, later called the Jubilee Group, which hosted conferences and published pamphlets. Rowan and John Saward were already meeting regularly on Thursday lunchtimes at what was then the Horse and Jockey pub on the Woodstock Road in Oxford; they now used these sessions to compose a manifesto for their colleagues. It begins by quoting another Russian theologian, Nikolai Fyodorov: 'Our social programme is the dogma of the Holy Trinity.' The document then declares that

> We are committed to the struggle of justice, liberty and peace, not because of some secondary interest in social theory, but because of the very foundation of the Catholic faith. We believe that man is made in the image of the Triune God, and is therefore social; that in Christ he is restored to his social capacity for social being. We believe that man is called to share the life of the Holy Trinity, the life and love of communion. We cannot, therefore, feign neutrality, or remain uncritical, in the face of a society based upon the ruthless pursuit of private gain and unlimited consumption. The institutional egotism of all forms of capitalism, including the Soviet collectivised form, must be challenged by Catholic Christians, if we are to remain faithful to the whole Gospel of Christ . . .
>
> We must above all revive the prophetical office of the Church. Now that we are in the death-throes of late capitalism, which threatens to inflict even greater violence on mankind than it has done before, we must make our stand with the oppressed, with the movement for liberation throughout the world.

Like Rowan's remarks on Bulgakov quoted above, this broadside is heavily theoretical. Even other members of the Jubilee Group judged the wording to be excessively gung-ho. John Saward has since disavowed it.

Rowan has proved more reluctant to revise his views on

economics: questionable judgements on the subject were still featuring in his diocesan messages during the 1990s.[16] It is perhaps easier in hindsight to identify the two main sorts of problem with his manifesto. First, it is based on a selective reading of Scripture. Although many contemporary Christian thinkers concentrate on the prophetic critique of injustice, there is a good deal of prosperity teaching in the Hebrew Bible. But while allowing for the power of the critique, one might ask what follows from the manifesto with respect to concrete problems of production, distribution and exchange. What can those who follow its line offer to businesspeople and other wealth creators? David Martin seems to me right in describing Rowan as 'very much the intellectual in avoiding the intricacies and moral dilemmas of [commerce and other areas, such as the military] as not all that existentially interesting, let alone within the ambit of Christian vocations'.[17]

Part of Rowan's economic vision matches that of the so-called distributists of the early twentieth century – figures such as Hilaire Belloc and Eric Gill. They and their associates were not only poor economists: they also hankered after the cultural uniformity seen in the Middle Ages. A further weakness of Rowan's manifesto is that it shows insufficient awareness either of the link between capitalism and modernity, or of distributism's theocratic associations.

* * *

His politics brought out the student's sensitivity to the darker side of life. So, too, in more convincing ways, did poetry. A sample of his best early work is preserved because he belonged to a six-strong group, the Gemini Poets, set up at Cambridge by Eleanor Nesbitt in 1971. The other members – Ian Florence,

Jane Hitchcot, Linda McCubbin and John-David Yule – were also students reading either English or theology. All had birthdays in either early or mid-June. Three volumes appeared under their joint auspices: *The Gemini Poets*[18] in 1972, *Gemini Twin* two years later, and *Gemini 3* in 1987. Rowan edited the first two, proceeds from which were donated to the Christian Movement for Peace.

All three contain fine material, though the quality varies. Rowan is the most adept of the group at uniting vision and technique in a range of idioms. For example, 'Counterpoint', from *The Gemini Poets*, begins by taking a playful pleasure in word sounds, before broadening the context to hint at a deeper, veiled reality:

One   the heavy fastswinging beat of a
       large cheap clock by the bedside lamp,
       with thick black hands that move to
       thick black tempo of a boiling kettledrum.

Two   the giggling hysterical patter of a
       small gold watch by my bookside fingers,
       with skeletal hands that dance to
       the scratching of an insect's fingernail
                            on glass.

Three the slow tumescent heaving of a
       large small pulse in my selfside veins,
       with wordfull hands that beat precariously to
       the muffled rhythm of a tide without
                         a shore.
           This syncopation to a
           Groundbass nobody can hear.

Elsewhere, his focus is overtly devotional. 'Song for Advent' gives a God's-eye view of the subject:

> I shut the city door, come out here
> On dark soil sucked by dark wind
> To throw my seedless words against the earth,
> Speaking myself to nakedness.
>   Here
> I must unknow that there was ever fire
> My hands that formed, that there was ever
> Light of my making. That there were ever
> Words my mouth had shaped. That I have ever seen
> A time that was not winter.
>
> Can there be any day but this,
> Though many suns to shine endeavour?
> And fail here in the unhelped night.
> I have forgotten how to raise the sun.
>
>   And must be taught
> To lean against the wind.
>
> The wind has taken my dropped words, I do not know
> If it will send them back again,
>   But give me words
> That speak my nakedness and do not clothe.
> 'Marana than'.
>   Even so come, amen.

There is technical accomplishment here, and an allusion (in 'Though many suns to shine endeavour?') to George Herbert.

The chief criticism that could be made of this poem is theological. Advent witnesses to the matrix of salvation, and is
therefore a time of joy as well as of repentance. Tone and
subject matter are more evenly balanced in 'Mass for Maundy
Thursday', also written early on in Rowan's time at Oxford:

> Here is the edge, the end
> Of the world, here are the mountains
> And the smooth sea, and afterwards
> The howling gulf, the dragon
> Shifting in his sleep.
>
> Today we gather on the mountain
> Under the scorching sun, to see him pass
> (His step wrinkles the standing sea),
> Dancing upon the mountain as he goes,
> Treading the vintage with his bloodstained feet,
> How beautiful upon the mountains,
> Mountain of spices, under the apple tree, my love,
> And casting grain behind him as he goes,
>
> Casting his corpse behind him as he goes,
> John Barleycorn upon the stone,
> And blackening in the heat, for he
> Has fallen on the outer scarp,
> And roused the hungry dragon, see!
> The flesh dissolving in the sun.
>
> Caught in the nomansland hysteria of despair,
> We parody his falling dance
> In savage and desirous mockery, only

> We find we cannot fall with him.
> But tipsy with his vintage, know
> His seed has rooted us and see!
> The Son dissolving in our flesh.
>
> Oh root of God and tree of man
> And sun that floods away the sky . . .
>
> Cup us to catch your falling light
> To warm us in tomorrow's night.

The influence of modernism is now more marked. Rowan is applying one of the lessons he had learnt from W. H. Auden, T. S. Eliot and others: that a poem can embody the sketchiness of experience – by juxtaposing fragments of speech, for example, or by dredging up words from a depth at which they might function symbolically.

It was Eliot who absorbed Rowan more than any other poet during his time as a graduate student. A passionate interest was reflected in his lectures on the *Four Quartets*,[19] delivered in New York in 1974, and to the sisters at Fairacres in 1975. The invitation to speak at General Theological Seminary in Manhattan was a mark of his growing reputation in itself. He enjoyed his first taste of America, and took the chance to visit Fr Georges Florovsky, a celebrated figure, at St Vladimir's Seminary in Crestwood, New York. (Anyone studying Russian Orthodoxy at this time would have found more research material in France or the United States than in the Soviet Union.) The lectures are not only based on a close reading of the text. They include a remarkably mature summary of Rowan's wider vision. Some commentators are uncertain whether the *Quartets* embody a truly Christian statement: they see traces of Manichaeism in Eliot's general avoidance of openly religious imagery. Others, certain that a committed Anglican could not have left his faith behind, have conceived of them as a labyrinth of coded Christian messages. The truth, in Rowan's view, is less straightforward. The *Quartets* are an essay in negative or apophatic theology (looking beyond human categories to the God who eludes our understanding), and their power therefore resides in their reticence:

> The vision of faith can be a 'torment', because its wholeness is so hard to retain, because, as 'Dry Salvages' proclaims, waste and failure in the world are constantly present to it; inevitably, then, faith is condemned to contradiction, to dialectic; and this the *Quartets* faithfully reproduce. The only nourishment of faith is, for Eliot, a doctrine of [the] Incarnation which some may regard as bleak and pessimistic, the doctrine of 'East Coker' IV, which – again, without explicitly dogmatic articulation – speaks of God, like us, 'defeated' for our liberation. In spite of everything, 'we call this Friday good', and, in spite of the insistence on such a theology of the cross, the vision of faith cannot ultimately be pessimistic: even if it *is* tragic, 'all shall be well'.

This argument is not strong enough to convince those who doubt whether the *Quartets* exhibit such coherence and theological sophistication. Rowan is especially vulnerable to a charge of special pleading when he argues that Eliot 'has imaginatively embodied his belief so faithfully that its . . . dogmatic structure is left almost totally unspoken'. But whether or not the lectures convince us about Eliot, they tell us a good deal about the lecturer. For this reason in particular, Rowan's conclusion deserves to be quoted in full:

Only if we are ready to look honestly at the depth of the world's dereliction and understand what is involved in claiming that *this* is the theatre of God's action can we begin to talk about transfiguration and healing; only when we have some idea of how difficult it is to speak of God's action *at all* can we intelligibly speak of His saving action . . . the *Four Quartets* recalls us, as so few other contemporary Christian statements, to an acknowledgement of the real difficulties of theology which are, at root, not intellectual, but personal and imaginative. It reminds us of the sheer *oddity* of witnessing to the Incarnation as an historical matter, the 'midwinter spring' of an otherwise unrelieved history, yet itself on the edge of nonsense. Theology's calling in the future is perhaps to rediscover the 'wisdom of humility'; to 'die with the dying', to accept the cost of 'simplicity', in order once again to hear, however faintly, the music of the spheres beyond the bewildering counterpoint of the world in which it begins.

* * *

Delayed by the fallout from Lori's death, Rowan's thesis was finished and passed in early 1975. It went without saying that a scholarly future lay within his grasp, but the job market for academic theologians was sluggish. The difficulty of getting a foot on the ladder was underlined for him when he applied unsuccessfully for a lectureship at Durham. Ann Loades, the internal candidate, got the job and held it down until her retirement thirty years later. Durham tends to keep its theologians for long stretches. Rowan's career may therefore have unfolded differently if he had secured a job there. But a few months later he was plucked from his temporary job labelling historic musical instruments at Oxford's Pitt Rivers Museum (and saved from the prospect of joining the dole queue) when

John Walters introduced him to Dennis Lloyd of the Community of the Resurrection at Mirfield. This quasi-monastic order runs its theological college on adjacent premises, and a new lecturer was being sought to teach history and doctrine there. Rowan was interviewed for the post, and was given a two-year contract straight away on an annual salary of £1,500. Board and lodging were free.

Founded in 1892 by Charles Gore, sometime Bishop of Oxford, in a former mill, Mirfield is more like an oratory (where priests share a common life under one roof, but come and go fairly freely) than a traditional monastic house. When Rowan arrived, it was in disarray. Hugh Bishop, the Superior, had left the community in 1974 to pursue a gay relationship; and one or two Mirfield men a year had been departing to become Roman Catholics for over a decade. Morale remained very low, and the governing council closed down the noviciate for two years. Those who remained included men of calibre, however, and Rowan thrived alongside figures such as Benedict Green, then principal of the theological college; Eric Simmons, the new Superior; and Simon Holden.

His liking for them was reciprocated. Green soon spotted the sombre side – he termed it 'a streak of residual Calvinism' – in his new colleague. But as in earlier phases of Rowan's career, he was also thought to be kind, likeable and endowed with something much rarer – a strong spiritual presence. Simon Holden speaks for others in suggesting that

> when you talked to him, it was as though you were in an arena of prayer. He never seemed to talk from either the head or the heart alone. Both were always firing equally. And there was a tremendous and unfashionable stillness about him . . . He made me

feel that what I was giving was as important as what he was giving.

His academic dash impressed the Mirfield men with equal force. Green judged that no one had ever possessed such an exceptional range, and that Rowan showed a 'perfect balance' between the analytic and the synthetic. 'That is very rare . . . I was constantly consulting him on matters of medieval thought. He seemed to have read virtually everything.'

Closer to the concerns of laypeople, as well as many theologians, was debate over the ordination of women – a subject that generated as much fervour in many quarters then as gay clergy today, or the theories of Darwin in Victorian times. The young lecturer first sided with the traditionalists, accepting their view that the apostles were male, and therefore that only a man may represent Christ at the altar. That this dispute serves as a bellwether for Rowan's evolution is borne out by the way his thinking changed in 1976 and 1977. Conservatives regularly complained of a tendency among liberals to mistake transient moments of development for permanent embodiments of the Church's founding principles. Opponents of change could make hay with this idea (the trendy vicar had fast become a figure of national fun), but many traditionalists failed to see how their argument might rebound on them. Slavery, patriarchy, a strict ban on usury: these, too, were part of the social landscape in ancient times and later, but had eventually been dismissed as relics of a superseded cultural milieu. When Pam Lunn told Rowan in his Wadham days that to oppose the ordination of women was like denying holy orders to black people, he at first dismissed her argument as a non sequitur. Further contact with feminists and their writings persuaded him that Lunn had a point.

If anything, he came to feel that the theological element in the debate was even more decisive, because the case for reform could be inferred from the incarnation itself. Early Christian reflection had been grounded in the claim that 'the unassumed is unhealed': and Christ had 'assumed' representative humanity, not only maleness. Much discussion in this area fostered the impression that there were only two options: accepting tradition, or jettisoning it. A glance at Rowan's view demonstrates the superficiality of such a picture. By the time he came to give his most important addresseses on the subject – at the 1988 Lambeth Conference, and during the Church in Wales's debate on women priests in 1993 – his argument had become very finely honed through frequent repetition. It runs like this. All Christian priesthood has its ground in the priestly work of Jesus. The *function* of ministerial priesthood is given to some by God's call, so that the *dignity* belonging to all may be received. To infer that women cannot be priests entails two assumptions incompatible with the New Testament model of priesthood: that the ordained priest's relation to the priesthood of Christ is different in kind from that of the baptised person; and that a baptised woman's relation to Christ's priesthood is substantially different from a baptised man's. For those who reject these assumptions, it follows that the ordination of women is perfectly compatible with Catholic orthodoxy.

Vatican opposition to the reform has been restated with growing vehemence in recent decades, beginning with Paul VI's 1976 encyclical *Inter Insigniores*. Eighteen years on, John Paul II's apostolic letter *Ordinatio Sacerdotalis* stated that '[i]n order that all doubt may be removed regarding a matter of great importance . . . in virtue of my ministry of confirming the brethren I declare that the Church has no authority whatsoever to confer priestly ordination on women and that this judgement is to be definitively held by all the Church's faithful'. In 1998, Cardinal Joseph Ratzinger took the very drastic step of stating that supporters of women priests were 'no longer in full communion with the Catholic Church'.[20] The future Pope assumed that ordaining women would be a denial of divinely revealed doctrine, and therefore of beliefs held 'always, everywhere and by all' (*quod semper, quod ubique et quod ab omnibus tenendum est*). But for Rowan, both at Mirfield and subsequently, this was to beg the question. It also explains why he has never been able to accept the strongest Anglo-Catholic argument against women priests – that reform constitutes too grave a sin against unity to be warrantable. His reply, as we have seen, is that to be an Anglican in the first place is to believe that there are circumstances in which gospel standards legitimise independent action.

The story of his change of heart over women priests would be incomplete without a reference to more subjective matters. As he put it to Angela Tilby, 'I had to change after looking around at my own side, and seeing the company I was keeping.'

*   *   *

The doleful periods in his mid-twenties were caused by an inconclusive and one-sided romantic attachment, as well as by politics and theology: the woman concerned remained a friend, but wasn't responsive to anything beyond friendship. This much he is prepared to admit, but almost all other details of the relationship (including the identity of the woman concerned) are still private. Since he was solaced by poetry, though, and wrote a sequence of eight sonnets called 'Crossings' about the liaison, we have some public impressions of the heartache it caused. The first and last stanzas give an idea of the whole:

While I sit mute, suspicious of my choice
(Reserve or fluency), how do I reach
You, then, across the acres of the room?
Yes, all the platitudes are clear enough:
Muteness is eloquence, silence is the stuff
Of sharing, while hands work a busy loom;
But on your flesh my hands will still be blind.
Your face is shut. Your body gives no voice,
But charts a distance. How do we avoid
A treaty with the compromising word?
Knowing that after, when we have destroyed
The ambiguity, the precious surd, we shall find
Our honesty still waits to be aligned? . . .

So did we ever have an assignation
Under the station clock? an intersection
Of complicated routes? Was there a break
Between connections when we might have snatched a word,
Unusual and hard and timely, stirred
By urgencies too close for us to make
Excuses, plead appointments for protection,
Slew our eyes round, sketch a retreat formation
Into the distance promised by the hiss
And echo of things setting to depart
All round? Eyes scattering far and anxious not to miss
Something or anything; travelling apart.
You never came, we both of us could say,
Angry, relieved, rejected, gone away.

Reflecting later on poetry's underlying importance to him,
Rowan cited W. H. Auden and Geoffrey Hill as his most

formative influences during his twenties alongside Eliot.[21] He 'perspired' over his own sonnets, counted syllables and stresses, recalled Dylan Thomas's verbal games, then 'lurched towards Hopkins and hastily recovered'. It was Auden who taught him how ideas-based poetry must face the challenge of 'acting in language', and Hill who said something central about religious verse by undermining his own music so as to leave a gap through which a deeper 'voice' is heard or hinted at. 'I can't imagine poetry without the awkward overlap with the territory of faith and sacrament and . . . redemption,' he concluded. 'Geoffrey Hill wrote years ago of poetry as "menace" and "atonement"; that seems about right to me as someone attempting in various modes the languages of both faith and poetry.'[22]

And what of his professional work at this formative time? Inevitably, Rowan's student writings had largely been expositions of other people's ideas. Mirfield was the place where his own identity as a theologian took shape. The intellectual ground he staked out commanded some very exciting views, but it was still an isolated place – at least until he acquired a larger posse of disciples and imitators during the late 1970s and subsequently. The distinctiveness of his vision appears even more striking in retrospect.

A sketch of the point he had reached by his mid-twenties might run like this. While obviously believing that the creeds definitively disclose the truth about the world, he was also starting to insist with growing emphasis that Christianity is a way of life – of loving, suffering, working, giving and receiving in relation to God and our fellow creatures. But since the rightness or falsehood of a way of life cannot be encapsulated in a single sentence, Rowan would have endorsed the Catholic literary scholar Nicholas Boyle's comment that: '[s]uch truth can be shown . . . but it is much, much harder to say it, to put it in a propositional form in which it can be affirmed or denied. Perhaps Wittgenstein was right, and it cannot be said. (And perhaps . . . Beckett was also right, and the obligations to say it nonetheless remain absolute.)'[23]

The coordinates offered by Ludwig Wittgenstein, perhaps the twentieth century's most influential philosopher, and Samuel Beckett, one of its most celebrated dramatists, were therefore critical. In the theological scheme to which Rowan felt increasingly drawn, liberals tended to err through saying too little, while many conservatives overlooked the dangers of saying too much. The most credible stance was based on a balance between two sorts of awareness – that religious truth (as opposed to the truth revealed in a test tube) can never be simple or slick, because it lies at a depth where things are often murky; but the burrowing process must be engaged with unflagging commitment nonetheless.

Rowan's spadework was and remains more genuinely traditional. While never ceasing to stress that the truth of God is too luminous to be apprehended by human beings, he maintained that the faithful mind may be brought by rational argument to see that the world's intelligibility points to a transcendent principle of truth and being. This, very broadly, is a central argument of St Thomas Aquinas, whose huge (8 million-word) oeuvre absorbed Rowan deeply during the 1970s. A key term in the Thomist lexicon is *manductio*: the Christian is 'led by the hand' of metaphysics into a reception of the revealed truth of God.

However they are judged, these ideas belong to the province of philosophical theology, and are therefore chiefly of interest to religious believers. But Rowan was a Renaissance man. More than almost any other British theologian of his age, he made it his business to investigate the ways in which secular thought might also lead to the threshold of a religious understanding, and for this task his principal guide was the later Wittgenstein. Though he is often assumed to have been hostile to Christianity, Wittgenstein's contributions to areas such as the theory of knowledge and the philosophy of mind are closely related to those of Aquinas. It could even be argued that Wittgenstein changed the course of Western thought by countering the legacy of Descartes and re-establishing a way of looking at the world which Christians had once taken for granted.

Descartes was himself an observant Catholic, but he is also held to have sown some of the most fertile seeds of modern atheism by introducing a hugely influential model of the self that sees us as isolated individuals prioritising our subjectivity above all else. This gave rise to the traditions of radical scepticism about the integrity – and even the existence – of the public world, and to what has been called the 'fundamental illusion' of modernity: belief in the solitary self as sole arbiter of meaning and value. In his supporters' eyes, it was Wittgenstein who rode to the rescue by reinstating a com- mon-sense or 'third-person' view of reality with his simple- seeming yet profound argument about the impossibility of a private language. This states that we can ask questions of meaning only if we have a language in which to phrase them, and no language can refer to a realm of merely private things. If we can think or speak about our thinking, then we must do so in a publicly accessible discourse, in which case we are part of an objective arena. It follows, therefore, that Descartes would have done better to say '*Loquor ergo es*' (I speak, therefore you are) rather than '*Cogito ergo sum*.' (On a lighter note, it also follows that Oscar Wilde expressed a profound insight when he commented that only very shallow people don't judge by appearances.)

Insights comparable to Wittgenstein's also bore fruit in the work of other twentieth-century philosophers, among them Edith Stein, the Jewish-born Carmelite nun murdered by the Nazis at Auschwitz. She focused on how our display of empathy – and especially so-called reiterated empathy, where I empathise with another's empathetic reaction to me – provides a route to self-knowledge and moral improvement that introspection cannot give. During the mid-1970s and subsequently, Rowan came to see that these arguments were still more significant when given a religious twist. If language itself involves an act of trust by expecting to evoke a shared world, then a profoundly suggestive inference may be drawn: that there is an affinity between the structure of thinking and the structure of reality – an affinity where love and imagination are integral to the picture.

These arguments also shed light on Rowan's true vocation. It was to lie not in the cloister, but at the crossroads between a variety of academic disciplines, spirituality and pastoral outreach. His eclecticism is especially evident in his first book, *The Wound of Knowledge*,[24] a study of spirituality from apostolic times to the sixteenth century. Although published in 1979 when he had been back in Cambridge for two years, it was written at Mirfield, and based on lectures Rowan gave there and at Westcott House. We are shown how St Paul and St John, St Ignatius of Antioch, Greek and Latin Fathers, monks of the East and West, various medieval theologians, and, finally, Luther and St John of the Cross wrestled with the business of articulating God's relation to the world and to human lives, finding the answer 'through their own exposure to a divine sovereignty centred in the event of Christ crucified', as Michael Ramsey wrote in a warm notice.[25]

The Wound of Knowledge is laden with insights from history that are at the same time important to Rowan personally – for example, his observation that the Greek Father St Gregory of Nyssa purged the notion of *arete* of its traditional Hellenistic associations with aristocratic dignity, and redefined it as the service of God and men after the pattern of Christ.

In *Rowan Williams: An Introduction* I attempted to summarise some of the book's other main arguments, especially regarding the Desert Fathers and works by St John of the Cross such as *The Dark Night of the Soul*.[26] A briefer discussion might focus on *The Wound of Knowledge*'s opening section, a vivid statement of the Williams creed in embryo. Christian faith, he declares, begins in an experience of profound contradictoriness. The gospel questions humanity because it reveals a God beyond human understanding and control. God is free to be gracious, to act in ways which confound human expectations, to break down human barriers and to form a community whose existence and calling question the existing order in the light of God's purpose. God is not to be captured or manipulated by people for their own ends.

There is a short but accomplished guide to the Church's New Testament foundations. The 'devastating finality' of Jesus' life and death means that, on the one hand, 'attitudes to the law and the chosen people cannot ever be the same again'. On the other, the believer is left with 'all the problems of living in a visibly untransformed world'. Christians must therefore live with a dual perspective. The resurrection, which creates reconciliation and in turn empowers the reconciling mission of the Church, also 'directs us to Calvary as an event which uncovers the truth, the resilient, inexhaustible, demanding objectivity of what God and God's work is like. From now on, all that can be said of God's action in the past or the present must pass under the judgement of this fact.'[27]

An implication of this is that God 'provokes crisis and division', in order to destroy the human illusion of self-dependence (what St Paul means by 'Law'). Because it is painful to be confronted with the knowledge that our projects often amount to empty self-serving, 'we readily turn to violence against the bearers of such knowledge'. In the language of John's Gospel, 'we have decided we want to stay blind when the light is there before us, claiming we can see perfectly well'.

But legalistic attitudes are not eradicated by the ministry of Jesus. The whole logic of the argument shows that new life is not a possession, and comes at a price:

> If we believe we can experience our healing without deepening our hurt, we have understood nothing of the roots of our faith; Jesus' obedience in the circumstances of his earthly life, in temptation and fear, 'with loud cries and tears' [Hebrews 5:7], is what opens the long-closed door between God and men's hearts, and, although that door is now decisively open, all must still pass through it to make the reconciliation their own.[28]

Powerful words, but not palatable to all tastes. Rowan continued to be highly self-critical: his tougher personal experiences had intensified his dread of shallow religious certainties. In theological parlance he was – and remains – an Augustinian, always insisting (just like the future Pope Benedict XVI) that divine grace transforms human nature from the bottom up: God's action is not merely like the icing on a cake. Paradoxically, the view of both Archbishop and Pope is more usually associated with certain strands of Protestantism. Many observers of a more typically Catholic mindset have judged it to be too negative. They counter that if we are made in the divine image, then 'grace perfects nature' – that is, God's gifts are a crowning of what God has already made.

In *Difficult Gospel*, a study of Rowan's theology, the Exeter theologian Mike Higton sides with the optimists, and discerns too bleak a view of human nature in the Archbishop's output:

> It sometimes seems that Williams is willing to risk muting the note of joy, of thankfulness, of release and rescue, appropriate to the news that God has stepped over all the barriers which separate us from him, and has accepted us despite ourselves . . .
>
> I suspect that the tenor . . . of his writings is too unrelentingly agonized – too aware of the possibilities of self-deceit, too aware of the dangers of cheap consolation, ever to relax in the Sabbath rest of God's love, feasting at table with the Son, despite all the dangers that attend such relaxation.[29]

Difficult Gospel is oddly structured, being essentially a very detailed and often repetitive report, shorn of context. Only rarely does description shade into evaluation: Higton's criticism is thus all the more noteworthy. It is also fair. Rowan could offer hostages to fortune (a sermon he preached at Mirfield in February 1976, 'To Give and Not to Count the Cost', is a forlorn riff on the idea that Christ will not wipe away our tears until we have learnt to cry), and he was willing to admit to Donald Allchin at this time that his outlook was shaped by what he called 'my Celtic gloom'. Theologians will also spot Rowan's large debt to the radical German theologian Dorothee Sölle (1929–2003).

Other arguments could be cited in Rowan's defence, though – above all, that Jesus himself regularly spoke in an 'Augustinian' register. Moreover, Rowan's aversion to the sheer banality of much preaching was sound enough. Second, though, Augustine's palette is richer than he is sometimes given credit for. *The Wound of Knowledge* contains a particularly strong chapter on the saint's work, and the extraordinary insight into spiritual struggle and reward set out in the autobiographical *Confessions*. For the soul to be 'at home', Rowan writes in a gloss on this text, is not to vanish into an impersonal cosmic unity, 'but to rediscover the eternal, faithful, patient love of our creator, who made us to enjoy him, so that "our hearts are restless till they come to rest in you" '.[30]

And Rowan is unrepentant in arguing that Augustine, with his insistence on the need for conversion, is closer to the heart of the gospel than Pelagius (the heretic who overstated humanity's unaided spiritual resources) – and 'Pelagian', or over-optimistic, attitudes down the ages:

> Neither despair nor bland assurance, but faith is the mark of the Christian. [And] faith does depend upon an ability to 'entertain' the Augustinian picture, an ability to see the world as unclear and the human spirit as confused and imprisoned in fantasies. The Pelagian (or rationalist or positivist) sees no schism in the heart and so no need for healing reconciliation. If Paul's understanding of the cross of Jesus was and is correct, the need for reconciliation is a basic human datum; and if that is so, the Augustinian's world is less closed to the Gospel than the Pelagian's.[31]

Another reply to Higton (and at the same time an indirect vindication of his charge) stems from Rowan's perennial open-ness to criticism. When John Binns, one of his Mirfield students, commented that John of the Cross's *Dark Night of the Soul* presupposes an eventual sunrise, Rowan agreed, but added that he needed to reflect more carefully on Binns's observation. Perhaps a talk he gave on spirituality at the 1983 Loughborough conference of Anglo-Catholics shows that he had revised his views in the meantime – and that gold was in any case never far from black in his theological colour scheme:

> Now I can always retreat, I can always manufacture mental busyness or emotional day-dreaming to fill these voids. Or I can choose them. I can say, this is the only way to dis-illusion my prayer and my life, by bearing the oppressive shapelessness of a dark without agency, blind desire, blind trust, the sparkle from the coal [a reference to *The Cloud of Unknowing*, a fourteenth-century spiritual classic], the single spark that pierces the cloud, the sheer act of willing love. Call it love, yes, only that can sound too emotional, or call it faith, and that can sound too cerebral. And what is it? Both, and neither. That sparkle from the coal, that sharp dart of longing love, the ache of wanting, the decision to be faithful, the patient, persistent refusal of easy gratifications, sustained as we look into the immeasurably more dreadful void of Jesus' prayer in Gethsemane and on the cross, that bloody crown of love and faith. That is how I learn finally of a God who will not be fitted into my categories and expectations. That is where I bring my projects and my fantasies and my loves and my hopes, that is where I bring my theology and my spirituality, to be judged in silent exposure to the living truth too great for me to see, trusting that he will see and judge and yet not turn me away, because in that void and in that terror at the heart of our prayer are the last fires of our salvation, the one release from sin and error. We only live, only suspire, as Eliot said, with either

fire or fire. That is the mercy which will never give us, or ever let us be content with, less than itself and less than the truth. I must be found in God. He cannot be tracked down to some corner of me. And so that void draws and calls us, the magnet of all our hearts and the lodestar of all truth. If we can bear it, it is because we have seen truth enacted in our world as mercy, grace and hope, as Jesus, the only-begotten, full of grace and truth . . .

A large proportion of twentieth-century theologians in Britain and elsewhere viewed spirituality as a private matter. Thomas Merton, the Trappist writer, famously complained about the compartmentalising of dogmatic and mystical theology, 'as if mysticism were for saintly women and theological study were for practical but, alas, unsaintly men'.[32] Rowan's Loughborough talk is among other things a resounding restatement of an insight he had drawn from Merton and others. The above passage reveals a virtuoso talent in fuller bloom, giving due weight to the blessings as well as the costs of discipleship.

At some level, the hosannas derived from Rowan's personal circumstances. By 1983, he had been back in Cambridge for six years. They were among the happiest of his life, before or since.

3

Where All the Ladders Led

After he had decided to pursue a teaching career, it was inevitable that Rowan would soon be lured away from Mirfield to a larger arena. The post of chaplain at Westcott House, Cambridge, which fell vacant in 1977, might have been tailor-made for him. He was ordained to the diaconate in the college chapel at Petertide that year, having passed a selection conference several months before. The bountiful decade that lay ahead was to be crowned by his marriage to Hilary Jane Paul in 1981.

Things almost turned out very differently, with what might have been calamitous results. Jane was not his first fiancée. In early 1979, Rowan suddenly became engaged to a Lutheran ordinand from Germany, Corinna, who was spending a year at Westcott on an exchange programme. The couple had been acquainted only since the previous autumn. The bride-to-be was well liked by some. But several of Rowan's closest friends found her forceful, even overbearing; Delphine and Aneurin were known to be uneasy about the match as well. Students who looked up to Rowan found it hard to associate him with an apparent lapse of judgement. Many were dismayed. Sarah Coakley felt that the relationship didn't ring true – that the couple were play-acting, rather than genuinely in love. Other friends, including Stephen Sykes, felt that Rowan was 'unmarriageable' in any case, because he had always seemed so self-contained. But a wedding date was fixed for the late summer, and a venue booked. John Walters (himself on the threshold of marriage) was asked to be best man, but found that he could not clear his diary at such short notice. When the engagement was broken at a very late stage, the relief felt throughout Rowan's circle was all the greater.

This story has broader ramifications, because in some respects his cloistered lifestyle had not left him much better prepared for leadership than for romance. Mark Santer, the principal of Westcott, later to be Bishop of Birmingham, emphasises Rowan's gentleness and tendency to recoil from conflict:

> Occasionally we had to let go of people. X or Y might find it very wounding to be told that they were unfit for ministry, but on occasion you have to be very blunt if you are to be fair both to individuals, and to the congregations among which they might otherwise be let loose. Rowan always sided with the underdog. Sometimes the overdog would have liked a bit of sympathy.

The sentiments behind Santer's reactions are echoed by John Milbank, one of Westcott's ablest students at this time. 'I now think that Rowan's generosity of spirit was a premonition of his future problems at Canterbury. He always saw every side to an argument, which can be a drawback as well as a strength.'

But the chaplain's record was still outstanding in most respects. It helped him, no doubt, that he had a following wind. Westcott – with Ripon College, Cuddesdon, near Oxford – is one of the two main liberal-Catholic clerical training grounds in

England. Its reputation for high pastoral and academic standards had been built up by Peter Walker (principal for a decade from 1962 and then Bishop of Ely) after the stewardship of Kenneth Carey (1945–61). Santer shared many of Walker's skills. Two other members of his team during the late 1970s were John Armson, the vice-principal, and Mary Tanner, a part-time lecturer on the Old Testament, who both went on to greater things.

Rowan was responsible for remoulding the student ethos a good deal, partly through his availability and informal teaching style. Milbank, who later abandoned his plans for ordination in favour of an academic career, recalls some of the attitudes that he terms 'public school meets 60s radicalism' – which lingered on and were potentially harmful:

> There was a good deal of badly absorbed psychology and sociology in evidence, including the idea that characters had to be 'broken'. You could not get married without the college's consent, because of the financial implications for the Church. Some people disapproved when I began going out with my future wife, who was an undergraduate. I was told I should be getting alongside the working classes and marrying a shop girl. The advice came from people whose own contact with wider society was modest at best.

By contrast, the new chaplain radiated good sense as well as kindness. He looked old for his age in Milbank's view, and could still sometimes seem 'rather anguished'. But perhaps the wonder was that Rowan did not look even more care-worn than he sometimes appeared. The trail of people seeking his advice and support remained long. He shone in one-to-one settings, but it was also noted that drama and ceremony mattered enormously to him. For all his modesty, he seemed to thrive on a podium at least as much as in private conversation. Westcott had a tradition of post-Compline addresses on a Monday night. Rowan's talks in this setting were legendary. And his acting days were not over. In 1978 he stepped in at a moment's notice to play Dogberry again when a member of the college cast fell ill. He was word-perfect in the role after a fifteen-year interval.

His reputation for consolidating the forces of theological orthodoxy appeared ever more robust. The tide was just starting to turn against reductive forms of liberalism – *The Myth of God Incarnate*,[1] a collection of essays questioning traditional belief about the person and work of Christ on assorted grounds, drew very mixed reviews, and even full-scale ripostes. Rowan's message invigorated a generation hungry for a richer theological diet. He recalled the changing times in an early interview as Archbishop of Canterbury:

> When *The Myth of God Incarnate* appeared . . . many people felt that this was about as far as a particular kind of rational revisionism could go. So it was one of those moments when people did begin to turn towards other sources, and . . . the growing profile in the British university scene of some Catholic theologians, Nicholas Lash [Donald MacKinnon's successor at Cambridge] being a very prominent example, did mean . . . that there was a bit of a turn against a certain kind of very insular Protestantism. A curious thing about *The Myth of God Incarnate* is that there is barely one reference to anybody outside the anglophone liberal Protestant world . . . The rest of theology might not have existed. And there is an awful insularity about the book in that way. Now, getting us away

from that insularity was . . . part of the important agenda of the years that followed.[2]

The scale of the chaplain's effect on his students at Westcott is expressed by Adrian Dorber, a graduate of Lancaster University and future Dean of Lichfield.

> We were offering ourselves for lifelong ministry, and needed to break out of what seemed like an old-fashioned Oxbridge consensus presenting Christ as essentially a moral mentor. Rowan liberated us from this. His theology was grounded, passionate, caught up in the life of God, and he was clear that everything came together in the Church, rather than the academy. New vistas were opened to us by his robust engagement with philosophy, politics and ethics, as well as history. We came to think that it was possible to out-think the Enlightenment, and defend the integrity of revelation.

The lectures that became *The Wound of Knowledge* were heard with awe. Dürer's painted grass was once described by the art historian Kenneth Clark as lifeless (like grass in a display case containing stuffed animals) compared with the real thing. This analogy may help to evoke the effect of Rowan's talks about Augustine and other early Christian thinkers. His accounts 'made spirituality mainstream', in Dorber's words.

Not everyone felt seduced. Alister McGrath, for example, a Wadham biochemist during Rowan's time at Oxford, had been converted from Marxism to Christianity before seeking ordination. As an Evangelical he was outside his milieu at Westcott, and the experience brought out an aggressive streak in him, according to several contemporaries. 'He was a nuisance, trying to pick fights with Rowan during lectures,' says one of his fellow students, now a vicar in London. 'Rowan generally didn't take the bait, but on occasion he could be firm. I think it's to Alister's credit that he gave a radio interview after Rowan's appointment to Canterbury describing him as head and shoulders above the other candidates.'

That the chaplain displayed steeliness with McGrath (and several other brilliant, slightly angular characters) belies the theory that he was entirely incapable of confrontation, or that his compassion always ruled his head. John Armson in turn was impressed by Rowan's understanding of mental illness, as was Jim Hume, one of the Fulbourn hospital's top psychoanalysts.

Rowan also gained a reputation for his frankness and occasional mordancy, especially among those close to him such as Thomas Seville, his first doctoral student, who went on to join the Community of the Resurrection. Seville asked his supervisor for advice on a choice of theological college, and was left slack-jawed, though grateful, by the frankness of the advice proffered. Rowan urged him to avoid St Stephen's House, on the grounds that its reputation for promiscuous homosexuality had not yet faded, despite the fresh broom then being wielded by the principal, David Hope. Salisbury and Wells fared no better in Rowan's estimation: he likened the regime there to a Butlin's holiday camp. Mirfield, though, was recommended as the place where Seville would 'really learn how to pray'.

Level-headed advice, delivered in no-nonsense terms. But his other-worldliness in other respects also drew comment. There was a wholly delightful side to it. Once, for example, Rowan collided with a man in the street, who apologised for his absent-mindedness before explaining that he had been thinking about Plato. The chaplain was all ears. 'What aspect of Plato?' He ended up inviting his interlocutor back to his rooms for what turned into a protracted discussion. On the other hand, Adrian Dorber says that his teacher could sometimes seem impractical. At one point, Rowan suggested having a prayer group across the Cambridge Federation, the umbrella term for the city's four main theological colleges. 'For a time we fell out over this,' Dorber adds, 'because he wasn't really facing up to how it was all going to be organised.' John Milbank's experience of the chaplain's less hard-headed side came during a parish placement at St George's, Chesterton, on the city's northern edge (where Rowan would later serve as a part-time curate): Milbank confesses that they were both 'hopeless' Sunday school teachers. 'Rowan looked at the chaos around him, shook his head, and said it was all proof of the doctrine of original sin.'

Intellectual brilliance, spiritual maturity and an unusual mixture of wisdom and artlessness – these, then, are among the main distinguishing features of Rowan's Westcott years, and part of the background to his relationship with Corinna. She arrived at the college in Michaelmas term 1978, at the start of Rowan's second year, and a few months before he led a pre-Christmas student tour of Christian holy sites in Egypt. As a child she had been severely burnt in a fire. The accident left her partially disfigured, despite a series of skin grafts and other treatment. But neither her appearance nor her status as West-cott's only woman student seemed to affect her self-belief. Rowan's friends thought her confident, clever and intense. She was a regular visitor at his flat; the two were often observed in highbrow conversation.

Early in the new year, the couple announced that they would be marrying a few months later. The bride-to-be – nicknamed Brünnhilde by the nuns at Fairacres, when Rowan showed her the convent during a visit to Oxford – insisted that she would be pursuing a career in her own Church. Rowan therefore agreed to move to Germany, and, given the thinness of the Anglican presence there, let it be known that he was thinking of joining the Old Catholics – the Church that broke with Rome after the First Vatican Council (1870–1) in protest against the declaration of papal infallibility.

Apart from feeling disorientated by the thought that his greatly admired teacher was making a 'big mistake', Peter Atkinson speaks for others in suggesting that Rowan was partly motivated by pity for Corinna. Her evident self-confidence tells against this; but whether it is true or not, Atkinson's broader verdict is widely endorsed: 'When the engagement was called off over the summer, we felt that this was a very necessary step in order to avoid frustrating one and possibly two vocations.'

Yet 1979, apparently a nadir for Rowan's personal life, was to prove the opposite. He had known Jane Paul, a very bright and popular graduate member of Clare, since the autumn of the previous year; they had been introduced at the D Society, a place of invigorating theological debate among dons and research students. Their eyes met as they both reacted in the same quizzical way to a dubious theological assertion. The break with Corinna freed Rowan to draw closer to his new friend; the two became an item in early 1980 and married on 4 July 1981 at St Barnabas's, Heaton, in Bradford. This time Rowan asked his friend Chris Morgan, a journalist, to be best man.

The success of the match had something to do with the differences between man and wife, as well as what they had in common. Jane was as steeped in religion as her future husband, but of another stripe. She and her four sisters had grown up in India, where her father, Geoffrey, worked for the Church

Missionary Society before his eventual appointment as Bishop of Bradford. The experience of studying theology might have led to a crisis of faith, but she had held fast to her Evangelical roots, and was active in the Christian Union at her college. 'I think some of the other members worried about me,' she explains, 'and at one point got me to co-lead a Bible study group with a scientist, to check that I was keeping on the straight and narrow. Their intellectual attitudes could be annoying, but they were lovely people.' Jane's faith in general was resurrection-shaped. She came from a tradition where speaking in tongues was relatively common, and suggested to her fiancé that the impulse to let God take over in this context had a parallel in the Catholic habit of silent contemplation. Above all, she was not too serious, and has always felt that her easy-going personality marked her out from the other women who had been in love with Rowan. In short, she liberated him from his earnestness.

There were important decisions to be made about their future life almost at once. The post of chaplain at Westcott was by definition transitional for someone of Rowan's abilities. Geoffrey Lampe, Regius Professor of Divinity at Cambridge and a well-known liberal, was eager to confer a full academic post on his former student as soon as possible. Though the two men were poles apart in theological outlook, their personal rapport had always been very good. The goal was realised when Rowan became a university lecturer in 1980. This significant honour had been withheld from several better-known names, including John Robinson (now berthed at Trinity, after his stormy period as Bishop of Woolwich), but was not accepted without much soul-searching. Rowan felt the lack of hands-on parish experience – a gap that would haunt him in his later career – and wondered whether he shouldn't take a full-time pastoral job for a few years, preferably in Wales. The news caused anxiety to Jane, who advised him that his gifts were best employed in Cambridge.

Rowan decided that the solution lay in a dual role. He would combine the lectureship with a part-time curacy at St George's, the parish straddling Milton Road. He met the vicar, Brian Watchorn, in 1979, after giving a talk to newly ordained clerics in Ely. A few weeks later, Rowan rang Watchorn to offer his services as assistant priest. It was agreed that he would live in the curate's house on the Arbury estate, which largely consisted of 1950s and 60s council housing, and minister every Sunday and on some weekdays.

Conditions looked unpropitious. Churchgoing was a minority pursuit, and petty crime was common. Court reports in the *Cambridge Evening News* suggested that many criminals came from addresses close to Rowan's home in St Kilda Avenue. Watchorn's arrival in 1975 had followed a lengthy interregnum, the diocesan quota had fallen, and it was hard to recruit churchwardens and PCC members. But the vicar refused to accept that slow death was the only option for St George's, and sought to emulate the example of his predecessor, Degwel Thomas, who had ministered energetically for twenty years. One of Thomas's most popular ideas had been to turn the parish magazine into a freesheet, in the days before circulars were commonplace. He had also introduced a so-called Fish scheme, with a warden on every street to serve meals-on-wheels, and other forms of support to the needy. Watchorn later saw an effective means of reaching out to parents through their children. When it was decided to bring the 100-strong Scout troop to church once a month, adults also appeared at the main service in numbers.

Like most recently ordained priests, Rowan was as keen as mustard in the face of a pastoral challenge, and relished the street cred conferred on him by his new address. (He had always lived with his parents or in institutional accommodation until now.) That the core congregation at St George's has remained small – about thirty or forty a week – is more a sign of deeper social trends than of clerical inertia. Rowan was asked to take over a satellite Sunday school operating elsewhere on the estate, and used a Scripture Union course that the vicar adapted to entail a less literalist reading of the Bible. The curate now had a better rapport with children than when he had parachuted into the Sunday school at St George's two years earlier. 'I'm not sure Rowan was entirely at home, but he did well and I was grateful,' Watchorn reports. His wider verdict on his colleague is also positive:

> He was sometimes a little in the clouds. I remember the Midnight Mass on Christmas Eve when he had prepared a sermon, even though I, as vicar, was due to preach. We both processed towards the pulpit during the gradual hymn, and I had to make it clear who would be speaking. In general, he produced fine, well-turned little homilies, though occasionally his register could be a bit off-target. He not infrequently mentioned Gilbert and Sullivan, without realising that many in the congregation would not pick up on these references. But even if he was sometimes hard to follow, it didn't necessarily matter. People knew they were being addressed by a holy man.

The curate is remembered with particular affection by Mick Gawthrop, a baker, and his wife Anne. However early they reached church on a Sunday morning, the familiar bearded, cassocked figure would already be there, praying in the sanctuary. Mick Gawthrop says that he had always been too self-conscious to speak in public, but Rowan alone gave him the confidence to do this.

When the Archbishop of Wales was translated to Canterbury twenty years later, Reg Tarrant, one of his former churchwardens at St George's, wrote in the parish magazine of Rowan's and Jane's 'wonderful gift of personal communication through word and deed'. He went on to describe how the vicar and curate had performed music hall numbers at parish shindigs, one of which featured a can-can danced by six parish ladies. On a less auspicious occasion, Rowan sang bass in a church performance of *Messiah*. He somehow made it through his final aria, 'The Trumpet Shall Sound', even though the trumpeter who should have been accompanying him had not made it to the performance.

It was partly through the proceeds of events at St George's that the Williamses were able to spend six weeks in India in 1981–2 on an exchange between Cambridge University and a Christian community, the Delhi Brotherhood. From the capital, armed with volumes of Trollope, the visitors took the long train journey south to Kerala, getting into several debates along the way. One evening, faced with Hindu, Muslim, Buddhist and atheist fellow passengers, Rowan conducted an impromptu interfaith seminar. He and Jane also visited Bangalore, to see how members of a Catholic institute for pastoral liturgy were taking up indigenous symbols in worship.

The trip meant much to Rowan – as well as seeing some of the places where Jane had spent her formative years, he got to grips with David Tracy's philosophical classic *The Analogical Imagination*. The plight of the poor filled him with dismay. In a busy street, a forest of hands would sway towards him whenever he reached into his pocket for a coin. He later told Reg Tarrant that the experience had left a permanent mark on him.

The Williamses' trip to South Africa in 1984 proved equally formative. Again travelling under church auspices, they spent some time in Soweto and other black townships among Anglicans involved in education and relief work. The suffering caused by apartheid was very marked. At a slum on the edge of Durban, in the company of a church worker called Helen, Rowan saw the truth of Paul Eluard's conviction that 'there is another world, but it is in this one'. After the Williamses had left, Helen was arrested and interrogated by the secret police. One of her tormentors turned her round and screamed, 'Who the hell do you think you're looking at?' Helen's courage in dealing with this question struck Rowan as profoundly revealing, as he later explained in his Alpha supper talk:

Is it possible for human beings – especially in circumstances of pressure and oppression like that – to look at something other than just the power and violence that is around them? Is there freedom even in the middle of an experience like that? . . . Is there somewhere else to go? Is there something else to see? Is there another world? 'Other worlds' may conjure up images of fairies, spirits and ghosts but I hope [Helen's story] may show what it is to live in another world and at the same time to live right in the middle of this one; to live with another vision; to step to a different drummer . . . because that is the heart – the hard essence – of faith.

The curacy at St George's counted as a success. Rowan was in charge for several months in late 1982 and early 1983, during the interregnum after Brian Watchorn's departure. Both men now went on to full-time university work, with Watchorn settling in as Dean of Pembroke College for almost a quarter of a century, and Rowan continuing his protean researches. He was himself eminently suited for the post of college dean – generally one-third pastoral and two-thirds academic – but resisted several invitations (including one from Trinity, where he judged that his duties would centre too much on arranging memorial services for deceased fellows) before accepting an offer from Clare in 1984. Not only was this Jane's college, and one of the most well-regarded in the university: it also had a venerable theological tradition. Rowan's predecessors included Charlie Moule, Maurice Wiles and John Robinson, as well as the banter-prone Mark Santer. Situated on the south side of the college, the dean's rooms provided a bewitching vista of King's College Chapel. It has sometimes been called the finest view in Europe.

So after three years of married life in the curate's house with Emily ('Em'), their ginger rescue cat, Jane and Rowan bought a two-bedroom cottage in Grafton Street beside the Kite, a park in central Cambridge. It was the only time they have lived in their own home: the house they later acquired in Charlbury, near Oxford, would be used only for holidays. Though generally happy, the Grafton Street years were also marked by a period of acute anguish. Jane suffered her first miscarriage. (Another was to follow in Oxford a few years later.) An addition to the family was later supplied by Jane's sister Celia, a highly accomplished artist. She gave birth to a son, Frank, by her partner Lucian Freud; the Dean of Clare had the satisfaction of baptising the great-grandson of Sigmund.

Rowan was admired across the board in his new college, even among the less easy-going of his colleagues. Tim Brown, the director of music, comments that administration was not of much interest to the Dean, which led to delays in decision-making over orders of service, and other chapel-related matters. 'It was not the easiest partnership from a managerial point of view,' Brown remembers. 'Rowan's rigour was in his thinking. He preached brilliantly, often without notes.' The biggest effect on the conductor's blood pressure famously came on Ash Wednesday in 1985, when Rowan took part in a Christian CND act of witness at RAF Alconbury, near Huntingdon. Having been arrested with several of his fellow demonstrators for scaling the fence of the base, he was obliged to make an urgent phone call explaining that he wouldn't be able to officiate at Evensong later in the day.

His move after so short an interval – to become Lady Margaret Professor of Divinity at Oxford, one of the top theological posts in Britain – was more a mark of his meteoric rise than of itchy feet. The very unusual combination of breadth and depth that he embodied can be gauged by a comparison with two of his elder colleagues, John Macquarrie and Henry Chadwick. Macquarrie (Rowan's predecessor in the Lady Margaret chair) devoted much of his career to demystifying Heidegger, and giving existentialism a theological twist. His *Principles of Christian Theology* is one of the most re-read single-volume compendiums of the twentieth century. But he largely confined himself to the bigger picture. Chadwick, on the other hand, was chiefly concerned with the study of patristic texts. Though serving on several important ecumenical commissions, he had less to say about contemporary doctrinal debate.

Rowan's bailiwick was the largest of the three. In 1978, for example – at the same time as *The Wound of Knowledge* was going to press – he was invited by Stephen Sykes (by then a professor at Durham) to collaborate with other young scholars, including David Ford and Richard Roberts, on the volume later published as *Karl Barth: Studies in his Theological Method*.[3] Rowan's chapter, 'Barth on the Triune God', handles an intricate theme with assurance. Two years later, he returned to Durham to deliver a paper on Augustine. Among the impressed members of the audience was Peter Sedgwick, another up-and-coming theologian. 'Rowan stood alone in the depth of his engagement with the tradition,' Sedgwick says. 'He illuminated Augustine's biography, and then, characteristically, he interpreted the text in a broader way. He was grappling with how you could speak about God's nature, and skirting very close to a doctrine of God's vulnerability, without making the mistake of saying that God suffers.' Shortly after this, Rowan rejoined Sykes's group (now augmented by Sedgwick himself and Nicholas Lash). This time their goal was to produce a book commemorating *Lux Mundi* (1889) – a collection of essays questioning traditional ideas about scriptural inspiration which had scandalised conservative opinion in its time. Sykes's project was eventually aborted. But the conversations behind it, centring on aspects of the incarnation, proved valuable to Rowan, who was also writing a 30,000-word encyclopedia article in German on the subject of medieval Christology.

At the same time he belonged to another team, including John Riches, Andrew Louth and Brian McNeil, charged with translating some of the major works of Hans Urs von Balthasar

(1905–88), often regarded as the twentieth century's greatest Catholic theologian. His genius was matched by his productivity: the Balthasar corpus amounts to more than 50,000 pages, and includes works on prayer, philosophy and literature, as well as a colossal fifteen-volume trilogy, *The Glory of the Lord*, *Theo-Drama* and *Theo-Logic*,[4] on the beauty, goodness and truth of God revealed in Christ. Balthasar's star has waned a little in recent years. Yet there is no question of his towering influence, which still extends to the Vatican's higher echelons. Rowan felt an enormous debt to him, witnessed in his willingness to render several hundred pages of dense German from *The Glory of the Lord* into English.

It is impossible to summarise Balthasar's achievement in brief. He was described more than once as Europe's most cultivated man. But among his core arguments was that theology had lost its way by forgetting that Scripture lays unstinting emphasis on the disclosure of God's glory. Through neglecting aesthetics, the Church had tended to understand revelation either in terms of 'the good' – with a corresponding tendency to reduce Christianity to an ethical code – or 'the true' – where discipleship is seen as no more than assent to a set of propositions. Balthasar held that the attempt to combine these two elements had often been awkward or unsuccessful, resulting in an opposition between moralism and dogmatism.

He evokes aesthetic categories as a cure for theology's wounds. Part of the argument in *The Glory of the Lord* is that the beautiful cannot only be set over against human beings objectively: it elicits subjective desire and delight in us as well. Aesthetic experience, then, is both self-involving and an 'unpliable' source of value. In the Christian arena a drama ensues, involving the soul's Yes or No to God. This process is simultaneously overshadowed by the greater drama entailed in God's Yes to humanity through the incarnation, and Jesus' apparently scandalous claim to be the Way, the Truth and the Life. Christ, therefore, both fulfils and overturns humanity's expectations. The question how 'one white cap atop a wave purports to be not only the sea and the seabed, but the generating matrix of the world as well', in the words of the Balthasar scholar Edward T. Oakes,[5] is a theme elaborated with unsurpassed sophistication in *Theo-Drama*.

Outside the academic labyrinth, Rowan could adjust to different kinds of track with rare ease. A good example comes from his (spoken) contribution to *The Case Against God*,[6] a book compiled by the BBC religious affairs correspondent Gerald Priestland and based on conversations with believers and atheists. The Dean of Clare evidently made an immediate impression as a defence advocate: Priestland introduced his description of their encounter by comparing Rowan favourably with an earlier interviewee, Keith Ward, who had spoken of his conversion to Christianity as an Evangelical experience. More attractive was the Dean of Clare's interlacing of what the BBC man had assumed to be contradictory sorts of argument. Rowan granted that religion forms part of the process of making sense. But he also flagged up the French philosopher Simone Weil's definition of God as 'the name we give to the connections we cannot make'. This amounted to a simplified expression of Balthasar's view that Christianity both answers our questions and questions our answers. Rowan made the point without highfalutin' references:

Looking back over experience as a whole, and relying on other people's experience as well, it seems a lot of the time that a consistency and pattern is there, just round the corner – something you can never quite lay hold of. It has constantly to live together with the sense that it may all be an elaborate wish-fulfilment. I have no means of checking here and now whether I am right or not. I have got to decide whether to do the next thing either in faith or not in faith. It's not just a once and for all commitment, it's a decision to look for sense in that way which means making certain choices, performing certain actions, not just holding certain ideas.

And then there's the difficult job, day by day, of seeing if that is workable. So there's no all-embracing solution to doubt, and I think it's a very important component to the religious enterprise; in that it makes you rightly suspicious of yourself, suspicious of your need to be consoled or cuddled by a cosmic friend. God's not necessarily consoling. The love of God is not a warm and cosy business very often, and you need always to be on the watch for that sort of wish-fulfilment. So insofar as doubt makes you aware of your capacity for self-deception, for . . . making it easy, then that negative moment is essential within faith.[7]

And it can be helpful to talk about God obliquely, by looking at the effects of belief:

I could only say, hang around with the representatives of one or another religious tradition – share the experiences of worship, entertain the images, the stories they tell. Look at the lives they point to as important lives, important saints, figures in their tradition: because I think it is profoundly true that the religious apprehension is caught, not taught.

Never mind the word God for the moment, I think sometimes one has to put brackets round it in order to get people to recognise what that sense of love, trust and openness to reality amounts to.[8]

Rowan pitched the argument at a more technical level in his essay 'Religious Realism: On Not Quite Agreeing with Don Cupitt'.[9] Cupitt, Dean of Emmanuel and one of Rowan's former teachers, was hanging on to Christian belief by his fingertips at the end of the 1970s: then he let go. In *Taking Leave of God*[10] and a stream of sequels, he dismissed belief in an objective deity as not only unwarranted, but undesirable. The language of spirituality and worship could be retained for its capacity to encourage moral striving, but only if Christians come of age accepted that words could not name any entity (such as the God of traditional belief) said to stand beyond the limits of language itself.

Questioned once during the early 1980s about Cupitt, Robert Runcie showed his theological limitations (or, possibly, his form as a scourge of swollen-headedness) by answering that 'the Dean of Emmanuel is much cleverer than me, but I'm Archbishop of Canterbury'. Rowan was a good deal closer to the mark in judging 'atheous' theology to be a flimsy phenomenon. Given his knack for ventriloquising other points of view, he typically began discussions of Cupitt by saying that his colleague had some hard but entirely necessary things to say about infantile dependence in Christian faith and practice. Like other sharp observers, though, Rowan instantly saw that *Taking Leave of God* was premised on a heap of questionable assumptions: that theology had never faced up to Cupitt's empiricist challenges before; that the natural sciences supply the only secure route to knowledge; and that human freedom is incompatible with submission to God's will. This latter claim (rooted in the work of Kant) is perhaps especially weak, and based on a Promethean rejection of God as a usurper of the space that human beings should be free to occupy. 'On Not Quite Agreeing with Don Cupitt' is in part a well-targeted philosophical attack on an often sloppy writer who was out of his depth without knowing it. The essay goes on to defend more credible forms of spirituality. As Rowan later summarised the matter, 'the challenge, the dynamism and the critical edge of the notion of an "objective" God are what saves the interior life from indulgence, stasis and insensitivity to the possibilities of self-deceit'.[11]

*   *   *

Resurrection,[12] Rowan's second published work, attempts to defend the integrity of the Easter narrative using an array of tools – literary and devotional, as well as theological. In this instance the critics were in two minds, judging the interdisciplinary emphasis to be a handicap as well as a strength. At the book's centre is an insistence that history and faith are ineradicable features of orthodox belief in the resurrection. Jesus appeared to people whose confidence in him had crumbled, not to believers. It was the resurrection that created the Church and its faith, not the Church that created the resurrection. Christians who see Christ's victory over death as only a metaphor can therefore be challenged on at least two grounds: not only that they risk circumscribing the power of God by laying down *a priori* what can and cannot happen, but that their supposedly rational understanding of Christian origins is in fact at odds with the historical evidence. For traditionalists, the witness of Christ's early followers is the most rational explanation of all the available evidence.

Yet this (according to Rowan's argument) is a necessary but not sufficient ground for resurrection belief, which cannot arise solely from textual or 'scientific' study. The mere fact of the empty tomb is ambiguous. On its own it does not constitute a compelling reason for believing in the resurrection. Orthodoxy requires that believers in every age reappropriate the experience of the first Christians, which is why doctrinal assent is also a matter of personal disposition. The ground for belief that Christ rose from the dead is not 'individual report', but the continuing existence of a fellowship marked by restoring grace.

Leslie Houlden, a New Testament specialist from the Church's liberal wing, judged the book to be too episodic. 'Any writer nowadays who breaks out of the enclosures in which the various theological disciplines generally live deserves applause for the very act. But there is a certain risk of not staying long enough in any of them to answer the questions which may properly be asked there.'[13] Houlden also pointed out that the term 'resurrection' was not coined de novo by the embryonic Church. It had already been used in Jewish eschatology for centuries before Christ. To understand the context in which the term had been used might provide grounds for denying its universal relevance.

Houlden in turn could be accused of overlooking the so-called scandal of particularity: tradition maintains that the gap between heaven and earth was bridged at one time and in one cultural setting, not others. From a more conservative stand-point, Donald MacKinnon complained of 'Dr Williams's tendency to substitute reverie for hard analysis'[14] in Resurrection – a charge voiced by a range of critics against other sections of Rowan's oeuvre (including some of his essays, and a book such as Lost Icons, where both the argument and the prose in which it is expressed are sometimes over-wrought). But MacKinnon's verdict was far from uniformly negative. He qualified his reservations by emphasising that Rowan's difficulties had much to do with his range, and his willingness to ask questions (for instance, concerning the nature of knowledge) that would not even figure on the radar of many other British theologians.

Resurrection originated in addresses given by Rowan to clergy in the East End of London at the invitation of Jim Thompson, then Bishop of Stepney. The move reflected Rowan's growing profile in the Church, as did his co-editing, with Kenneth Leech, of *Essays Catholic and Radical*,[15] published in 1983 to mark the 150th anniversary of the Oxford Movement. The book's title recalled that of *Essays Catholic and Critical* (1926), written by an influential group of Anglo-Catholic scholars who held that the terms 'Catholic' and 'critical' were not necessarily opposed. Rather, the two elements should be harnessed to yield a fuller grasp of historic Christianity.

Produced under Jubilee Group auspices, *Essays Catholic and Radical* applies this argument to the political sphere, after a more theological introduction by Rowan encapsulating some of his most dearly held ideas. Orthodoxy, he writes (employing the Wittgensteinian idiom that was now second nature to him) should not be a matter of inflexible boundaries and limits on free discussion: rather, it is the shared speech of a community – the Church – with the resources for encompassing all provinces of human experience, including deep shifts in historical consciousness.

Many were and are attracted by the idea that being orthodox is less a matter of parroting off correct answers than of remaining faithful to certain points of reference. But some observers (not only Roman Catholics, who might have been expected to complain of a certain murkiness in *Essays Catholic and Radical*) wondered whether orthodox belief wasn't being redefined rather wishfully as meaning little more than keeping in touch with tradition, without necessarily agreeing with what it says.

We shall return later to Rowan's defence of his position. But of even broader interest is how his understanding of orthodoxy cashes out. If asked during the 1980s, he would probably have cited his support for women priests as a major instance of authentic development in doctrine. And he might have built up his case with reference to Chesterton, who pointed out that '[w]hen we talk of a child being well-developed, we mean that he has grown bigger and stronger with his own strength; not that he is padded with borrowed pillows or walks on stilts to make him look taller . . . Development is the expansion of all the possibilities and implications of a doctrine . . .'[16]

The second equally important example of this style came in Rowan's change of mind over sexuality. As reported, shift came about after he had read a church-sponsored report on the subject released in October 1979, *Homosexual Relationships: A Contribution to Discussion*. It was produced by a working party under the chairmanship of the Bishop of Gloucester, John Yeats. While reaffirming that marriage should be the Christian norm, and thus denying that gay and heterosexual lifestyles are equally valid, the document nevertheless held that same-sex partnerships could be justified in some contexts.

Pro-gay campaigners seeking full parity of treatment for sexual minorities were not satisfied, but the lion's share of indignation came from traditionalists. For their part, the report's authors insisted that they had approached their task with due rigour: 'we have indeed taken great pains to interpret [the Bible] rightly', the chairman wrote in his preface. On the other hand, he added, the working party had 'not felt bound' simply to repeat Scripture's every utterance:

Rowan Williams in 1955

... as a choirboy at All Saints',
Oystermouth in 1963

... on his first visit to London
in 1959

... and as a young man,
1968

Graduation in 1971

With Jane Paul, on their wedding day, 1981

Rowan (second from right) as a deacon at the wedding of Alison and John Milbank in 1978. The other clergy are Mark Santer (left), John Armson (second from left) and James Owen (right)

Consecration as Bishop of
Monmouth, 1992

Rowan sitting on the
ground in his cassock during
the diocesan retreat in
Walsingham, 1997

With some of his fellow participants, including George Carey (second from left), during the 1998 Lambeth Conference

Diocesan pilgrimage to Uganda, 2002

Children's event to meet the
new Bishop of Monmouth

Enthronement as Archbishop
of Wales with Rhodri
Morgan, Wales's First Minister

Garden in Newport, 2002

With Barry Morgan (right), Rowan's successor as Archbishop of Wales

Accepting its authority as witness to the ways of God with men, and listening carefully to its teachings, we have at the same time laid claim, under the guidance of the Holy Spirit, to a liberty of judgement in discerning what God is saying to us here and now . . . In following such a method . . . we believe that we have continued in the mainstream of Anglican theology.[17]

Given the Gloucester report's importance in shaping Rowan's outlook, it is worth rehearsing its contents in more detail. There are six chapters: on the 'social setting' of homosexuality, the medical factors, the biblical evidence, theological and ethical considerations, the legal perspective, and pastoral care. The first highlights the multi-textured nature of sexual identity. There may be a genetic component; in which case moral condemnation of gay people would be dubious in principle. And even if environmental factors play a part in determining a person's sexual identity, this does not necessarily provide grounds for taking up cudgels: 'at this point it might be useful for those readers who are convinced of their own heterosexuality to ask whether this depends on any element of choice on their part'.

The second chapter avers that homosexuality is not an illness, and that talk of cure is therefore inappropriate. Turning to Scripture, the report defines the story of Sodom in Genesis 19, and references to same-sex acts in Leviticus 18, as 'the only directly relevant passages' on the subject in the Old Testament. The former is described as a legend, providing 'a stereotype of the peculiar wickedness and corruption of Canaanite culture'. And since it is not historical, 'it cannot be taken, as so commonly in the past, to record an instance of divine action intended expressly to condemn and punish homosexual behaviour. It is a reflection, rather than a cause, of existing attitudes and beliefs, the nature and origin of which must be sought elsewhere.' By contrast, the laws of Leviticus are held to have been intended to regulate a community in particular circumstances. They did not purport to be universally applicable, but were framed to strengthen the family group, which was the only social organisation familiar to the Israelites. 'The main concern is to establish the separateness and distinctiveness of the people of God.'

Traditionalists could be forgiven for seeing this argument as corroboration for their own beliefs. If the people of God were called to a distinctive standard of life over against 'the world' in ancient times, then it may be equally important to maintain the standard in the face of contemporary neo-paganism. But overall, the report provides the germ of an argument which would be seen in later decades as central to the debate: that the Old Testament assumes all to be heterosexual, and therefore knows nothing of the distinction between gay practice and gay identity. Granted this, then it is conservatives who may be reading Scripture with blinkers, since the text does not reckon with monogamous same-sex partnerships. (Vatican pronouncements in this department are also based on the idea that gay people are defective heterosexuals.)

Homosexual Relationships also sees Paul's condemnation of same-sex relations in Romans 1:18–32 as part of an argument against the sinful state of the world outside the Church. In any case, adds the report, this passage 'has to be considered in the light of the underlying message of the Bible, especially the New Testament; and, in assessing and interpreting this, we need to take account of knowledge not available to biblical writers, and moral institutions formed in the Christian tradition'. This tradition includes an apparently unwavering ban on gay sex, which does indeed constitute a weighty consideration. But Yeats and his team sound a cautionary note: 'as can be seen from the case of contraception, which has also been traditionally condemned, this fact cannot of itself be decisive for the Christian conscience'.

Though in some respects a prophetic document (its arguments have weathered well), the Gloucester report was swept under the carpet after the initial fuss had died down. Looking back, Yeats granted that the document had alarmed Graham Leonard – Bishop of Truro and chairman of the Church of England's Board for Social Responsibility – who saw that it would divide Anglo-Catholics, especially, at a time when hopes of reunion with Rome were still credible. 'Perhaps it would have been cannier to express ourselves more moderately,' Yeats told me.

Aged twenty-nine, Rowan was unswayed by political calculations of this sort. The principle was clear to him. Reading the New Testament in the light of historical analysis and contemporary knowledge of human sexuality could allow the Church to recognise same-sex relationships, but recognition should depend on discerning in those relationships the covenantal pattern of faithful self-giving, rather than the deliberate rebellion against nature and wilful self-indulgence that are condemned in Romans 1.[18] There was talk of his producing a reflection for the doctrine committee of the Church Union but, in the end, more influential figures in the organisation went cold to the idea. 'He saw this as hypocritical,' Thomas Seville recalls. 'A number of senior Anglo-Catholics were publicly critical of the Gloucester report, even though some of them had unacknowledged gay partners.'

The assumption that Rowan's early career was unaffected by his pro-gay stance is inaccurate. In 1983, before accepting the deanship of Clare, he applied unsuccessfully to be Professor of Christian Doctrine at King's College London. The job went to Colin Gunton, who stood at a slight advantage through being the internal candidate and a little older. A little beforehand, Rowan was turned down when he applied to be principal of St Stephen's House in Oxford (a more conservative college than Westcott, though with much else in common), because he was by now thought of as too liberal. Eric Kemp, Bishop of Chichester and chairman of the governors at St Stephen's, had determined on blocking his path. If Rowan had secured the appointment, he would have undoubtedly worked to soften opposition to the ordination of women; some believe that his influence on Anglo-Catholicism might have been much greater. But the Lady Margaret chair was a considerably more prestigious destination, and at thirty-five he still had plenty of unfinished academic business.

*   *   *

The high hopes vested in the Lady Margaret Professor were not disappointed – despite an early hiccup. He looked pale and unsettled during a service in the cathedral one day: this caused some of his new colleagues to fret about his reliability. It turned out that both he and Jane had eaten some poisonous berries in their garden, and were clutching their stomachs in agony. Fortunately, they soon got better.

With enthusiasm came surprise. It was as unusual to find literature and philosophy cited at length in theological lectures as it was to hear the Fathers expounded as though they were of more than archival interest. Rowan's style was no less novel. His lectures would regularly begin with a request for several moments' silent thought, and end with an invitation to a weekly At Home co-hosted by Jane. A bracing evening's conversation might move from the novels of Patrick White or Anita Mason to the thought of Cornelius Ernst, one of Rowan's Dominican heroes, to politics and film and back to theology. Contact between undergraduates and professors of divinity was commoner at Cambridge than at Oxford. Rowan's initiative proved popular in a department with no great reputation for conviviality.

Part of the problem was connected with surprisingly poor facilities. Despite its high reputation, Oxford in the 1980s seemed chronically ill-equipped in some respects, with a theology faculty that was housed in a cramped, usually empty annexe of Regent's Park College. The focus of the Williamses' lives now became Christ Church Cathedral (which doubles up as a college chapel) along with other members of the chapter and their families: Eric Heaton, the Dean; Frank Weston, the Archdeacon of Oxford; John Fenton, residentiary canon and father of the poet James Fenton; and the two other canon professors, Maurice Wiles and Oliver O'Donovan. At seven o'clock most mornings, this fellowship – accompanied by John Norsworthy, a retired schoolmaster who ran the cathedral office as a labour of love – would gather for Matins and the Eucharist. Choral Evensong followed in the late afternoon. After a while Jane and Rowan established links with a parish, St Alban's, Cowley, in a less well-heeled area of east Oxford.

The canons' living quarters are palatial. Tom Quad, the main space in Christ Church, largely consists of half a dozen clerical dwellings. Rowan and Jane lived in one of the four canonries there for a year until their longer-term residence – the thirteen-bedroom Priory House, in the cathedral cloisters – had been refurbished. Both homes were furnished sparsely with cheap chairs and sofas decked in ethnic throws – a mark of the couple's disquiet about the size of their new surroundings, as well as their general lack of interest in interior décor. In Priory House, this unease was softened by the presence of lodgers, and by the fact that one of the bedrooms was used as a study by Catherine Osborne, a Cambridge friend now also teaching in Oxford. Em was diagnosed with feline AIDS in the late 1980s, after which her owners took on Sophie, another rescue kitten from the same litter. At one point she briefly escaped to Corpus Christi College, which adjoins Christ Church, and was made an honorary member of the Junior Common Room there by a group of devoted students.

From 1988, when Jane gave birth to Rhiannon Mary after another difficult pregnancy, the space in Priory House was put to better use still. Rhiannon's arrival brought further elation, given the suffering Jane had already been through. Her life remained challenging in important respects. She had a very late miscarriage before leaving Oxford, and at one point pressed Rowan to shoulder more of the childcare. This may be surprising, given his deserved reputation as a devoted father. But it can be readily explained in terms of a heavy workload (including many evening meetings or services or lectures) and regular absences abroad.

Among his peers, Rowan appeared more than ever to be the man of the moment. Some of the other dons were on different theological wavelengths – not only the liberal Maurice Wiles, but also philosophers such as Richard Swinburne, Nolloth Professor of the Philosophy of Religion. Rowan held Swinburne to be guilty of 'foundationalism' – the belief that Christian discourse can be based on 'neutral' reasoning. In effect, the Lady

Margaret Professor thought that Swinburne and Don Cupitt had more in common than either of them realised, and that they essentially agreed about the caricature of God that Cupitt rejected and Swinburne believed in. But although Rowan could be scathing in private (and regretted that his friend D. Z. Phillips from Cardiff had not been awarded Swinburne's chair when the post was filled in 1985), he did not allow differences of view to shade into public animosity. Humour, as always, was powerful medicine. Likewise, he felt a strong personal liking for Eric Heaton. But when the Dean preached what struck him as a Laodicean sermon one Easter, either Rowan or Oliver O'Donovan whispered, 'Christ is risen: he is *possibly* risen indeed,' as the two processed out of the cathedral. Each now ascribes the comment to the other.

There were other colleagues for whom the new arrival's writings were like rain on a barren landscape. Figures as diverse as Geoffrey Rowell (later Bishop of Gibraltar in Europe) and Timothy Gorringe (a Barthian devotee of liberation theology) saw Rowan as a fellow traveller, as did Tom Wright, the New Testament specialist lately returned to Oxford as chaplain of Worcester after a stint at McGill University in Canada. In significant areas of biblical interpretation, the two men were largely on the same page. A good deal of the liberal exegesis in which both had been steeped as students rested on belief in a sharp difference – even a contradiction – between the creeds and the biblical raw data from which they apparently derived. Wright has consistently challenged this idea (and allied assumptions about the New Testament's unreliability) in a major series of books on Christian origins.[19] The seminar he co-led with Rowan on the links between early and more developed forms of belief proved highly popular.

Rowan's own largest scholarly work, *Arius: Heresy and Tradition*, was completed soon after his arrival in Oxford. A sabbatical at the University of Chicago in 1985 had given him a rare chance to make uninterrupted progress on the manuscript, though he almost lost it when his baggage went astray in transit back to England. It is a technical study of the heretic condemned at the Council of Nicaea in 325 for denying the full divinity of Christ. Part of Rowan's thesis rested on some audacious claims about Arius's debt to different shades of Platonist philosophy.[20] The book also underlines the conservatism and scriptural literalism presupposed by the Arian outlook, and savours the irony of this. Both the epigraph (Alasdair MacIntyre's maxim that 'traditions, when vital, embody continuities in conflict') and a long Postscript signal that Rowan was partly writing with an eye on much later disputes.

* * *

Yet for all the Lady Margaret Professor's popularity, his second phase in Oxford must also be seen in the light of his decision to quit the job after only six years. Then and subsequently, the official explanation was that he wanted a broader challenge. This was true, but there were other reasons besides – above all that the theology faculty was lustreless. Christoph Schwöbel, a German theologian who taught at King's College London during the 1980s, noticed the enduring lack of a common ethos when he was involved in external appraisal of Oxford's set-up twenty years later. He notes the competing influence of colleges vis-à-vis the university. Others who recall the 1980s feel that this problem was augmented by a rigid syllabus allowing very little undergraduate choice, and few mechanisms for consultation with students. It is telling that John Webster, Rowan's successor, also spent less than a decade at Christ Church before defecting – in his case to a chair at Aberdeen. Several other past and present professors have echoed his complaints about institutional cobwebs.

To criticise Rowan for failing to overhaul an awkward structure single-handedly would obviously be unjust, especially as others were also defeated by the challenge. Perhaps it was intractable. But the Lady Margaret Professor's lack of interest in the nuts and bolts of the faculty's workings has left former colleagues divided about his legacy. Christopher Rowland, professor of New Testament studies from 1992, believes that his old friend and Cambridge contemporary could have shaped the department but did not do so. O'Donovan (who lasted twenty-four years as Regius Professor of Moral and Pastoral Theology, but also took the unusual step of moving to another job before retirement age) has a more positive assessment:

> Rowan worked terribly hard. He never declined an invitation, and often faced an administrative backlog. Some of his graduate students had problems with him, because he did so much, and was therefore less available to them. It is true that he didn't have an agenda for changing the faculty, but he could have developed one, along with the necessary clout, if he'd stayed.

Christoph Schwöbel sees justice on both sides of the argument:

> I see Rowan as a very generous person who would always go out of his way to help individuals. But to change the ethos of a place you need to understand the workings of structures. This is not Rowan's main forte. As an outsider, I could see that a place like

Oxford tended to generate the same type of person in university politics – figures with the right social connections, who also understand the role of Oxford and Cambridge in the British establishment. Rowan, with his left-wing background, is likely to have been viewed as rather a maverick.

As we have seen, Cambridge's divinity faculty was different from Oxford's, whatever the broader likenesses between the two universities. For this and other reasons, the job offer Rowan received in 1989, to become Regius Professor of Divinity at his old university, looked very tempting indeed. This vacancy was unexpected. The incumbent, Stephen Sykes, had been in harness for only five years, but also felt the pull of a senior church post – as Bishop of Ely. Had he remained Dean of Clare, Rowan would almost certainly have stepped into Sykes's shoes. He now appeared ineligible for the post, not only through having been in Oxford for a mere three years, but also because he was the external adviser for the panel that would choose the successful candidate. In the event, he was asked to leave the room while his colleagues discussed his own credentials. When they offered him the job shortly afterwards, he felt disorientated and (as he later told O'Donovan) upset.

To have accepted Cambridge's offer would have been odd, perhaps, though not unprecedented. But Rowan now knew that his next move should not be to a similar but better-run university – especially one so far away from his parents, who were now considerably less robust. A bigger change was needed. Having spent almost his entire adult life in Oxford or Cambridge (long seen respectively as the right and left ventricles of the heart of the Church of England), he wanted to minister in different sorts of places.

Intimations that his future lay on a larger stage were numerous. In 1987, for example, he wrote a 'theological response' to the AIDS crisis for the Oxford Diocesan Board for Social Responsibility.[21] Reproduced in other church publications around Britain, his reflection called for solidarity with gay people and others affected by AIDS at a time when unthinking prejudice in Church and society was still rampant:

> In any situation of acute and widespread suffering, the first and most important theological assertion to be made is that we are called on to see God in the sufferer . . . to respond to the sufferer as to God, in clear-minded, attentive, self-forgetful love and in readiness to serve . . .
>
> Nothing in the New Testament suggests that our response should vary according to the 'moral' standing of the sufferer. So we should at once clear our minds of any remaining feeling that the person with AIDS who has been promiscuous has a lesser claim on our loving attention than the one who contracts the disease through a blood transfusion. Equally, whatever our views on the morality of active homosexual relationships, the partner of a dying man has no less claim on our love and support than the husband or wife, child or parent, of a person who has not contracted the disease by sexual transmission.

Rowan then countered the notion (still surprisingly widespread in those days) that HIV infection is a divine punishment, pointing out that a great deal more is said in Scripture to deny a link between adversity and God's anger – by Jesus himself (Luke 13:1–5 and John 9:1–3) as well as others – than to support it.

Even from a progressive standpoint, Rowan's arguments are uneven in some respects. He downplays the role of

African heterosexuals in spreading HIV, and ignores the disastrous view, common among African church leaders in the 1980s, that AIDS was only a problem for the 'decadent' West. In general, though, the generous sentiment behind this essay did his reputation little harm and much good. Certainly, he was held by liberal-minded onlookers to have acted heroically in June 1988, when the Archdeacon of London, George Cassidy, took legal action to eject the Lesbian and Gay Christian Movement (LGCM) from their office on church premises at St Botolph's, Aldgate, on the City's eastern edge. A ruling in Cassidy's favour was given by the diocesan chancellor, George Newsom QC, who also imposed a gagging order on the LGCM and the rector of St Botolph's, Malcolm Johnson. Rowan's reaction carried greater weight because he was by this time chairman of the Theological Education Committee at ACCM (the Advisory Council for Church's Ministry). In a statement, he declared that 'the deliberate will to humiliate which seems to be evident in the way this case has proceeded is very scandalous for the Church'. Newsom in turn said that he deplored the Lady Margaret Professor's criticisms.[22]

Cassidy and Newsom got their way, but Rowan did not let the matter rest, especially given the broader ecclesiastical and political climate. The late 1980s saw a bid by Margaret Thatcher's government to end the alleged promotion – termed discussion by its supporters – of homosexuality in schools. (A part of the Local Government Act, the provision was known as Clause 28.) This period also saw a bid by Tony Higton, an Essex-based Evangelical cleric, to secure the sacking of clergy in gay relationships. His General Synod motion was eventually replaced by one upholding traditional teaching on sex, but the damage had been done. Acrimonious debate flared up across the Church and outside it.

In 1989, Rowan would give a theological underpinning to the pro-gay case in 'The Body's Grace', his Michael Harding Memorial Lecture given under the LGCM banner. This is generally judged to have been the most contentious speech of his career. Yet beforehand, he said his piece with equal bluntness in a preface to *Speaking Love's Name*,[23] a collection of 'Catholic and Socialist' reflections on homosexuality published by the Jubilee Group. His multiple denunciations – especially of the tabloid press and of the mixture of ignorance, cruelty and hypocrisy he saw reflected in church attitudes to gay people – mark a profound contrast with his later caution. Conservatives and liberals would later use his words against him, as well as in their respective diagnoses of the way forward for Anglicanism. For this reason alone, the preface needs to be quoted in some detail. 'The past year [1987–8],' Rowan wrote,

> has been a wintry one for the Church of England; a time in which it has often been difficult to believe that it is possible to be an Anglican with integrity. We have shown ourselves to be self-destructive in our inner conflicts, in some very dramatic ways; above all, we have shown a degree of collective neurosis on the subject of sexuality that is really quite astounding in this century and this culture. We have, it seems, been happy to collude with the paranoia of populist homophobia, fuelled by the AIDS epidemic and by myths of gay 'propaganda' in schools – fuelled, that is, by tragedy on the one hand and lies on the other. Last November, the General Synod passed a resolution whose force remains ambiguous, declaring the undesirability of gay clergy being allowed to express and experience their sexual identity in

the way most people do. Even the most superficial analysis of the debate shows how the Synod was simultaneously cajoled and panicked into this move: well-meaning 'liberals', equally afraid of the harshness of [Higton's] original motion (about which the less said the better) and of getting involved in a genuinely theological debate on sexuality, joined hands with some of the most disturbing elements in the contemporary Church of England, those who are determined to make it an ideologically monolithic body, to produce a vote which has, in practice, delivered much of what the original motion aimed at. This shabby compromise has been held up by bishops as representing the 'mind' of the Church, and accorded something like legislative force. Bishops have appealed to it in justifying their actions against gay clergy and ordinands. *It is becoming harder all the time for a gay person to be honest in the Church. We have helped to build a climate in which concealment is rewarded – while at the same time conniving with the hysteria of the gutter press, and effectively giving into their hands as victims all those who do not manage successful concealment* [my italics]. And the lowest point has come with the vendetta conducted by the Diocese of London through its legal officers against the parish of St. Botolph's, Aldgate, and the Lesbian and Gay Christian Movement . . .[24]

Supporting gay liberation was not to commend a free-for-all in a 'bland situationist paradise', he went on, but to ask that this issue become part of 'collective and public reflection' in the Church. 'If we have no integrity here, we cannot expect to carry conviction elsewhere, because the issues of victimisation and disempowering are the same here as with the questions of race, sex and class.'

Rowan now had the bit between his teeth. It was therefore unsurprising that an invitation to deliver the Michael Harding

Lecture should have come his way. The address included a forthright defence of sex outside marriage in some cases:

> . . . an absolute declaration that every sexual partnership must conform to the pattern of commitment or else have the nature of sin and nothing else is unreal and silly. People do discover . . . a grace in encounters fraught with transitoriness and without much 'promising': it may be just this that prompts them to want the fuller, longer exploration of the body's grace that faithfulness offers. Recognising this . . . ought to be something we can do without . . . weakening . . . our Christian understanding . . . of what sexual bonding can be.
>
> Much more damage is done to this by the insistence on a fantasy version of heterosexual marriage as the solitary ideal, when the facts of the situation are that an enormous number of 'sanctioned' unions are a framework for violence and human destructiveness on a disturbing scale: sexual union is not delivered from moral danger and ambiguity by satisfying a formal socio-religious criterion.[25]

Turning to same-sex relationships, Rowan revisited ground already covered by the Gloucester report before building on a pivotal revisionist argument: that the link between companionship and gay practice cannot be properly acknowledged and sanctioned without an acceptance of homosexual identity. For historical reasons (the thesis runs), this recognition was not made until after the Enlightenment.

Side by side with this came the equally significant claim that views about homosexuality hinge on the prior question of attitudes to birth control, and connected beliefs about whether there is a psychological dimension to sex independent of procreation. The Vatican has maintained a consistent (albeit heavily criticised) line by opposing artificial contraception, in part justifying its stance with the argument that support for birth control implies tolerance of homosexuality. The Anglican Communion changed its mind on contraception during the 1930s, however, and the implications of this adjustment were knitted into Rowan's conclusion. In a Church that accepts birth control, he argued,

> the absolute condemnation of same-sex relations of intimacy must rely either on an abstract fundamentalist deployment of a number of very ambiguous texts, or on a problematic and non-scriptural theory about natural complementarity, applied narrowly and crudely to physical differentiation without regard to psychological structures. I suspect that a fuller exploration of the sexual metaphors of the Bible will have more to teach us about a theology and ethics of sexual desire than will a flat citation of isolated texts.[26]

Though a major source of Rowan's later problems at Canterbury, 'The Body's Grace' was a ground-breaking piece of work. By implicitly challenging liberals to be more serious about scriptural principles, the Professor was subverting conservative arguments all the more comprehensively in the process.

The chief criticism of his stances – whether on sexual ethics or, as outlined in *Essays Catholic and Radical*, on the nature of orthodoxy – has been that he wants to have his cake and eat it too. We are now in a stronger position to understand his response. The Bible, as he has observed in an important academic essay,[27] is itself a history of the re-reading of texts. It has generated 'an enormous family of contrapuntal variations'.[28] Moreover, although the Church is committed to understanding the world in the light of its own foundational narratives, the interpretative process affects the narratives, as well as the world. For example, something happens to the Exodus narrative as it is absorbed into the black slave culture of America: and in the light of this and other examples, the Church 'is itself enlarged in understanding and even in some sense evangelized'.

He rearticulated this insight in a celebrated address at the inauguration of Affirming Catholicism – the network for liberal Anglo-Catholics established in 1990:

> I've heard it said that one of the greatest triumphs of Catholic Christianity is its ability to *train its own critics*. And this means surely that Catholic tradition ought to be concerned with presenting a depth and range of resources that will stop anyone from too easily believing that the Church at any one moment has got it all wrapped up, has fathomed the meaning of Jesus Christ. And this isn't polite agnosticism or do-it-yourself modernism – making up Christianity as you go along – but the fruit of trying to keep eyes and ears and heart open to the wholeness of what's being passed on to us – including the awkwardnesses, the half-hidden points of conflict, the half-muffled voices.[29]

*   *   *

Rowan was doing far more than weighing into arguments about sex during the late 1980s. He taught theology to non-university students such as the novelist Sara Maitland, and began a close friendship with Gillian Rose, Professor of Social and Political Theory at Warwick University. A Jewish left-winger, Rose was gradually propelled towards religious belief by her political and ethical convictions. She died in 1995 at the age of forty-eight, and was baptised into the Church of England on her deathbed. Among much else, she can be credited with sharpening Rowan's interest in Hegel during his time at Christ Church.[30]

Halfway through this period, he was guest speaker for Holy Week at St Albans Cathedral, and riveted his audience. Colin Slee, later Dean of Southwark, reports that the congregation were 'blown out of the water' by the depth of Rowan's sermons, which were all delivered without notes. 'One woman was so moved during the talks marking the Passion that she couldn't handle the emotional turnaround entailed by Easter,' Slee remembers. 'That was one sign among many of how deep an impact Rowan had on people.'

A short break gave him the opportunity to visit Launde Abbey, a handsome manor house in Rutland serving as the Leicester diocesan retreat house. Here Rowan enjoyed the hospitality of the warden, Canon Henry Evans, and wrote part of his book *Teresa of Avila*.[31] Another service he performed to the Church at this time came from his membership of the Anglican–Orthodox International Commission. The official dialogue had begun in 1973 and had seen notable progress, especially when some Anglican provinces agreed to drop the *filioque* ('and from the Son', a clause added unilaterally to the creed in the West during the first millennium, which encapsulates differences in Trinitarian doctrine between Eastern and Western Christianity). But by the late 1980s, ecumenical progress had been damaged in Orthodox eyes by the ordination of women. Part of Rowan's achievement consisted in the smoothing of ecumenical feathers. 'He commanded huge respect,' according to John Riches, his former teacher, who also sat on the commission. 'We met at the monastery of New Valamo in Finland, and the Orthodox saw Rowan as a man of great devotion.' Much of the encounter consisted of a sustained dialogue between the Lady Margaret Professor and Archbishop John Zizioulas, perhaps the most influential thinker in the Eastern tradition today.

Further academic garlands came Rowan's way – he was awarded a doctorate of divinity in 1989 and made a Fellow of the British Academy the following year. But his pastoral concerns and relative dissatisfaction with Oxford were tugging him away from the ivory tower.

4

Fox and Hedgehog

Rowan Williams is even more absorbed by the life of the mind than were William Temple and Michael Ramsey, his two most cerebral twentieth-century predecessors; and what is true of the intellect applies still more to spirituality. To get the measure of this, we need to look more closely at the underground streams that have nourished him.

As reported, Rowan developed an exceptionally disciplined early-morning prayer routine from an early age. How did he fill the hours before breakfast when he wasn't reading or meditating on Scripture and devotional works? A clue comes from a frequent observation about his style as a lecturer: he has an unusual gift for making figures from the remote past his contemporaries. The Desert Fathers, Meister Eckhart, St Teresa of Avila and St John of the Cross speak not only to him, but for him. Rowan's writings and talks about these and other authorities tell us much about his own inner life. An example of this is his 1984 essay on Dom Cuthbert Butler's great book *Western Mysticism*. The exercise of 'simple loving will' in prayer, Rowan comments, 'without complicated schemes of meditation and efforts to stir the imagination', is truly contemplative, and basic to what the 'mystics' are writing about. Butler also contends that the mystical aspect is to be viewed as one of religion's four elements, alongside the institutional, the intellectual and the charitable. 'We're not talking here about the cataloguing of paranormal experiences,' Rowan explains, 'but the deepening, habitual awareness of loss, recovery and transformation in relation to the paschal focus of Christian commitment . . . Christian contemplation, in short, is about having the image of Christ formed in us.'[1]

Amid all the turmoil he has faced as Archbishop of Canterbury, it may be easy to forget that Rowan has a merited reputation as one of Anglicanism's finest spiritual directors. The bravura passage from his Loughborough conference address quoted in Chapter 2 gives some idea why. Further signs of his know-how came in the reply, both straightforward and subtle, that he gave when asked in a *Daily Telegraph* interview for his advice on praying:

it doesn't much matter at first how much time you can give so long as you can give some regular time. The challenge is to find enough time to become quiet enough and still enough. And all the [emphasis on] the need to attend to your body is not about exotic yoga techniques. It is how do you use your body in such a way that you can actually centre it to be where you are. Somebody once said that the deepest problem in prayer is often not the absence of God but the absence of me. I'm not actually there. My mind is everywhere. So take a few breaths, use a simple formula like the Orthodox, 'Lord Jesus Christ, Son of God, have mercy', and sense in that that the line is anchored somewhere in the depths. That's back to where we started, really. Familiar formulae and the rhythms that come naturally actually matter quite a lot and I've sometimes advised people to try to find a verse of a hymn that means something to them or just a single phrase. It doesn't have to be the Orthodox formula that I mentioned. It can be 'Jesu, Lover of my Soul, Let me to thy Bosom Fly', or 'Immortal, Invisible, God Only Wise'. Things that people only half remember but phrases that stick and, if you let them, sit in your mind, that's a beginning of getting there. And when you are there God can relate to you. God cannot speak to you if you are not actually there.[2]

A valuable insight into Rowan's spirituality comes in his presentation of Teresa of Avila's most celebrated writings: *The Life*, her autobiography; and *The Interior Castle*, a spiritual classic.[3] *The Life* includes a well-known digression on what Teresa terms the four levels of prayer, in which she describes the path of a Christian from a state where he or she is shouldering the burden, to one where God does the work. The levels are sometimes called the Four Waters, by which Teresa means four methods of spiritual irrigation. She invites us to think about ways of watering a garden. The first involves taking a bucket to the well, a process that grows irksome with frequent repetition. Later, we might erect a water wheel with buckets on it. This may help, until we see that it would be more satisfactory to dig an irrigation channel. The simplest way of all to water a garden is through rain. Rowan interprets this 'very powerful parable' of the levels of prayer as follows:

We begin with the bucket and the well, laborious concentration, colloquy – that is, speaking to God – using our imagination, cranking it up. Hard work, but everybody starts there really. After a while you get used to that, and it's more like the water wheel and the buckets. Your recollections, your sense of focusing on matters of the spirit and the mysteries of God become easier, more natural, though your memory and your imagination aren't yet fully harnessed. You arrive at some sort of quiet, some sort of inner peace, where your intelligence is stilled a little bit. You become a bit more passive to what's going on. That's the water wheel. You're still doing the rounds, you're still performing the meditational techniques, but it's getting a bit easier . . .

The stream running through the garden is another matter, though. Something is happening in you, whether or not you are doing anything.

And that's the deeper level still where you're increasingly aware that it's not you making the running. And in this state there may be a kind of arrest or seizure of your mental faculties . . . Then there's heavy rain. God's action just soaking in, straight down, and all you know is that you are glad to be there under the rain. It's a fruition, an enjoyment, which you can't find words for . . . In this fourth state, you're united with God.

St Teresa charts this process with much greater sophistication in *The Interior Castle*, where she likens the soul's journey towards God with progress between the outer and inner layers of a fortification. There are seven resting places or 'mansions' in this structure. The first, strictly speaking just outside the castle, is occupied by many Christians. They practise formal prayer of some sort, but are only dimly aware of their spiritual matrix. The second resting place is peopled by those who are becoming more actively religious. Their emotions are engaged, and they are starting to show greater discipline in their prayer lives. The third stage is both transitional and perilous. Rowan makes its universal relevance clear. It is

> where you're really enthusiastic about religion. In fact, you're so enthusiastic about religion that the impulse to get right to the middle to meet Christ can actually be a little bit weakened. This is a stage where, Teresa says, you're full of zeal for the souls of other people and very ready to try and bring them up to your standard. She hadn't lived in convents for nothing. Or, indeed, the Church. And although, in this third stage, the roots of sin are beginning to be eradicated, and there is genuinely growing a natural affinity, a taste, as you might say, for God, the problem is that also sin can be more deeply hidden. The roots of sin are beginning to be tackled, but also there's so much religion going on that those may be overlaid.

The third resting place is thus a point from which one can easily slip backwards. The priority is to advance with some speed. But the Christian on this path will encounter a good deal of disorientation, because he or she is letting go of familiar bearings as the supernatural, in the strict sense of the word, begins to take effect. A measure of spiritual irrigation is taking place (though this stage cannot be tied in neatly with the Four Waters), and the will is directed more systematically towards God. The intelligence, however, tends to fall behind, not least because the soul's previously ordered prayer life has been churned up.

This renders the fourth resting place an even more unsettling spot than the third. You will feel confused, spiritually parched, and may undergo some of the profound trials that St John of the Cross describes with particular insight and integrity. Yet Teresa's point is that the process is underwritten by God. The fifth resting place is a zone of assurance, the 'spiritual betrothal'. God has united himself with the soul at a fundamental level. A deep choice, made possible by God, has been made. Rowan is quick to note a parallel here with the apparently Protestant conviction about a relationship with God that cannot be lost. The sixth resting place involves a process of further spiritual refinement. Teresa writes of the need to shun afresh false ideas about religion, but she also lays a strong accent on the incarnate Jesus as the source and destination of the soul's journey. (Other writers, both in the Middle Ages and beforehand, had urged that meditating on Jesus' humanity should in due course give way to a greater focus on his divinity. Teresa is doubtful about this on practical as well as theological grounds, and urges her sisters and others to hold on to a crucifix, or keep a small image of Jesus in their pockets.)

The final resting place marks the consummation of a spiritual marriage, but it is not a source of visions and other special experiences. On the contrary, life is normal again. Teresa sums this up with the image that Mary and Martha are united. Almost all other theologians had seen Mary, representing the contemplative calling, as superior to her sister Martha, who embodied the active life. Teresa is very unusual in seeing them as two sides of the same coin. Rowan explains that

> when you've got used to living in the stream of God's action, then actually you settle down again. And what's striking there is [the similarity] not only [with] what St John of the Cross says but to that old chestnut from the Zen Buddhist world. Before you begin meditation, mountains are mountains, and rivers are rivers, and trees are trees, and when you start meditation, mountains stop being mountains, etc. When you arrive at enlightenment,

mountains are mountains again, and rivers are rivers, and trees
are trees. The journey is to come back where you started and
know the place for the first time, as T. S. Eliot puts it.

The resting places (like the interior castle itself) are metaphors, of
course. Teresa is aware that the coordinates of a Christian's
evolution cannot be tracked precisely. But her map can help
people in any era avoid common spiritual blunders.

Much the same could be said about Meister Eckhart (*c*1260–
1327), the most notable of the fourteenth- and fifteenth-
century Rhineland mystics. Eckhart's reputation has been
damaged by two groups: those of his more nervous contemporaries who doubted his orthodoxy, and some wishful modern interpreters who conceive of him as a Buddhist or Hindu
in a Dominican habit. Rowan's lecture on Eckhart to a mainly
lay audience in Bristol is characteristically stimulating.[4] Early
on, he refers to Eckhart's belief that there is a divine spark in
everyone – a notion feeding the sense among his critics and
fans alike that he was a kind of pantheist. Not so, Rowan
maintains, granted Eckhart's insistence that we can say something about *our* apprehension of God – known as Father, Son
and Holy Spirit, as creator and redeemer – but absolutely
nothing about what God is in himself. When the being of God
somehow 'overflows' into creation, God does not cease to be
God, just as a mirror may reflect the sun without becoming the
object it reflects.

So there is a form of continuity between God and ourselves,
by dint of the divine spark (Eckhart's word is *Funkelein*, twinkle)
in human beings. Much closer to the present, this insight is
memorably conveyed by Thomas Merton, who influenced
Rowan profoundly during his student days. 'At the center of

our being is a point of nothingness which is untouched by sin and illusion,' Merton writes,

> a point of pure truth, a point or spark which belongs entirely to God, which is never at our disposal, from which God disposes of our lives, which is inaccessible to the fantasies of our own mind or the brutalities of our own will. This little point of nothingness and of *absolute poverty* is the pure glory of God in us. It is so to speak his name written in us, as our poverty, as our indigence, as our dependence, as our sonship. It is like a pure diamond, blazing with the invisible light of heaven. It is in everybody, and if we could see it we would see these billions of points of light coming together in the face and blaze of a sun that would make all the darkness and cruelty of life vanish completely . . . I have no program for this seeing. It is only given. But the gate of heaven is everywhere.[5]

How, though, is the spark to be cultivated? Once more, Eckhart's perspective broadly coincides with what Rowan himself believes. In the first place, you don't wander around looking for your own spark of divinity. Be still, close your eyes, stop thinking, don't look for anything. The spark will kindle when you are dead to the world:

> it's rather like the child's game [that] comes up in the folklore of various nations: don't think of the word 'hippopotamus' for the next five minutes. Or [there is] a Norwegian saying, that you are perfectly safe crossing the polar icecap so long as you don't think about polar bears. So with Eckhart, you discover who you really are by absolutely not thinking about it. Don't go in search of your inner self. That's absolutely fatal, for Eckhart. Don't even

think about it. Just shut up and go into the dark. And the more you go into the dark, the nearer you get to an absolute darkness and stillness, the nearer you're getting to the moment of birth, the moment of renewal.

These ideas might seem like standard fare for mystical writing, but Rowan is quick to warn that they are only the foundations of Eckhart's structure. As a Dominican, he believed that contemplation should be a spur to action and not a substitute for it. Rowan quotes the twelfth-century Cistercian writer William of Saint-Thierry here, who declared that love of the truth drives us from the world to God, and the truth of love sends us back from God to the world. In other words, as Eckhart commented, if you were in the seventh heaven of ecstasy and a poor man knocked on the door to ask for a bowl of soup, then the bowl of soup should come first. He added that you would perform a labour of love more effectively through having first drawn close to God, the fount of all truthful and effective action.

Eckhart's emphasis on God's birth in us (and his use of sometimes astonishingly graphic similes to depict the process) has led some of his disciples to see him as a positive, world-affirming thinker; others, focusing more on what he says about the sacrifices entailed by mystical prayer, have drawn the opposite conclusion. Rowan's crossbench verdict – complete with a damning verdict, showing his sometimes very sardonic sense of humour, on the American theologian Matthew Fox – is revealing about himself, as well as his subject:

So is [Eckhart] positive or negative? Well, neither quite works. And it's very interesting to see how commentators have leaned on one side or the other. I mentioned that for a long time people thought Eckhart was a kind of Hindu in disguise, and [his work] was all about being absorbed into the divine, but I hope I've shown you why that isn't really accurate. On the other hand, you have this man Matthew Fox, the great guru of creation spirituality, [once] a Dominican, now, I'm sorry to say, an Anglican, and [he] really wants to make Eckhart a prophet of late-twentieth-century Californian eco-feminism, and he works very hard at that, but again that's only part of the picture. I don't read very much in Eckhart myself that suggests that that would be his natural homeland today.

A more convincing link drawn by Rowan at the end of his lecture is between Eckhart and Luther, given their mutual insistence that Christians do not do good in order to please God, but because God is pleased with them. 'If Eckhart and Luther can exchange a rather wry smile across the wreckage of divided Christendom between them, that's a promising sign for all of us.'

*   *   *

The rationale for a report on Rowan's account of the creed is based not only on his scholarly stature. As he prepared to move to Lambeth in late 2002, the Archbishop was accused of heresy in a pamphlet, *The Theology of Rowan Williams*, by his namesake Garry Williams. Written from a hardline conservative Evangelical standpoint, it challenged the common assumption that the Archbishop is a doctrinal traditionalist whose only contentious views are about sexuality. On the contrary, Garry Williams held, the argument about sexual ethics is 'merely the presenting symptom': the defects in the Archbishop's theology extend to the core, embracing the doctrines of revelation and salvation.

Other Evangelicals (not to speak of liberals and Anglo-Catholics) discounted the pamphlet as poorly argued and even malicious in intent. But it nevertheless helped intensify the pressure on the Archbishop in an already febrile situation. Unsurprisingly, we get a more reliable idea about Rowan's views from his own writings. The most lucid statement of his faith comes in *Tokens of Trust* – edited transcripts of talks given in Canterbury Cathedral during Holy Week 2005.

The book begins light years away from the small world of church wrangles:

> Why, if every specific form of active existence is going to stop being what it is and turn into something else, is there never a moment when the entire network collapses into incoherence, into complete randomness? We recognize randomness at the smallest, most primitive level of existence, yet the big picture is never random. Just what is it that holds the balance, that makes what we encounter a true universe, a bounded, self-consistent, interdependent system?[6]

With this question – a variation on the challenge to Richard Dawkins quoted earlier – Rowan turns the tables on the sceptics. Atheism should not be seen as the neutral or default world view: to believe that the universe does not have a creator is at least as taxing as to hold that it does.

The Christian's gauntlet springs from a phrase common to the Apostles' and Nicene Creeds: 'maker of heaven and earth'. It is not unreasonable for the atheist to say that we can't know about God, and no set of human scales is equal to the task of weighing questions about the ultimate purpose (if any) of creation. In reply, Rowan underlines the widespread and dogged impulse to push against the boundaries of what can be said. This leads us to consider the idea that the universe is 'related to a reality that does not stand alongside it but somehow holds or includes it, a reality that is simply action, movement, without restriction or qualification'.[7] The child's question, 'Who made God?' is natural enough, but its redundancy becomes clearer the more we think about the unique context of the discussion. During the High Middle Ages, St Thomas Aquinas attempted to get to grips with the problem by defining God's being in very sophisticated philosophical vocabulary. Rowan presents this reasoning much more accessibly: 'in referring to God, we are no longer talking about levels of explanation within the same system; we're trying to get our minds around the idea of an activity that is so utterly consistent with itself, so unaffected by any other activity, that it is, so to speak, its own explanation, its own "cause", eternal and unchanging.'[8]

Tokens of Trust then moves straight to dispel a misconception common among both religious believers and their secular critics – that God made the world and then stood back from it. In the great monotheistic faiths, God is held to be energising and sustaining his creation at all times. There is indeed a beginning point, Rowan writes, but it is the beginning of an active relationship that never stops. Eighteenth- and nineteenth-century deists famously drew on a comparison between God and a watchmaker: the universe was held to have been 'wound up' and left to tick. In Rowan's eyes, a less misleading analogy could be drawn from the relation between electricity and light. A light shines because of electric current, but we do not infer from this that power is around only at the moment when a switch is turned on, 'so that the light itself is a rather distant result'. No: 'the light is shining here and now because the electric current is flowing here and now. In the same way, it is the "current" of divine activity that is here and now making us real.'[9]

There are radical implications to such claims, among them that

> within every circumstance . . . every person, God's action is going on, a sort of white heat at the centre of everything. It means that each one of us is already in a relationship with God before we've ever thought about it. It means that every object or person we encounter is in a relationship with God before they're in a relationship of any kind with us. And if that doesn't make us approach the world and other people with reverence and amazement, I don't know what will.[10]

This vision excludes pantheism (the identification of God with the universe *tout court*): God is not 'exhausted' by creation, and would not be in any way diminished if the universe did not exist. And since the creeds' account of reality is metaphysical, not quasi-scientific, Rowan concludes that science and religion are not, after all, in conflict.

The discussion turns to theodicy – the defence of Christian belief about God's attributes in the face of widespread evil and suffering. *Tokens of Trust* adopts a version of the so-called freewill argument. Creation, by definition, is not God, and is therefore subject to change and collision. If processes were engineered so as never to clash with one another, it is doubtful whether the world could be looked on as having any integrity of its own. In our context, evolution has given rise to beings who can think and plan: among much else, they may (whether through choice or other circumstances) end up living near the site of a natural disaster:

This does absolutely nothing to make it emotionally easier to face something like the Asian tsunami [which claimed several hundred thousand lives in December 2004], nothing at all; it won't stop us questioning God or protesting to God. But we have to try and keep our heads clear enough to recognize that natural disasters are just that, the laws of nature going ahead. It is unspeakably terrible that people and animals are caught in the flow, so to speak; but can we imagine a world where certain processes were always halted in their tracks by God if there were a risk to living creatures? If the world is not just a veil for God's reality, not just a matter of appearances with no continuity in them, there is no quick way through this. And what makes it possible to find God credible even in this context will not be a knockdown argument explaining why evil occurs but . . . the experience of how actual people find God real even in the middle of these terrors.[11]

But orthodox Christianity entails belief in miracles, so it is still reasonable to ask why God does not intervene (or, if he does intervene, why he does not do so more often) to avert disaster. For Rowan as for many in the classical tradition, help comes from further resistance to knee-jerk ideas about God and the universe. As we have seen, orthodoxy does not picture God as standing at a distance from creation, but rather as a 'steady swell of loving presence, always there at work in the centre of everything that is, opening the door to a future even when we can see no hope'.[12] And if God is always present in and around his creatures, then we must reject the impulse to think of divine action and worldly processes as jostling for space. Where miracles are concerned, Rowan's deduction (again indebted to St Thomas and his modern interpreters) is that there are times when events come together in a way that is more 'transparent' to the underlying act of God:

> Perhaps a really intense prayer or a really holy life can open the world up that bit more to God's purpose so that unexpected things happen. We're never going to have a complete picture of how that works, because we don't have God's perspective on it all. But we can say that there are some things we can think, say or do that seem to give God that extra 'freedom of manoeuvre' in our universe. And whether we fully understand what's going on or not, we know that it's incumbent on us to do what we can to let this happen. We pray, we act in ways that have some chance of shaping a situation so that God can come more directly in.[13]

'A Man for All Seasons', the chapter on Christ in *Tokens of Trust*, is especially light to read and weighty in impact. The difficulties of discussing Christian claims that Jesus is both human and divine are formidable. Part of the picture tends to be overlooked, or lost altogether. Before the late twentieth century, the Church itself did much to feed the fantasy that its Lord was more a supernatural visitant than a real man. These days, many believers, let alone secularists, are happy to strip away what they see as the thick mythological crust affixed to a charismatic first-century carpenter. 'A Man for All Seasons' thus amounts to a fresh statement of the case against *The Myth of God Incarnate*.

All the main points are there. First, that the creeds do not betray Jesus' message. Within a few decades of the crucifixion, the author of Colossians wrote that in Christ, 'all the fullness of God was embodied'. Here, Rowan urges, 'is a human life so shot through with the purposes of God, so transparent to the action of God, that people speak of it as God's life "translated" into another medium. Here God is supremely and uniquely at work.'[14]

This text is not isolated. Some of the most audacious claims about Christ's identity belong to the New Testament's primitive strands. The message emerging from the Gospels is correspondingly bold: 'live in Jesus's company, and you become a citizen of a new world, the world in which God's rule has arrived'. You will still be residing in the here and now, with all its pressures, and in which 'many other powers claim to be ruling; but you will have become free of them, free to co-operate or not, depending on how far they allow you to be ruled by God'. No sphere of human life is therefore untouched by this message. The Beatitudes, for example, have profound social implications, but their message cannot be caught by political action alone. Change can only spring from a personal acceptance of the gospel message – and this subverts the spiritual self-sufficiency implied by Jewish ritual observance in Jesus' day.

Judaism during the inter-testamental period was awash with speculation about angelic beings who bridged the gap between the supernatural and created realms. Some Christians might have settled for language of this kind to describe Jesus, Rowan explains, but it didn't ring true: 'Awkwardly and slowly and with much complication and even apparent contradiction', the New Testament felt its way towards 'the extraordinary notion' that the creator of the universe and Jesus are one in action. But Christ is also represented in the Gospels as one who prays, and speaks of doing his Father's will. Here, Rowan moves to explain how the doctrine of God was itself reforged in response to Jesus' career. 'Somehow, the divine presence in Jesus, if it's really a presence in all he does and says, is working itself out in this humility and responsiveness.'[15] In other words, our definition of

God cannot just embrace power, but includes an element of loving response, an outflowing and a reflecting back, an initiative and a depending.

The Christian conception of God's nature therefore differs substantially from that of Jews or Muslims; and what is more, it has deep implications for our own self-understanding as moral agents:

> It means, among many other things, that we human beings, who live in relationships where we are both givers and receivers, both depending and controlling, can reflect the life of God in every aspect of what we are; we are no less in God's image when we acknowledge our dependence or when we offer thanks than when we are taking decisions or showing God's love to another.[16]

Yet the world Jesus enters, like our own, is sinful – steeped in 'blocked choices, wrong turnings and drastically false accounts of who and what we are'. Anyone embodying unrestricted love will be 'terribly unsafe' in such a setting; so when Jesus is rejected by the religious and political establishments of his day, 'we can say that he "embodies" not only the purposes and possibilities of God but the effects of the self-destructiveness of human beings'.

Rowan harnesses the various elements in atonement theory with deceptive skill. Jesus on the cross in his agony and wretchedness is

> a sort of picture of our ultimate fate [which is] . . . being cut off from what is true . . . In that sense, at least, he is carrying the burden of our sin – bearing the results of what we habitually do . . . It isn't that a vengeful and inflexible God demands

satisfaction, more that the way the world is makes it unavoidable that the way to our freedom lies through the self-giving of Jesus, even to the point of death. In the kind of world that you and I inhabit, the kind of world that you and I make or collude with, this is what the price of unrestricted love looks like.[17]

Tokens of Trust's discussion of Jesus' triumph over death is redolent of Rowan's approach in *Resurrection*. This miracle 'displays God's triumphant love as still and for ever having the shape of Jesus'. But there is something else. According to John's Gospel, Jesus ' "breathes into" his disciples his "spirit", the breath of his life, so that they become equipped to do what he does and to speak with his voice with God and to the world. By breathing into his disciples, he sets up a chain of human contact coming down to our own day . . .'[18]

The New Testament thus plants the seed of Trinitarian belief. In time, the Church saw this seed's momentous fruit. As Rowan said in another context, if we were to picture God only as Father and Son, we would be stuck with an image of static reflection: two just looking at each other. Belief in the divinity of the Holy Spirit was codified when Christians acknowledged that God is more than a mirroring of Father and Son. There is 'an excess and a flow of love always and eternally more than just that . . . reciprocity. And it's because of that that a world can appear that may be drawn into the life of Father and Son. God is eternally open to the world joining him. That's partly what the doctrine of the Holy Spirit says.'[19]

'God in Company', the penultimate chapter of *Tokens of Trust*, includes an explanation of the Eucharist as the place where worshippers encounter Christ in the action of the Spirit. Technical terms are avoided, but the influence of recent Roman

Catholic thinking is clear when Rowan says that the Christian receiving communion is given 'what the literal flesh and blood have within them, the radiant action and power of God the Son, the life that makes him who he is'.[20] No less agile is the section on scriptural authority. The Bible is not a Christian Koran. It does not itself purport to be a divine revelation – Jesus Christ is that – but revelation's primary witness. The inspiration of Scripture resides in 'its capacity to be the vehicle of the Holy Spirit, making Jesus vividly present to our minds and hearts, and so making his challenge and invitation immediate to us'.[21] If you make the category mistake of reading the Bible 'as a single book between covers', you may end up fretting about whether every verse of it is inerrant. If one episode or other is shown to be mythological, then doubts may be sown about the text as a whole. But if, on the other hand, Scripture is seen as

> a collection of texts consistently used by the Holy Spirit to renew and convert the Church . . . [then] the issue of whether it is all totally accurate by modern standards of history or science becomes less important. Genesis may not tell us how the world began in the way a modern cosmologist would; but it tells us what God wants us to know, that we are made by his love and freedom alone . . . And while we are on a different kind of ground with – say – the Gospel stories, which were written down so close to the time of the events narrated, it is still true that contradictions of detail between Gospels are not the end of the world . . .[22]

The Trinitarian faith elaborated in *Tokens of Trust* might be described as the enduring melody in the Archbishop's writings, and thus provides a useful gauge by which to assess the complaints of Garry Williams. True, Rowan has regularly underlined the difficulty of speaking about God. Garry Williams is not alone in thinking that the Archbishop has sometimes overstated the implications of divine transcendence and of the priority of silence over speech. As reported in the Introduction to this book, another conservative Evangelical, Oliver O'Donovan, thinks so too, though this has never caused him to doubt the Archbishop's underlying orthodoxy. O'Donovan would agree with numerous other observers who hold that Rowan's core Christian theme is always reasserted, even when it has been reconfigured in multiple variations, some darker and further away from the home key. It is Garry Williams's neglect of this point, above all, that has fed the idea that his intentions were mischievous. A biography is not the place for a detailed discussion of his pamphlet. Given the alarm he stoked up among traditionalists in an already combustible situation, though, a few sentences on his main conclusions are in order.

Garry Williams believes that the Archbishop's theology is radically negative or apophatic, and sabotages all claims to revelation.

> Gone is the clear, content-full revelation of God in Christ. Gone is the perspicuity of Scripture as an inspired witness to revelation. Gone is the illuminating work of the Spirit in opening our minds to the clear truth which God has given us in his Word . . . The only truth which remains is the truth that all truth is in question.[23]

His conclusion is that 'the theology of Rowan Williams puts souls at risk of perishing. The tragic consequence, a consequence which we can only greet with heavy hearts, is that we find ourselves bound to oppose his appointment.' Garry Williams seems unaware that the critique of cut-and-dried theologising has a long impeccable pedigree. Among other sources, the Archbishop bases his views on the biblical denunciation of idolatry, St Paul's argument that the cross of Christ subverts human wisdom, and much of the classical tradition from the Greek Fathers onwards, not to mention philosophical and political diagnoses of power, both modern and postmodern. Garry Williams also takes exception to Rowan Williams's admittedly intrepid likening of God to a spastic child. But the criticism ignores the context in which the remark was made. Rowan was meditating on the solitude of Jesus on the cross, where God passes beyond words and, like the spastic child, 'can communicate nothing but his own presence and his inarticulate wanting'.[24]

Garry Williams is especially appalled by the Archbishop's support for gay couples, and his suggestion in 'The Body's Grace' that not all pre-marital sex between men and women is wrong either. Even if you discount Garry Williams's view that such teaching will lead people to hell, 'The Body's Grace' does offer some ammunition to conservatives, coming as it does from a future church leader. Again, though, Garry Williams overplays his hand. In office, the Archbishop has not endorsed heterosexual sex outside marriage, and this fact is ignored in *The Theology of Rowan Williams*. Garry Williams is also unreliable in implying that the Archbishop approves of gay sex as such, as opposed to monogamous partnerships expressing God's love through fidelity. The pamphlet's invocation of Romans 1 and 1 Corinthians 6 begs the question, since Paul is speaking about a pattern of life in alienation from God, not one based on faith in Christ.

The Church of England was sufficiently concerned about Garry Williams's charges to commission a briefing paper for the House of Bishops from Christopher Jones, then an Oxford theology don. It gives short shrift to the Archbishop's antagonist, describing the 'menacing tone' of Garry Williams's conclusion as 'perhaps an inevitable consequence' of the pamphlet's 'distorted' portrait. 'There may well be grounds for taking issue with Rowan Williams's thought at particular points,' Jones added, 'but that is a very different matter from finding him unorthodox or a "false teacher".'

Published four and a half years after this furore, *Tokens of Trust* was very well received. Any weaknesses in the book are unconnected with the terrain covered by Garry Williams: they lie (as more searching commentators have pointed out) with the Archbishop's ecclesiology, and his view of the relation between Church and world. His accent is more on an idealistic account of churchly attributes than on the institution as such:

> Just as we can trust God because he has no agenda that is not for our own good, so we can trust the Church because it is . . . a community of active peacemaking . . . where no one exists in isolation . . . So a well-functioning Christian community is going to be one in which everyone is working steadily to release the gifts of others.[25]

In other words, the Church is described primarily as a set of human communities, working more or less effectively, as marriages work, according to how much give and take is displayed. The historian Lucy Beckett[26] was one of several Roman Catholic critics to note the lack of an explicit sense of the Church's double nature, as both a divine society, the bride of Christ ('a very different use of the marriage analogy') and a human institution, which has a difficult and sometimes horrifying history, always includes saints and sinners, and which will be judged by God alone. Some also queried Rowan's definition of ministry as the inhabiting of a common life with 'particular intensity'. That the Church needs to teach and conserve orthodoxy is implied but never asserted in *Tokens of Trust*.

The faultlines in Rowan's doctrine of the Church have already been brought out by Theo Hobson in his stimulating broadside, *Anarchy, Church and Utopia: Rowan Williams on Church*.[27] The clue is in the title. The Archbishop, in Hobson's eyes, is in the anomalous position of being an undeclared anarchist utopian who is yet steeped in traditional language, as well as leading a traditionally structured Church linked to secular power. Rowan therefore combines what are at bottom Protestant ideas about how the Church is constituted with a Catholic sensitivity to the importance of sign and ritual in community-building. As we have seen, his decision to remain an Anglican was partly negative: if he had been able to accept papal infallibility, he might have left the Church of England during the mid-1970s. But for those who cannot accept Roman Catholic teaching, ecclesiology is likely to be a less clear-cut business in principle. Rowan's supporters also argue that inconclusiveness can be creative as well as unsettling. As one proudly Anglican reviewer put it, 'institutions, with their inherent hierarchies and boundaries, can still conserve radical visions, including unbounded love'.[28] Nor does the vision stay behind closed doors. It is 'able to fructify as picked up by the world'. We shall return to this subject: as the prospect of a schism loomed after the consecration of Gene Robinson in 2003,

Anglican ecclesiology itself began to change, and with it the ecclesiology of its leader.

*   *   *

What, though, of Rowan's attitude to the interface between the Church and politics? This area, too, is of the highest importance, and much depends – as David Martin has argued – on 'whether you stand back at a safe distance from tough choices, thereby risking being accused of bardic lament, or whether you come up close and risk your authority in the cut and thrust of the public square'.[29] Martin does not doubt that Rowan belongs too much in the former camp, and that his most significant weakness lies in his political thinking, rather than in his theology. A surer path, in Martin's view, is based on the so-called Christian realism of a figure such as Reinhold Niebuhr, which entails focusing on what can be done now within the limited available options, rather than exercising a roving commission of free-ranging moral judgement, ignoring real constraints or alternative costs, and big on hindsight.

This subject is not an exact science, of course. Thoughtful Christians usually seek to balance a set of constantly shifting variables as situations change. They will also guard against complacency: Niebuhr's critics have been quick to argue that the gospel presents us with a world which has broken into this one through the resurrection, and therefore requires a fundamental redefinition of power. In Rowan's case, though, the suspicion remains that witness literature (devotional or exclamatory material about the power of the risen Christ, for example) is a substitute for practical analysis. This argument was summed up by Angela Tilby in a television documentary about the newly appointed Archbishop of Canterbury in 2002.[30] She spoke of how her friend's politics had always come out of a different and less sophisticated part of him.

Archilochus, the ancient Greek poet, wrote that the fox knows many things, and the hedgehog one big one. The Oxford philosopher Isaiah Berlin later applied this saying to point up the distinction between those with a multifarious view of the world and those with a more unitary vision. By this standard, Rowan is a theological fox and a political hedgehog. Some of the main elements in his political world view are set out in *The Truce of God*,[31] a volume written with more flair than care.

Explanations for the ambivalent reaction of Archbishop Robert Runcie, who commissioned it as his 1983 Lent book, are not hard to find. Overall, it says a good deal about why Rowan's experience in the public square as Archbishop has sometimes been bruising by comparison with the adulation heaped on him in the more protected arenas provided by academia and the peace movement. He begins *The Truce of God* by identifying a deep spiritual malaise behind the disaster and horror films that were especially popular during the 1970s and 80s. These movies are said to have much in common, including the idea that pain and injury and sudden death are unplanned, not of our making, not our fault. 'Violence does not belong in the moral world; it has nothing to do with human responsibility, with the kinds of choices by which we make up our lives from day to day.'[32] From this, Rowan infers that *The Exorcist*, *The Towering Inferno* and similar works reflect a society incapable of turning a critical eye on itself. 'Instead, it chooses to see itself as innocent and vulnerable, recognising that the world is full of destructive potential, but refusing to deal with this recognition in human moral terms.'[33]

Nothing if not self-critical – some might say self-lacerating – Rowan then points to 'the embarrassingly obvious' context into which the fantasies of Western society fit:

We have been living for several decades with the knowledge that we are at last capable of obliterating the greater part of the human world in war . . . Because the possession and development of [nuclear] arms . . . is, on the face of it, morally outrageous, justification has been provided by the notion of 'deterrence': the Other Side must be the aggressor, and we shall never be other than the innocent victim, driven to retaliation by the horror of our circumstances.[34]

These comments could readily be classified as bardic lament: their credibility depends to a large extent on whether one sees the Soviet threat during the Cold War as dangerous, or just dangerously exaggerated. The peace campaigners who demonstrated against the deployment of Cruise missiles during the 1980s were accused by their opponents of favouring a policy that would leave the British population at increased risk. They judged differently, of course, and such divergencies of view are not only possible but to be expected between thoughtful people.

But *The Truce of God* takes a more absolutist line as it moves from generalities to a specific judgement on military strategy. Rowan starts, naturally enough, from Christian just-war theory, and especially the premise that any military action must be proportionate. Nuclear deterrence, summed up in the doctrine of Mutually Assured Destruction (MAD), involves the threat to inflict mass indiscriminate slaughter on the enemy. Like others in the peace movement, he directs particular criticism against a new military doctrine: that 'tactical' nuclear weapons, targeted on silos, not cities, would make the West more secure. His reasoning is straightforward. You don't fire weapons at an enemy silo *after* their weapons have been discharged, but before. Cruise, Trident and other new-generation weapons thus mark a qualitative shift in military thinking because they are designed to be used in a first strike. Nuclear war becomes more likely in consequence. As Rowan puts it: 'There is certainly less reluctance to admit that we might after all be the first to use nuclear weaponry in an international conflict if things are going badly. The idea of a deterrent as a tragic necessity imposed on an innocent and peace-loving society becomes less and less convincing.'[35]

This is simplistic, as well as simple, because the new generation of weapons opposed by peace campaigners was developed precisely in response to church-backed misgivings about MAD. It was *because* Christian leaders (Catholic bishops especially) had lobbied successive American presidents against deterrence that Jimmy Carter resolved to turn the development of NATO's weaponry from the morally unusable towards the morally defensible. Oliver O'Donovan confesses to have become 'very cross' with the peace movement, on the grounds that it got into 'the self-contradictory position of obstructing every attempt' at nuclear disarmament:

> While Moscow and Washington were gingerly trying to trade disarmament moves, the peace movement found nothing better to do than complain that each new disarmament package made nuclear war more possible. But who ever thought that nuclear war *wasn't* entirely possible as things stood? Only the true believers in nuclear deterrence! So the great lie at the heart

of deterrence, the idea that you could make your weapons so destructive that they would prevent war breaking out, was swallowed hook, line and sinker by the peace activists.[36]

O'Donovan draws an ironic lesson, directed at Rowan and others, from this: 'You see why political theology has to exist: to prevent those who love peace from scoring own goals.'[37]

The point of a detailed example such as this is that it demonstrates how a much larger discussion can be impaired by a neglect of detail. *The Truce of God* takes refuge in generalised comments and gives little or no quarter to the often serious-minded and ethically committed figures actually responsible for policy. Niebuhr was not a cynic. But he could not agree with those Christians, shielded from experience of power, whose fears about its misuse prompted a contempt for power per se. The rise of Christianity need not be treated as a spiritual calamity, nor its waning in the modern era as a recovery of original innocence and dynamism. A theologian such as Stephen Sykes stands on firmer ground here in seeing Augustine's two cities as a basis for dialogue between spiritual and secular power. It is neither necessary nor desirable to draw a firm line between the two: power may be put to beneficial as well as harmful use. Admittedly, authority and ritual have been responsible for gross abuses, but there are compelling grounds for thinking that, without them, no good can be achieved at all.[38]

Much of what Rowan has written about politics suggests that he would regard such a view as based on a serious dilution of Christian standards. But this attitude is not only questionable in the light of his ecclesiology – starting with his willingness to accept senior office in an established Church. It is also unfair to the achievements of pastoral theology over recent decades.

O'Donovan – who accused Rowan of being 'conceptually slack' about politics in an otherwise enthusiastic comment on his appointment to Canterbury[39] – is scathing about those who downplay the Christian shape of just-war theory. Not only does he think it wrong to say that the just-war idea is simple rationality; it is not even the simple rationality of the West, for just-war theory has had its high tides and low tides in the history of Western thinking. He points out that one can search the debates of the Second World War without finding any extensive moral scruple about non-combatant casualties. Even Bishop George Bell of Chichester defied the wartime thirst for vengeance by appeal to consideration of non-Nazi Germans, rather than of non-combatants. In the second half of the twentieth century, however, the category of non-combatant immunity recovered its value. During the war in Afghanistan in late 2001, O'Donovan observes, 'a controversy arose in the USA because commanders in the field were expected to have every potential target cleared by lawyers in the Pentagon for risk of excessive non-combatant collateral damage. A set of moral factors had come into our thinking that weren't there when the Second World War was fought.'[40]

One of the curiosities of *The Truce of God* is that Rowan repeatedly rejects total non-violence without showing due awareness that the non-pacifist faces some very tough choices in the real world. This oversight is not uncommon. Pope John Paul II was among many late twentieth-century church leaders to condemn all armed conflict, thereby feeding the impression that the just-war tradition mandates functional pacifism. History tells otherwise. The Iraq war has blackened the reputation of pre-emptive conflict, but if, for example, the liberal democracies had been able and willing to strike against Hitler in 1936, then incalculable suffering might have been avoided. They were by then consumed with guilt over the terms of the Versailles treaty, however, and would have been condemned by the Left for war-mongering had they sought regime change in Germany. One clear inference of this is that disablement by guilt has become a Christian and liberal speciality.

We shall return to *The Truce of God* in a later chapter, because it was heavily revised in 2005 to take account of developments since the Cold War and the aftermath of 11 September. In the meantime, though, several further observations are worth making about the book's first edition. The following quotations – including an undernoticed suggestion that hell may turn out to be an empty place – give a flavour of the whole:

> This is what the Church exists to say, and to sing, play, paint, act in all the ways it can: that human destiny . . . is in fact a single pattern organized around the magnetic centre of Jesus[41] . . . Cold War confrontation says that 'the others' are finally dispensable; they have nothing to give us that we could not do without. The existence of the Church contradicts this flatly, maintaining that we all need each other for our fulfilment, and that when mutual sharing breaks down this is a . . . wound in the whole human race. The logical conclusion is indeed what a great Russian saint of this century said, that no one could truly know the joys of heaven so long as anyone remained in hell.[42]

Nothing if not deeply serious, Rowan also turns the spotlight on his own side in a chapter called 'Illusions of Peace'. No right-wing pundit could have indicted with more precision the ramshackle anthropology underlying sections of the peace movement from the 1960s onwards:

> When . . . 'peace' became so much a . . . slogan among . . .
> youth movements, it came as part of a package which included a
> deep suspicion of public life and social planning . . . and what
> might be best summed up as a disbelief in original sin – a
> conviction that humanity could be drastically reconstructed by
> good will or love . . .[43]

'Peace' was thus seen as what we are left with when social
constraint is taken away – a very callow idea indeed, by Rowan's
own admission – and very much at odds with his theology in
general. At the end of the book, he describes the blind spots of
the Left even more sharply:

> Multilateralists are right: there is always a danger of peace movements
> and disarmament campaigns becoming narrow and one-sided in
> their aims. They may castigate their own societies and apologise or
> even condone the militarism of others. They may reproduce with
> uncanny accuracy the neuroses of the military establishment, re-
> directed now against governments and allies, instead of enemies.
> It is, for a British 'disarmer', a real temptation to build up fearful
> caricatures of the brutality, untrustworthiness and inhumanity of
> the United States, as vivid as many American (and British) caricatures
> of the Soviet Union. We have to remember to love our allies as well
> as our enemies. And they [disarmers] may represent a desperate
> eagerness to withdraw from the arena of public life, from the real and
> weary business of creating approximations to justice and under-
> standing between states. They may long for instant and total
> reconciliation, the immediate dismantling of all our arsenals.[44]

He cannot, in consequence, be accused of overlooking the
weaknesses of his own side in the nuclear weapons debate. The

surprise lies in his failure to think through the implications of his own insights more systematically.

A corollary of these comments might be that Christians can disagree in good conscience about nuclear disarmament, and that unilateralism is not the only (or even necessarily the best) path. Rowan appeared to grant this point in his address to the 1998 Lambeth Conference on making moral decisions. His coded message to bishops who read absolutist messages about sex from the Old Testament was simple. You believe that being anti-gay is the litmus test of Christian integrity; but there are others of us who hold that no Christian worth his or her salt can sanction the possession of nuclear weapons. We both need to listen and learn – and to appreciate that sexuality is not an issue carrying unique status. That many bishops from the Third World stopped their ears to this message is obvious enough. But amid all the emphasis on sex, fewer people have seen that in the political domain, Rowan, too, might be accused of reluctance to think outside the box. As Archbishop of Canterbury, for example, he said in a radio interview that he was against the replacement of Trident because he opposes nuclear weapons as such. Since there is no chance that the United States will forgo its nuclear arsenal, to find itself under threat from (say) North Korea, and given that Britain's rejection of such weapons leaves it enjoying American protection, this was moral free-loading. The ethical point of his remarks does not relate to some grand moral gesture at all, but to a margin where money spent on Trident could be spent more profitably on other things.

In the light of the compromises Rowan has been obliged to make in the ecclesiastical arena, the irony of this will be clear. What David Martin and others observe is an academic uncomfortably ensconced in a restrictive ecclesiastical role. In that role he finds himself with the outlook of a monk – almost, indeed, the outlook of a Quaker – while having to negotiate deals, and manage and manipulate outcomes. In church politics, he is not commenting from the touchline, but placed on top of the ball. As a consequence he is able, on the one hand, to talk in the world at large about nuclear armaments, a sphere where he can have no impact whatever, while on the other hand he has kept his counsel about the day-to-day politics of the Church, where he has considerable impact. He experiences the standard political imperative, which is to suppress some personal convictions in order to keep the show (whether Church or party or nation) on the road.

Before saying more about his time at Canterbury, though, we must return to Wales.

5

The Newport Years

The place to which Rowan went back was unfavourable mission territory. Therein lay part of the appeal. As we have seen, much of Wales was still socially cohesive and Evangelical in spirit during his youth. Within twenty-five years, the position had changed at a profound level through a mixture of secularism, migration and social mobility. Much of the Principality, like the rest of the UK, had become post-Christian, with churches that were serving a mainly older and female generation. This trend had affected the Nonconformists above all, but Anglicans, though protected to a degree by the parish system, were hardly immune. It is perhaps ironic that the man appointed to lead the Anglican Communion in 2002 came from a diocese that saw a faster rate of decline during the 1990s than almost any other in England or Wales.

The downward trend has been traced by Bob Jackson, Archdeacon of Walsall, in a report unveiled in May 2004.[1] This document reveals that adult attendance across the see of Monmouth fell from an average of 8,621 in 1990 to 5,540 in 2002, a drop of 36 per cent, which was steeper than most other parts of Wales. 'Along with Llandaff,' Jackson revealed, 'Monmouth has seen the fastest attendance falls of any diocese in the UK.' The fall in the number of children attending Sunday worship was even greater. Figures sank from 1,777 in 1996 (the first year in which they were counted) to 1,132 in 2002, a reduction of 36 per cent in only six years. Jackson's conclusion was bracing: 'with its small size and rapid decline, the diocese has no guarantee of a viable independent future'. Monmouth has remained intact, and towards the end of Rowan's time the effect of church-planting and other initiatives meant that fresh recruits slightly outnumbered those who were falling away. The diocese is now a tighter ship. Dominic Walker, Rowan's successor, is often described as a professional bishop. There has been much talk of mission action plans, and other forms of appraisal, since his arrival in 2003. The Representative Body, the Church in Wales's financial arm, has far less money to contribute to stipends than during the 1990s. By 2013, clergy numbers in the Monmouth diocese are due to have fallen by 30 per cent – from just over a hundred to under seventy.

The rest of the Church in Wales is also feeling the pinch. Within a year of Rowan's departure for Canterbury, the new primate, Barry Morgan, had implemented a radical plan to cut the number of priests and rebalance church finances. This initiative, named after its main architect, David (now Lord) Rowe-Beddoe, has also entailed drastic reductions in bureaucracy. The impact on clergy morale has been large; the number of those coming forward for ordination plummeted for several years running. Prompter action would have softened the blow, according to a senior priest who did not want to be named. 'But in this respect Rowan was part of the culture of the Church in Wales, which refused to think about managerial reform till it was too late.'

Other sobering developments naturally predated Rowan's appointment to Monmouth by many years. The impact of broader social currents had been intensified by the poor records of his immediate predecessors: Derek Childs, Bishop from 1972 to 1986, and Cliff Wright, who served for the following five years. The former was thought by his critics to lack both imagination and spirituality; the latter had been known for an imperious style. Hopes that the new Bishop would be a dynamic spiritual leader and not (as often in Wales) a product of the Church's old boy network were therefore especially strong. Several influential figures, including the Archdeacon of Newport, Barrie Evans, dared to hope that England's most impressive theologian might be coaxed back across the border; but the waters needed to be tested with care. Older observers could recall the disappointment felt when another Oxford professor, Leonard Hodgson, had declined an offer to become Bishop of Monmouth during the 1940s. As a result, Patrick Thomas – an incumbent in rural Pembrokeshire who had known Rowan since their Mirfield days – was sent to sound his friend out by the then primate of Wales, Archbishop George Noakes. Thomas received a positive reply. Rowan revealed that he had been spoken of as the possible leader of an English diocese – probably Durham, because it had a tradition of scholar-bishops – but that he would prefer to serve in a disestablished Church.

There were now several hurdles to clear. Bishops in Wales are chosen by a college consisting of forty-seven electors: twelve (six clergy and six laypeople) from the diocese in question, six (three laypeople and three clergy) from each of the other five dioceses, and the five bishops already in post. The successful candidate needs to win majorities in each section of the college. Not everyone was delighted by the prospect of a chief pastor who had never run a parish and who lacked strong ties with the area of Wales between eastern Cardiff and the English border. This point was not lost on Peter Woodman, Archdeacon of Monmouth from 1993 to 2001, and thus one of the Bishop's right-hand men. Soon after his meeting with Patrick Thomas, Rowan wrote privately to Alwyn Rice Jones (who had by now succeeded Noakes as Archbishop), spelling out his views on sexuality and his opposition to nuclear weapons. This document alarmed some who read it. Woodman, who favoured the appointment of Rowan, always liked and admired him, but later worried about his pastoral savoir-faire, had a simple message to his fellow electors when the Bishop of Monmouth was chosen as Archbishop of Wales eight years later: 'Don't worry about his radicalism. Watch for his romanticism.'

Rumours about the Lady Margaret Professor's possible move spread to England before a formal announcement was made, and Bishop Richard Harries raised the subject with Frank Jenkins, the recently retired Dean of Monmouth. Harries said that he'd heard the Church in Wales was 'thinking of appointing a prominent theologian' to Monmouth, adding that Oxford 'couldn't afford to lose one'. Jenkins replied tactfully that Wales's need of a distinguished thinker was at least as great. Privately, he couldn't believe his luck that Rowan was on side.

There was gloom throughout the cathedral community at Christ Church. Henry Chadwick (by now retired and living in Oxford) worried that Rowan's intellectual promise would not now be fully realised, but later granted that his former protégé had made the right decision. Oliver O'Donovan begged his colleague not to leave, but in time reached a conclusion similar to Chadwick's. Had he remained a professor for longer, the academic community would have gained 'a couple of good but not irreplaceable works on patristics', O'Donovan suggested to me. 'The Church as a whole benefited far more by his becoming a bishop.'

Jane was also among the doubters, and her opposition to the move grew before it abated. Her first instincts were understandable. Rowan's salary would now be £18,000 – half that of an Oxford professor. They would be exchanging Priory House for a featureless post-war home in Newport, and leaving an internationally renowned city for what was then a depressed backwater. Having not voiced strong opposition to the plan when it was first mooted, she felt angry and upset when there was no option but to go ahead. In time, though, she accepted that the grounds for her opposition had been 'bad as well as good', and that the task of applying theology outside academia was a noble one. The challenge applied to her, as well as to her husband. She worked as an editor for the publishers Darton, Longman and Todd from 1994 to 1996, took a break after the birth of her son Pip in 1996, and was later appointed part-time lecturer in pastoral theology at Trinity College, Bristol.

Frank Jenkins's impression of his new colleague encapsulates the view of many. Rowan was quite unlike any other Bishop of Monmouth in living memory. He was above all a man of God rather than a manager. He did not stand on ceremony, and was happy to be called by his first name. His appearance was as unassuming as his manner. He never wore a purple clerical shirt. He had a very good memory for faces. To some, he recalled the deeply loved Glyn Simon, probably the only other Welsh prelate in modern times to enjoy a substantial reputation throughout Britain. And while Rowan's approach to administration 'left a lot to be desired', Jenkins adds, 'his effect on people was a kind of conversion experience. Once you entered into his ambit, you never forgot it.'

A chronicle of his individual acts of kindness would be very long indeed. He was a magnet for the walking wounded. One man, for example, had a reputation for making heavy emotional demands on the clergy. He was frequently shunned by them in consequence, but the Bishop was among the few who could always be relied on to give him a sympathetic ear. When the man's mother died, he asked Rowan to conduct her funeral: the wish was granted. Some of the Bishop's hangers-on were unstable – severely so in one case. The woman in question obtained details of his diary engagements, and for a time stalked him at every service he attended. Sometimes she shouted insults at him during worship, once calling him the spawn of the Devil. Even in the face of this extreme provocation, he remained calm but not unduly detached. At other times he could give vent to strong emotions. When Sara Maitland came to tell him that she was going to become a Roman Catholic, he burst into tears in the street.

What did Rowan himself think he was doing? Though he was obviously far more approachable than many other prelates, his view of episcopacy corresponded to classic definitions of the office in important respects.[2] A bishop encounters unbelief or indifference or moral turpitude, and needs to identify the deeper sources of these attitudes. He should understand the conditions in which the members of his flock work and spend their leisure time. He should be sensitive to demographic change, so that people who move to a new estate, for example, will be able to hear the Word and receive the sacraments. He needs to reflect on how to match ministers, laypeople, members of religious orders and others to different kinds of pastoral challenge. This will in turn require him to weigh considerations including accommodation, stipends and church buildings. But practical matters should never displace the care of souls, the need for clergy and people alike to refresh themselves in the truths of the faith, and avoid lapsing into versions of it that miss what Michael Ramsey called 'its height and depth and wonder'.

So much for the general picture. A more detailed answer to the question comes in an essay Rowan published on the subject in 1995.[3] He concentrated as much on the Welsh dimension of his work as on episcopal ministry as such. The piece started with a revealing set of observations. No diocese in Wales has more than 180 clergy, and bishops therefore tend to be closer to the grassroots than in England. Rowan reported that this was initially resented after Welsh disestablishment in 1920, when two new dioceses (Monmouth, and Swansea and Brecon) were created, but said that smaller sees came to be seen as a strength in due time. This development accorded with the vision of Charles Howell Green, the second Archbishop of Wales, who saw in it a heaven-sent chance to restore the discipline of the early Church, where a higher proportion of bishops guided their clergy directly. While acknowledging the frequent clash between vision and reality (Green was in some ways an old-style auto-crat), Rowan suggested that the model still has much to commend it. It meant, he said, that he could devote far more time than many bishops elsewhere to face-to-face pastoral engagement, and operate on a shoestring by First World standards, with no chaplain or PA to cushion him, and only part-time secretarial help. He therefore spent many hours on the phone. 'A priest who has just broken off his engagement, a woman complaining about litter in the graveyard where her grandfather is buried, a local Age Concern volunteer wondering if I can come to a Christmas dinner for pensioners in Bedwellty – all of these can get through straight away.'

The modest dimensions of the Monmouth diocese gave Rowan further scope for practising what he preached. He would visit most of his eighty-five parishes once a year, and go more often to the big churches in Newport and the edge of Cardiff. He took a hands-on part in episcopal visitations: these usually extended across five evenings in different centres around Gwent, and involved meetings with Readers and churchwardens, as well as clergy, and a look at parish accounts and responses to questionnaires. He spent one day a week, and sometimes more, sharing a parish priest's rounds. This might entail anything from a morning in a primary school to fish and chips with the church council, celebrating a house communion or taking part in a question-and-answer session with sixth-formers. His innovations included the introduction of a diocesan pilgrimage to Walsingham each summer, which regularly attracted about a hundred people for a week of prayer and relaxation. But he was not partisan. Evangelicals came to look on him as their protector, and he became an enthusiastic backer of Evangelical initiatives such as Victory Outreach, a scheme helping ex-offenders. He befriended Anglican Charismatics, and was himself 'slain in the Spirit' during Easter worship one year. Archbishop Rice Jones encouraged the Bishop of Monmouth not to let go of theology; diary spaces were thus cleared for him to supervise doctoral candidates and do some part-time teaching at Bristol University. He continued to lecture widely, both in Britain and abroad. For peace and extra time to pray, Rowan went frequently to Ty Mawr, the rural Anglican convent near Monmouth.

The essay owns up with candour to certain problems – above all that accessibility can make you vulnerable to attack – but it is evident from his tone that Rowan did not regard himself as being at fault. A difficulty he reported concerned a request that the parishes make larger financial contributions to help fund a deployment of extra clergy in some of the neediest parts of the diocese. He described the consequent impulse to blame the Bishop for mistakes or other setbacks as 'a kind of corporate immaturity, looking to the patriarch to solve the problems, and hitting out when he can't'.

A second source of tension that he cited was the campaign for women priests – voted down by the Church in Wales's Governing Body (its equivalent of the General Synod in England) in the spring of 1993, but narrowly supported when the reform was reconsidered four years later. During the lead-up to the first of these votes, Rowan and other bishops were attacked both by conservatives, for allowing the legislation to be considered in the first place, and by liberals, for not securing its passage. One lesson to be drawn from such stories is that episcopal office carries acute risks, he concluded.

I can well understand why some people in and out of the Churches think the idea of having bishops is just bad in principle. Isn't it practically unavoidable that this sort of infantilising will go on? That all sorts of crippling projections will be dumped on this figure who, in Anglican and Catholic terms, carries so much mystique, so much glamour (no, not exactly in the Susan Howatch style)? We had better be honest and admit that much of this is unavoidable; and that for this reason, being a bishop is – in all seriousness – potentially very bad for the soul.

But he still thought that the advantages outweighed the drawbacks:

the thing that keeps me convinced that the risk might be worth it is not the dangerous glow of charismatic leadership or efficient problem-solving, but something that the Eastern Christian tradition has often been better at articulating than the Western. A bishop is a visible and personal sign of the Church's unity through time and over space. And that implies that the bishop's job is to make personal the kind of unity in and through conflict or misunderstanding that the Church has to believe in if it's to stay sane and not become either a totalitarian empire or a free market.

The discussion ends on a pious note, glossing Michael Ramsey's conviction that being a bishop itself makes you do theology, 'forces you to reflect on power and freedom, grace, faithfulness and failure'. Rowan added that he had had no regrets about his change of career plan. '[I]n spite of the ironies, frustrations and institutional quagmires, there is nothing I'd rather be doing.'

*   *   *

What was going on under the surface, and why, in particular, was Rowan judged to have performed less well in some respects, as well as outstandingly in others? The answer arises from his sincere attempt to address the diocese's deepest problems. The Cliff Wright era had been marked by procrastination over appointments, and low morale in the parishes tended to be intensified by lengthy interregnums. Rowan frequently avowed to colleagues that Jesus' followers make up a Spirit-led community; and that he was not going to 'strategise the Church'. In so far as he had a management plan, though, it centred on staffing. He offered his first diocesan conference a choice between having as many priests as possible, or cutting back, with consequent savings. The gathering gave him the green light to appoint more priests. Three negative consequences followed from this: a severe financial shortfall, from which Monmouth could only hope to recover through the sharp retrenchment already outlined; the selection of a number of unsuitable candidates for ministry; and a relative lack of appraisal when they and others took up their posts.

'Plenty of people came forward to offer themselves for priestly training,' one diocesan observer told me.

Some had made a mess of their earlier careers in secular employment, or as clergy in other denominations. Several had been turned down for ministry in the Church of England. About half a dozen – an unprecedented number – left or were turned away from St Michael's, Cardiff's Anglican theological college, because they caused trouble there. Others made it into parishes, with mixed success. That Rowan supported them was a mark of his warmth, his undying instinct to give people a fresh start and to see the best in them thereafter. But ordination is not a right, and there are financial implications in commending someone for ministerial training. Leniency could shade into holy naivety in Rowan's case.

Comments as bracing as these need to be viewed in a biblical context if we are to get the measure of Rowan's policies. The New Testament clearly abounds in holy naivety: Jesus himself selected for his inner circle a man who would eventually betray him. But Jesus was not running an institution, and the scope for leniency is always circumscribed when third parties are involved (to cite a well-known example, John Paul II was free to forgive his would-be assassin, but could not proclaim release for the captive without undermining the moral order). Rowan now concedes that his 'reckless generosity' – a term used both by himself and others – got him into difficulty at times – though in mitigation he argues that most of his unsuccessful ministerial candidates were not approved by him alone. (In Wales, those offering themselves for the priesthood go before a Diocesan Ministry Committee, and then the Provincial Selection Committee. But it is the Bishop of the relevant diocese who has the last word on whether someone will be ordained.)

Those who think of him as too tender-hearted to have been a good judge of character are reluctant to revise their verdict. Several cite an especially difficult episode concerning an alcoholic priest who ran up six-figure debts during the 1990s, and was eventually forced into early retirement. Rowan maintains that he disciplined the man concerned when the source of his misdemeanours became apparent. Richard Tarran, a former banker who became the Monmouth Diocesan Secretary in 1995, believes that the Bishop ought to have acted sooner: 'The man was alleged to be spending much of the day in the pub. He was declared bankrupt but still allowed pastoral care of a group of parishes. His congregations suffered as a consequence.'

A broadly comparable example is given by a retired bishop who oversaw an important Church of England see during the 1990s. 'At one point Rowan sent me a priest who had caused difficulties, assuring me that he could be placed in my diocese. Yet this man caused chaos in his new job as well. In his desire always to show charity towards individuals, Rowan sometimes lost sight of the good of the broader Church.' More widely reported was the saga of a cleric who had to be sacked on the day of his planned induction after eleventh-hour revelations about his past. He had come to Wales from Scotland, where his record was unblemished, but had earlier been banned from ministry in England. This meant that his name appeared on the so-called

Black Book at Lambeth Palace. Critics felt that Rowan was at fault for not consulting this volume.

If you were down on your luck, then, Rowan was your friend. He took gospel precepts on forgiveness very seriously indeed. Two further consequences of this style were noted. The first was that the Bishop's devotion to those in difficulty left him with less time for more average clergy who did not claim his attention. Some of them therefore felt neglected, especially if they were serving in more economically prosperous parishes. The second consequence was that Rowan's approach reflected a perceived paradox in his nature – that he was not a team player, despite his consensual impulses. Peter Woodman was 'captivated' by Rowan's generosity, but felt that his Bishop made rods for his own back. Rowan would often see a difficult cleric alone, despite being advised that he would be in a stronger position if supported by one of his archdeacons or by the diocesan chancellor. 'I said it would be less painful,' Woodman recollects. 'But Mirfield men have a reputation for turning suffering into an art form. If Rowan could have shared more, he would have anguished less. I couldn't work out whether it was because he didn't trust us, or because he was sure he knew best.' In other respects, though, the Archdeacon found the Bishop unassertive. 'I told him that there were times when he needed to thump the table to get somewhere, but he replied that that wasn't his way. While some clergy wished he would give more of a lead, he maintained that it wasn't for him to take sides.'

The method had other negative consequences. Rowan's support for permanent deacons (two dozen of whom were ordained for Monmouth during the 1990s) is a case in point. This form of ministry has been rare in the Anglican Communion. The Bishop encouraged it to buttress a belief – shared in the Roman Catholic and Orthodox traditions – that the diaconate should not be seen simply as a stepping stone to the priesthood. But this did not stop people who had previously been turned down for ordination training from being accepted as trainee deacons, and thus gaining access to holy orders by the back door. Most became priests in later years, contrary to the original judgement of the selectors.

'Rowan didn't make the case for permanent deacons,' according to Tudor Griffiths, who was diocesan missioner from 1996 to 2003. 'In some cases his choices were inspired, but in others they were disastrous. He chose one man whom I had judged unsuitable for ministry. He lacked the necessary gifts and had no depth of spirituality. But he could say the right things.' The want of planning reflected in this policy was also evident to Barry Morgan, Rowan's friend and successor as Archbishop of Wales. 'He would have great ideas,' Morgan says, 'but would then leave it to others to think through their implications. The experiment with permanent deacons was not adequately monitored.' This view is endorsed by Huw Jones, Bishop of St David's from 1996 to 2001, who suggests that most other members of the Bench viewed the scheme with unease, and felt that the deacons-to-be were not being properly trained.

So Rowan was not thought to be lacking in drive. The debate about him centred more on the wisdom of his targets – though in his defence, he points out that there was a formal system for the nomination of permanent deacons through the parishes, and that the Welsh bishops did vote in favour of the scheme. Given that mistakes were also made, however, a query can be raised about whether the Bishop's modest staffing arrangements really constituted a benefit. Had he gone to an English diocese, he would probably have been assisted by a suffragan with substantial pastoral experience. Rowan did not want an assistant bishop, feeling that such a figure would come between him and his people. As a candidate for election as Archbishop of Wales in 1999, he was obliged to leave the room during the bishops' meeting that discussed his candidacy. Some of his colleagues advised in frank terms that he should take on an assistant bishop. When this message was conveyed to Rowan he again demurred, but agreed to take on a chaplain, Gregory Cameron, who won respect for his firefighting skills, as well as his intelligence. (Friends of both men suggest that the Archbishop's first years at Lambeth would have been less punishing if he had been able to retain Cameron as his chaplain on moving back to England.)

The evidence of alleged mistakes should not take away from the record of Rowan's achievements: as I have reported, they were also substantial. Tudor Griffiths speaks for many in expressing deep gratitude to his former boss. Their professional relationship got off to an awkward start, because Rowan expected him to combine his work as missioner with a parish post. 'I think being diocesan missioner and vicar, albeit part-time, was not realistic,' Griffiths comments. But the Bishop paid serious attention to Griffiths' writings on the subject of church growth, sending him with a colleague, Nick Hawkins, to Sabah to see what a growing Anglican church looks like.

Griffiths cites several examples of the Bishop's involvement in strategic thinking. Rowan sponsored an evangelistic venture known as Good News in Wales, the only Welsh bishop to do so. He was an ardent supporter of church plants – new, extra-parochial congregations – notably in Duffryn, part of Maesglas parish, and in Wyllie, a mining village in the benefice of Pontllanfraith. (Opposed by the local rector, this initiative was led by a laywoman, Marian Barge, whom Rowan later ordained deacon.) As Archbishop of Wales, he appointed Griffiths and Peter Hayler, an industrial missioner, as his chaplains, thus flagging his commitment to this sort of outreach. He expressed unceasing support for the Jubilee 2000 campaign to cancel Third World debt; and in 2002 he gave the keynote address during 'God@work.monmouthdiocese' – a conference, not a website – which was lay-led and saw numerous personal testimonies of faith.

The Bishop's messages in his diocesan leaflet – whether on doctrinal or social issues – were invariably stimulating and sometimes unusual. His thoughts on the Muslim model of God are worth quoting for what they reveal about attitudes that he would be obliged to keep under his hat as Archbishop of Canterbury:

> Islam has a wonderful vision of divine majesty, generosity and glory, and its demand for unreserved loving obedience has great nobility. But it is a faith that cannot find room either for the idea that God longs to share his very life or for the vision of a God who can only win through defeat. It is not intrinsically a violent faith, but it is one that sets high store by victory. And it is not able to pray to God in God's own 'voice', to say 'Father' in the Spirit of Jesus.

Rowan's personal qualities shone through all the while. In 1998, Tudor Griffiths' first wife, Nelleke, died in a car accident. The Bishop's support at this time was unflagging. Griffiths remained composed during the funeral, but burst into tears after the interment. It was on Rowan's shoulder that he wept. Overall, Griffiths' only cavil concerned his reliability as a judge of others:

The Dean, Richard Fenwick, was unsupportive of mission initiatives. Generally, Rowan appointed to senior positions men (I use the term advisedly) who were fairly set in traditional modes of thinking and church life. This meant that those of us who were with him in his vision were left vulnerable on his departure. Someone said he didn't like rival stars. This was too bitchy. But his distaste for management meant that he surrounded himself with people who didn't have the necessary complementary gifts.

The Bishop was therefore not a hands-on leader. His understanding of episcopal authority did not allow it. We can see a variation on this theme in relation to his handling of major debates, especially over the ordination of women, which in turn tells us a good deal about his understanding of his role as Archbishop of Canterbury. Long before his decision to withdraw support for Jeffrey John, he was a conciliator as well as a campaigner, with a keen belief that any decision reached by *the Church* needed to be owned by as many of its members as possible.

An example of him in action as both campaigner and bridge-builder is his address to the Governing Body in April 1993, seconding the motion in favour of women priests. Much of his speech appeared unequivocal – about the timing, as well as the principle: 'I don't believe . . . that much is now to be gained by delay, because I don't think there are new facts or new arguments that will suddenly make things clearer, and because I think also that delay can polarise and embitter things still further.' But then came a change of gear. The Bishop warned that 'we must be prepared to be *taught* by each other in the debate; and, if the final result is not what we prayed and hoped for, to ask what God is saying to us in that'.

Some might have thought that Rowan was resorting to a formula here. Few supporters of women's ordination, I suspect, feel they have much to learn from their opponents. That the sentiment behind the Bishop's comments was anything but formulaic would become progressively clearer over time. It emerged when he was asked by several English dioceses to preach at the ordination of their first women priests in 1994. All these invitations were declined on the basis that Wales had not yet approved the reform. When the moment came, Rowan did not insist (as many wished) that the minority should accept the majority decision. On the contrary, he pressed more than any other senior Welsh cleric for the appointment of a provincial assistant bishop to oversee traditionalist congregations. His wish bore fruit with the consecration of David Thomas. Rowan's backers saw a simple reflection of Catholic and consensual impulses in his move. The doubters divided into two groups. Some wanted what they saw as a victory for justice to be endorsed without equivocation. Those who accepted conscientious opposition to women priests were more worried about the practical results of Rowan's plan. Thomas was a respected figure, but some of his backers were viewed as troublemakers by more liberal clergy. One bishop told me that he felt undermined when theological college students began announcing that they were only prepared to be ordained by Thomas, rather than by their respective bishops.

As well as championing an unpopular conservative cause (Thomas retired in the summer of 2008, and was not replaced), Rowan leant over in the other direction as well. As Archbishop, he supported the appointment of an 'ecumenical bishop' to serve in eastern Cardiff. The idea was thrown out by the Governing Body in 2002, when every other denomination involved (Methodist, Baptist and URC) had welcomed it. 'The move was probably too bold,' comments a well-placed source, 'and its failure left a great deal of ecumenical hurt in Wales.'

            *   *   *

The strains – personal, as well as theological – endured by the Bishop of Monmouth were also laid bare during the 1998 Lambeth Conference. The 800 or so participating bishops were divided into four groups dealing respectively with ministry, education, sexual ethics and mission: Rowan was appointed to chair one of these (the fourth) because of his consensual style, as well as his charisma. The conference is chiefly remembered for an unedifying dialogue of the deaf – at one point a Nigerian, Bishop Emmanuel Chukwuma, tried to exorcise Richard Kirker of the Lesbian and Gay Christian Movement – and for the passing of a hardline resolution, 1.10, deploring all sex outside marriage. A sub-clause committing the Church to listening to the experience of its gay members seemed paradoxical to both liberals and conservatives in different ways. Sexuality had been discussed by only one of the groups, and it had taken members of this subsection a full fortnight to start heeding each other. The plenary debate that followed was perfunctory, and yet the subject assumed disproportionate importance in the media and the wider Church. George Carey's critics blamed him for the perceived imbalance.

The sexuality debate was (and to some extent remains) novel in that it sprang from the lifting of a taboo. Inasmuch as the matter turns on the nature of Scripture and its interpretation, however, it has a very long lineage indeed. A historical illustration is instructive. The Lambeth Conference of 1958 focused on biblical interpretation, and Michael Ramsey, then Archbishop of York, was the man charged with drafting a report on the subject.

How to reconcile a contemporary scientific world-picture with one based on Scripture? Ramsey exhorted his audience to develop theological maturity. The Bible has authority over the Church, not vice versa. It diagnoses humanity's spiritual sickness and offers the necessary medicine. At the same time, he warned Anglicans to beware those who are so eager to impose the Bible on others as to display extravagance or sectarianism. Moreover, it was vital to defend the legitimacy of free enquiry. Scripture is not infallible on points of science or history, and the Holy Spirit speaks through textual expositors in every age, as well as via the texts themselves. God, in any case, cannot be encapsulated in words, even when they are inspired. Treated so, Ramsey concluded, the authority of the Bible is not diminished but enhanced.

Thirty years on, it was obvious that such arguments had been imperfectly absorbed by the next generation – or, rather, that the Communion remained deeply divided about them. (Much the same could be said about Roman Catholics, although clashes of view are easier to mask in a far more centralised Church.) Rowan's plenary address, 'Making Moral Decisions', entailed a variation on Ramsey's theme, though the matter was approached obliquely. He concluded that Christian discipleship is less a matter of ticking certain boxes than of embodying a particular form of life:

What we are looking for in each other is the grammar of obedience: we watch to see if our partners take the same kind of time, sense that they are under the same kind of judgement or scrutiny . . . This will not guarantee agreement; but it might explain why we should always first be hesitant and attentive to each other . . . If another Christian comes to a different con-

clusion and decides in different ways from myself, and if I can still
recognise their discipline and practice as sufficiently like mine to
establish a conversation, this leaves my own decisions to some
extent under question.[4]

He drove home the message by citing his conviction that no
Christian should ever sanction the possession of weapons of mass
destruction, while granting that others disagreed – not moral
pygmies, but precisely those who also 'make themselves ac-
countable to the central truths of our faith'.

The speech was densely argued, and most members of the
audience were not supplied with texts. Although the Bishop of
Monmouth's underlying plea for generosity towards gay Christians was only lightly coded, it seemed clear to me and other
reporters in the press gallery that many of the delegates had not
caught his drift. One senior English churchman observing the
scene said that 'Rowan talked and Africa slept'. This verdict
needs to be qualified. Many American prelates appeared som-
nolent as well. A high proportion of African bishops had caught
the anti-intellectual contagion from Britain and the United
States in the first place, because of the Church of England's
historic aversion to theology and abstract thought in general.
Moreover, the African conservatives seemed to have short
memories. During the 1988 Lambeth Conference, they or their
predecessors had warned white bishops to consider African
mores before delivering lectures about the evils of polygamy.
This evidence of double standards fuelled the perception that
some lifestyles were being treated as more equal than others.

Rowan was among a forty-strong minority who abstained
in the vote that concluded the sexuality debate. By avoiding
polemics and demonstrating his skill at chairing meetings, he

emerged from the conference with his reputation enhanced, even though aspects of it depressed him deeply. His dejection was shared by scores of other participants. In recognition of this, they released a pastoral statement to lesbian and gay Anglicans. While diplomatic, their choice of words clearly signalled dissent:

> Within the limitations of this Conference, it has not been possible to hear adequately your voices, and we apologise for any sense of rejection that has occurred because of this reality. This letter is a sign of our commitment to listen to you and reflect . . . on your lives and ministries. It is a deep concern that you not feel abandoned by your Church and that you know of our continued respect and support.
>
> We pledge that we will continue to reflect, pray, and work for your full inclusion in the life of the Church. It is obvious that Communion-wide we are in great disagreement over what full inclusion would mean. We ourselves have varied views and admit, as the Human Sexuality Subsection of the Conference says, that there is much we do not yet understand. But we believe it is an imperative of the Gospel and our faith that we seek such understanding.[5]

Most of the signatories were from North America and Britain, though their ranks were boosted by Archbishop Khotso Makhulu of Botswana, Bishop John Osmers of Eastern Zambia, and Archbishop Lgauco Soares de Lima of Sao Paulo. This letter is often referred to by those who feel that, as Archbishop of Canterbury, Rowan has betrayed his earlier undertakings on the gay issue.

* * *

The end of the 1990s was almost as momentous a time for him as the dawn of the new century. It is often suggested that he failed to secure nomination as Bishop of Southwark in 1998 because of his refusal to toe the official line on sexuality. There is no clearly identified teaching authority in the Anglican Communion to match the Roman Catholic magisterium, but in England, Anglicans could choose between the 1987 General Synod resolution outlined in Chapter 3 or, slightly less hardline, *Issues in Sexuality*, a 1991 House of Bishops document stating that gay relationships were permissible for the laity, but not the clergy. Rowan knowingly ordained at least one gay man in a relationship while Bishop of Monmouth, partly because the Welsh bishops had not agreed an equivalent discipline. He nevertheless insists that 1998 would have been too soon for a move back to England, and that he was not seeking a new job. Moreover, his parents were now both very frail and in residential care near Swansea. They died within just over a fortnight of one another in 1999.

But the need to support Del and Aneurin did not preclude a career development closer to home. Two posts, those of Archbishop of Wales and Bishop of Llandaff, were to fall vacant with the respective retirements of Alwyn Rice Jones and Roy Davies. It was possible in principle for Rowan to succeed both men. Wales has no primatial see, and an archbishop remains in charge of his former diocese. But Llandaff, embracing almost all of Cardiff, covers a more populous area than Monmouth. Translation would not have been unprecedented, and life in the capital would have suited Jane better than Newport. Some people even thought that the Williamses were anticipating a move when in 1998 they moved Rhiannon from her state school in Newport to Howell's, an independent in Llandaff. This view can be discounted. Jane and Rowan were unhappy with local provision, fought with their consciences about private education, and concluded that their daughter's needs should come first.

Rowan nevertheless told Barry Morgan that he was 'not averse' to a change of see. In the end Morgan himself was selected for Llandaff, partly because he had had difficulties as Bishop of Bangor, and partly because Rowan was considered by some of the electors to be unsuited for the heavy administrative load that went with a larger patch. He was also viewed unfavourably by some traditionalist Anglo-Catholics in Cardiff because of his consistent support for the ordination of women. Given his own Catholic pedigree, this made him too eager to be all things to all people in their eyes. Morgan's broad churchmanship hardly matched their own, but they felt they knew where they stood with him.

The Bishop of Monmouth's disappointment was softened by his election to succeed Rice Jones on 7 December 1999. The result was announced formally during the Governing Body meeting in April of the following year by Barry Morgan, who had these words of commendation:

> Sparing his blushes – you know that he is a scholar of international standing, and although one of the newest primates, is well known and respected throughout the whole of the Anglican Communion already, not only because of his learning, which he wears lightly, but because of his willingness to make himself available to lecture and to lead retreats, and not least because of his own spirituality and holiness . . .

Morgan's words were not premature. Rowan was judged to be more of a round peg in a round hole as Archbishop: still a skilful and courteous chairman of debates, a charismatic media performer and an effective ambassador for his country. He won the affection of other Christian leaders through his work in Cytun, Wales's main ecumenical body. And he was especially glad to become patron of the Bevan Foundation, a think-tank promoting regeneration. The experience provided a backdrop to several of the main arguments in his 2002 Dimbleby Lecture. Two events stand out from his thirty or so months in office – 11 September 2001, and the start of the drawn out crisis in Anglicanism internationally.

The ecclesiastical storm brewed slowly. One of its portents was the illicit consecration of two American traditionalists, Charles Murphy and John Rodgers, by a pair of serving archbishops in Singapore in January 2000. Murphy and Rodgers condemned what they called the 'apostasy' of the Episcopal Church of the United States of America (ECUSA), where some dioceses had openly dissociated themselves from Lambeth 1.10. Rowan was among the primates who assembled in Oporto, Portugal, to try to iron out the ensuing tensions. Soon after the meeting ended on 28 March, he wrote an article for *The Tablet* revealing much about his general view of Anglicanism, as well as his ideas about managing disagreement.[6] His conclusions – especially that Anglicanism has no need for centralised structures, and that homosexuality should not be rated a Communion-breaking issue – seem optimistic in hindsight.

Tellingly, the piece began with an explanation for the primates' venue: Portugal is hardly a powerhouse of Anglicanism. The participants were marking the 120th anniversary of the Lusitanians – a group (like the Old Catholics in Germany and Switzerland) who could not accept the declaration of papal infallibility. Rowan saluted the Lusitanian protest against centralised authority, and voiced a hope that the Anglican Communion, too, would resist calls to tighten the reins of government.

The consecration of Murphy and Rodgers had marked an unprecedented breach in church order, since neither George Carey nor the Episcopalian leadership in the United States had been consulted. Yet for the renegade bishops, canonical irregularity was the lesser evil by comparison with an *à la carte* approach to Christian belief in general. Revealingly, given his later ambivalence towards ECUSA during the years that followed, Rowan showed a precise grasp of conservative anger: divisions between Episcopalians over sexuality had been, 'for a vocal minority, the last straw in a long process that is seen as the uncritical adoption . . . of a liberal, multicultural, relativist agenda'. There followed an unsparing reference to John Spong, formerly Bishop of Newark, New Jersey, whose apparent jettisoning of historic Christianity had prompted a rebuke from Rowan during the Lambeth Conference two years previously.[7] Spong's theological fireworks are described as 'cutting long swathes through pretty well every received doctrine and ethical conviction of historic Christianity', and as contributing 'a lot' to the dissent.

The article then spoke of the rising exasperation of African bishops about the gay issue – and presciently about the influence of American lobbyists, 'hanging around in doorways', to stiffen the sinews of archbishops from the developing world. Here is his verdict:

But what emerged was – perhaps predictably – a less dramatic outcome, which some will undoubtedly see as a typical bit of Anglican evasiveness . . . [M]any primates, especially the Africans, while they are uncompromisingly traditional about sexual ethics, can see the risk of the Communion either becoming completely mired in this question for years or breaking up over it. It was very clear that they wanted neither. One influential African archbishop declared forcefully that a lot of the discussion had been a waste of time for him, faced as he was with civil war, the effects of the AIDS pandemic and the debt crisis: 'Some of us,' he said, poker-faced, 'are tired of sex . . .'

. . . The meeting seemed to have no appetite for denunciation, or even direct appeal to the United States for a moratorium on gay ordinations; the seriousness of the concern was registered, and the presiding bishop of the Episcopal Church [Frank Griswold] was left to work out with his house of bishops what the implications might be.

A fudge was also evident in another statement to have emerged from the meeting: that a province excludes itself from the Communion only by public rejection of any part or parts of the so-called Lambeth Quadrilateral (the fourfold marker of Anglican identity consisting of the supremacy of Scripture in doctrinal matters; the two greater sacraments; the creeds of the first four centuries; and the historic episcopate). Rowan recognised that this was to beg the question, since conservatives view support for practising gay clergy as a breach of the first principle, but argued that the behaviour of Anglican liberals – as of Evangelicals in Australia who support lay presidency at the Eucharist – amounted to an implicit, rather than explicit, rejection of the Quadrilateral. On this basis he ended hopefully, and with a parting shot at Roman authoritarianism: 'The next few years will undoubtedly be increasingly painful and difficult for many Anglicans; but this particular meeting suggested that

the classical Anglican method was not dead yet . . . and unin-
hibited theological conversation may yet save Anglicanism from
its own variety of the Vatican I débâcle.'

*   *   *

Although much of Rowan's time as Archbishop of Canterbury
has been described as a personal Calvary for him, the events of 11
September provide a truer context for analogies with Christ's
Passion. This is not just for the obvious reason that Anglicanism's
possible fragmentation cannot be compared with a terrorist
atrocity. It is also because Rowan found his faith further refined
amid scenes of nameless horror.

He was due to address twenty-two spiritual directors from
across the United States in a church-owned building next to
Holy Trinity, Wall Street, on 'the shape of a holy life', and
reached the venue, 74 Trinity Place, at 8.35 a.m. His host was
the Revd Fred Burnham, director of the Trinity Institute, an
educational foundation attached to the neighbouring church.
The two met in the lobby and went up to the twenty-first floor –
notionally to give the speaker a few minutes' quiet reflection
before his address. Burnham was sitting in his office next door
when the World Trade Center's north tower was hit at 9.03
a.m.; and even though Flight 11 came from the opposite
direction (Trinity Place is south of Ground Zero), the noise
sounded like a sonic boom. Fred Burnham sprang to his feet,
raced to the room where Rowan was, and cried that 'some
cowboy' had just gone through the sound barrier. Then came a
scream: one of the secretaries working on the same floor could
see what had happened through her window. Burnham, Rowan
and the others joined her to look. Though aghast, they assumed
that the crash was accidental.

After a few minutes of watching smoke spurt from the north tower and debris flying by, they decided to go down to the studio where Rowan would give his speech. It was not until the second tower had been hit that everything changed. Hindsight tells us that people in the areas near the World Trade Center should now have evacuated their buildings. But that was not obvious at the time, because many concluded that Manhattan itself was under some sort of attack. Suddenly, as Burnham recalled later in language matching his sense of confusion, 'we knew we were in the middle of a war zone and this was not a happy day'. He approached Burt Medley, one of his colleagues, and asked what they should do. Medley suggested that the Archbishop be asked to lead prayers, and this happened almost spontaneously. Rowan's words were like balm; the group began to feel more composed. Not only did he pray about all of the obvious things – the loss of life, the general anguish – he also began to lift up to God the anxieties of everyone in the room.

For twenty minutes they were able to watch a television monitor showing what was happening at the World Trade Center, but then the first tower disintegrated with a colossal roar, 74 Trinity Place itself began to shake, and the monitor went blank. When it flashed back on again a short while later, the group became more aware of what had happened. At the same time, smoke and soot began to enter their auditorium. The urge to move was confirmed by security staff, who came to guide them towards the bowels of the building via a service stairwell. It was thought that the absence of windows and air vents on this route would make respiration a little easier, but this hope proved to be misplaced. Some of Rowan's companions went back upstairs to the nursery that was also housed in the building; there they found blankets which they tore up and moistened with water, to provide impromptu face masks.

Scarcely able to breathe, yet convinced that the atmosphere in the street was yet more treacherous, Fred Burnham felt close to death:

> We were pretty much told to stay where we were and the most profound moment of the whole day, for me, was when five or six of us were gathered on the landing in the stairway, where the air had become virtually suffocating, and I began to think to myself, Well, it's worse outside, and I don't know how much longer we can tolerate this, maybe we've got fifteen minutes, and beginning then to realise I would die.[8]

Elizabeth Koenig, a friend of Rowan who teaches at New York's General Theological Seminary, now laid a hand on the Archbishop's shoulder and said, 'I can't think of anyone I'd rather die with.' At that moment, Burnham felt enclosed in 'a circle of love' that he would never forget.

> None of us will ever forget it. We were bonded for life. We became comrades in the face of death. And there was in the group a total submission and resignation to the prospect of death. No fear. And I discovered for the first time that I am not afraid of death and that has totally changed my life. My experience, my every breath from that moment on has been different from anything prior to that. That transformative moment, discovering that you are not afraid to die, can . . . totally transfigure your life.

Then their thoughts of the hereafter were interrupted by screaming harbingers of the here and now. Police officers had broken down a back door of No. 68 and were ordering everyone to evacuate, knowing that the second tower would almost certainly collapse soon. Rowan's group descended two flights of stairs and emerged into a cataclysmic scene on Greenwich Street, parallel to Trinity Place. Everything lay covered in ash and shards and personal belongings – bags, books, shoes.

They began making their way towards the southern tip of the Financial District, from where ferries and buses were escorting people to safety. The distance was small – barely 700 metres – but before the group had covered a block and a half, the second tower came down. They turned to see the elephantine dust cloud, stamped on the collective memory through repeated broadcasting, sweeping towards them. For the second or third time, the group thought it highly likely that they would die.

Fred Burnham again recognised Rowan's courage. Not all of their companions were able to run away from the enveloping smoke. A woman on the staff of Holy Trinity was paralysed by fright. One of her colleagues asked the Archbishop if he would help; he put his arm round her and walked her down the street. They were all breathless and coated with soot by the time they reached the Staten Island ferry terminal, but the immediate danger had passed. Instinct told Burnham not to enter the building; instead, the group approached a trailer with an open door, and were welcomed inside by a group of construction workers. As in certain fictional tragedies, a macabre scene was briefly tinged with humour. One of the builders was an Evangelical of strong faith who decided that everyone needed to turn to the Lord. He began to lead prayers himself, unaware that there were clergy at his side, because they weren't wearing their collars. Burnham remembers that he 'went on and on and on, but it was a great moment, really. One of those moments . . .

where people who'd never otherwise be together bonded in a significant way.'

Half an hour later the air was clearing, and the police began evacuating people on buses. The Trinity group were driven slowly up East River Drive, on Manhattan's eastern edge, and down 32nd Street to the junction with Fifth Avenue. Their route was lined by thousands of pedestrians. From there, Fred Burnham walked with Rowan to his hotel near by. The Archbishop was able to contact his secretary, Hazel Paling, by phone, and to leave a message for Jane that he was all right. Over lunch and a bottle of wine, the two men began to shed tears for the first time. Burnham set off for home towards the end of the afternoon, leaving Rowan to work on a brief article for that week's *Church Times*. 'I'm obviously very glad to be alive,' he wrote, 'but also feel deeply uncomfortable, and my mind shies away from the slaughter.'[9]

The following day he had an early breakfast with the Presiding Bishop of the Episcopal Church, Frank Griswold, and managed to reach St John the Divine Cathedral, where he was due to give a lecture, with time to spare. He was immediately asked to celebrate an unscheduled Eucharist at the high altar, and agreed to do so. A congregation of 200 to 300 people, most of whom were in the building for solace, took part. Fred Burnham was inspired:

When [Rowan] got to the rubric for the homily he was totally surprised; he hadn't expected to preach, so he preached off the cuff, completely. And he went back to an encounter that he had with an airline pilot on the streets of New York at 7 a.m. that morning, when he was walking over to [meet] the presiding bishop, and the pilot said to him, 'Where the hell was God?' And Rowan's answer was that God is useless at times like this. Now that's pretty shocking, but actually what he then went on to unpack is that God didn't cause this and God [was not] going to stop it, because God has granted us free will, and therefore God has to suffer the consequences of this like we do. So in a sense he exonerated God . . .

The intercessions were improvised; Rowan gauged each one so as to address a different facet of the disaster. At first the response ('Hear our prayer') to the invocation 'Lord, in your mercy' was quiet. Then Burnham and others sensed a swell of feeling throughout the congregation:

As they began to get what he was doing and they got into the rhythm of the intercessions, and they realised where he was going and how he was touching them, each one individually, they began to shout their response and by the time he finished, the response was just like a football game . . . I was standing there with tears streaming down my face and I could hear people on all sides of me sniffling . . . in a magnificent way Rowan had liturgically connected with the people. And it was profound.

The spontaneity was sustained after the service, when the Archbishop put aside the prepared text of his lecture and spoke without notes. In brief, his approach was to see the events of the previous day as a revelation of humanity's radical vulnerability in the face of death, of the need to live 'with courage and generosity from one day to the next':

It seems to me that when we are faced with the real, concrete possibility that death is going to happen to us, we immediately have one of the deepest possible challenges posed to the way . . . we think about ourselves. We're brought up against a situation in which we have no ability at all to think about the future. So often we as humans construct our sense of freedom and worth around our capacity to change the future. What happens when we cannot? When you and I are frustrated, the temptation is to try to do something, which, while it won't or might not let us change the circumstances, at least makes us feel better. A great deal of the life of the Church, not to mention international relations, is based on this principle, as you may have noticed. But if the powerlessness is real, and if you're prepared to look it in the face, what happens?

Our Buddhist friends tell us that when we've learnt to let go of the craving to leave our thumbprint on the wall, what is left is compassion. Because when we are released from the urge to leave that thumbprint, to scribble that signature on the wall, the urge to act so as to seem to be making a difference, one thing that happens is that a space is created. A space that is otherwise occupied by anxiety . . . becomes vacant space into which someone else's reality may come.

I want to suggest that ultimately, all authentic pastoral activity has to be activity in the face of death . . . Arising out of this is a further feature of what death teaches, which we might want to think about: something to do with self-doubt. Suddenly you've joined the vast majority of human beings living or dead for whom human dignity is not a matter of living only, but living with courage and generosity from one day to the next. Those of us in the United Kingdom and in North America who are used to living lives that are not usually thought of like that may have cause to give thanks, strange as it may sound, for an experience that puts [us] a little, just for a moment, in touch with the experience of most humans. And if that's indeed true, as death teaches solidarity, death teaches humility . . .

An encounter with death . . . puts us radically in touch with people whose experience is generally unlike our own. I thought of that again as I listened to the Epistle at Mass, to those remarkable words about how the cross of Christ brings near those who are far. The distance in question is first of all, of course, distance from God, but that is also, necessarily, distance from each other. Scripture is definitely clear that to be drawn near to God is always to be drawn near to each other, and there is no way of separating those two . . .

We may think as we begin the pastoral priestly ministry, that we know ourselves and we know what we're vulnerable to, [but] the reality and words are different things entirely. And I found, being confessional for a moment, that one of the really difficult things in being a bishop is that some of the things I thought I was good at I discovered I'm bad at, and some of the circumstances where I thought I would be able to rise to challenges in crises have been the source of my greatest failures. So again we're brought up against this very alarming insight – the future we're not in charge of.

Not, of course, that he wanted the experience suffered by so many to be repeated. The lecture included a strong warning against the thirst for revenge:

I don't want anybody to feel what others and I were feeling at about 10.30 yesterday morning. I've been there . . . if the first word spoken is an indiscriminate slaughter, if the first word spoken is the sad but inevitable cost to the innocent and I reply in that language, I'm saying this is how we go on. This is our currency. Again and again in human transactions at every level, personal, communal, interracial, intergender, international, the question of what language we are going to speak together is one of the most important moral issues that we have. Do we want the conversation to continue, and in what terms? And when there is pressure for . . . retaliation, that is perhaps one of the moral questions a Christian might want to address. How do we talk? How do we make sense?

Even by his own standards, Rowan was on impressive form here. Not all of the political lessons he drew from the tragedy were considered judicious, however. The problem was focused in his presidential address to the Governing Body on 19 September, where solid spiritual observations preceded some curious conclusions. In the former category lies the familiar idea that anger 'always blurs the real human features of those we're angry with . . . No one treats me as human, as a conversational partner; so my anger grows to the point where I don't want conversation but release at all costs, a terrible self-affirmation even if it destroys the other.'

Few would quarrel with his supplementary comment that Israelis and Palestinians (especially the latter) feel angry and helpless; the problem lies with the minor premise in Rowan's syllogism: that the 11 September jihadists counted as powerless victims who believed they had nothing to lose. 'They may be wrong in that belief,' Rowan continued,

but what matters is the belief itself. Someone else apparently has all the power there is, and they are frustrating change; my condition is such that I and my family, my culture, my religion, seem doomed to die unless there is change. Sometimes people talk to me about negotiations that will save us from dying, or at least from dying quite so quickly; but this is abstract, I can see no evidence. When my voice is raised, I am promptly silenced. So my anger rises, to the point where I can't listen to anything outside the situation. If I have to die, at least I don't have to concede victory to my oppressor . . . That is where terror of the kind we have seen in the last week begins.

But it is not at all clear that al-Qaeda were 'silenced' before 11 September: the bombers themselves were mainly middle-class men with university educations, and the network to which they belonged grew out of American backing for the Afghan Mujahedeen resisting the Soviet occupation of their country during the 1980s.

Rowan naturally expresses a psychological truth when he adds that 'only in . . . forgiveness . . . can the way open up, precarious and narrow . . . out of a burning building, that might take away some of the zero-mentality in which we're trapped'. The question is how forgiveness can apply at the level of state conflict, notably in the overthrow of the Taleban, and what place judgement should take. Though indispensable to a Christian world view, judgement is held by Rowan's friends and critics alike to be underplayed in his sermons and writings.[10]

A similar tension can be discerned in *Writing in the Dust*,[11] the challenging little book he wrote within a few weeks of 11 September. With typical modesty, he says very little about his own experience, concentrating on broader spiritual and political themes. For example, the Archbishop remarks on the contrast between the religious murderers who made 'a martyr's drama out of a crime', and the secular witness through desperate mobile phone calls to what religion purports to be about, namely the victory of altruistic love. At the same time, he offers a further hostage to fortune by claiming that the terrorists experienced their world 'as leaving them no other option'[12] (the book's blurb goes so far as to say that the attacks were 'prompted' by 'feelings of powerlessness').

You don't need to be a supporter of George W. Bush's version of the war on terror to judge that comments such as these fragment uncontrollably in different contexts. They are also music to the ears of the deranged. To take one example, Muhammad Siddique Khan, ringleader of the 7 July bombers in London, justified his action on the grounds that Muslims were being killed in the Middle East. Much has been made of the moral squalor of this comment, but far less said about its incoherence. The lion's share of violence in Iraq has been visited by Muslims on their co-religionists. Worldwide, Christians are harassed and killed by Muslims in far larger numbers than vice versa, a fact easily verified by a glance at the situation in Sudan, or at the embattled position of Christians living in most countries between Morocco and Pakistan. The position is under-reported for the simple reason that young Christians in the West do not become 'radicalised', and persecuted Christians tend not to respond with terrorist violence.

Rowan's stance was later exploited by the more venomous of his critics. On the eve of his appointment to Canterbury, for instance, the *Wall Street Journal* carried a withering attack on him by Peter Mullen (a British cleric), headlined 'a terror apologist may soon head the Church of England'. Mullen wrote that

> Dr Williams is sometimes described . . . as something of a saint. In fact he is an old-fashioned class warrior, a typical *bien-pensant* despiser of Western capitalism and the way of life that goes with it. Perhaps this would not matter much in ordinary times, but when the future of Western civilisation itself is under threat, such posturing is suicidal. What havoc this man might wreak from the throne of Canterbury.[13]

*　　*　　*

Rowan's output during the decade 1992–2002 naturally consisted of far more than political salvos. He wrote prolifically by any standard, let alone that of a diocesan bishop with a young family. His record in this department was not immediately obvious: no large-scale work appeared for almost a decade after *Teresa of Avila* (1991), although he published a collection of sermons and addresses, *Open to Judgement*,[14] in 1994, and edited a substantial volume on Bulgakov's political theology during the late 1990s.[15] Several other projects absorbed him at this time. In 2000 came *Christ on Trial*, a comparative study of Jesus' arraignment as portrayed in each Gospel; *Lost Icons: Reflections on Cultural Bereavement*,[16] principally a work of social analysis; and *On Christian Theology*,[17] a wide-ranging collection of technical essays. To mark the millennium he also co-edited *Love's Redeeming Work*,[18] a monumental anthology of Anglican spiritual writing.

Lost Icons revisits familiar Rowan Williams landscapes. The Archbishop acknowledges a good side to the Enlightenment protest against unaccountable forms of authority, but worries about its unforeseen legacies: the introspective, atomised self, together with consumerist doctrines of choice and value. But the subject is viewed from a fresh angle. In a series of chapters elaborating an alternative vision, Rowan concentrates at first on a need to respect the integrity of childhood, and to resist a widely acknowledged drift towards treating children as quasi-economic and sexualised objects. By apparently growing up more quickly than before, he argues, young people are forfeiting the chance to become genuinely mature through moral growth and the exercise of imagination.

At the same time, *Lost Icons* amounts to a piece of indirect apologetics very different from the explicit defence of Christianity that we find in a work such as *Tokens of Trust*. The argument – close in substance to that of the Archbishop's Raymond Williams Lecture,[19] given at the 2002 Hay-on-Wye literary festival – is that human persons are knitted together by bonds that 'precede' rivalry and negotiation. As we saw earlier, language itself presupposes a world of shared meaning in Rowan's scheme, which is why he sees a philosophical warrant for the biblical idea that we are members one of another. What is more, our selves never belong to us alone. A person's identity derives from his or her being seen and responded to by another. The next stage of the argument lies in the suggestion that humanity's ultimate 'anchorage' comes from our being held in the gaze of a non-contingent Other who does not compete for space and resources with us. The Archbishop does not press a Christian interpretation here, though it is this argument that drove his friend Gillian Rose towards faith.

As often before, Rowan has harsh things to say in *Lost Icons* about that constant object of his scorn, 'the North Atlantic world'. For reasons already rehearsed, many would want to lay greater stress on the West's role in bettering the planet, as well as harming it. Another sort of imbalance in *Lost Icons* is stylistic. Sometimes the book calls out for the attentions of a disciplined editor. At one point, for example, Rowan warns about a situation in which there are 'all kinds of difficulty about appealing as a moral sanction to the danger of diminishing the solidity of the self by ignoring the perceptions of others'. He is talking in a diffuse way about the danger of selfishness. After giving the Raymond Williams Lecture, Rowan received letters beginning 'Dear Archbishop, you are very clever, but . . .'. Several highly intelligent reviewers of *Lost Icons* made a similar point. After the summer of 2002, when his pronouncements were scrutinised as never before, the reaction was sometimes far more hostile.

Reading *On Christian Theology* has rightly been likened to scaling a peak, though here the author is less vulnerable to criticism. The book was written for other mountaineers. It begins with a threefold definition of the subject.[20] There is 'celebratory' theology, which aims at expressing a 'fullness of vision', especially through hymnody and preaching; 'communicative' theology, which 'experiments with the rhetoric of its uncommitted environment' – through the early Church's encounter with Platonism, say, or the contemporary dialogue with feminism; and 'critical' theology, which broaches the awkward questions, and 'nags at' questions of continuity and coherence. The essential point is that Rowan's work employs all three registers. Those who accuse him of unorthodoxy tend to marshal their case by giving disproportionate weight to his grapplings in the third of his categories. *On Christian Theology* proceeds in careful dialogue with philosophy and the arts, among other disciplines, and includes sections on metaphysics, incarnation and Trinity, New Testament exegesis, and interfaith discussion.

His creative output did not flag either. The Newport years afforded him many opportunities to meet other Welsh poets, including Gillian Clarke, Jeremy Hooker, Ruth Bidgood and Gwyneth Lewis. As the latter revealed in a television documentary about Rowan shown on Advent Sunday 2002, her whimsicality could draw vivid putdowns from the Bishop – 'Bollocks, Gwyneth!' among them. (The programme was called *An Archbishop Like This*, and showed its subject changing places for a day with a schoolgirl, among other eye-catching events in his timetable.)

The extension of his poetic range was underwritten by growing technical skill. His first two collections, *After Silent Centuries* (1994)[21] and *Remembering Jerusalem* (2001),[22] were combined with some unpublished work in *The Poems of Rowan Williams* (2002).[23] Among his finest mature pieces of verse is 'Winterreise', a sequence reflecting on the death of Gillian Rose inspired by the great Schubert song cycle. It ends with three stanzas entitled 'Night':

> Dying by degrees, perhaps, is a winter journey:
> connections cancelled unexplained, the staff,
> their patience ebbing, closing amenities, one by one, around
>   you.

> The temperature falls, and for an hour you sit
> on a plastic bench, aching for sleep,
> under the surly light that strips you

> For some always–delayed inspection; so even,
> so hard, that for so long you cannot see the dark:
> the homely dark, with its fierce small fires.

There is musical subtlety in the use of repetition ('so even / so hard, that for so long', 'the dark, the homely dark'), and, as the critic John Greening has suggested, the surprising adjective 'surly' is not merely surprising.[24] In early middle age, Rowan had found his own voice and shaken off the influences of Dylan Thomas or Vernon Watkins or R. S. Thomas, evident respectively in poems such as 'Oystermouth Cemetery', 'Great Sabbath' and 'Drystone'. Other successes include 'Thomas Merton: Summer 1966' and the group of poems about Jerusalem. The collection ends with a dozen translations – from the German of Rilke and the Welsh of Ann Griffiths, T. Gwynn Jones and Waldo Williams. The latter is sometimes hailed as one of the finest twentieth-century British poets writing in a language other than English, and his qualities are brought out in Rowan's well-crafted rendering of a work such as 'After Silent Centuries', composed for the Catholic martyrs of Wales. It begins with a memorable conspectus on faith:

> The centuries of silence gone, now let me weave a celebration;
> Because the heart of faith is one, the moment glows in which
> Souls recognise each other, one with the great tree's kernel at
>   The root of things.
>
> They are at one with the light, where peace masses and gathers
> In the infinities above my head; and where the sky moves into
>   the night,
> Then each one is a spyhole for my darkened eyes, lifting the
>   veil . . .

Apart from the visit to New York in September 2001, his most notable foreign trip was to Uganda in the spring of the following year. Rowan was accompanied by Tudor Griffiths, who had ministered in the country during the 1980s, Helen Van Koevering, the diocesan world mission officer, Margaret le Grice, a chaplain to deaf people, and Ian Beston, a lay representative from Magor parish.

An otherwise successful trip began unpromisingly when the group visited Uganda Christian University and its stridently conservative American Vice-Chancellor, Stephen Noll. The tension between the Archbishop of Wales and his host was evident from the start of their meeting. On returning to his base at the home of Archbishop Livingstone Nkoyoyo, Rowan received an envelope containing writings by Noll and others critical of his stance on homosexuality. He was 'furious' about this, Griffiths comments, especially as Noll had apparently lacked the courage to confront the Archbishop openly.

The Monmouth team then moved on to visit a large prison on Luzira, near Lake Victoria, where they entered the condemned section for an act of worship conducted by inmates. Here Rowan addressed more than 300 men who had been condemned to death. He spoke of his visit to Jerusalem in 1998, which had included a tour of ancient cells where Jesus might have been held. The visitor then preached on the resurrection, and assured his hearers that no situation is hopeless. After the service, he was presented with a petition and was begged to give it to Uganda's President, Yoweri Museveni, whom he was due to meet the following morning. The Archbishop did as he was asked. The schedule included a day in Namirembe diocese with Canon Gideon Byamugisha, an important force in ministry to AIDS patients. Rowan was especially moved by this work, and made personal donations to it.

Uganda's natural beauty stirred him to verse. At Nebbi, in the north-west of the country, he stopped at Murchison Falls, which supplied the title for a poem he wrote soon afterwards about the experience. The tone is playful, and the words themselves form a kind of cascade through frequent enjambment (where meaning overspills the bounds of line division):

> Physics gets nervous sometimes: can we manage?
> Can we keep upright on the narrow board of law
> In a tight corner with the speed rising?

– so sets itself these adolescent dares: go on,
solve this! Jump; walk the wire; dodge
the zigzagging traffic. Push unlikely bundles
down canals too tight for them, spring them
from world to world, water to air,
and catch them as they drop. Tighten the passageways
so that the pitch goes razor-sharp, and the flow bumps
over more stones along the jostled path
and sounds come thicker. Squeeze, stretch,
strike; and the equations, sweating, give their answers.
Turn up heat and choke the roads: come
to the edge of things and sounds, and look!
says physics, I can do it, I can jump and land,
and leave a map vibrating in the cloud, I move
so fast you must stand still.
                              The mica
shines in the rock as though the spray
has petrified. Physics relaxes as the stone
and water drop to the levels where the idle crocodiles
wait for what physics sends them in crushed parcels
down the chute. The test is passed, the lung
forced open; something has crossed the plaited
crossfire currents to hang steadily in the rapid air
as if said, as if written, once for all.

The voyage also prompted the poetic draft that is 'Kampala; the
El Shaddai Coffee Bar':

> The patron sometimes calls in for a glass,
> perhaps; sits with his back
> to the door.

Eyes shine and water in the woodsmoke;
who can tell who might be
welcome here?

The Archbishop's fellow travellers noted further signs of his informality during the visit, and his imperviousness to physical discomfort. When they all crossed the Nile to see Bishop Henry Orombi of Nebbi – Nkoyoyo's successor as Archbishop of Uganda – their host turned out in full episcopal fig. Rowan wore a dusty open-necked shirt. The two men established a speedy rapport. Back in Kampala, the Welsh visitors attended a Eucharist celebrated with sweet and crumbly bread typical of the region. Ugandan Anglicans tend to communicate through intinction (consuming bread dipped into consecrated wine), with often messy results. Rowan's reaction was wry. He told his Evangelical companions that Catholic sensitivities must sometimes be suspended.

Noll was not the only senior churchman in Uganda to view the Archbishop of Wales with unease because of his liberal views on sexuality. Several senior clergy displayed initial suspicion on meeting him. But the Vice-Chancellor was the only figure not to be won over by Rowan's evident godliness. The trip ended with an especially companionable evening at Nkoyoyo's house during which the guests sang 'Calon Lân' in harmony. This was the last low-profile foreign trip that Rowan would make in a professional capacity. His move to the cockpit of Anglicanism was announced several months later.

PART II

6

On the Front Line

In January 2002, while still three years shy of his official retirement date, George Carey announced that he would be bowing out the following autumn. Steps to choose a successor then began under the auspices of the Crown Appointments Commission. The burden faced by this thirteen-strong group of clergy and laypeople, including representatives from the Canterbury diocese and the General Synod, was made heavier by a widely held view that the Commission had done a poor job when last faced with the same task. In 1990, the crop of electors had been chaired by Viscount Caldecote, a Tory peer of Evangelical churchmanship with a background in industry. He had an ally in Robin Catford, the Downing Street appointments secretary: they were united by suspicion of Anglo-Catholicism and a disdain for church-based critiques of Conservative economic policy. They also shared the impression that members of a putative liberal elite were over-represented in top ecclesiastical posts. While questionable, this view had become firmly rooted through frequent repetition.

The best-qualified candidate to succeed Robert Runcie had been the Archbishop of York, John Habgood, known as the best brain on the Bench. He excelled also at administration, and his personal qualities were only lightly veiled by shyness, sometimes mistaken for aloofness. In such a climate, however, his self-description as a 'conservative liberal' (not to mention his Eton education) amounted to a handicap. There were enough opponents of Habgood on the Commission to get their way, as well as to see off the supporters of David Sheppard, Bishop of Liverpool, a prominent advocate for the urban poor whose left-wing sympathies were a matter of record.

To Caldecote, Catford and those who thought like them, the choice of George Carey, then Bishop of Bath and Wells, had seemed sensible, as well as imaginative. Though only lately raised to episcopal rank, he had been a well-liked principal of Trinity College, Bristol, and a successful vicar of St Nicholas's, Durham. He was not one of the usual suspects. Raised in a working-class household in Dagenham, east London, he had gained his first degree and subsequent doctorate the hard way.

Carey would have made an effective diocesan bishop. As Archbishop of Canterbury, though, he proved to be out of his depth, and especially vulnerable under the media spotlight. Not that there was anything to hide. He and his wife Eileen were models of respectability, evinced a firm and uncomplicated adherence to the Christian faith, and were capable of touching acts of kindness. But over time, the Lambeth staff – especially Jeremy Harris, the Secretary for Public Affairs, and the press officer, Jonathan Jennings – opted to shield the Archbishop from journalists as far as possible. It was probably the least damaging policy. Carey's memoir, *Know the Truth*, ends by listing some genuine achievements of his primacy, but the underlying tone is complacent:

> . . . no one could now point the finger at so-called 'unbelieving Bishops'. The ordination of women to the priesthood was now a

fact, and women were visible at practically every level of Church life . . . The financial crisis created by the Church Commissioners' problems in the early nineties had resulted in reformed and clearer structures. Mission and evangelism were priorities in Church life . . . Ecumenical relations were firmly on track, and beginning to bear fruit. Inter-faith co-operation and dialogue were significant realities in the Church and the nation, with the Archbishop of Canterbury taking a leading role . . . The Anglican Communion was in good heart, and the Lambeth Conference . . . had revealed the strength of the Church in the developing world. As we [Dr and Mrs Carey] drove away we felt confident about handing on to my successor, Rowan Williams, a national Church that was in good heart, even if, like other great institutions, it faces many challenges . . . I had no doubts that Rowan's considerable gifts would be appreciated by many, and would be used significantly in the time to come.[1]

Those with a clearer sense of the Church's problems – and of the very mixed success of the Decade of Evangelism, which Carey had tirelessly championed – were a good deal less positive. Twelve years after Caldecote and his fellow electors had laid a hand on the Church's tiller, many in both Church and state were ready for a change. One of Carey's greatest limitations was his dependence on conventional Evangelical language of little appeal outside his own constituency. Many Christians (not only Anglicans) wanted a successor of greater acuity who could frame the Christian message in ways that addressed those with serious intellectual misgivings, and unsettle those indifferent to run-of-the-mill pieties.

To his credit, Carey had the insight to set up a working party around the turn of the millennium to consider a recasting of the

Archbishop of Canterbury's role. Chaired by Douglas Hurd, a former Foreign Secretary, the group produced a report, *To Lead and to Serve*, with a revealingly long list of proposals for reform. It recommended that among other things the Archbishop of York should be the normal chairman of the Archbishops' Council (the Church of England's new executive body, which was part of the Carey legacy), as well as of the Church Commissioners; that some other bishops, especially the Bishop of London, should be given more definite national roles; and that almost all diocesan work in east Kent should be transferred to a bishop based in the area. The idea was to lighten the Archbishop of Canterbury's administrative load, so that he could focus on spiritual leadership.

David L. Edwards, the church historian and former Provost of Southwark, suggested in a newspaper article that this agenda should be enlarged. 'The Archbishop should be allowed time for the . . . acceptance of worthwhile opportunities in the House of Lords and the media, and for lectures. His trips overseas could be quick, but not fewer, being primarily chances to talk with other bishops and clergy . . .' Edwards made it clear not just that Rowan matched the template, but that the template should be further moulded to match Rowan: 'In brief, [the new Archbishop] should be enabled to make an impact in his own style as one of the world's leading religious thinkers, theological scholars, and spiritual guides, with ecumenical vision and equipment. Also, he should have some time for his family, as well as for prayer, study, and undistracted thinking.'[2]

Carey, however, disagreed about Rowan's eligibility, and let his feelings show. It was an open secret that he wanted another Evangelical, Bishop Michael Nazir-Ali of Rochester, to succeed him. Yet an Archbishop of Canterbury has far less influence over the choice of his successor than of diocesan bishops; and although Rowan's Welshness was a mixed blessing – he was a relative outsider, but accordingly had fewer enemies in England – a host of senior figures were rooting for him.

Articles on the Canterbury stakes were carried across the press in 2002. A cluster of names were thrown up, apart from the Archbishop of Wales. As well as Nazir-Ali, the list included James Jones of Liverpool, Kenneth Stevenson of Portsmouth, Graham James of Norwich, Michael Scott-Joynt of Winchester, Peter Forster of Chester, Tom Butler of Southwark, Christopher Herbert of St Albans, and Richard Chartres of London. Several were weighty figures, but the exercise was chiefly a matter of convention. It had something in common with the lists of *papabili* cardinals (always featuring at least one African, however unsuitable) that also appeared at this time as John Paul II drew closer to death. In the Church of England, only Chartres and Nazir-Ali were considered strong candidates for the top post. From the majority point of view, though, the Bishop of London was compromised by his refusal to ordain women. Nazir-Ali's problem was different. Critics described him as lacking in social graces, and unduly ambitious. His churchmanship posed a further difficulty: custom suggested that it was now an Anglo-Catholic's turn.

William Chapman, Tony Blair's appointments secretary and a non-voting member of the Crown Appointments Commission, was a principal conduit for the many representations from Rowan's supporters. They included the Dean of Southwark, Colin Slee, who urged in the strongest terms that the line-up consisted of only one outstanding figure, and that the Church would miss a historic opportunity if it did not make him its first recommendation. This message was repeated by Peter Thompson (the Australian priest nicknamed Blair's guru, who had known the future Prime Minister since their Oxford days). Slee and others who shared Thompson's assessment – it would probably be safe to say that the Archbishop of Wales had the whole of the Affirming Catholicism movement behind him – were not denigrating Rowan by referring to the paucity of other suitable bishops. Their support would have remained firm (it only began to drop off after 2003) even if the Church of England had been able to field a stronger team.

Yet he was far from being a shoo-in. The Crown Appointments Commission was chaired by Elizabeth Butler-Sloss, a former High Court judge. Its other members were Archbishop David Hope of York, and Bishop Timothy Stevens of Leicester; four representatives of the diocese of Canterbury: Bishop Stephen Venner of Dover, Brian Chalmers, David Kemp and Caroline Spencer; and six permanent members of the Commission: the Revd Hugh Broad, the Ven. Judith Rose, Professor Anthony Thiselton, Gill Brentford, the Revd Ian Garden and Brian McHenry. Six – a highish fraction – were Evangelicals, and some suggested that Carey was exiting early in order to take advantage of this.

The rumour mill ground on for several months – at one point Jane Williams got an apparently 'clear idea' from a church source that the Commission would choose someone other than Rowan. She rang to let him know (he was away at the time); both 'heaved a sigh of relief'. In other words, the successful candidate was not much better informed than anyone else. The truth emerged through the ferretings of Ruth Gledhill from *The Times*, who published her scoop on 20 June. When the official announcement was made on Tuesday 23 July, Rowan began his speech to reporters at Church House, Westminster, with a comment on the twists and turns of the previous weeks: 'It is

ON THE FRONT LINE

a curious experience to have your future discussed, your personality, childhood influences and facial hair solemnly examined in the media, and opinions you didn't know you held expounded on your behalf.' Then he moved on to the crux of the matter: 'I hope with all my heart that I can serve to nurture confidence and conviction in our Church and to help Christian faith to recapture the imagination of our people and our culture.' Later in the day he returned for a second press conference, in Welsh and in Newport. Several Lambeth Palace staff members were taken aback by the idea that there was any call for a separate event in Wales. To the Williamses, this reaction was early confirmation of their hunch that their future minders held them to be an other-worldly pair in need of firm management.

The great and the good were almost universally enthusiastic about the appointment. Rhodri Morgan, Wales's First Minister, said: 'Rowan Williams is a man in a million, and people of his calibre come along every 200 or 300 years.' There was also praise from around the Communion. Bishop John Paterson of Auckland, New Zealand, Vice-Chairman of the Anglican Consultative Council, described the appointment as 'undoubtedly right . . . at this critical time'. Archbishop Robin Eames of Armagh, the Church's longest-serving primate, said that he had greeted the news with 'delight and confidence'. 'Dr Williams will quietly identify with the needs of our diverse family. His sincere spirituality, allied to personal courage, will, I am sure, make him a great leader of the Church, at home and abroad.' Ecumenical approval was summed up in a *Tablet* editorial drawing attention to Rowan's record of political dissent: 'He is a prophet and theologian. He is not a "safe" man. If Tony Blair decides to hitch his wagon to the American star and back an attack on Saddam Hussein, Rowan Williams is unlikely to be found cheering him on.'[3] The article went on to praise Tony Blair for not choosing a more politically docile figure. Even the *Daily Mail*, no uncritical fan of the Church of England, carried a positive reaction:

> One thing is sure. Even leaving aside his liberal views on such issues as gay clergy, the ordination of women and the remarriage of divorcees, Dr Williams is not going to be a cautious archbishop. But this primate has more important things to offer than mere controversy. A renowned theologian, a gifted pastor, and a priest of luminescent spirituality, he has the qualities to lead and inspire. In this secular, sometimes cynical age, there is nevertheless a yearning for spiritual fulfilment. Perhaps under Dr Williams's guidance, the Church of England can at last begin to satisfy that hunger. We wish him every blessing.[4]

The Archbishop's responses to press questioning on 23 July were typically sure-footed. Less remarked on were his bids to dampen the euphoria during the press conference. Asked whether he had had doubts about accepting his new post, he said:

> I think, frankly, you'd be a maniac not to have doubts about accepting a job of this kind, and the . . . things which . . . worried me most were that it's a job that inevitably carries huge expectations and projections, and living through that, you live through other people's fantasies in a way, and to try and keep some degree of honesty, clarity and simplicity in the middle of that is going to be hard work – so that frightened me a lot.[5]

Expressions of modesty such as these were perhaps only to be expected. With hindsight, however, you might suspect that the

Archbishop knew something most others did not. To see why this was not only possible but likely, we need to probe Carey's attitudes and legacy in a little more detail. Though often unsuccessful at home, Rowan's predecessor made a bigger impact overseas – especially in the developing world. But as the Catholic commentator Damian Thompson noted in an article shortly after Rowan's nomination, the achievement came at a price. Bishops in Africa and elsewhere expected him to uphold conservative teaching on gay sex. This partly explains why the issue became a litmus test of orthodoxy during the 1990s. As attitudes shifted in the Church, let alone in secular society, before the turn of the millennium, the risks entailed by this policy grew more obvious. Thompson drew a prescient conclusion: that Carey's 'meticulously engineered alliance' between the Church of England and the Anglican Communion would fall apart. 'Williams's Welshness notwithstanding, [his appointment to Canterbury] has been, in some respects, a very English coup. Using the instrument of the Crown Appointments Commission, the establishment has squashed the ambitions of an evangelical lobby which reflects the prejudices of the developing world, not cosmopolitan London.'[6]

It may now be easier to see that Rowan's misgivings about accepting the top job were genuine. For one thing, the reaction to his appointment was far more polarised than suggested by Fleet Street coverage. A fringe Evangelical group such as the Church Society, which condemned the new Archbishop in operatic terms (and even disapproved of Carey), counted for little. Other hardline bodies such as Reform were more influential, though hardly mainstream. But primates and other senior bishops from the developing world were another matter. Rowan did not lack influential Evangelical friends keen to offer assistance and, in doing so, to buttress their own influence over church teaching on sexual ethics. One such was his Oxford friend Oliver O'Donovan. Anticipating Rowan's appointment earlier in the summer, he invited three primates – Donald Mtememela of Tanzania, Drexel Gomez of the West Indies, and Yong Ping Chung of South-East Asia – for an evidently lavish dinner in Christ Church in early July. He then reported back to the Archbishop in the following letter, marked confidential:[7]

Christ Church
Oxford
4 July 2002

Dear Rowan:

Well, I met with the three primates, and I spoke to my brief. There were only the four of us, they having decided to exclude senior bishops and administrators to make the occasion as confidential and intimate as possible; and whether it was the effect of that decision, the soothing atmosphere of the Freind Room on a summer evening, the effectiveness of [the chef] in the kitchen or the deft unobtrusiveness of [a college steward] as he waited on our needs, the predicted fire did not stream from their nostrils. Indeed, we became congenial, and as we warmed to our theme a good deal of sympathy was expressed for you in the situation in which you are presently placed.

These fathers in God are clearly inclined to like you personally and to appreciate your contribution to the primates' Meeting. Part of the vigour of their initial reactions, I guess, was sheer shock. There is also, as you are doubtless well aware, a palpable anti-American animus, stoked up (through a confusion of categories, perhaps, but understandably) by political circumstances. One question about you which I could not answer concerned your 'friendship' with [the Presiding Bishop of the Episcopal Church] Frank Griswold.

At the end I was charged with a message for you, which I reproduce as much like a good CD player as I can, complete with the emphases with which it was declared to me:

> In the event of Rowan Williams' appointment, he must say something *as early as possible* to reassure the Communion; and in giving such reassurance *emphasising the authority of Lambeth* [1.10] *is crucial.*

Should the moment arrive, you know what these primates at any rate are hoping to hear from you. It will require a twofold portion of all the sevenfold gifts to attune such a message appropriately for the whole Communion.

On the broader front it now appears that the efforts of the harder elements of this Conference, initially inclined to focus upon you, are to be directed more constructively, to the general question of accountability and authority within the Anglican Communion – the agenda of something called *Mending the Nets*, of which I have only now been apprised.

In all this drama (since my quiet life sees little such, you will forgive me if I make too much of it), a critically constructive negotiating role has been played by two figures, both of them Oxford men who had experience of you in your time here. They are Tim Dakin, the new General Secretary of CMS, and Bishop John Chew of Singapore. As I said on the phone, a disinterested friend would do anything to protect you from appointment to Canterbury; yet if that burden should be laid upon you, I hope you will not forget that even the fire-breathers can sometimes be tamed, and that there are one or two determined and skilful tamers out there in the field, on whose good will you can count.

With my prayers,
Your friend,
Oliver

In this light it becomes easier to see why Rowan saw it as not only politic but vital to allay fears that he would be seeking to impose his pro-gay views on the Church at large. The message was conveyed in a circular to fellow primates on the day his appointment was announced; by early August the letter was in the public domain after its appearance on the Sydney diocese's website. The Archbishop-designate granted that Lambeth 1.10 expressed the mind of the 'overwhelming majority' of the Communion; he then issued a warning to liberals in New Westminster, Canada, where the diocesan synod had on three occasions approved a rite for the blessing of same-sex unions. Any unilateral action by an individual province or diocese would pose 'a substantial problem for the sacramental unity of the Communion'. Evangelicals expressed qualified relief; gay campaigners appeared unperturbed. Richard Kirker of the Lesbian and Gay Christian Movement used a form of words that he would later have reason to rue: 'Rowan's record of the past twenty years stands for itself.'[8]

What did 'Rowan's record' amount to? Consisting of a highly forthright lecture, an open-handed pastoral policy, and a declaration of deference to the collective mind of the Church, it was more comparable to a mosaic of fragments than to a seamless garment. The third of these elements was summed up by the Evangelical theologian Alister McGrath, in an article for the

Church of England Newspaper which quoted with approval a definition of the episcopal role Rowan had given twenty years earlier: 'The bishop does not make decisions, doctrinal or disciplinary, alone: the Church decides, and the bishop's unique role is to guarantee *all* that the Church decides.' McGrath glossed this remark as follows:

> I . . . judge that Rowan would see himself as free to make his own views known, and to commend them to the Church – yet in a personal, rather than institutional capacity (as *doctor privatus* rather than *doctor communis*, to use an old distinction). He will see his role as raising uncomfortable questions, and keeping them open, catalysing the crystallization of the 'mind of the Church'. But in the end, it is the Church that must decide its own mind, and the bishop who must seek to maintain unity during and after that decision . . .[9]

McGrath, by now one of Britain's most respected Evangelical theologians, ended with a positive verdict on the new Archbishop of Canterbury: 'Evangelicals will find in him someone who understands their position and concerns, and will want to encourage them in their mission and ministry.'

Aside from all the chin-rubbing about ecclesiology, a further taste of the future came in a stream of silly-season stories centring on the new Archbishop. Word had got out about his love for *The Simpsons*. Rhiannon enjoyed the cartoon series as a child, and her father had described it as one of the finest pieces of propaganda around in the causes of sense, humility and virtue. Prompted by this, reporters from the *Sun* doorstepped him in Newport with a hamperful of *Simpsons* merchandise. Less trivially, he was excoriated by some conservative Evangelicals for attending that year's Eisteddfod. The ceremony is cultural and Christian in origin; and in any case, the Archbishop was being honoured for his achievements as a poet. This did not stop journalists from suggesting that he had taken part in pagan ceremonies – and attempting to validate their claims by circulating pictures of him in white bardic robes and a headdress. Village-pump theologians had a field day. Among them was the novelist Anne Atkins, who used her 'Thought for the Day' slot on Radio 4 to deplore the allegedly confused signals sent out by the Archbishop to African clergy battling against syncretism. He went off for his summer holiday with a greater sense of relief than usual, but remained angry about the criticism for years afterwards.

McGrath's words formed part of the informal campaign to support Rowan already organised by O'Donovan, and some Evangelicals were mollified. But in practice, August 2002 marked only a lull in hostile exchanges over the new Archbishop. The broader Evangelical picture is worth outlining. In November two prominent Evangelicals, Francis Bridger and Christina Rees, wrote of the seismic implications of Rowan's appointment for their wing of the Church.[10] The rise of Evangelical scholarship over recent decades had led to more nuanced attitudes: it was no longer enough simply to recite mantras such as 'the Bible says . . .'. While the Church of England's General Synod faced a heavy agenda centring on the looming Iraq war, abortion, pensions and mission, Bridger and Rees predicted that the subject of Rowan's credibility among Evangelicals would dominate all others in the tea rooms and corridors of Church House. The fault, they insisted, lay with hotheaded conservatives who had no time for diversity, and a nostalgia for the period (before the late 1960s) when Evangelicals were less integrated with other Anglicans.

The difficulty was that hotheads were by definition unlikely to cool down. Those who rejected McGrath's arguments had a simple rejoinder. It was not enough to be told that Rowan would not seek to impose his views on the majority. Only a full-scale recantation was adequate. Principle was here entwined with politics – obviously so, since the Church would be a laughing stock if it made as much noise about sex between unmarried men and women as about the gay variety. With the softening of attitudes to divorce on all wings of the Church of England, opposition to homosexuals had become the new banner under which many conservatives could rally.

Rowan got the measure of his more extreme opponents when he agreed to meet a delegation from the Church Society at his office in October. This amounted to a further act of 'reckless generosity': the group had been invited for lunch, but they announced on arrival that they had eaten beforehand. An already awkward encounter grew more so as the Archbishop, unsupported by his chaplain, ate sandwiches while the visitors eyed him in silence. There was no meeting of minds.

His valedictory address to the Monmouth diocesan synod, delivered at this time, is revealing in this context.[11] At one point, as reported, he likened himself to St Augustine of Canterbury, setting off from France to evangelise the 'savage' English; but the main aim was to defend a classically Anglican model of scriptural authority. The building blocks of his argument are familiar. Orthodox Anglicans saw the Reformation as 'a colossal and liberating discovery of the Bible as the place where God's challenges were to be heard'. But some had drawn a false inference from this – that the Bible also provides a blueprint for how the Church was to be run. A smaller minority even argued that the Law of Moses ought to be the law of England

and Wales: 'Think of that next time you eat a prawn cocktail,' Rowan joked.

More persuasive voices maintained that the Bible was a touchstone – 'a rule in the sense of a standard rather than a legal regulation' – with the result that the Church of England needed to give weight to history and common sense, listening to what earlier generations had said, and to the best of contemporary wisdom. A degree of untidiness was therefore inevitable:

> it is not fair or accurate to see this as a quarrel between people . . . who think the Bible is just a human book, and people who think it's inspired. You might have thought, from some of what has been in the press lately, that I regard the Bible as an outdated text with no more authority than last week's newspaper. I hope that isn't what you have heard me say as pastor and teacher.[12]

Only one of his final comments – 'I have always been committed to the Church's traditional teaching on sex before marriage' – seemed doubtful. The point of 'The Body's Grace' had been precisely to defend the view (almost universally shared in modern Western society) that sex outside marriage is not always wrong. Perhaps he would have been better advised to stress that he was talking about his stance during his time as a bishop, rather than implying that everything he had ever said and written cleared the far higher bars set for the Primate of All England.

Yet it was hardly surprising that he felt anxious to present his views as unexceptionable. The actions of some of his antagonists had been demonic. Fundamentalist Evangelicals had been sending him a stream of hate mail, including faeces, and Jane had been reduced to tears more than once. One correspondent had sent him a copy of the Bible. His sense of apprehension – dread is probably not too strong a word – was augmented by some intensely disappointing news: that he would not be allowed to retain Gregory Cameron as his chaplain at Lambeth. A consequence of *To Lead and to Serve* not foreseen by Lord Hurd himself was a requirement that the incoming Archbishop would inherit his predecessor's staff (as newly appointed government ministers inherit their officials), in the interests of continuity. When Rowan asked if he could take Cameron, he was told that Carey's people were on contracts and could not be moved. This, say some, was the moment at which he should have insisted on getting his own way. Rowan disagrees. One of his friends later told me that the Archbishop thought civil war would break out in the palace if he had refused to give Cameron up. Besides, confrontation was not his way. Having consented to become Archbishop of Canterbury in the first place, he decided that he should accept everyone whom God had placed in his orbit. So his first years were spent with David Marshall as his chaplain, and relations between the two became very warm. When asked now about staffing, however, he replies uncompromisingly that his successor will have a freer hand from the start.

The sense that he was too boxed in during the early days is borne out by the story of his ill-fated visit to the *Guardian* in late 2002. Alan Rusbridger, the paper's editor, had been highly impressed by the Archbishop on hearing him lecture at the Hay festival several months beforehand. He invited Rowan to a *Guardian* lunch – a regular fixture allowing editorial staff to meet well-known people in an informal atmosphere. Conversation at these gatherings is conducted off the record. Rowan agreed to come without hesitation. But Harris, learning of the engagement a fortnight before it was due to take place, reacted suspiciously. In the end he insisted on being at the Archbishop's side for the encounter. A journalist who was present at the lunch recalls a deeply embarrassing turn of events:

> Alan Rusbridger asked Rowan Williams what he intended to do about gay clergy. Jeremy Harris rolled his eyes and tutted, as if to imply that the question was absurd. This struck us as very ill-mannered. The Archbishop himself grew quieter and quieter. The lunch ended after only forty minutes. These events normally last one-and-a-half or two hours. The story provides evidence of poor judgement on Harris's part, and Rowan Williams's weakness in not being firmer with his own people.

Foreboding aside, there were still many positive developments in which Rowan could take pride during the second half of 2002. His statement to the primates had bought him time, and in the five months before Christmas – palmy days compared with the trauma that would erupt over Jeffrey John and Gene Robinson the following year – the public were regularly reacquainted with the value of a stimulating Anglican voice on the national stage. Just after his appointment, for example, *The Times* spotted an opportunity, and reprinted one of the most persuasive passages in *Lost Icons* under the headline 'Defending the Unborn Human'. The flaw, as Rowan sees it, in pro-abortion arguments is a muddled notion of choice. By discouraging a pregnant woman from smoking or drinking alcohol, we are taking it for granted that she is morally constrained by interests not completely defined by her. Choice, therefore, is not the decisive moral issue, and anyone who treats it as such is reducing ethics to a trial of strength –

that is, to 'who is able more successfully to defend their interest against others'.[13]

This argument lies at the heart of his protests against the rhetoric of choice in state education – successful schools attract 'customers' away from the competition, leaving a spiral of failure in less effective establishments – and his anxiety about the rise of the so-called market state generally. The term derives from the American political thinker Philip Bobbitt, and provided the Archbishop with one of the central ideas in his Dimbleby Lecture,[14] delivered just after his move to London. In environments where there is acute deprivation, he said, 'including deprivation of everyday habits of mutuality and respect, a school bears an impossible burden of trying to create a "culture" practically on its own, because the institutions that help you shape a story for your life are not around'. Acutely uneasy about these empty spaces, the state was advertising for partners to re-establish contact with the people it was supposed to be looking after. The Churches and their associated charities were the obvious partnership candidates, Rowan argued.

In some ways, the verdict on this text reflected standard Left–Right divisions: a *Guardian* leader-writer called the address 'magnificently authoritative', while the former Tory MP Matthew Parris accused Rowan of doom-mongering, and of ignoring the reasons for Britain's economic gains during the 1980s and 90s. 'The nation state is not being torn away. The citizen has never in history enjoyed a higher level of protection and shelter from government. Individuals are no greedier today than they were two, 20 or 200 decades ago.'[15] But the picture overall was more complex. Ferdinand Mount, a former adviser to Margaret Thatcher, praised the lecture for drawing attention to 'a sphere where public morality, local loyalty and a sense of community used to be'.[16]

That not everyone appreciated what Mount saw was partly a mark of Rowan's murky style. Like his speech on the place of sharia in UK law five years later, the Dimbleby Lecture was allusive and very short of concrete examples. As one senior Anglican priest in the audience put it to me, 'you were just left feeling, "Well, so what?" It was a great pity that he couldn't have earthed the lecture a bit more and made it more straightforward. All the more so as talk of his supposedly clotted style is often exaggerated. There are occasions when he can be luminous about things, and beautifully simple and direct and challenging . . .'

The countdown to war made the six months before March 2003 an especially febrile period. Tony Blair had apparently decided that the UK should join any American-led attack on Iraq well beforehand, so counsels of caution from prominent public figures – or any other quarter – were unlikely to be heeded. The tragedy was compounded by the good counsel coming from church sources. Although some of Rowan's earlier writings on war and conflict had been utopian, his statements on ways of dealing with Saddam Hussein were pragmatic, as well as doveish. He told the *Guardian* that he had three pieces of advice for MPs debating the so-called dodgy dossier on Saddam Hussein's alleged stockpile of weapons of mass destruction:

First, that the removal of unjust regimes without reference to international law is a Pandora's box. We need UN inspections; we also need due process in bringing the regime to justice over its human rights abuses in the appropriate courts. Second, that pre-emptive action on a supposed threat is a deeply destabilising matter – what message is being sent to India and Pakistan? Third:

that any action without some regional consensus invites a spiral of terrorist retaliation . . . If Arab neighbours are convinced they are excluded from the process of containment of Saddam, the results will be disastrous. If they are willing to sign up to diplomatic containment and indictment in international courts, we should work with this. The moral case against Saddam is overwhelming. We should not imperil it by compromising legality or ignoring the region's long-term justice and stability.[17]

This admonition in turn reflected equally sane instincts about the Israel–Palestinian morass which the Archbishop had expressed a while earlier. He asked his audience to imagine a situation in which there had been a military withdrawal and ceasefire in the Holy Land; the Israeli government had given an undertaking not to build new settlements, and had even dismantled a few recent ones; and Yasser Arafat had handed over negotiating powers to a small group boosted by representatives from Lebanon, Jordan, Egypt and, possibly, Syria, on the basis that all these countries repudiated suicide bombings. Rowan went on to envisage a body akin to South Africa's Truth and Reconciliation Commission, operating under the joint auspices of the US and UN, which could try to say what had been unsayable in the history of both parties. The signatories of the Alexandria Declaration would be invited to review the status of Jerusalem. 'What would make this possible? We can't know, and it is a fairly remote dream. But we do need to think a bit laterally, to get ourselves out of the iron grooves of violence and simple territorial battling.'[18]

The Archbishop restated his opposition to war in a wide-ranging interview with the journalist Paul Handley, a few weeks before Christmas. His answers to questions about his general role were in keeping with several of Douglas Hurd's main recommendations. He said he could live with not attending every meeting of the Church Commissioners, and hoped to concentrate on teaching and commending the faith in the public arena. In an echo of his reflection on the Porto Primates' Meeting two years earlier, he denied that Anglicanism needed to tighten up its structures:

> I don't think [the Communion] needs to have a more centralised executive. That would be a mistake; it would be following a model that, on the whole, in Anglican history, we have not followed. We've seen ourselves as a federation of essentially local churches. The difficulty is not so much central management of the Communion as communication . . . [G]iven that different parts of the Communion do take, and have taken, controversial decisions that are not easily going to be put back into the bottle by strong executive action, how does the Communion grow into a situation where people are simply in communication with each other, either to allow or to refrain from this?[19]

Writing shortly afterwards, he summed up his rationale for Anglicanism as a grown-up form of Christianity well equipped to confront the contemporary world:

> Anglicanism 'answers' modernity because it has bothered to listen to it, and thinks it worth talking with. In a good conversation, something is genuinely contributed towards a common future, but always in response to the reality of what's presented, rather than in lecturing or preaching mode.
>
> It is easy to pretend, with some affection of superiority, that this is a weak and unconfident style . . . But conversation, in fact,

assumes quite a bit of confidence, since it requires quite a high degree of confidence to enter into an unstructured conversational exchange, convinced that there will be opportunities for what you believe to emerge strongly enough to challenge, and even transform, whomever you are talking to.[20]

Hindsight is not needed to see how attractive this is in some ways, and how idealistic in others.

*   *   *

The Williamses moved to Lambeth at the end of November. As recently as the 1970s the Ramseys had lived in the State Rooms at Lambeth, but when they were *en famille* the Coggans, Runcies and Careys had confined themselves to a flat on the palace's upper floor. This arrangement had worked satisfactorily for the three couples concerned. But Rowan was the first Archbishop in almost two centuries to have school-age children, and this made his new home rather cramped. The problem was eased by having a second official residence, the Old Palace at Canterbury, which the family were determined to use whenever possible. Diary commitments would keep them at Lambeth for most of the time, however.

Rowan formally became the 104th Archbishop of Canterbury on Monday 2 December, when he received the 'spiritualities' of his new see in St Paul's Cathedral. Though not as grand an affair as his enthronement three months later, this ceremony, known as the 'confirmation' of his election, also drew a sizeable tally of bishops, bewigged lawyers and big hats. 'It had been a rough ride to this point,' reported Glyn Paflin in the *Church Times*, 'but the Archbishop's most vocal critics were notable by their absence. There were no protesters like those who shouted through

Bishop William Wand's confirmation in 1945, and whose successors still shop at Kensit's bookstore in Fleet Street, and read about "Sodomites" in *The English Churchman*.'[21] Archbishop David Hope of York declared his fellow primate to be 'a man both prudent and discreet, deservedly laudable for his life and conversation', and was accompanied by eight other bishops, 'by Divine Permission', who heard Rowan's oaths and the Declaration of Assent. Perhaps out of respect for the Archbishop's own preferences, the ceremony was made more of a musical occasion than it had ever been before. Jane was visibly moved.

The lighter side of things included a well-nigh obligatory appearance on Radio 4's *Desert Island Discs*. Rowan gave an engaging performance, despite the occasional condescension of the presenter, Sue Lawley. At one point, she expressed deep surprise about her guest's lack of a South Wales accent, implying that he had deliberately jettisoned any aural mark of his background. The Archbishop explained that there had never really been an accent to lose — a pattern common among grammar school recruits of his generation.

Unsurprisingly, his musical choices said at least as much as his words. He started with the first of five variations on *Dives and Lazarus* by Vaughan Williams – the tune known as *Kingsfold* in the hymn books. Next came 'Calon Lân'. Rowan's third choice, 'The Hedgehog Song' by the Incredible String Band, was anything but predictable. He explained that he had never been much of a rock fan, but someone had given him this track as a twenty-first birthday present. Its lyrics – 'You know all the words and you've sung all the notes, but you've never quite learned the song . . .' – formed 'a powerful summing up of the problems people have with relationships, and with life in general'.

In the fourth and fifth slots were *Ave Maris Stella* from Monteverdi's Vespers, and the opening of Bach's G major cello suite. Monteverdi's inhabiting and development of earlier musical forms was analogous to Christian discipleship itself, Rowan suggested. He added that Bach provided him with a uniquely powerful springboard for meditation, and that this was an essential source of nourishment in a pressured life. It became clear that the Archbishop's pre-modern musical preferences were of a piece with his theological traditionalism. His final three choices were the climax of the Act One quintet from Mozart's *The Magic Flute* (one of the most exquisite moments in music), the *Herr dein Mittleid* duet from Bach's Christmas Oratorio, and a setting of Compline for Christmas Eve by the Russian composer Alexander Kastalsky.

Lawley did not pull her punches. Among other things, she questioned whether the Archbishop really had a strategy to avert decline, and why he had knowingly ordained a priest in a gay relationship. Evidently taken aback by the second of these questions, he asked for a moment of silence before replying. Then he said that bishops take soundings on the suitability of candidates before ordaining them, and he had 'never' overridden the advice he had received. (This may have been true with regard to gay ministerial candidates, but as we have seen, several of his Monmouth colleagues would not have seen this as an accurate description of the broader picture.) During the 1990s, he continued, the Church of England had had a clearer policy on gay clergy than the Church in Wales; and he would abide by the practice of his new province. His strategy for arresting decline would focus on 'New Expressions' of Church alongside the parish system rather than in competition with it. Go and open a community centre on an estate and see who comes, he suggested. If pastors made themselves known and trusted in areas like that, the approach would pay dividends.

He gave one of the customary defences of establishment. The Church of England shoulders a responsibility for the local, accessible expression of religious concern. It is committed to performing its rites all over the country, some of which remain a resource for the majority in circumstances of stress and loss and transition. The status quo allows people to hear what God might be saying, 'without too much prescription about what they are permitted to hear', as Rowan said in another context.[22]

Lawley predicted bumpy times ahead. 'I think it could be very interesting,' her guest replied with a laugh. Castaways on the programme are asked to choose their favourite musical work – the Bach suite, in Rowan's case – a luxury, and one book apart from the Bible and the complete works of Shakespeare. Rowan opted for a piano (but admitted that he would pine for supplies of chocolate ginger) and the collected poems of W. H. Auden.

The Archbishop spent several weeks after Christmas on retreat at Bose, the ecumenical community for men and women near Milan. Winter's last days were dominated by preparations for his enthronement, and by efforts to change the Prime Minister's mind about the Iraq invasion. Rowan and his Roman Catholic opposite number, Cardinal Cormac Murphy-O'Connor, summed up their case in a joint statement on Wednesday 19 February. They questioned the moral legitimacy of the imminent invasion, and urged that 'all sides in this crisis engage, through the United Nations – fully and urgently – in a process, including weapons inspections, that could and should render the trauma and tragedy of war unnecessary'.[23] Other parts of the statement read less tautly. This was because the Catholics found Rowan's first draft too convoluted: versions of the text had to be passed back and forth between Lambeth Palace and Archbishop's House. On Monday 24 February, Rowan restated his view in person to an unbending Blair during a private encounter at 10 Downing Street.

The enthronement took place three days later amid pageantry in Canterbury Cathedral, and protest outside. Walsingham Witness-style Protestant demonstrators were outnumbered (and drowned out) by a larger group of anti-war campaigners targeting the Prime Minister: the scale of their action persuaded the police to block off the entire Precincts. Inside the cathedral were gathered a large array of senior clergy and politicians, including bishops from the Orthodox and Oriental traditions as well as Free Church leaders, Catholic prelates and the Primates of the Anglican Communion.

At 3 p.m. the Archbishop, vested in an almost plain mitre and golden cope with a dragon clasp – both made for him by Welsh craftspeople – arrived at the west door. He knocked three times with his crosier to gain admittance, and the choir sang a setting of the Jubilate Deo by Lassus. After prayers and further music, Rowan made the Declaration of Assent and took his oath before the lessons: Isaiah 6:1–8 ('In the year that King Uzziah died . . .') and Revelation 19:1, 5–9 ('I heard what seemed to be the loud voice of a great multitude . . .'). Then, from the nave, John Walters' daughter Bethan began a 'Pennillion' on her harp beside the Compass Rose (the symbol of the Anglican Communion) set in the floor. Performances in this genre are traditionally led by a harpist; after a time, Bethan was joined by a soprano, Rachel Grey, who performed a setting of words by Ann Griffiths that Rowan had translated. *'Wele'n sefyll rhwng y myrtwydd wrthrych teilwng o'm holl fryd . . .'* she sang: 'Under the dark trees, there he stands, there he stands; shall he not draw my eyes? . . .' The poem also speaks of Jesus as a 'stranger to them all'.

After the Archbishop's installation in the quire throne, the choir began to sing 'Amen Siakudumisa', a South African song, to the beat of drums played by members of the Frititi group, who wore traditional costumes with feather headdresses. Having taken his seat in Augustine's chair and received a blessing from Archbishop Robin Eames, Rowan rose for the Peace. More music followed before the Gospel (Matthew 11:25–30) and sermon.[24]

The Archbishop picked up on the theme of God's 'secrets' from this reading, and asked why a jaded, secularised society might need to listen to strangers, 'the children; the exhausted; the ravaged and burdened and oppressed'. 'They know the secret,' the Archbishop explained. 'It's the really hungry who can smell fresh bread a mile away.' The weightier secret was that Jesus had been given the freedom to give God's own life and love: he was the bread of life. 'The one great purpose of the Church's existence is to share that bread of life,' Rowan continued,

> to hold open in its words and actions a place where we can be with Jesus and be channels for his free, unanxious, utterly demanding, grown-up love . . . Once we recognize God's great secret, that we are all made to be God's sons and daughters, we can't avoid the call to see one another differently. No one can be written off; no group, no nation, no minority can just be a scapegoat to receive our fears and uncertainties. We cannot assume that any human face we see has no divine secret to

disclose: those who are culturally or religiously strange to us; those who so often don't count in the world's terms (the old, the unborn, the disabled).

Was there a point where Anglicans couldn't recognise the same Jesus, the same secrets, Rowan asked, in a reference to divisions in the Communion.

The Anglican Church is often accused of having no way to answer this. But I don't believe it: we read the same Bible and practise the same sacraments and say the same creeds. [And] I do believe that we have the very best of reasons for hesitating to identify such a point too quickly or easily – because we believe in a Jesus who is truly Lord and God, not the prisoner of my current thoughts or experiences.

His prayer for the Church was that it would be given confidence, courage, 'an imagination set on fire by the vision of God the Holy Trinity', thankfulness.

The Church of the future, I believe, will do both its prophetic and its pastoral work effectively only if it is concerned first with gratitude and joy; orthodoxy flows from this, not the other way round, and we don't solve our deepest problems just by better discipline, but by better discipleship, a fuller entry into the intimate joy of Jesus's life.

The Archbishop revealed that he had come to realise twelve years beforehand that Jesus was 'simply there' at the heart of everything. 'Simply there; nothing anyone can do about it; there he is as he has promised to be till the world's end. And nothing of value happens in the Church that does not start from seeing him simply there in our midst, suffering and transforming our human disaster.'

Reform and the Church Society reacted scathingly to the sermon. The Evangelical Alliance, an inter-denominational umbrella group, wished Rowan well, but said its members remained concerned that 'he has adopted positions which, if maintained and promulgated by him as Archbishop of Canterbury, will undoubtedly undermine the unity and biblical mission of the Church'. Some commentators felt that he should have spoken more of secular politics. Others judged that talking to Christians about God was exactly what an archbishop should do. 'It is where he gets the capital that he spends with his excursions into public life,' one pundit argued.[25]

*   *   *

Several further events from early 2003 stand out. In retrospect, these months continued to provide signs of how Rowan's primacy might have unfolded but for the Jeffrey John affair. On Maundy Thursday, he became the first Archbishop of Canterbury since the Reformation to perform the traditional foot-washing ceremony during the Liturgy of the Lord's Supper – though another own goal from Lambeth Palace almost stopped the world from seeing it. Rowan's staff judged the event might generate bad publicity if it were photographed; Jonathan Jennings even advised journalists that the Archbishop did not want a camera crew in attendance. Puzzled by this, the Dean of Canterbury, Robert Willis, went over to the Old Palace to question the decision. Rowan replied that he had never been against a press presence. The service duly generated front-page photos of Rowan kneeling before a group from the cathedral congregation, and some admiring comment on his humility.

This was more than a PR exercise. The new Archbishop's actions were in character, and were duplicated on many occasions away from the media glare. One notable example has already been reported.[26] Not long after moving back to England, Rowan spent a Sunday at a church on the outskirts of Maidstone. After morning worship he went back to the vicarage with the local incumbent for a drink, but they were interrupted by a churchwarden who announced that a couple had brought their baby to be baptised. The ceremony had been booked but the vicar, who had cancer, had forgotten about it. Rowan offered to officiate, and did so without fuss or fanfare. The family had no idea who he was. On another occasion, he visited an old people's home in Margate. As the Archbishop approached the lift, a male member of staff looked at him quizzically and asked, 'Should I know you?' 'I don't think so,' Rowan replied. 'Ah,' the man answered. 'For a moment I thought you was the Archbishop of Canterbury.'

May saw him being sucked back into church politics via the Primates' Meeting – held that year at Gramado in Brazil. Although Rowan earned wide praise for his preaching (including some fine reflections on John's Gospel), the meeting was held against the background of the earlier decision in the Canadian diocese of New Westminster to allow the public blessing of same-sex relationships. The primates issued a unanimous warning that 'we as a body cannot support the authority of such rites', because there was 'no theological consensus' in support of gay relationships. Within hours of this, though, Michael Kalmuck and Kelly Montfort were united at a ceremony performed by the Revd Margaret Marquardt at St

Margaret's, Cedar Cottage, in Vancouver. The event attracted coverage across the world. Liberal–conservative tensions intensified. Both sides noted that Marquardt had allowed the happy couple to exchange rings – a feature that had been deliberately excluded from the official New Westminster rite for seeming too redolent of the sacrament of marriage.

Events in New Westminster – and the election of Gene Robinson to succeed Douglas Theuner as Bishop of New Hampshire on 7 June – overshadowed the crisis over Jeffrey John which was about to break in England. An explanation as to why so many reacted to this and subsequent events with bewilderment, above all, could begin with reference to the international context. Rowan was faced with not so much an accident as a tragedy of timing. Modern communications also played a commanding role. Just as claims about universal papal jurisdiction had been made possible by the railways in the nineteenth century (the doctrine had previously been more a matter of theory than practice), email and the internet in 2003 made the Anglican Communion seem a much smaller place. Computers provided previously unknown opportunities for networking and alliance-building – especially among the well-drilled ranks of Dr John's opponents. Those who saw homosexuality as a secondary issue, and therefore judged the John affair to be trifling, had not taken this into account. Anglicanism's tectonic plates were about to collide.

The story has already been vividly told by Stephen Bates of the *Guardian* in *A Church at War: Anglicans and Homosexuality*;[27] and a complementary account comes in John S. Peart-Binns's biography of Richard Harries, John's sponsoring bishop.[28] One lesson that emerges from these and other narratives is that Rowan would have been cannier if he had questioned John's suitability from the outset, or else stuck by him. He could have told Harries that opportuneness was essential to securing John's appointment as a bishop – but that Oxford was not the right diocese, and 2003 (so early in his own tenure at Canterbury) not the right time. Alternatively, the Archbishop could have warned Harries that he would face strong opposition, but that Lambeth would back him if he were resolved to press on. Rowan's eventual change of heart created the damaging impression that he had caved in to pressure (and could do so again). But the blame did not lie in one quarter alone. It was Harries who proposed Jeffrey John in the first place, and who assured Rowan, probably wrongly, that diocesan opposition to the appointment would fade away in time. Despite employing what appeared to be consensual selection procedures, he misjudged the mood among many of his colleagues. Several of Harries's most senior clergy ended up telling Lambeth what they were unable to tell their bishop to his face: that they felt inadequately consulted, and would have resigned if John's appointment had gone ahead.

In this light, both Rowan's initial and his later attitudes are easier to understand. Archbishops do not have simple powers of veto over the choices of suffragans: bishops in the province of Canterbury consult with Lambeth, but do not need formal permission to forward their nominations to the Prime Minister. If an incoming primate is assured by one of his most senior bishops that the opponents of a potentially controversial appointment can be won over, it would usually be undiplomatic to disagree.

Harries had two vacancies to fill in 2003. Buckingham, the patch of the diocese adjoining Reading, also required a suffragan bishop. He rightly considered Reading to be in need of a high churchman 'with a heart for mission', because of its preponderance of Anglo-Catholic parishes in rundown areas. He also saw that John (who had been a successful vicar of Eltham, in south-east London, before becoming a canon of Southwark in 1997) was eminently qualified for the job, even though not necessarily a safe option. Not one to lead a double life – his colleagues knew of his long-term relationship with Grant Holmes, a hospital chaplain, and the moral conviction that went with it – he had publicly supported a change in church teaching on homosexuality. His involvement with the launch of Affirming Catholicism had brought him into close contact with Rowan a decade or so previously (they had been colleagues in Oxford). Under the network's auspices he had written a booklet, *Permanent, Faithful, Stable*, that spelt out the theological arguments for accepting long-term gay partnerships on an equal footing to those of heterosexuals.[29]

This made John a hero for many, but unsound in establishment eyes. A further aspect of his situation had been unduly down-played. He had grown up in the Rhondda valley, and would have been happy to return to Wales. John thought that he had a decent chance of succeeding Rowan at Monmouth, but it was a vain hope. He was tarred as too liberal, and therefore as unelectable, by senior Church in Wales figures at an early stage. This episode influenced Rowan's initial reaction to Harries's proposal: he was in part motivated by sympathy over John's recent disappointment. Others (especially in Wales) have drawn an equally valid con-clusion: if John was deemed unsuitable for Monmouth in 2002, alert observers – including Rowan – ought to have foreseen that he was the wrong man for Reading the following year.

If this point had been put to Harries at the consultative stage, he might have replied that Oxford was a more liberal place than Monmouth. Furthermore, any concern he felt about a possible backlash against an openly gay bishop had been softened through a panegyric about John penned by Colin Slee as the selection process was getting under way. Slee knew that his colleague was no firebrand; that he did not live with his partner; and that their relationship had been celibate for many years. He was also confident that if John became a bishop, he would uphold current church teaching on sexual ethics. The reference made much of John's evident skills as a bridge-builder, and of his popularity among at least some conservative Evangelicals in the Southwark diocese, where he was chancellor and Canon Theologian.

In early 2003, Harries contacted the Archbishop by phone to check that he would support John's inclusion in the line-up of candidates. The Bishop expected his superior to request more time to reflect on the matter, and was pleasantly surprised by Rowan's immediate expression of support. 'If we'd been doing things differently, we would have met to discuss the matter,' Harries told me. 'I acknowledged that there would be opposition, but said I felt we could overcome it.' In May, Harries and the members of his advisory panel interviewed the shortlisted candidates, four of whom, including John, were asked to give detailed presentations of their proposed strategies. The canon from Southwark was thought by Harries and two of his colleagues to have been particularly impressive. But another member of the panel, Philip Giddings, warned of the substantial opposition to John in Evangelical parishes. Dr Giddings, a lecturer in politics at Reading University, would later take a central part in orchestrating resistance to John's appointment.

The Bishop of Oxford rang Lambeth Palace again, this time to announce that he would like to propose Jeffrey John formally if the Archbishop were prepared to consecrate him. For a second time, Harries felt that Rowan was giving him a remarkably easy ride. 'I fully expected that we would meet up and talk the matter through,' he later told Peart-Binns; 'indeed I said over the telephone that he [the Archbishop] would want time to think about Jeffrey's nomination. In fact by the end of the conversation he had agreed to it.'[30]

It was not only events in New Westminster and New Hampshire that caused grey clouds to blacken in England. John's position was undercut with the unveiling of a hitherto virtually unknown address he had given in 1998. Speaking to a small Affirming Catholicism group in Keble College, Oxford, he had lambasted Lambeth 1.10, and spoken of the perceived hypocrisy entailed by having different sexual standards for the clergy and the laity. The talk had not been published, but John's words had evidently been recorded. They were now posted online by his enemies, who also alerted the *Daily Telegraph*. John's repeated claim that he would not use his episcopacy to campaign on gay issues may well have been sincere. But to his critics, his pledge was severely undermined by the Keble talk.

A full-scale campaign was now launched against Jeffrey John, spearheaded by Giddings and a squadron of Evangelicals based in the city of Oxford. They put out a sharply worded statement bewailing the nomination. The 120 signatories expressed their 'astonishment that someone can be entrusted with the responsibility of a bishop in the Church of Christ when they have so strongly and consistently opposed the Church's moral teaching in relation to same-sex unions'. Giddings's associates included Chris Sugden, an outspoken hardliner from the Oxford Centre for Mission Studies, Andrew Goddard, tutor in ethics at Wycliffe Hall, the Evangelical theological college; and the incumbents of several city-centre parishes. Giddings and

Sugden recruited many of their allies to a new body, rapidly christened Anglican Mainstream, which aimed to bring together 'orthodox Anglicans who are united on the controlling authority of Holy Scripture for the life and work of the Church'.

Harries defended John as an able and upright pastor, assuring his diocesan synod on 7 June of his nominee's celibacy and willingness to abide by church teaching. This did not satisfy the opposition, most of whom wanted to see John openly repent of his views and earlier lifestyle, and give a public endorsement of Lambeth 1.10. Nine days later, the crisis assumed national proportions when *The Times* published a letter from nine diocesan bishops (Bradford, Carlisle, Chester, Chichester, Exeter, Liverpool, Rochester, Southwell and Winchester) opposing John's nomination. 'We are glad at the reassurances from the Bishop of Oxford that Jeffrey John's life is now celibate. But it is the history of the relationship, as well as Dr John's severe criticism of orthodox teaching, which gives concern.'

The letter was drafted by the Bishop of Carlisle, Graham Dow. To some extent it reflected Harries's unpopularity among several of his episcopal colleagues, and a sense in conservative quarters that his championing of John entailed a bid to pre-empt the conclusions of an unfinished debate. (A follow-up document to *Issues in Human Sexuality* was due to be published later in the year.) But the implications for Rowan himself were even more profound. Liberal-minded onlookers viewed the action of Dow and his colleagues as an unprecedented breach of collegiality; even many non-aligned voices felt that the Archbishop's authority had been torpedoed.

Liberals now raised their own standard in reply. Eight other bishops (Hereford, Leicester, Newcastle, Ripon and Leeds, St

Edmundsbury and Ipswich, Salisbury, Truro and Worcester) expressed full-throated support for the appointment in another dispatch to *The Times* carried on 20 June; their views were echoed in an open letter signed by 100 clergy in the Oxford diocese.

The Archbishop, facing heavy pressure to intervene, issued a press release on 23 June. It appeared deferential towards John's critics and expressed a vain hope that the Oxford diocese's problems could be resolved internally:

> The concerns of many in the diocese of Oxford are theologically serious, intelligible and by no means based on narrow party allegiance or on prejudice. They must be addressed and considered fully. Confidence in the ability of a new bishop to minister to those in his pastoral care is an essentially important matter, and it is clear that serious questions remain in the diocese. To consider these with prayerfulness and maturity needs time and a measure of calm. It is not for anyone outside the diocese to override or pre-empt what is obviously a painful and complex process . . .

The Archbishop said that he had 'neither sought to promote nor to obstruct' the appointment, but stood by Richard Harries's decision all the same:

> Despite what some have claimed, I do not believe this overall process weakens the commitment of the House of Bishops to what we have declared as our common mind. Nor do I believe that Canon John's appointment either subverts current discipline or forecloses future discussion. It would certainly be deplorable if it were assumed that the existing approach has been abandoned

by stealth, or that the forthcoming guide to the debate on sexuality that we have agreed to publish was slanted towards a change in that policy. So, let us be clear: there could be no question of trying to pre-empt, undermine or short-circuit the reflection of the church as a whole.[31]

Confirmation that the debate was not a local matter came when Conservatives hosted a conference attended by several foreign bishops and representatives from groups such as Reform, the Church of England Evangelical Council, and the American Anglican Council. The gathering resulted in an uncompromising restatement of opposition to John. Hackles were raised around the Communion. Archbishop Akinola wrote to Rowan threatening to sever ties with any Anglican province – including the Church of England – that elected a gay bishop: 'we are mindful of the backlash this strong stand can engender from the rich Churches in Europe, America and Canada who have long used their wealth to intimidate the financially weak Churches in Africa. Our boldness in condemning the spiritual bankruptcy of these Churches must be matched by our refusal to receive financial help from them.'[32]

John's fate was probably sealed on Friday 4 July, when Rowan had a conference call with several of his most senior bishops, including conservatives (on this issue) such as Michael Scott-Joynt and Tom Wright, the newly consecrated Bishop of Durham. Richard Harries and Jeffrey John were then summoned to a meeting at Lambeth Palace early the next morning. The Bishop of Oxford expected a debate on how to contain the opposition, and reacted with astonishment on learning that the Archbishop was no longer prepared to give John his backing. As Harries told Stephen Bates, 'Rowan made absolutely clear to me that he had made an agonising decision, which was very hard for him to make because he agrees with Jeffrey John's views and Jeffrey John was a very old friend. He had agonised long and hard and there was nothing we could say to change his mind.'[33]

John's appointment was backed by Bishop Tom Butler of Southwark, as well as by Dean Slee: for this reason, perhaps, neither was permitted to accompany John to his interview with the Archbishop. Anxious about John's well-being, Butler obtained David Marshall's number, and rang the chaplain on his mobile phone during the encounter. The Bishop demanded to speak to the Archbishop, and then entreated both him and John to reflect for twenty-four hours before reaching any resolution. Butler was told that the die had already been cast. He replied tartly that John's treatment had been shameful.

Butler was a late convert to the pro-gay cause: he had not previously been known for supporting those of his clergy in same-sex relationships. Slee's relations with John had always been warmer. The strategy of Rowan's aides – Jeremy Harris especially – was to sideline the Dean as far as possible. Harris saw that Slee would want to stiffen John's resolve in any confrontation with Lambeth, and that he had the presentational skills to champion his friend in the media. Two palace staff members even asked John not to contact Slee, though the two men managed to have a brief meeting that evening, after the Dean and his wife had attended a wedding.

Slee was woken up at 7 a.m. the following morning, Sunday, by Ruth Gledhill, who asked him to confirm whether John had resigned. The Dean drafted a statement for the Southwark Cathedral congregation and read it out at the end of the morning Eucharist. There was consternation all around; Jeffrey John went into hiding. Several hours later, Rowan himself made a detailed press statement explaining his change of heart:

As most of you will know already, Canon Jeffrey John has announced his intention of withdrawing from his appointment as Bishop of Reading. The road that has led him to this point has been extremely arduous; and I must pay the warmest public tribute to the dignity and forbearance he has shown throughout, often under the most intrusive and distasteful personal scrutiny . . . We have to grasp that Canon John's appointment has brought to light a good deal of unhappiness among people who could by no means be described as extremists, many of whom have willingly testified to their personal respect for Canon John. They are convinced, however, that there is a basic issue at stake relating to the consistency of our policy and our doctrine in the Church of England – and that this issue has arisen in this particular case in a way for which there are no obvious parallels. Such unhappiness means that there is an obvious problem in the consecration of a bishop whose ministry will not be readily received by a significant proportion of Christians in England and elsewhere. For the divisions we have seen do not exist only at diocesan and national level but internationally as well. The perspective of the Anglican Communion demands careful consideration here. The estrangement of churches in developing countries from their cherished ties with Britain is in no one's interests. It would impoverish us as a Church in every way. It would also jeopardise links with other denominations, weaken co-operation in our shared service and mission worldwide, and increase the vulnerability of Christian minorities in some parts of the world where they are already at risk. Any such outcome would be a very heavy price to pay . . .

Let me add that some of the opposition expressed to Canon John's appointment has been very unsavoury indeed. A number of the letters I received displayed a shocking level of ignorance and hatred towards homosexual people. Our official policies and resolutions as Anglicans commit us to listening to the experience of homosexuals and recognising that they are full and welcome members of the Church, loved by God. Not everyone, it seems, takes equally seriously this element in the teaching of the Anglican Church; and some letters that came from non-believers suggest that the level of foolish and hurtful prejudice in our society is still uncomfortably high. Christians who collude with this are simply not living out their calling.

In short, a good man was being sacrificed on the altar of church unity – the cause that a church leader is especially likely to rate over almost all others. Many Anglicans were not especially perturbed by the Communion's possible break-up. If the cost of treating gay people fairly was the loss of a gangrenous limb, they urged, then the price was not too high. But Rowan did not merely subscribe to the main practical argument against this – namely that the Anglican Communion is necessary to do all sorts of things that have nothing to do with sex, including service of the poor and countless other expressions of global solidarity. He was also desperately worried about the possible fragmentation of the Church of England. If the briefings he had received behind the scenes were accurate, then a number of the largest parish congregations in Oxford and elsewhere in England might have opted out of diocesan control and established ties with the province of Nigeria, or other conservative outposts.

Such was the scale of Rowan's dilemma. It is possible – as Richard Harries and others in Oxford still believe – that the anti-

John campaign's bluff ought to have been called. But no one had foreseen quite how toxic the atmosphere would become. Grant Holmes became ill as a result of the ordeal, and several friends of John – who had to move out of his house for a time – concluded that he had made a lucky escape. Rowan knew that his own decision looked neither brave nor noble. If he had reaped a whirlwind by imposing a contentious bishop on a divided diocese, however, his own primacy might have been written off at an early stage.

Colin Slee still concluded that Rowan had surrendered to strong-arm tactics. He condemned the Archbishop's decision on the airwaves and wrote to the nine bishops who had signed the *Times* letter, upbraiding them for their conduct. One – James Jones of Liverpool – subsequently apologised, explaining that they had not appreciated the non-sexual status of John's relationship. Outside the Church, things tended to look very different, especially to younger observers. The damage to Rowan's reputation would have been smaller if this story had unfolded during the 1980s, when the attitudes of tabloid journalists were a closer match for those of church tradition-alists. But Britain in 2003 was a vastly more gay-friendly place than in 1987, when the *Sun* had carried headlines such as 'Pulpit poofters to stay'. Several leader-writers could not see what the fuss was about, and accordingly judged the Arch-bishop to be a hollow man. Others accused Richard Harries of acting with undue haste, and said that precipitate action could only impair the cause of gay equality. A third widely held view was that there would never be a 'right' time, in this sense, to appoint a gay bishop; that the pursuit of justice demanded courage; and that Harries had been right to take the bull by the horns.

Rowan's many fans were still prepared to give him the benefit of the doubt. They duly portrayed him as the prisoner of Carey's men. This was only partly true, if at all. As the journalist Paul Vallely pointed out, it was impugning the Archbishop's intelligence to suggest that he could 'shrug off responsibility' to a gang of officials. He had simply concluded that there did not exist a critical mass of support for a change in church teaching on homosexuality – just as, for that matter, Anglicans had been unprepared to accept the ordination of women half a century earlier.[34]

A further twist in the affair tells us about the sometimes fitful policies of Lambeth Palace. A few weeks after the débâcle, Jeffrey John asked if he could discuss his future with the Archbishop, but was told that he would need to wait for several months. Outraged by what he saw as off-handedness, Grant Holmes informed the palace of his partner's extreme state of distress, and warned that unless a meeting were arranged quickly, the press would be briefed about the Archbishop's apparently hard-hearted attitude. Lambeth jumped to attention. A slot in Rowan's diary was then made available shortly afterwards. The encounter was confidential, but it is known that the two men prayed together, and that Rowan got down on his knees to ask his visitor's blessing. Jeffrey John obliged. (Years later, however, he remains too angry and upset about the Reading affair to discuss it in public.)

Much of this story is a matter of record. Less has been said about Rowan's frame of mind, even though the politics of the situation were shaped by personal factors to a considerable extent. Several aspects of his style, all emphasised by people who have worked with him closely, are worthy of note. First, what Oliver O'Donovan once dubbed his 'carefully judged unclarity'[35] can cause different people to think that he means different things. In the words of another former colleague, 'Rowan will hardly ever gainsay someone he's talking to. This means that often, unless you listen very, *very* carefully to what he is saying, you can emerge from a meeting thinking that he agrees with you, even if this is not necessarily the case.' (The comment may suggest that Harries's upbeat assessment of his phone conversations with the Archbishop was wide of the mark.) Second, although Rowan does not yield to full-on bullying, he is susceptible to forcefulness. If people make it abundantly clear that they are not to be challenged on a particular subject, he is less likely to act against them. Third, as a friend puts it, 'he can be so able to see the other side in an argument, that he almost doesn't know his own view'. If this is right, then the Archbishop's uncertainties may well have been trumped by the certainties both of Harries and, later, of Harries's critics. This insight also points to a paradoxical consistency in Rowan's conduct throughout the Jeffrey John crisis. He systematically mistrusted his own wisdom and deferred to other people's.

Vallely, in his article, concluded unhesitatingly that Rowan Williams was the statesman rather than the man who blinked first. But others had grounds for being less decided – and many who couldn't make up their minds in 2003 were, if anything, yet more confused by events that were to come.

7

The Windsor Way

The Archbishop's personal flair for seeing both sides of an argument has had major political consequences. To fathom his actions, we should attach special weight (as he does) to the opinion cited at the outset of this book – that the kind of person given to putting his foot down 'would only have messed things up'. This has a tactical component. Rowan's room for manoeuvre on the national stage was always going to be limited in important respects. For example, it is hard to defend an establishment institution in decline, particularly when you have a reputation for being anti-establishment. It is hard to defend English culture, of which the Church is a part, when you are committed to multiculturalism. That role is more easily assumed by a Jewish leader such as Jonathan Sacks, or an African-born churchman such as John Sentamu. And it is hard to avoid compromising yourself by taking conservative views into account, whether Evangelical or Roman Catholic, when you are committed to ecumenism and mutual respect.

The theological component of our quoted comment is more significant still. Leading the Church of England can seem a near impossibility, because it is dominated by congeries of clerics with entrenched views and dissatisfactions which get displaced onto surrogate questions. Only a few of the laity are as fired up about these matters as many of the clergy are, but the clergy often call the shots. In such a climate there were obvious advantages in appointing an archbishop whose views could not be pigeon-holed – and thus endorsed or rejected – as liberal or conservative. No choice would have been cost-free, however.

What is more, around the turn of the millennium, many thought that Anglican structures were in need of a shake-up. This points us back to another comment quoted in the Introduction of this book – that relations between Anglican provinces had come to look less like an old-fashioned game of cricket than a bad-tempered football match calling for a referee's attentions. Such a state of affairs was anticipated in the *Virginia Report*, a document produced by the Inter-Anglican Theological and Doctrinal Commission in 1997. It pointed out that none of the international Anglican forums – the Primates' Meeting, the Lambeth Conference and the Anglican Consultative Council (a representative body including clergy and laity meeting every three years) – has executive powers. They are merely consultative. Accordingly,

> [t]here is a question to be asked whether this is satisfactory if the Anglican Communion is to be held together in hard times as well as in good ones. Indeed there is a question as to whether effective communion, at all levels, does not require effective instruments, with due safeguards, not only for legislation, but for oversight. Is not universal authority a necessary corollary of universal communion?[1]

The evidence of his writings and comments shows that Rowan would not have agreed with this argument before 2003. But the trauma of the Jeffrey John and Gene Robinson affairs changed his mind.

The process was incremental. His presidential address to the General Synod's York session in mid-July 2003 offered no real clues: it amounted to a general apologia for Anglicanism, and a plea for peace. He began by describing the different ecclesiological views common among English Anglicans. One holds that the reconstruction of the Church along biblical lines has barely even begun; another that the Church of England is and should remain more like a mosaic than a seamless garment. Rowan's appeal for tolerance was addressed as much to conservative Evangelicals as to liberals, but he cannily prefaced it with a swipe against *bien pensant* opinion formers, a legitimate if softish target:

> Lately we have seen another version [of the Church of England] as well. It is surprising to see how liberal intellectuals in Britain so often express similar yearnings for a national spiritual hinterland. And the result is that, when the Church shows signs of believing and acting upon things that do not derive from, or are at odds with, a progressive consensus, much anger and disappointment is voiced (our discussions not only about sexuality but about embryo research touch this very closely).

The Archbishop then called more forthrightly than ever for the antagonists to drop their pretensions to infallibility:

> I now have a really remarkable collection of letters which say, 'Every Christian I speak to, and most people I know outside the Church, agree that . . .' – whatever view it is that the writer holds. And these views are dramatically incompatible. It's hard to avoid concluding that most of us speak and listen mostly to those who share our world, and assume it is indeed the natural one to belong to.

The way forward lay in an acknowledgement of 'what makes us a Church at all', namely 'the call of Jesus Christ, and our freedom and ability, helped by grace, to recognize that call in each other'. It was this vision that really sustained Christ's followers and the 'real' Church of England – overlooked both by the commentariat and by clerical tub-thumpers. It was visible where the parish priest chairs the school governors in the estate, sits with the asylum-seeker to help them complete an official form, negotiates the grant that will allow the crypt to be developed for a drop-in centre, organises the distribution of goods from a farmers' market or the rota of lifts for a pensioner to get to church and shops, 'and where he or she is equipping their people to do all this and more'.[2]

Soon after getting away from the synod hothouse, Rowan made his first visit to Russia. It was a brief but stirring trip. Seraphim of Sarov (1752–1833), one of his favourite saints, had been canonised a hundred years earlier, and the Archbishop was invited to take part in the centenary celebrations. The site of Seraphim's hermitage near Sarov can now be visited. But throughout the Soviet era and afterwards, the city housed a centre for nuclear research and was a restricted area. Seraphim is especially revered for his asceticism and simplicity. Even as a schoolboy, Rowan felt devoted to him. He now keeps an image of the saint beside his computer keyboard at all times.

Back in Britain, media verdicts on Rowan's performance in York were largely predictable. The *Daily Mirror* ranked Rowan ninety-ninth on its list of Britain's 'least influential people', and suggested that his retreat over Jeffrey John would leave his credibility tarnished for good. Libby Purves in *The Times* was equally plain-spoken, perhaps bearing out Rowan's point. She confessed to disappointment at his not having told 'narrow-hearted Evangelical rebels (in a kindly, humble and caring way) to go and boil their heads'. Purves had at first thought that Rowan Williams seemed like a wild card, an inspirer, a holy man from the West come to revive the faith. 'Alas,' she wrote, 'the dreadful suspicion grows that he is just another Archbishop of Canterbury.'[3]

But the *Guardian* was sufficiently impressed by the speech to carry most of it on an op-ed page under the title 'Forget the Soap Opera'. An accompanying leader opined that 'Rowan Williams yesterday demonstrated why he was chosen as Archbishop of Canterbury. He is a wonderful speaker – always thoughtful, fluent, profound, provocative and witty . . . If words alone were enough, [his address] was a speech to unite a Church bitterly fragmented . . .' The editorial then drew a curious corollary:

> It is agreeable enough to make a pulpit appeal for fundamentalists to behave like pluralists. Unfortunately, life isn't like that. In the real world, the fanatics who forced out Dr John are feeling rather emboldened by their success. Sooner or later Dr Williams will discover there is, indeed, no third way on such matters. He will have to fight for what he believes in.[4]

But a third way of sorts was exactly what the speech was about, and the path that, despite himself, Rowan would increasingly cleave to.

The first major staging post on this path was the Primates' Meeting in October 2003 and the epoch-making consecration of Gene Robinson the following month. First, though, came several developments that put further pressure on Lambeth Palace. In August a new group, known as Inclusive Church, was launched. Its founders sought to counter the impression that conservative Evangelicals were making all the running, as Colin Slee emphasised in a speech at the network's launch in Putney, south-west London. In late September came Britain's largest Christian gathering of 2003: the National Evangelical Anglican Congress (NEAC) at Blackpool. Rowan was hailed in advance by the Bishop of Thetford, David Atkinson, among other Evangelical leaders, as possessing 'a unique ability to address our nation effectively in the name of Christ';[5] but the Archbishop was not invited to deliver a full-scale address (a courtesy extended to Robert Runcie in 1988) and had to settle for a briefer slot. The initial applause for Rowan was not ecstatic; a group of hardliners even boycotted his talk, decamping for prayers in another venue. But he won over many who remained by joking that he had resisted an urge to give the audience a Bible study based on Psalm 71 – 'I am become, as it were, a monster among many.' He then spoke briefly on the Congress themes of Bible, Cross and Mission. His desire for the gathering was that it would 'renew everyone's eagerness to listen to God, speaking his nature and his name in such a way that others will be able to hear and believe and give thanks'.

In late September, there was an unequivocal restatement of traditionalist teaching on sexual morality during a meeting in Nairobi of delegates from twelve African provinces, and a warning from the Archbishop of Sydney, Peter Jensen, that Rowan's 'peaceable approach' had 'run out of time'. Writing in the traditionalist publication *New Directions*,[6] Jensen suggested that the Archbishop of Canterbury had three options in the face of Gene Robinson's imminent consecration. The first was to do nothing. But this would encourage conservatives to secede, 'and invite others to act in support of [them]'. The second was to recognise both liberal and traditional positions as valid. This would also make the Communion more of a federation than a Church. The third would be to expel 'erring' dioceses, such as New Westminster. This would alienate many, but 'would send a powerful moral and spiritual message to the Churches of the West, that our flirtation with secularism has gone too far'.

Jensen's sympathies are stridently low-church – Sydney has long been a centre of the campaign to allow lay presidency at the Eucharist – but he was anything but a voice in the wilderness on the gay issue. That the forces of conservatism were galvanising themselves with a strong commitment (financial, as well as theological) was clear from a glimpse at the situation in North America, where traditionalists and liberals had long been at odds over points of faith and morals. An emerging conservative leader was Robert Duncan, Bishop of Pittsburgh, who with nineteen fellow bishops had branded Gene Robinson's confirmation at that summer's General Convention a 'pastoral emergency'. About one-fifth of Pittsburgh's eighty or so parishes were affiliated to the American Anglican Council (AAC), a body formed in the late 1990s to uphold 'biblical authority and Anglican orthodoxy'. From the outset, it sponsored numerous missionary organisations and received strong financial backing from Howard F. Ahmanson Jr, a reclusive California-based multi-millionaire. AAC meetings in 2003 and subsequently would involve representatives from virtually all of ECUSA's 109 dioceses, and hammer home a message of conservative 'fidelity' to Anglican teaching, and of liberal 'betrayal'.

Evangelicals and Roman Catholics may disagree on many matters, but sexual morality is an area where levels of convergence are high. The point was impressed on Rowan in early October, when he realised an ambition to meet John Paul II in Rome. The Pope had an explicit message for his guest: that the 'differences' between the Catholic and Anglican Churches did not concern only matters of discipline: some touched on 'essential matters' of faith and morals. 'Faced with the increasing secularism of today's world, the Church must ensure that the deposit of faith is proclaimed in its integrity,' John Paul warned.

Rowan offered an encomium to the Pontiff, and thanked him for an invitation he had issued several years earlier for Christian leaders to advise him on the shape of the Petrine ministry. As Bishop of Monmouth, Rowan had taken up the gauntlet, and had explained in robust terms why he could not accept papal infallibility.[7] In Rome as Archbishop of Canterbury, though, he took the diplomatic course, saying to John Paul: 'I will be glad to participate in the reflections on the possible sharing of a primacy of love and service.'

The symbolism of the visit meant most. Though normally inclined to dress down – he had made a trademark of wearing a black cassock and purple cincture (a somewhat plainer outfit, that is, than most Anglo-Catholic canons) – Rowan wore a bishop's soutane for his journey through the marble halls of the Apostolic Palace. At first chaperoned by tail-coated ushers and Swiss Guards, the Archbishop and his party were then met by a brace of cardinals before being conducted to the papal library. John Paul's failing health had long formed a source of almost limitless speculation; it was even suggested that he would die with the Archbishop on his doorstep. This was fanciful, but few would have predicted that he could survive a further eighteen months. The Pope sat slumped in his high-backed chair, and greeted his visitor in heavily accented English, each word a struggle. One of the reporters present wrote of how 'silent compassion' emanated from Rowan – an attitude underwritten when he sank to his knees to kiss John Paul's ring. In an unprecedented move, the Pope then kissed the Archbishop's as well. Several onlookers were in tears at the spectacle, though its significance to John Paul was uncertain. Clerical sources provided a frightening stream of anecdotes about his mental degeneration at this time. One story had it that after Rowan's departure, John Paul turned to his aides and said, 'Tell me, who *were* those people?'[8]

* * *

A few weeks before the visit to the Vatican, Rowan signalled that his own views were shifting when he wrote an article of his own for *New Directions*. He was both resigned to the likelihood of further fragmentation, and extremely worried about it:

> I suspect that those who speak of new patterns, of the weakening of territorial jurisdiction and the like are seeing the situation pretty accurately . . . I don't expect the next few years to be anything other than messy as far as all this is concerned. The question is not whether we can afford mess, but whether we can hang on to common convictions about divine grace and initiative . . . The danger to avoid is an entirely modern or post-modern map of church identity in which non-communicating and competing entities simply eradicate the very idea of a communion of churches.[9]

The Primates' Meeting was dominated by discussion of Gene Robinson's forthcoming consecration. In a sombre statement, the archbishops and presiding bishops said that they had reached 'a crucial and critical point in the life of the Anglican Communion. If [the consecration] proceeds, we have to conclude that the future of the Communion itself will be put in jeopardy.'[10] The new bishop's ministry would not be recognised by most of the Anglican world, and many provinces would then be likely to consider themselves out of communion with the Episcopal Church. The primates also announced the setting up of a seventeen-member body[11] under the chairmanship of Archbishop Robin Eames of Armagh and encompassing a variety of views, which would study the theological and legal consequences of Robinson's election, and complete its work by October 2004. This was to become known as the Lambeth Commission. The fruit of its labours was later christened the Windsor Report, after the place where two of its meetings had taken place.

So much for the big picture. Behind the scenes, conservatives from ECUSA had ready access to Rowan, and were encouraged by a private breakfast meeting they held with him the day after the statement was released. Among those breaking bread with the Archbishop were Robert Duncan and the Bishops of Albany, Central Florida and Fort Worth, and two other members of the AAC, David Anderson and Martyn Minns. Duncan then posted an outline of the meeting in note form on his diocesan website:

> The Communion will experience significant realignment. New Hampshire will proceed despite ultimatum. Uncertain whether Presiding Bishop will participate. Most provinces will break with ECUSA and/or participants. An orthodox (in Communion) network in US will emerge. In the US, the 'territorial principle' will give way to something more complex, more like celtic missionary model. The 'Network of Confessing Dioceses and Parishes' has Archbishop Rowan's encouragement. Specifics will be developed stateside.[12]

Jonathan Jennings later sought to dispel the impression that Rowan was supporting centrifugal forces in the Episcopal Church, saying that the Archbishop was keen for the self-styled 'Network of Confessing Dioceses and Parishes' to work as closely as possible with the Primate of ECUSA, Frank Griswold.

Some liberals, though, were inclined to take the conservatives at their word and to agree with their assessment that Rowan was moving with the anti-gay majority. Light was shed on his style, as well as his attitude to matters of substance, when he gave an interview to BBC Radio 4's *Today* programme after the meeting.[13] The broadcast was a rarity in itself. The editors of *Today* had been trying all year without success to get the Archbishop to make an appearance; in the event, the interview was overshadowed by Rowan's handling of an unexpected question. He was cross-examined about the threat of schism for ten minutes off-air at 7 a.m. by his fellow Welshman, John Humphrys, who rounded off the encounter by asking whether the Iraq war was immoral. The Archbishop paused for twelve seconds – an eternity in radio terms – before replying that ' "immoral" is a short word for a very long discussion'.

In the hour before the exchange went out, Lambeth Palace lobbied the BBC ferociously for the silence to be edited out. Humphrys was reported to be 'livid'; others wondered at the apparent naivety both of Rowan and of his advisers. Jennings insisted that the interview was scheduled to last just ten minutes, and that it had been agreed beforehand that the Archbishop would only be asked about the Primates' Meeting. The wish to dwell on a subject likely to reflect badly on the Church was surprising in itself. More so was the assumption that a zealous interviewer would not try to squeeze in a question to Britain's principal religious leader about the hottest political topic of the moment. Ominously, media attention became focused on Lambeth Palace's lack of media savvy and the Archbishop's perceived reluctance to face awkward questions. This was unfortunate, given his fluency during most of the exchange. The heart of the conversation ran as follows:

RW: I think that what we have achieved this week is at least to find some way of talking through the crisis without instantly jumping into what appear to be quick solutions.

JH: So, where do we go from here?

RW: When and if the ordination of Gene Robinson goes ahead, we shall immediately have some responses around the world, but what we've done is to give ourselves a twelve-month-plus thinking time, inviting provinces to reflect on their reactions, and also having a central Commission in the Anglican Church, which will look at the possible implications of a split, because there are constitutional and legal questions for all the Churches involved . . .

JH: Do you believe that Canon Robinson should become a bishop?

RW: No, I don't, because I believe that on a major issue of this kind, the Church has to make a decision together, and one of the things that has emerged most painfully in the last couple of days in our conversations is the large number – the very, very large number – of Anglican provinces who feel that, quite simply, a decision has been made which commits them or involves them in some way, and yet in which they have had no part at all.

JH: Where does that leave the Church?

RW: It leaves the Church with a huge challenge about co-ordinating its discipline and its legal systems across the world, which we've never had to do before. It leaves the Church with a number of very untidy relationships . . .

JH: Are you prepared, as the Archbishop of Canterbury, to accept as bishops, and indeed priests, homosexuals who are celibate?

RW: The position of the Church and my own position is that a celibate homosexual is always eligible for consideration as a priest or indeed as a bishop, but the question is always with a bishop whether such an appointment – such an election – is genuinely the mind of the Church.

JH: So why was Jeffrey John not allowed to become bishop?

RW: The situation with Jeffrey John's nomination was one complicated very considerably by the level of internal dissension in the Church of England over this, but also the level of dismay, incomprehension and difficulty felt by sister Churches across the world, and that certainly factored into the discussions that went on.

JH: But isn't there a degree of hypocrisy here, because the Church of England seems to be saying it's all right for people to be homosexual, indeed even to express their homosexuality through sexual acts, but not for priests of the Church of England?

RW: I think that the position that the Church of England has held in the document *Issues in Human Sexuality* for the last ten years recognises that public ministry imposes certain constraints, and that, if you like, a minister – a bishop, a priest or whoever – is never appointed, never works, in the abstract, but works within the expectations that the wider Church may have.

JH: So is there a contradiction then between your own private conscience and your position as the head of the Church?

RW: My belief has always been that on this, as in any other matter, if the Church were ever to change its view, it would have to be because the Church as a whole owned it, not because any one person's conviction prevailed . . .

JH: What is more important: the unity of the Church in the long term or individual morality?

RW: What's more important in the long term is, of course, what the unity of the Church is for: that is, mission to the world. Individual morality is emphatically a part of that, and yet in witnessing to the wider world, what we have to do is to try to consider what we can do and say together without some feeling completely squashed or excluded by that process.

Now, the paradox here is, of course, that there are two groups that feel as if they are excluded by a process. One group, of course, is the homosexual community, here and elsewhere. The other group is those from small and struggling Churches, often in the developing world, who feel excluded, overruled and ignored in some of the discussion that's gone on. Therefore, we don't have a morally black-and-white situation of how the Church responds.

Several commentators spoke of a breakdown of relations between Lambeth Palace and the BBC in 2003, and of the way Rowan's *Today* interview served to highlight his generally low media profile. The policy of keeping beneath the radar may have done the Archbishop less damage than his actions during the Jeffrey John affair, wrote one pundit. 'But sooner or later [Dr Williams] is going to have to say things to remind the world why everyone thought he was the last best hope of the Church of England. The longer he puts off contact with the press, the more the unanswered questions will pile up.'[14]

*   *   *

Gene Robinson's consecration went ahead on 2 November 2003 at the University of New Hampshire's ice arena. Security was strictly enforced. Bishop Griswold was the chief consecrator at the ceremony; both he and Robinson wore bullet-proof vests. The ceremony was described by the Anglican Communion News Service as 'one of the most controversial and momentous occasions' in the Church's history, and by ECUSA's own news service as 'a glorious mixture of music, wise and humorous words'. Between 3,000 and 4,000 people attended the service; the other consecrators included Griswold's predecessor, Edmond Browning, and Barbara Harris, the Church's first woman bishop. Fifty-five other bishops, twenty-two of them retired, took part. The references in the opening hymn, 'The Church's One Foundation', to 'By schism rent asunder, / By heresies distressed', were not lost on the reporters and other members of the congregation. Outside the venue, about 200 student supporters of Robinson confronted a smaller collection of protesters, including a posse of Primitive Baptists from Kansas with posters bearing the message 'God Hates Fags'. Led by their pastor, Fred Phelps, this group are notorious for acrid anti-gay demonstrations.

The service included space for formal objections. Griswold asked that the opposition be heard with respect. One clerical dissenter, Earle Fox, gave a graphic description of the medical consequences of certain forms of gay sex. Meredith Harwood, a locally based dissenter, called the consecration 'the defiant and divisive act of a deaf Church'. Bishop David Bena of Albany read a statement on behalf of nineteen serving and seven retired ECUSA bishops, and ten of their Canadian counterparts, which argued that '[t]he consecration poses a dramatic contradiction to the historic faith and discipline of the Church. We join with the majority of the bishops in the Communion and will not recognize it. We also declare our grief at the actions of those who are engaging in this schismatic act.'

The message was repeated by other conservative groups in the United States and overseas, including the AAC, the Anglican Mission in America (AMiA) – a network of breakaway Churches under episcopal oversight from the Province of Rwanda – and Archbishop Akinola, speaking on behalf of primates from the traditionalist grouping known as the Global South. He declared that '[a]s ECUSA has wilfully disregarded the strong warnings given at Lambeth that such an action would "tear the fabric of the communion at its deepest level", we can now have no basis whatsoever for any further confidence that ECUSA will pay any regard to the findings of the recently announced Commission set up by the Archbishop of Canterbury'.

Rowan himself expressed 'deep regret' over the divisions resulting from the consecration. It was clear, he went on, 'that those who have consecrated Gene Robinson have acted in good faith on their understanding of what the constitution of the American Church permits . . . The autonomy of Anglican provinces is an important principle. But precisely because we rely on relations rather than rules, consultation and interdependence are essential for our health.' Richard Kirker of the Lesbian and Gay Christian Movement said that he had felt privileged to attend the consecration. 'Our love in Christ for each other is a communion that cannot be broken. We must all resist the pressures to exclude rather than build a community of faith where the diversity of God's creation can be celebrated by all.'

This chapter began with some comments on the Church of England's relation to British society. A word about some aspects of Anglicanism's transposition into an American cultural key is now overdue. Help comes from one of Mark Twain's best-known quips – that the British do things because they have been done before, while Americans do them because they haven't been. Next to this stand considerations about ECUSA's unusual history. As pointed out by an American priest who backs Gene Robinson but is sensitive to the problems stoked up by his ministry, the Episcopal Church did not have bishops for almost 200 years before the late eighteenth century: 'The truth is that the country's most powerful Anglican clerics are the so-called Cardinal Rectors [incumbents of very large and wealthy parishes such as Holy Trinity, Wall Street] rather than the bishops themselves. Most American Anglicans don't have much sense of being in a diocese, let alone a national Church, let alone a worldwide Communion.'

Views about Gene Robinson were thus affected by cultural attitudes. His supporters lay stress on the canonical regularity of his election, and see his eligibility for high office as a simple matter of justice. (This argument in turn echoes the case advanced for women bishops during the 1980s.) Opponents see an undue sense of American self-sufficiency reflected in the process, and defend the Archbishop of Canterbury's reaction in the light of the doctrine of mutual submission taught in Philippians 2 and elsewhere in the New Testament. Some conservatives have also tended to accuse Robinson's supporters of an *à la carte* approach to Christianity as such. William McKeachie, Dean of South Carolina, was one of many American traditionalists to write at this time about an apparent emergency facing the Churches as a whole. His words echo those of the future Pope Benedict XVI:

The crisis is this: do we who profess and call ourselves Christian still share, in all our theological and cultural diversities, a common understanding of Christian truth? Do we still share a common conviction about the priority for Christian theology of biblical revelation? Do we still share a common faith in the biblical God of Abraham, Isaac and Jacob, the God and Father of One who is the Way, the Truth and the Life? Do we indeed still worship one and the same God?[15]

The sentiment behind these comments will seem either prophetic or alarmist, according to your point of view. Certainly, some leading American liberals, especially Bishop Jack Spong, appear to have abandoned traditional Christian belief.[16] But Gene Robinson is keen to stress his own orthodoxy. Conservatives, he feels, 'perceive that the fuller inclusion of gay and lesbian in the Church is the precursor . . . to the deconstruction of other essentials, whether that be the divinity of Christ, or the Trinity, or the resurrection. That could not be further from the truth about me.'[17]

Robinson's consecration nevertheless had immediate consequences for Rowan. A month later, the Vatican suspended formal talks with the Anglican Communion, citing 'ecclesiological concerns'. Yet the announcement about the Lambeth Commission also gave Rowan a breathing space in which to pursue his ministry. In mid-November, he went to Turkey to meet the Ecumenical Patriarch, Bartholomew I, and the Armenian Patriarch of Istanbul, Mesrob II. The visit began just after twenty-four people had been killed, and 300 injured, in a suicide bombing at Istanbul's Neva Shalom synagogue. The Archbishop conveyed a pastoral message from Britain's Chief Rabbi, Jonathan Sacks, to the victims, and made a good impression on his Orthodox hosts.

Back at Lambeth, Rowan gave his backing to a church-led campaign against the Lord's Resistance Army, the terrorist band responsible for destabilisation and mass carnage in Uganda, and published *The Dwelling of the Light*,[18] a short, popular guide to praying with icons of Christ. It formed the companion volume to *Ponder these Things*,[19] a slightly earlier study of icons of Mary. Both of these books are at times a little cavalier with art-historical detail.[20] But this drawback is offset by the wealth of spiritual wisdom distilled into a short space, and the clarity of Rowan's prose. His account of Christ's nature revealed in the icon known in Greek as *ho ōn* (The Existing One) gives a flavour of the whole:

> What we see is Jesus of Nazareth, a human figure in modest, not royal or priestly, clothing; a recognisably human face and figure. Yet of this face and figure we say: 'This is truth, this is reality'; what is alive in Jesus is life itself, the very act of being which is God.
>
> Although this human being, like any human being, is vulnerable to what happens in history (and the cross in the halo reminds us of just what that means), [he] is in every moment, even in the deepest vulnerability, acting out the act of God. Divine action appears to us in all the human detail of this life; not as an extra to it; not as a mysterious something or other floating above the surface of history, but embodied in it.

The Archbishop scored a similar hit in 2003 with *Silence and Honey Cakes: The Wisdom of the Desert*, edited transcripts of talks that he had given in Australia a few years earlier.[21] Though focusing on a group of fourth-century hermits, the book also has much to say about emotional flourishing more generally.

In Advent he criticised the government's anti-terrorist legislation as likely to alienate moderate Muslims, a complaint leading some to question his right to speak for those of other faiths. His response was spelt out in his Christmas sermon, and amounted to a defence of a strong church voice in politics. Faith threatened no one, he said; instead, it provided 'a glimpse into a richness surrounding all that we are, without which all our vaunted values and principles would soon corrupt and die'. And he went on to defend the 'outward expression' of religious allegiance: the Muslim headscarf, the Jewish skull cap or the Christian cross.

These remarks appeared unexceptionable to all but a few mavericks. But January was the period of calm before the storm. When the Archbishop visited the Holy Land the following month, he was given a taste of the far greater obloquy to come involving his judgement on Muslim–Christian relations. The subject would dog him more than any internal church matter, and provides a further demonstration of the way the internet could be used against him.

Things began encouragingly. Rowan's six-day timetable included meetings with President Moshe Katsav of Israel and the Palestinian leader, Yasser Arafat. The Archbishop visited church and community projects in Jordan, Israel and the Palestinian Territories, as well as the Church of the Nativity, the Bethlehem Peace Centre, Nazareth, the Mount of the Beatitudes and Lake Tiberias. Speaking at St George's Anglican Cathedral alongside the Bishop in Jerusalem, Riah Hanna Abu El-Assal, he voiced finely balanced feeling for both sides in the world's most intractable conflict.

During the trip, a Palestinian Authority policeman detonated a bomb in West Jerusalem, killing ten people. This outrage followed the deaths of eight Palestinians in skirmishes in the Gaza Strip twenty-four hours earlier. Rowan voiced compassion for the suffering on both sides. He met Arafat on the day of the carnage in Jerusalem. The Palestinian leader announced that he would present the Archbishop with the so-called Bethlehem 2000 medal, though the nature of the award remained a bit of a mystery. A photo was taken, and the myth that Rowan was being honoured for services to the Chairman of the PLO took root. Melanie Phillips of the *Daily Mail* responded hawkishly, describing the Archbishop as a 'disgrace to his calling' at the end of a lengthy philippic on her blog. Her complaint was over-pitched: it appeared that the Archbishop's offence was to have sympathised with Phillips's enemies as well as her friends. But this is not to say that the Arafat meeting was well handled, or that Rowan could be forgiven easily by powerful sections of Fleet Street.

A sense of his beleaguered status came when he granted the Press Association an interview to discuss his first year in office. The only thing that had kept him sane as he attempted to be 'a sort of vicar for the whole country', while also trying to hold the Anglican Communion together, was doing the next thing that had to be done 'as carefully and prayerfully as possible', he said. The Reading affair had focused 'most painfully . . . what it means to try and hold and articulate what the Church overall is thinking and wanting'. But he was more upbeat about the broader situation. Britain was a nation not of unbelievers, but of 'rather confused thinkers'. Young people, especially, had 'very little of what we could call lively contact with the Church, with any sense of what religious language is about'. He added that while he found London a fascinating and absorbing place in which to live, he continued to miss Wales. 'It is my home, quite simply, and that is how I still feel. I miss the particular strengths of being a small Church in a small country. I miss friends, and I miss contacts in the political and cultural life of Wales, and sometimes I miss the language, too.'[22]

His bid to persuade educated people of Christianity's coherence – a project soon nicknamed 'the Mission to Waitrose' by parts of the press – took root in 2004, notably when the Archbishop had a public debate with Philip Pullman, the children's author. Behind *His Dark Materials*, Pullman's best-selling trilogy, lie several hoary misconceptions about mainstream Christianity – for instance, that it takes a negative view of the body, that spiritual experience is an essentially solitary matter, and that worship entails submission to a cosmic tyrant.

Rowan challenged these ideas in a *Guardian* review of the National Theatre's adaptation of Pullman's work, but had the grace to grant that Christians could learn much from atheist polemic. The apparently godlike 'Authority' in *His Dark Materials* is killed in the name of freedom: the Archbishop revealed that he had been approached by a group of Essex teenagers in the interval who had asked whether he found this shocking. He surprised them by saying no, and then asking what kind of a church it is that lives in perpetual anxiety about the fate of its God: 'What the story makes you see is that if you believe in a mortal god, who can win and lose his power, your religion will be saturated with anxiety and violence.'[23]

Rowan agreed to a public debate with Pullman at the National Theatre the following week. As well as repeating some of his arguments from the *Guardian* article, he also spoke about Christian formation. His comments about education were a restatement of arguments he had voiced a few days earlier in a talk at 10 Downing Street – that it is not helpful to present faith 'from the outside in' as a set of strange practices tacked on to ordinary life. Some religious textbooks didn't give you much sense of 'what it feels like to be religious, why it's difficult to be religious, why it hurts to be religious, why people want to stop being religious, and why people want to start being religious'.[24]

He drew a parallel with good art, and spoke about the writings of the American writer Flannery O'Connor, who refuses to steer her readers, but indirectly constructs 'a world in which certain things may become physical or tangible'. This was what made Just Betzer's *Babette's Feast*, which the Archbishop described as his favourite film, such a great work of religious art. It is a simple tale of a Frenchwoman who moves to rural Denmark in the late nineteenth century, and eventually hosts a pointlessly sumptuous banquet for her employers and their friends during which sins are confessed and reconciliation achieved between the diners. The film itself is not overtly evangelistic, Rowan granted, but 'watching it, and absorbing what I call the animated icon of it, gives me all sorts of things to reflect on in my own belief system'. In contrast to this, the mistake made by producers of Hollywood biblical epics from the 1950s onwards lay in trying to depict 'religious things happening' – all packaged with soft music and a glow round the edges. The lesson of *Babette's Feast*, however, was that religion complicates and challenges our humanity – and this was a lesson that government ministers, as well as religious educators, could profit from.

At around this time, Rowan initiated a House of Lords debate on custodial sentencing, and attacked the empty-headedness of much TV drama in an Easter message to the diocese of Canterbury. (He instanced the ITV series *Footballers' Wives* as especially gross.) Renewed charges of other-worldliness were thrown at him when he preached the Mere Sermon – an address given at St Benet's, Cambridge, under university auspices – which was interpreted as a sharp attack on the Iraq invasion, and the policy failures in Britain and the US associated with it. Two weaknesses in particular were laid bare by the episode: the Archbishop's occasional obscurity, and Lambeth Palace's continuing problems with trouble-shooting.

Even though Bush and Blair were not mentioned by name, it seemed clear enough that Rowan had the two leaders in his sights. 'Credible claims on our political loyalty have something to do with a demonstrable attention to truth, even unwelcome truth,' he said.

> A government that habitually ignored expert advice . . . habitually repressed criticism or manipulated public media – such a regime would, to say the least, jeopardise its claim to obedience . . . Its policies and its rhetoric would not be designed to secure for its citizens an appropriate position in the world, a position that allowed the best kind of freedom because it did not deceive or encourage deception about the way the world is. It would be concerned finally about control and no more; and so would be a threat to its citizens and others.

The Archbishop's meaning was blunted by the wedging of these comments into a discourse about obedience and 'attention'. His message ran like this. Just as Christians should pay attention to the demands of the gospel, so governments should pay attention to moral complexity.

The Times's report was headlined 'Archbishop Accuses Labour of Damaging Democracy'; the paper also carried a fiercely worded leader suggesting that it had withdrawn its earlier support for Rowan. The *Daily Mail* assumed him to be saying in code that 'Blair lied' over Iraq. But when journalists from other newspapers sought clarification from Lambeth on the afternoon the sermon was delivered, they were told that Jonathan Jennings was ill. No one else could give a proper steer. It was a further mark of amateurishness in the press office, especially as journalists could also be treated with an unwarrantably firm hand in some other contexts. But it also reflected Rowan's slowness to adapt to the less forgiving media climate compared with Wales. Shortly after the débâcle, someone with constant access to him asked me why the press could not simply have viewed the sermon as pitched at a Cambridge audience alone. The answer to this complaint should have been obvious: because the preacher was the *Archbishop of Canterbury*.

Rowan took the point. In an interview two months later with Mary Ann Sieghart for *The Times*, he opened up more than he had done to the Press Association: 'The sheer level of attention is one of the things I hadn't quite expected, and perhaps that was silly of me.' He compared speaking in public to talking to someone who is hard of hearing, as his mother had been in her later years. 'As you pitch your voice like that, and try and keep it audible, you become more self-conscious about what you're saying, and perhaps more stumbling . . . People are listening quite hard for nuances. But when you're speaking in the public register and nuance is hard to get, you get self-conscious.'[25] As for the clarity of some of his speeches and sermons: 'Yes, I know, I know, I know it's very clotted, and when it is, it's partly having to try and formulate something quickly, and partly that sometimes the subject matter isn't wrestled to the ground very easily.'[26]

He also had a clear answer to the question of whether it might not be better to loosen the ties between different parts of the

Anglican world. A federation might have 'practical attractions', but fell short of God's will for the Church. Communion, though a high-risk enterprise, nevertheless went 'a bit closer to the heart of the New Testament than just slightly shoulder-shrugging co-existence. I do feel that federation, loose parallel processes, are less than we've got, less than we could have, and, in the very long run, less than what God wants in the Church.'[27]

Soon afterwards he granted an interview to Roy Hattersley, the Labour politician, for an *Observer* profile. This encounter was less successful (Hattersley later told me that he had found the Archbishop very hard to follow), and appeared to bear out the concerns of liberals. Asked to say that anti-gay discrimination is wrong, Rowan gave an equivocal reply: 'The voices in the developing world, people who regularly feel marginal in pretty well every respect – this is another turn of the screw for them. I'm serious about the international dimension here. That is probably what weighs with me most, personally and emotionally.'[28] It is not hard to spot a logical flaw in this argument. The idea that Africans and others are ignored by the First World, and therefore that their chauvinistic views on homosexuality should be tolerated by Europeans and North Americans, does not hold water. What the interview really disclosed was that Rowan the politically correct left-winger feels nervous about criticising black clerics. It was this impulse that stopped him from taking Thabo Mbeki to task when the two men met in 2007, even though the South African President had become infamous for questioning the link between HIV infection and AIDS. (The Archbishop of Cape Town, Njongonkulu Ndungane, had been a lot firmer, describing Mbeki's attitudes as even more calamitous than the apartheid system itself.)

Unsurprisingly, however, Rowan fared a lot better when not confronted by the gnawing sexuality question. In July, he and the Archbishop of York, David Hope, wrote to Tony Blair on behalf of the whole Bench deploring the treatment of Iraqi detainees at the Abu Ghraib prison near Baghdad. Rowan spoke eloquently about prison reform, among other issues, at that summer's General Synod meeting in York, and supported an unsuccessful attempt to end pay differentials between bishops and clergy. Then he departed for the Solomon Islands, in part to honour seven members of the Melanesian Brotherhood, an Anglican order, who had been murdered by separatist militants the previous year. The Archbishop praised the community's 'mighty witness' in promoting peace on its home turf and in several parts of Papua New Guinea and the Philippines; he also addressed a 6,000-strong ecumenical congregation at a football stadium in the capital, Honiara. For James Rosenthal, editor of *Anglican World* magazine, who has accompanied the Archbishop on most of his overseas travels, the Melanesian visit was the highlight. Inside the country, they partly travelled by water. Rosenthal judges that

> the flower-bedecked chair mounted on a canoe was the most incredible mode of transport I had ever seen, especially as when we landed on Isabel Island, slightly clad muscular men ran into the river and lifted the Archbishop high and carried him to his next preaching engagement. I took more shots of that than of anything else, including the signs saying DON'T FEED ALLIGATORS. I sensed Archbishop Rowan was wishing either my camera disk would run out of space, or that I would fall into the river . . .

* * *

Several weeks later came the Beslan tragedy, in which at least 350 people, half of them children, died after Chechen terrorists took them hostage at a school in the southern Russian town. The carnage made headlines around the world, and Rowan was again summoned to the *Today* studio to articulate a Christian response. Asked the age-old question as to where God was, he gave a resonant reply foreshadowing his response to the vastly greater loss of life after the Asian tsunami several months later. He showed similar deftness in Egypt a few days later, using an address at the al-Azhar al-Sharif Institute, one of Sunni Islam's main centres of learning, to appeal for greater concord between Christians and Muslims.

But there was little peace for the virtuous. A further sense of how some Evangelicals had poisoned the wells for the Archbishop came in early October, when Phillip Jensen, Dean of Sydney, accused Rowan of 'theological and intellectual prostitution' in an address to Reform's 2004 conference.[29] The Dean berated the lobbying group's members as a 'bunch of old women' for their alleged timidity, and complained that he knew 'our side had lost' when Rowan had persuaded the primates to receive communion together at their meeting the previous autumn. Reform later apologised to Lambeth Palace.

The Windsor Report, published on 18 October, marked a victory for conservatives. The Lambeth Commission's seventeen members had met three times – once at Kanuga, North Carolina, as well as twice at Windsor. Rowan had been the only archbishop allowed to read the report beforehand: Eames and the Commission's secretary, Gregory Cameron, showed him an advance copy in late September. Among other things, the document urged that the provinces of the Communion should sign up to an Anglican Covenant and adopt a basic 'common law'; that church leaders whose actions had caused recent divisions should say that they regretted the breach, and should consider withdrawing from 'representative functions' in the Communion; and that the Archbishop of Canterbury should 'exercise very considerable caution' in inviting or admitting Gene Robinson 'to the councils of the Communion'.

The sense that Anglicanism now needed a clearer rule book was brought out by Archbishop Eames at the launch of the report in St Paul's Cathedral. The Commission had been urged in some of the submissions it had received that Robinson's appointment was an expression of legitimate diversity. But most of the primates had rejected this and said that it was 'not appropriate' to regard the move as an example of waiting for a development to be 'received' by the Communion. Eames went on to underline the scale of the crisis as he saw it:

> In all honesty, I dare to suggest this is one of the Communion's
> last opportunities. If it's not grasped, I really do not know where
> we are going. The report, of itself, is not going to prevent
> disintegration, but it could help, if people are prepared to take
> this opportunity. God may be using this crisis to make us really
> look in new ways at what keeps us together.[30]

Support for this view came from Tom Wright, who had also served on the Commission:

> Frank Griswold, the presiding bishop of the Episcopal Church,
> has repeatedly urged that we 'celebrate difference' and 'embrace
> the Other'. In other words, we must have a broad church
> without nasty, rigid boundaries. These concepts are problematic
> even in their own terms, though this is usually ignored in the

public discourse which has made them central to its (ironically narrow) new morality. But invoking them in current Anglican debate simply begs the question. We all agree that some 'differences' are to be celebrated. We all agree that some 'Others' are to be embraced.

But . . . random 'embracing' risks colluding with behaviour which should instead be questioned . . . The question then is: 'Which things come into which category? Which differences make a difference?'

Wright emphasised that the Lambeth Commission had focused on questions of process, rather than on homosexuality as such:

The charge against the US churches, for which they have been invited to express regret, is not that they took certain decisions, but that they thereby knowingly ignored, and hence damaged, the 'proper constraints of the bonds of affection' which . . . hold us together. That is why the report also criticises interdiocesan invasion, however well-intentioned.

So far, the only expressed regret has been that actions taken have hurt other people. That is not the point. What matters is a refreshed understanding, rooted in scripture and common tradition, of how 'communion' works.[31]

Inevitably, perhaps, the report went too far for liberals, and not far enough for some traditionalists. Peter Akinola expressed fury over both the document's failure to call for outright repentance from ECUSA, and its rebuke to those offering alternative episcopal oversight for traditionalist American parishes without the consent of their bishops. Marilyn McCord Adams, an American priest who had recently become Regius

Professor of Divinity at Oxford, wrote an article portraying the report as a tool for suppressing principled disagreement. Fresh consensus on issues of race, gender and sex was the work of decades. The Windsor Report's built-in demand that member Churches wait for multicultural consensus 'would have the consequence of quenching the Spirit'. Worldwide cultural flux meant that 'too much agreement' between the provinces was unnecessary, she added. 'Instead, we should stick with the loose federation that has enabled us to work together to meet the world crises of war, hunger, poverty, disease and disloca-tion in the past.'[32]

* * *

Church storms were put in perspective by the tsunami of Boxing Day 2004, in which hundreds of thousands lost their lives, and millions their livelihoods. A footnote to the disaster is the misreporting of Rowan's views about it: the *Sunday Telegraph*'s main headline on 2 January 2005 read: 'Archbishop of Canter-bury: This Has Made Me Question God's Existence'. The story's apparent basis lay in an article about the problem of evil and suffering that Rowan had written for the paper. What he actually said was that it would be wrong if Christians were not challenged by the tragedy. There was no neat explanation for the suffering of the innocent. And yet, he added, some forms of response could console the believer:

> The extraordinary fact is that belief has survived such tests again and again – not because it comforts or explains but because believers cannot deny what has been shown or given to them. They have learned to see the world and life in the world as a freely given gift; they have learned to be open to a calling or

invitation from outside their own resources, a calling to accept God's mercy for themselves and make it real for others; they have learned that there is some reality to which they can only relate in amazement and silence. These convictions are terribly assaulted by all those other facts of human experience that seem to point to a completely arbitrary world, but people still feel bound to them, not for comfort or ease, but because they have imposed themselves on the shape of a life and the habits of a heart.[33]

Bishop Glyn Simon had said something similar in response to the 1966 Aberfan disaster in Wales, when dozens of children were killed by a landslide. Rowan gave a pithy account of Simon's message:

> I can only dare to speak about this because I once lost a child. I have nothing to say that will make sense of this horror today. All I know is that the words in my Bible about God's promise to be alongside us have never lost their meaning for me. And now we have to work in God's name for the future.[34]

The Windsor recommendations were formally approved in a statement by the Church of England's House of Bishops in early 2005, and a motion based on the endorsement was moved by Tom Wright at the General Synod's London meeting in February. He warned that the report was not a discussion document. Nor could the process it had generated be likened to the range of routes a group of friends might consider before a ramble in the hills. It was 'more like the urgent discussions, high in the crags with evening coming on, snow threatening and two of the friends suffering frostbite, as to the best and quickest route back to the valley. Wrong choices could be disastrous; but to delay would be the worst choice of all.'[35] Rowan, too, spoke in favour of the report, agreeing with those who had termed it 'the only game in town'.

Many eyes were now fixed on the Primates' Meeting, which took place a few days later in Northern Ireland. All but three of the thirty-eight leaders attended: the venue was the Dromantine retreat centre, a Roman Catholic establishment near Newry in County Down. On the face of it, the bishops and archbishops presented a united front. A final communiqué announced that the Anglican Churches in the United States and Canada had been asked to withdraw from the ACC for the three years leading up to the Lambeth Conference in 2008, though representatives from both provinces were invited to a 'hearing' at the 2005 ACC meeting (due four months later) to discuss the rationales behind their actions. A moratorium on the appointment of non-celibate gay bishops and the blessing of same-sex unions was urged, but familiar pieties were also voiced about the evils of homophobia and the need to listen 'unreservedly' to gay people.

The majority had reason to be complimentary about the Archbishop's leadership. Henry Orombi, the newly appointed Primate of Uganda, said that he was 'very touched by the way [the Archbishop of Canterbury] allowed us to be open with each other'. Gregory Venables, the British-born Presiding Bishop of the Southern Cone, was equally pleased. 'Under Archbishop Rowan's leadership . . . we've been able to get to a stage where we can talk very openly, very strongly even, but somehow keep the thing open and keep going. We're very grateful for that.'[36]

But things were bloody behind the scenes, mainly because parts of the conservative camp had shown old-fashioned chauvinism to be alive and well, and had resorted to the methods of the school playground to get their way. The scene was set when Peter Akinola told Rowan peremptorily that the Windsor Report must take precedence over the twenty or so other subjects on the agenda for discussion. The Archbishop of Canterbury at first stood his ground, but then yielded when Akinola became even more insistent.

The Archbishop of Nigeria and his allies then pressed home their advantage. One member of this company did not shrink from being personally offensive about the Primate of All England behind his back, saying at one point that Rowan would 'do what we tell him'.[37] Moreover, a clutch of campaigners – including Martyn Minns and David Anderson of the American Anglican Council, Robert Duncan (purporting to be on a golfing holiday in the vicinity) and the terrier-like Chris Sugden – were on hand at a neighbouring hotel to stiffen the sinews of conservative prelates. Africans were provided with mobile phones and a taxi service, in an obvious breach of Rowan's request that the primates should not have dealings with third parties; and Akinola was given money to host a dinner for nineteen of his colleagues. On the last day, Rowan asked his peers to join him for a valedictory Eucharist. At least fourteen failed to come, on the grounds that Frank Griswold was taking part in the service as well.

Gene Robinson later identified this as a watershed for Rowan:

> I would like him to have insisted that everyone stay at the table . . . I think that to absent oneself from the communion table because of the presence of other perceived sinners is blasphemy against the sacrament. And I think that if the Archbishop of Canterbury had named that for what it was, and had called it not just inappropriate but sacrilege, we would be in a better place.[38]

In his Easter message several weeks afterwards, Rowan suggested that the press had not given due weight to the good things that came out of Dromantine, including a renewed commitment to assist with AIDS education. Given the actual turn of events, this complaint seemed other-worldly. It was now a matter of record that Akinola and the primates of Uganda, Central Africa, Kenya, Rwanda, Congo, West Africa, Tanzania and Sudan considered Gene Robinson's consecration to be a more pressing subject for debate than the fight against one of the greatest threats to human health. Akinola, indeed, had recently gone further. During a meeting of conservative archbishops in Nairobi in January, called to discuss tactics during the Dromantine showdown, he had been asked why he appeared obsessed about gay sex to the exclusion of war, corruption, HIV and poverty in Africa. He replied: 'I didn't create poverty. This Church didn't create poverty. Poverty is not an issue. Human suffering is not an issue at all.'[39]

Preachers in the Global South tend to be uninterested in German biblical criticism and other forms of exegesis largely associated with elite Western universities. In Africa, a more self-confident generation of Anglicans have digested Christian teaching in situations closer to the Old and New Testaments than to those of contemporary Europeans or North Americans. There is a much wider take-up of messages about prophecy, exorcism, healing, miracles, liberation of all kinds, promised lands, and also of the victory of the righteous. As David Martin has observed, 'From a postmodern perspective, readings of scripture are up for grabs; and what one might call an Afro-Jewish take on the good and "the goods" has great appeal.'[40]

None of this is to imply that Akinola was reasonable. On the contrary, his words were crass. We haven't heard the last of him.

8

Multiple Echo

Rowan Williams's circumspect approach to the global side of his ministry has a parallel in his attitude to home affairs. The reasons for this are grounded in the Church of England's changing polity. Peter Sedgwick, Principal of St Michael's College, Llandaff, and formerly a senior official at Church House, Westminster, puts further flesh on this matter:

> To be an archbishop until the end of Runcie's era, you needed three things. First, you had to believe that you could give a moral and spiritual lead to the nation as a whole on particular issues. Runcie believed that, and Habgood believed it even more. Carey shared that belief, but could not make it a reality. I question whether Rowan even wants to try. He is sceptical about what 'leadership' means (it is not a biblical word), and he prefers to witness to what he believes. That is a different issue from leadership.[1]

A second necessary attribute, Sedgwick says, was to be *in a position* to give a lead. During the Second World War, Runcie had served in the same regiment as Willie Whitelaw, Margaret Thatcher's first Home Secretary; Michael Ramsey had been at university with Selwyn Lloyd, later Foreign Secretary and

Chancellor. Though he enjoys warm relations with Gordon Brown, Rowan has never had political friendships of this kind, and is in any case ambivalent about exploiting such contacts. Third, Sedgwick argues,

> the nation has to want the Church to give a lead. It could still do that – just – in the 1980s when the C of E published *Faith in the City*, its very critical report on Thatcher's urban policy. But in the 1990s a pluralist nation lost interest in what bishops or religious leaders had to say, unless they were exceptionally talented, as Jonathan Sacks is. When Rowan gave the Dimbleby Lecture, the press coverage suggested that people felt that the clock may have been turned back. But the moment was a fleeting one.

Sedgwick's prognosis is either sobering or liberating, depending on your point of view. 'Rowan confronts the dilemma of the Church of England as it is today,' he adds.

> It is now de facto disestablished. As Archbishop of Canterbury he does not want to give a lead; he does not know closely, and over a long time, those politicians he might seek to influence; and the nation does not care. That is a very difficult platform to stand on, and as the sharia law episode showed, it sometimes goes badly wrong.

The Archbishop's name will be associated with the sharia lecture for years to come, even though he has made many contributions to interfaith discussion, most of which have been well received. That the majority have not reached a larger audience also says something about the more hostile climate in which Rowan has worked.

With the third main element in the Archbishop's official responsibilities, his oversight of England's senior see, the picture is different again. The evidence gathered in Chapter 5 suggests that his life would have been easier had he accepted more support in Monmouth, but back-up is of course what he had in abundance from 2002. A mixed blessing at Lambeth Palace, it has been an unqualified benefit in Canterbury itself. The cathedral and its community 'are a kind of home', he says simply. 'It's the family I belong to. And although there are other families, this is the centre of it.'[2]

Much of the credit for Rowan's outright success in the Canterbury diocese should go to him personally. The source of his know-how lies as much in Oxford, where he was one of the cathedral chapter's best-loved figures, as in Monmouth. His monastic links form another positive influence. Canterbury is haunted by its Benedictine past. Above all, there is the Williamses' simple wish to spend as much time as possible in the shadow of Anglicanism's mother church. Rowan is in Canterbury a good deal more than most of his recent predecessors. The family spend at least one weekend a month at the Old Palace, and are also there at Christmas, in Holy Week and Easter Week, and for several spells over the summer. Jane has lectured to the diocesan clergy; Pip belongs to the cathedral's Sunday Club. Although the Bishop of Dover, Stephen Venner, has full delegated powers, Rowan ordains the deacons at Petertide, confirms the cathedral choristers, and makes about fifteen Sunday-morning parish visits a year. His chaplain, Martin Short, has resisted pressure to stage-manage these events. The accent is on informality. Local newspapers are rarely informed of the Archbishop's impending arrival. Just as in Monmouth, his addresses to his clergy during the Chrism Eucharists of Holy Week are savoured.

Relations with the Dean of Canterbury, Robert Willis, are especially warm. 'Rowan had a natural affection for our community from the start,' Willis comments. 'That made things very easy. Not all of his visits are scheduled. It's a delight to come to Matins sometimes on a weekday morning to find him there, unannounced, alongside members of the chapter.' The Archbishop has put his lecturing skills at his colleagues' disposal. The talks published as *Tokens of Trust* have been followed by further series of Holy Week addresses. And Canterbury's profile has grown further in his time. This is partly because the International Study Centre, a smart new building in the cathedral precincts, opened its doors just before George Carey's retirement. Almost all recently consecrated bishops from across the Anglican world now spend ten days there shortly after Christmas. In August, the centre hosts visits from theological college students, many of whom get bursaries from the dean and chapter. The visitors are often greeted personally by Rowan, who has made himself available even if it means shortening his family holiday – now usually spent in Cornwall.

Nor did his commitment to Canterbury flag after asbestos was discovered in the Old Palace two years after his enthronement. At Easter 2005, the Williamses decamped to a small modern house normally used by the cathedral's assistant organist, and returned to their official residence for a clan gathering (with Jane's sisters and their families) at Christmas the following year. There is a firm rhythm to the seasonal celebrations. The streets of Canterbury fill up on Christmas Eve for a torchlit programme of carol-singing: the Archbishop, other clergy and civic dignitaries are usually joined by a crowd of several thousand. On Christmas Day, Rowan pays visits to the prison and the Scrine Foundation, a shelter for the homeless, before presiding at the cathedral's main Eucharist. Other acts of worship follow; the Williams family celebrations do not get under way until the late afternoon.

Another task on Rowan's Christmas menu is the recording of his New Year message, always broadcast on television. Here, too, his qualities have emerged as he has reflected on the darker corners of contemporary life. One December, he was filmed at a drop-in centre in Deptford, south-east London, listening to young unemployed people (several with drug problems) and pensioners suffering from illness or bereavement. Other great and good visitors might easily have dealt in platitudes. Rowan sounded both compassionate and unsentimental. 'At times,' he said, 'the most we can do for each other is to say, "I can't promise to keep you safe, but I'll do all I can to make sure there is someone with you in the worst moments."'

His combination of warmth and wisdom has gone down well in the House of Bishops, where he is not only admired but loved – even by some whose loyalty was put in question when they wrote to *The Times* in 2003. It is hard to describe in detail the views of such a diverse body, but at least three main perceptions are apparent. Conservatives, sensing that the Archbishop has moved their way on the sexuality question, tend to be especially approving. Several see strategic skill, as well as a return to orthodoxy, reflected in Rowan's policies. Liberals tend to be less united. Some agree that he has played a difficult hand as well as could be expected, both in 2003 and subsequently. Others draw a distinction between his personal traits and his deficiencies as a politician. The more favourable liberal verdict is summed up by one of the shrewdest figures on the Bench. He is in no doubt that the Archbishop towers over all his colleagues and provides both the gravitas and the sense of collegiality that were in short supply during the Carey era. 'Everyone's voice is welcome,' according to this source, 'and Rowan has taken us into his confidence over matters close to his heart – especially the unity of the Communion. He understands that the Church is built on relationships, and should not operate like a political party.'

An Evangelical bishop from the opposite end of the theological spectrum is equally positive:

> Rowan is his own man, he does his own thing, he listens very carefully. People who don't like what he does accuse him of being in the pocket of advisers going this way or that. I really don't think that's true. I think he has a rich spirituality and an amazing wisdom which enable him to think through issues and round corners that many of us haven't quite seen yet. I have an enormous respect for that, intellectually and personally.

Until 2007, the House of Bishops met three times a year – at Leeds in the spring, at Lambeth in the autumn, and at Leicester in the summer. The Leicester meeting includes the suffragan bishops for three days out of four. The overall success of these encounters has led to the scheduling of a fourth annual get-together for the diocesans. Many examples of Rowan's acumen at these meetings could be cited: here is one. Soon after his move to Lambeth, the House of Bishops was addressed by Elizabeth Templeton, an academic theologian. She told the story of a question put to applicants for a job in her faculty. Candidates were asked to say how they would answer a man who came up to them in the street and said, 'My bus leaves in two minutes. Tell me about the resurrection in the time remaining.' The bishops reflected on this before Dr Templeton told them the answer that her fellow panellists had hoped to hear: 'If you really want to hear about the resurrection, be prepared to miss your bus.' On hearing this, Rowan began to scratch his beard – a sign that he didn't think this reply quite hit the spot. Then came his own solution: 'I think I'd have asked the man where he was going, then said that I'd accompany him on the journey.'

This comment throws a sidelight on his difficulties, as well as his generosity. A member of the Archbishops' Council who esteems him very highly, yet feels he has made rods for his own back, offers a more ambivalent assessment of the years leading up to the 2008 Lambeth Conference: 'Rowan was more fearful than he needed to be of conservatives. Quite a few liberals feel out of it. I would want to argue that the Church of England contains a huge liberal Catholic constituency that's basically pretty quiescent.' This complaint, an echo of another already cited in the Introduction to this book, shades into anxieties about the Lambeth Palace staffing. The top aides to Robert Runcie and George Carey were bishops. But Rowan opted to have a lay Chief of Staff and appointed Chris Smith, an accountant with a City background, in the summer of 2003. Smith's Evangelical churchmanship has been cited by those who fear that conservatives have the Archbishop's ear. For his part, Smith argues that neither he nor the Archbishop can be blamed for the superior organisational skills of traditionalist groups, and that in any case, listening to people does not imply endorsement of their views.

Another reservation about the choice of Smith comes from bishops who feel that his post should still be occupied by one of their own number. A critic says: 'It breaks the sense of priestly solidarity when disciplinary issues, for example, have to be raised with Chris and other senior administrators such as Andrew Nunn.' Other observers see advantages in Smith's lay status.

His record in the commercial world constitutes an asset, and he is considered a genial colleague. But his presence may nevertheless have fuelled the arguments of another senior cleric, who feels that the Archbishop has not developed qualities such as boldness and decisiveness. 'Rowan has seemed emotionally isolated over the past few years,' this source suggested in 2007,

> and he has looked like a captive of people whose expertise he respects. This has come out in several ways. When Jonathan Goodall was appointed to succeed David Marshall as the Archbishop's chaplain in 2005, the interviewing panel did not include Rowan himself. On other occasions I've seen him asking lawyers what he should do about this or that, but I haven't seen this process in reverse. The overall impression is that we have command and control mechanisms for someone who is not himself especially keen to implement them.

These views come from serious people, not mischief-makers. But they need weighing alongside a record of genuine achievement. Rowan could not turn water into wine. The worshippers had had exorbitant expectations from the start. Yet the same could be said for the doom-mongers who were writing off his primacy by 2005, and judging that a series of unrelated mishaps had congealed into a narrative of failure. It would be fairer to say that both weaker and stronger points tended to be duplicated. The truth, in other words, remained tangled.

*   *   *

One story that wouldn't go away centred on the ineffectiveness of Rowan's press office. The 2005 general election campaign

Druid induction by Dr Robyn Lewis (left), Arch Druid of Wales, 2002

Meeting Pope John Paul II and Cardinal Walter Kasper (centre) at the Vatican, 2003

With Anglican Primates at Lambeth Palace, 2003

Frank Griswold and other Episcopalian bishops consecrate Gene Robinson
as Bishop of New Hampshire, 2003

Receiving a medal from the Palestinian leader, Yasser Arafat, during their meeting in the West Bank city of Ramallah, 2004

At Lambeth Palace, London

With the new Archbishop of York, Dr John Sentamu, after the service to confirm Sentamu's election to the See of York, 2005

In conversation with Archbishop Peter Akinola of Nigeria during the Global South meeting in Egypt, 2005

Dr Jeffrey John (left), newly installed as Dean of St Albans with Bishop Christopher Herbert, 2004

Greeted by singers and local officials, Rowan Williams meets the Archbishop of Sudan at Malakal airport, southern Sudan, 2006

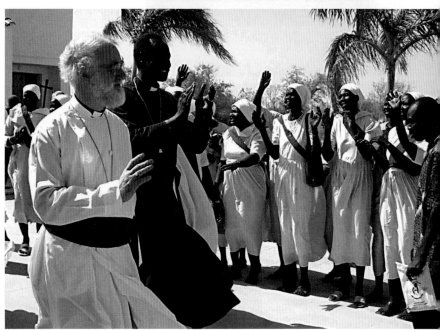

With Pope Benedict XVI,
at the Vatican, 2006

With Bishop Katharine
Jefferts Schori on their way
to a press conference in
New Orleans, 2007

With Philip Pullman, 2004

Travelling by boat around the Solomon Islands, 2004

The Archbishop and other religious leaders, including Britain's Chief Rabbi, Sir Jonathan Sacks (second from left), on an anti-poverty march through central London, July 2008

Speaking at the 2008 Lambeth Conference

began in March, and early on the *Daily Mail* complained on its front page of the Church of England's alleged silence on abortion. Stories – or, rather, opinions dressed up as news – such as these could easily have been anticipated by the House of Bishops, as well as by Lambeth Palace staff. In the absence of an oven-ready rebuttal, however, Rowan restated his deep concern about pregnancy terminations in a hastily composed article for the *Sunday Times*. His challenge was to avoid a mistake already made by Cormac Murphy-O'Connor, who had implied that the issue could be linked with a particular party. Michael Howard, the Tory leader, had won praise from the Cardinal by signalling his support for reducing the legal time-limit to twenty weeks into pregnancy. But this was not official Conservative policy. Rowan recognised this fact with a simple warning: 'The plain fact is that no party has made, nor is likely to make, commitments on this matter as part of a set of its electoral pledges. No party has given the least indication that it would seek anything but a free vote on any related question.'[3] He also had a tart rejoinder for (mainly) liberal women commentators who argued that male religious leaders had no right to intervene on the subject: 'the idea that raising [the issue] is the first step to a theocratic tyranny or a capitulation to some neanderthal Christian right is alarmist nonsense,' he said. Several days later, he put out a statement that listed four electoral priorities: the environment, the arms trade, prison reform and

a growing number of young people who are severely emotionally undernourished and culturally alienated. Ask anyone who works with children or young people in any city. The climate of chronic family instability, sexual chaos and exploitation, drug abuse and educational disadvantage is a lethal cocktail. To call for more public support for stable families and marriage is not in this context a bit of middle-class, Middle England nostalgia; it's life and death.

From an international perspective, the election naturally counted for little by comparison with the death of John Paul II on 2 April. Many Roman Catholics, let alone secularists, were taken aback by the outpouring of affection for one of the longest-serving popes in history. His time in office had been identified with a steady centralisation of power, and intolerant attitudes to dissent. To some, of course, this was the right medicine for contemporary ills. But John Paul was also liked by many more liberal members of his flock, who tended to distinguish between the singer and the song. At least five million mourners came to pay their respects at his lying-in-state.

The Archbishop's tribute to the Pope was deeply felt. By the manner of his death, said Rowan, John Paul had given 'a message to the whole of the Christian world, and in fact to the whole human world, that won't be readily forgotten'. He also made clear that attending John Paul's funeral on 8 April was a higher priority for him than conducting a service of dedication after the marriage of Prince Charles and Camilla Parker Bowles. The couple's plans were duly changed: Charles also travelled to Rome for the funeral, and their wedding was postponed by twenty-four hours.

Rowan's difficulties at this time were largely shrouded from view. As had become customary, he stayed at the English College with Cardinal Murphy-O'Connor. The two preached at Compline on the eve of the funeral, in their very different registers, to seminarians and a select group of reporters. One of these journalists interviewed Rowan beforehand, and recalls being discombobulated by the behaviour of Jeremy Harris:

He [Harris] seemed to want to control both the Archbishop and the line of questioning. For instance, he said that I wasn't to ask about the royal wedding. As it happens, I hadn't thought of doing so. But if I'd wanted to press ahead, any attempt to muzzle me would have been counter-productive. An archbishop is like a Cabinet minister. He has his own specific beat, but it ought to be possible to ask him in passing about any big issue of the moment.

Harris is admired in some quarters, but it is clear that he and Rowan did not see eye to eye. When he was offered an administrative post at Oxford University in 2005, the Secretary for Public Affairs took the chance to move on. The more relaxed style of Tim Livesey, an urbane former Foreign Office man who succeeded Harris in early 2006, has been much more to the Archbishop's liking. Some, however (bishops included), still complain of a certain haughtiness displayed by other staff members at Lambeth.

April 2005 was a momentous month. John Paul was succeeded by Benedict XVI (formerly Cardinal Joseph Ratzinger) on 19 April after a very short conclave. The Archbishop hastily returned to Rome to greet the new Pontiff: he was received alongside other Christian leaders at a special audience in the Vatican's Clementine Hall. Rowan was already brushing up on his linguistic skills by reading several of Benedict's books in the original German. He now took the chance to greet the Pope in his native tongue as well.

As the Vatican's chief doctrinal watchdog, Ratzinger had proved a highly divisive figure during the 1980s and 1990s. His election as Pope was a clear sign that John Paul's restorationist agenda would be consolidated still further. It also meant that the already strained relations between Rome and the Anglican

Communion would not ease quickly. When I asked the Archbishop how he planned to address this challenge, he emphasised the common ground occupied by Christians vis-à-vis secularists:

> Recent events in the Anglican Church haven't made things easy for us ecumenically in many directions, and that's one of the facts we live with. What I do think is significant, and have discussed with Cardinal Kasper [President of the Pontifical Council for Promoting Christian Unity], is a common interest in the character of the Christian presence in Europe now. It links up with a conversation I had some months ago with Cardinal Schönborn of Vienna. We agreed that we weren't talking about Christianity ruling or directing culture, just about how to make it visible and attractively visible. We agreed that we weren't doing terribly well on that front. Where Christianity was visible, it was often [seen] in either negative or retrograde terms.[4]

The Archbishop hoped that the Anglican–Roman Catholic International Commission (ARCIC) would be revived, but did not think that this would occur 'for a couple of years'. As it happened, a favourable announcement on renewed ecumenical talks came within a few weeks. This was interpreted in some quarters as a reward for Rowan's newfound conservatism over gay clergy – a shift signposted more clearly than ever in the Archbishop's presidential address at the ACC meeting, held that summer in Nottingham. The debate over sexuality, he said,

> could be described either as 'The Churches of the North are tired and confused, losing evangelistic energy', or 'The Churches of the North have been made aware of how much their life and

work has been sustained in the past by insensitive and oppressive social patterns, with the Bible being used to justify great evils'.

On the question of what the Church required in its ordained leaders and what patterns of relationship it would explicitly recognise, the Communion was not persuaded that change was right. And he had a warning. Where there was a long consensus of teaching in Christian history, and a widespread ecumenical agreement, 'it may well be thought that change would need an exceptionally strong critical mass to justify it'.

Within a few weeks of meeting Benedict, Rowan set off to woo another constituency during the Building Bridges conference for Christians and Muslims. Sarajevo provided the venue. In a speech, 'Christianity, Islam and the Challenge of Poverty', he talked of the 'common agenda' uniting adherents of the two faiths, including the encouragement of local credit schemes:

> Whether in the shape of the Anglican 'Five Talents' initiative in Africa, or the Grameen banks of Muhammad Yunus in South Asia, there is a way of furthering economic maturity that belongs, most obviously, with religious conviction, simply because it assumes that a dependable local community, bound by trust and common commitment, is an ideal unit in which economic empowerment can take place.

The address contained an indictment of the protectionism stopping Third World goods from reaching Europe and North America – a de facto call for *more* globalisation, not less. Absent, still, was due awareness of the steep falls in malnutrition arising from free-market reforms.

This gap in Rowan's reckoning was also evident a few days

before, when he preached at a service in St Paul's Cathedral marking the sixtieth anniversary of Christian Aid. In an argument bearing his own fingerprints, not his advisers', he portrayed economic liberalisation as an often destructive force. The address drew a poor notice from *The Economist*, among other publications.

He continued to plough the religion-and-culture furrow in a trenchant lecture about the media at Lambeth Palace in June. His charges against the newspaper trade – that it distorts debate, fuels a climate of national cynicism, and unjustly attacks institutions over their secretiveness – reflected views he had expressed in private, with even greater vehemence, for decades.

The lecture began with a distinction said to be ignored by many journalists, between exposing deceptions that sustain injustice and attacking confidentialities that protect the vulnerable. Yoked to this were assumptions about 'an unblinking (and probably discreditable) agenda in every public statement or decision'. Rowan then quoted with approval the characterisation by Peter Wilby, a former editor of the *New Statesman*, of reporters in the parliamentary lobby: 'What does an NHS reorganisation or an "initiative" on behaviour in schools mean for doctors, patients, teachers or children? The political journalists cannot tell you. They can tell you that this is a Blairite or Brownite idea, that it shows the minister is "getting a grip" or losing it, that it will pacify backbenchers or enrage them.'

The implied parallel with religious affairs coverage here was clear. News editors often favour material that ticks the boxes marked 'sex' or 'strife': as one weighty Fleet Street figure put it several years ago, 'the Church of England getting its act together is not a story'. Much of Rowan's lecture thus formed a justified protest against what the New Testament terms 'idle' speech: speech that debases the currency because it is inflated, untruthful, aggressive, contemptuous or salacious. The Archbishop had this conclusion:

> good journalism is one of the models of good conversation and communication in the wider social context. That is, it may be and should be at times argumentative and one-sided, but it must leave room for reply . . . It must work with a sharp sense of what it is that different kinds of community know and how they know it. Without this, it will move constantly further into its parallel universe.

Critics were dubious about some of the lecture's more solemn claims. At one point Rowan suggested that the rationale for journalism 'is that it promises to deliver what other sources can't, information that is needed to equip the reader or viewer or listener for a more free and significant role as a human agent'. Several commentators thought that by lifting his eyes to the hills in this way, he was showing his unawareness of what makes the industry tick. One old hand was quick to remind him that journalism exists to deliver readers to advertisers, or to entertain and inform readers so much that they are willing to pay for it. 'These aren't mutually exclusive reasons,' said one, 'but you won't find any journalism of which neither is true.'[5] Another general point made was that although much journalism is indeed puerile or one-sided, newspapers nevertheless provide the first draft of history. For an organisation such as the Church, with its own values and priorities, there are more and less canny ways of engaging the media.

＊   ＊   ＊

Though aspects of Christian–Muslim relations continued to provide the press with periodic chances to attack Rowan, his woes during the remainder of 2005 centred on Anglicanism's likely fragmentation. It will be obvious from the story told thus far that disputes over homosexuality had largely become a dialogue of the deaf long before the middle of the decade. Conservatives who saw the matter in terms of fidelity to the Bible, and liberals whose priority lay in keeping up with the times, were all frustrated in their different ways. Both sides continued to claim the victim's mantle. For Rowan, who was emphatically not hard of hearing, the effect was like a tinnitus of rancorous and endlessly repeated messages.

The pretext for the year's eruption of summer madness was a church response to the British government's civil-partnerships legislation. This new law posed a conundrum for the Church of England, since the official requirement that clergy forswear same-sex relationships was now undermined by the newly enshrined right of all citizens to register such unions in public. In the absence of other options, the House of Bishops opted for a fudge. A pastoral statement declared that gay clergy would not be stopped from entering into civil partnerships, as long as they were celibate.

This gave Peter Akinola his chance. He ridiculed the statement, asking whether bishops intended to place cameras in the bedrooms of their clergy. Calling for stricter discipline, he said: 'I believe that temporary suspension of the Church of England [from the Anglican Communion] is the right course to take. The Church will [sic] be subjected to the same procedures and discipline that America and Canada faced.'[6] Akinola was also quoted as saying: 'Lambeth Palace upholds our common faith. It will now lose that place of honour in the world. Must I come to Lambeth Palace in order to go to heaven? The answer is no!'[7] One of the Church's liberal spokesmen, Giles Fraser, found fault with the pastoral statement on the more reasonable grounds that it had failed to mention the word 'love' a single time. Gay sex was bound to appear morally inadequate if divorced from a context of loving relatedness. 'The love that dares not speak its name isn't sex; it's love itself,' Fraser wrote.[8]

There was no doubting which side of the argument carried greater ecclesiastical weight. Rowan's resolve to keep on the right side of conservatives was evident in his willingness to attend a meeting of leaders from the Global South, held in Cairo in late October. Some saw his very presence at this conclave as a sign that he had become the traditionalists' pawn. That he remained to some degree disabled by feelings of guilt about African Christians was clear when he made an ill-judged apology for the conceit allegedly reflected in 'the mass export of *Hymns Ancient and Modern* to the remote parts of the mission field'.

The best part of his speech squared up to the conference theme, 'One, Holy, Catholic and Apostolic Church', and painstakingly defined the common ground. 'If our unity is about standing in the one Christ, then it's quite clear that those who seek to stand in another place are automatically breaking that unity,' he told the hundred or so delegates. This gave him the foundation for a reply to Akinola. 'Someone said recently that the path to heaven doesn't lie necessarily through Lambeth. I agree. The path to heaven lies solely through Jesus Christ our Saviour and the unity he gives, and the only use and integrity of our instruments of unity comes when they serve that.'

All the same, the final communiqué was dominated by the prospect of further division:

Our own Anglican Communion sadly continues to be weakened by unchecked revisionist teaching and practices which undermine the divine authority of the Holy Scripture. The Anglican Communion is severely wounded by the witness of errant principles of faith and practice which in many parts of the Communion have adversely affected our efforts to take the gospel to those in need of God's redeeming . . . love.[9]

The leaders endorsed the idea of an Anglican covenant 'rooted in historic faith and formularies', and committed the Global South alliance to being 'full partners in the process of its formulation'.

Once more, Rowan had opted to play the patient peacemaker rather than assume the more glamorous mantle of the hero or martyr. And again, the stance bought him more time – especially as it was Akinola, himself often an able tactician, who now overplayed his hand. He and several other primates drew up a confidential letter criticising the Archbishop of Canterbury's leadership, and purporting to command the backing of several archbishops who hadn't even seen the text. The document, a response to Rowan's address to the Global South encounter, thanked him for his 'unequivocal words' on the sexuality question, but continued with a rebuke: 'We wonder, however, whether your personal dissent from this consensus prevents you taking the necessary steps to confront those Churches that have embraced teaching contrary to the overwhelming testimony of the Anglican Communion and the Church. We urge you to re-think your personal view and embrace the Church's consensus and to act on it.'[10] The primates then charged the Church of England with 'giving the appearance of evil' by not seeking an exemption from the Civil Partnerships Bill. They continued: 'We are troubled by your reluctance to use your moral authority to challenge the Episcopal Church and the Anglican Church of

Canada . . . We do not see why you cannot warn these Churches now, based on the Windsor report, and your own convictions about unity, that they will not be invited to Lambeth 2008 unless they truly repent.'[11]

The signatories were listed as the primates of Nigeria, West Africa, Congo, the West Indies, Rwanda, Jerusalem, Central Africa, Sudan, Kenya, Uganda, the Indian Ocean, the Philippines, the Southern Cone and South East Asia. The other three primates at the meeting – those of Tanzania, Burundi and South India – were listed as present but obliged to leave 'before the final draft had been circulated'. But it was clear that this draft – which included the claim that Europe was a 'spiritual desert' – had not done the rounds as claimed. A first draft was given to the primates with other documents at the end of a meeting on the final evening of the encounter (29 October). Nothing more was heard of it until a copy arrived at Lambeth Palace on 16 November, while Rowan was addressing the Church of England's General Synod. Before he had read it, the letter was circulated on conservative websites.

Early the following week, it was denounced by Archbishop Drexel Gomez of the West Indies as 'an act of impatience and a disrespect for process'. This view was echoed in private. Some ascribed Akinola's maverick tendencies to his temperament. Others sought to spread the blame, maintaining that he was being steered by traditionalist lobbyists in the United States. Rowan himself maintained a dignified silence amid the storm, but several influential liberals decided that the biters should be bit. Among them was David L. Edwards, Colin Slee's predecessor at Southwark and a leading church historian, who published an open letter[12] to the primates of the Global South. It provided a shrewd estimate of Rowan, as well as a welcome burst of sense:

Dear Archbishops

. . . I don't want to discuss the civil registration of single-sex partnerships, except in two sentences.

You say that such partnerships illustrate 'the severing of the grace of Christ from his moral commandments', but you cannot quote a single reference to this issue in the Gospels. You complain that the Church of England ought to have sought exemption from this Act, but you ignore the principle that in our democracy a state may provide legal facilities if these accord with public opinion, but will leave continuing questions of conscience to personal decisions, after listening to advice from any source that a citizen may choose.

Nor do I concentrate on your completely unprovoked attack on the Archbishop of Canterbury. He is a Bible-based and Catholic-minded theologian, whose view of homosexuality has been influenced by the modern knowledge that this unalterable condition is natural for some. But he does not insist on that opinion now, when he has accepted the burden of pastoral leadership of a Communion most of whose members do not share it.

That is an honourable position, to be expected both from a mind that is more fairly accused of being so well-informed and so honest as to be unclear, and from a soul dedicated to humble service in response to the needs and invitations of others.

But the example of insensitivity or ignorance that I find most offensive is your description of Europe as a 'spiritual desert'.

Of course, Europe and its Churches have massive problems, as is surely true about your own situations. But please note that these are discussed freely, frequently, and expertly, to an extent not matched in any other region of our troubled world . . .

You are men in positions of leadership, but you should also appreciate the liberation of women in contemporary Europe as part of the acknowledgement of human rights. The admission of women to the ordained ministry is not yet complete, but it is already a key example of the release of the God-given talents of one half of humankind.

The recognition of rights for the traditionally marginalised of both genders, now firm in Europe-wide and national laws and courts of justice, can be seen as a reflection of the attitude that Jesus took to women and to the poor, in the context of the dawning of the Kingdom of God. Should you not applaud?

You are right to say that progress in society is not enough if there are no standards in private life, particularly in sexual behaviour . . . The big difference is not that Europeans have ceased to have consciences or souls. It is that they have a more sophisticated awareness of their bodies, with their instincts to explore and compete (look at any sport), and also to express love and to build co-operation in some way that involves sexuality. So Europe is embarked on the discovery of a new morality, as well as a new unity. For example, in Europe, marriage has become a union of equals, attracted and held together by love.

That does not make it a cesspit or a barren desert. It is a laboratory, as the desert was in the time of Moses. Some of its experiments go tragically wrong, and then it needs to repent. But don't we all? You have consciences like us Europeans. Do they never make you uneasy like us?

*　　*　　*

Away from the limelight, Rowan was notching up some quiet triumphs, most of which barely registered outside the religious press. In this category could be placed his visit to Pakistan at the end of November, hosted by Alexander Malik, Bishop of Lahore. The Archbishop met the country's President and Prime

Minister in separate meetings, repeatedly urging his hosts to do more to protect Christians from persecution. He also called for a review of the blasphemy law (under which anyone accused of desecrating the Koran or insulting Muhammad can receive the death penalty), suggesting that the legislation gave far too much scope for the settling of private scores. As well as visiting a *madrasah* and comforting victims of the earthquake that had lately caused devastation in Kashmir, the Archbishop gave two presentations at the International Islamic University of Islamabad. In the first, he outlined to an audience of students some popular misconceptions about Christianity. In the second, his focus was on the need for greater concord between the faiths: 'dialogue is not proselytism . . . When I enter into dialogue with a person from another religious tradition . . . I am not out to secure agreement, but to secure understanding.'

In late January 2006, he hosted the launch of the Christian–Muslim Forum, an initiative that had emerged from several years' consultation. The Forum has four Christian and four Muslim Co-Presidents, and includes specialists in the fields of community affairs, education, media, family and international relations. Standing next to Tony Blair, Rowan gave a rationale for the Forum which shaded into a general defence of the religious voice in public life: 'This is not about élites. This is about ordinary people talking to each other in ordinary circumstances and working together on the needs and the challenges that face us all.' The object, he said, was to remind society

that faith is a perfectly normal activity for human beings . . . Instead of being an eccentricity, practised by slightly weird British people and very, very strange foreigners, it's just something that belongs to the fabric of civic life in this country . . .

We are not people of faith because we want to make a contribution to civic life: we are people of faith because we believe that what we believe is true. Nonetheless, we need to say in a society that's both sceptical and chaotic at the moment that the commitments of faith to human dignity and liberty are essential to the life of a healthy society.

The importance of this subject was again shown a few days later, as furious Muslims in Europe and elsewhere demonstrated against the printing of caricatures of the Prophet produced by a well-known Danish cartoonist. Some of these protesters became very violent; many carried placards inciting murder. Privately, Rowan shared a common view that the agitators were behaving hysterically. In public, though, he said that the exercise of free speech should be tempered by sensitivity to cultural differences. This meant that once more his fire was chiefly trained on the secular mindset: 'Enlightened attitudes are, understandably, seen by minorities as a refusal to believe that others take their convictions seriously,' he remarked.[13]

The Archbishop's next sally in support of Muslims got him into hotter water. The occasion was a successful motion at the General Synod during its February sessions calling for the Church to review its commercial interests in Israel, and to disinvest from Caterpillar Inc., an American company making giant bulldozers used by the Israeli army to demolish homes in Palestinian areas. Rowan supported the motion (the Church of England had shares in Caterpillar worth £2.5 million), which was also backed by the Anglican Bishop in Jerusalem.

The debate drew familiar charges of bigotry from those who conflate any censure of the Israeli government with anti-Semitism. Cooler heads laid more stress on the overall context:

this included a pledge by the Palestinian group Hamas, now in control of the Gaza Strip, to wipe Israel off the map. Rowan wrote an awkward letter to Jonathan Sacks regretting the synod's decision 'at a time when anti-Semitism is on the rise'.[14] In mitigation, he said that the Church had not decided to do anything, except send a fact-finding mission to Israel. The observation naturally prompted questions about why the debate had taken place at all. Then the Archbishop was handed a lifeline. Sacks denounced the motion in an article for the *Jewish Chronicle*. This gave others a chance to point out that Jewish leaders rarely criticise the Israeli government, despite its seizure of Palestinian land and non-cooperation over nuclear weapons, the evidence of war crimes in Jenin, and the use of bombs in residential areas.

Rowan was not off the rack for long, however. His visit to Sudan in late February provided a further lesson that noble intentions do not speak for themselves in an era of twenty-four-hour news. Shocked by the scale of suffering at camps for displaced people, he issued several plangent appeals for more international aid. But when asked by a BBC journalist whether he could still believe in God after encountering deprivation on such a scale, the Archbishop gave a donnish reply, beginning 'I can't prove that God exists in the way that that tree exists . . .' Although the theological wine-drinker could talk the beer-drinker's language on occasion, this time his common touch had deserted him. The interviewer was left nonplussed, and later remarked to me: 'If the Archbishop of Canterbury can't provide simple Christian reassurance in such circumstances, then who can?'

The broader criticism centred on Rowan's allegedly indul-gent attitude towards Sudan's Islamic government and its support for genocidal policies in the western province of

Darfur. The hook for this implausible story came from a television interview with David Frost, in which the Archbishop deplored at some length the Bush administration's policy towards detainees in Guantanamo Bay. David Blair, Africa editor of the *Daily Telegraph*, then drew the low-minded conclusion that Rowan was more concerned about the fate of 500 Islamists in American custody than that of two million Sudanese refugees. The Lambeth Palace press office responded angrily that the Archbishop had flagged up the woes of Darfur in other interviews. This had been 'all over the Khartoum papers', Jonathan Jennings said. 'Surely the Africa editor reads the Khartoum papers?' This was assuming too much – like imagining that a European correspondent would be up to speed with the Lithuanian press, as Andrew Brown put it.[15] Primates, like politicians, must be prepared to repeat messages ad nauseam, especially on platforms as large as David Frost's, if they are to avoid giving ammunition to their enemies.

Rowan's reluctance to think of himself as a leader surfaced again in a long interview he gave to Alan Rusbridger, editor of the *Guardian*, in March.[16] Rusbridger lifted the lid on a hitherto secret meeting that had taken place between the Archbishop and several senior journalists and clerics a few months previously. Nearly all of the media representatives thought that Dr Williams was insufficiently visible. 'Here', in Rusbridger's words, 'was someone of tremendous intelligence, warmth, integrity and personal charisma and yet . . . for the most part he remains hidden from view.' In reply, Rowan sought to make a strength out of this apparent weakness:

> I know that I'm not the world's greatest strategist . . . but I think
> I need to take more advice on what makes sense. It's a great

temptation to try and do everything or be good at everything. You can't be . . . I just feel that the centrality of highly individual drama – individual struggles, individual views – is not a comfortable place for a Christian to be, perhaps for anyone to be. So I guess the unease is . . . a recognition of the fact that a lot of my professional background has been such as not to make me feel very confident in this.[17]

But didn't most people expect the Archbishop to be a spiritual and moral guide? Rowan queried what he described as the common expectation that archbishops should make statements, usually of a negative, condemnatory kind:

I just wonder a bit whether, when an archbishop condemns something, suddenly in, I don't know, the bedsits of north London, somebody says, 'Oh, I shouldn't be having pre-marital sex,' or in the cells of al-Qaeda, somebody says, 'Goodness, terrorism's wrong, the Archbishop says so. I never thought of that.' I'm not sure that's how it is.[18]

He added that two of his most admired twentieth-century predecessors, William Temple and Michael Ramsey, were sparing in their public interventions. Yet intervene they did. Again, depending on your standpoint, Rowan's reticence will seem either refreshingly in touch with the times, or a missed opportunity. A third view that does not contradict either of these interpretations is that the Archbishop was very keen indeed to avoid confrontation. In Nigeria, the row over the Danish cartoons of Muhammad had led to a wave of anti-Christian violence in which eighty people had died. Archbishop Akinola, writing as President of the Christian Association of Nigeria

(CAN), had then warned Muslims that 'they do not have the monopoly of violence in this nation . . . CAN may no longer be able to contain our restive youths should this ugly trend continue.' When asked about these reckless remarks, Rowan put an extremely benign spin on them. What Akinola meant, he said, was 'Don't be provocative because in an unstable situation, it's as likely the Christians will resort to violence as Muslims will.' Akinola was a man 'who will speak very directly and immediately in crises', Rowan continued. 'I think he meant to issue a warning, which certainly has been taken as a threat, an act of provocation. Others in the Nigerian Church have, I think, found other ways of saying that which have been more measured.'[19]

Were Rusbridger and his colleagues fair in accusing the Archbishop of invisibility? It is certainly true that Rowan had kept a low profile during the second half of 2003. Two years later, though, he complained to me about a lack of media interest in many of his ventures. His website gives proof of intense industry, especially as he has always written most of his own speeches. Taking a brief period – August to November 2005 – almost at random, we can see ample evidence of the Archbishop's presence at the stump:

7 *August*: 'Forget the Tea and Cakes. How the Mothers' Union is Riding to the Rescue of Africa' (article for the *Independent on Sunday*)

29 *September*: 'Law, Power and Peace: Christian Perspectives on Sovereignty' (David Nicholls Memorial Lecture at the University Church, Oxford)

26 *October*: 'The Laws of Ecclesiastical Polity Revisited' (Richard Hooker Lecture at the Temple Church, London)

1 November: Sermon at the St Paul's Service of Remembrance for the victims of the 7 July London bombings

7 November: 'Religion, Culture, Diversity and Tolerance: Shaping the New Europe' (address at the European Policy Centre, Brussels)

10 November: 'Becoming Trustworthy: Respect and Self-Respect' (Temple Address, Church House)

Social outreach remained one of his central concerns. And he remained well able to use the subject strategically, as a means of encouraging the Church's factions to look beyond their own navels. In mid-2006, anti-poverty action took centre-stage with the launch of a church report, *Faithful Cities.*[20] The document appeared twenty-one years after a similar publication, *Faith in the City*, which drew a volley of largely unjust attacks from right-wing politicians in reply. Like its precursor, *Faithful Cities* protested against wealth inequality. It argued that the gap between rich and poor in some places had become so wide that society's different elements were leading parallel but entirely separate lives. The Churches had a duty to 'challenge the thoughtless accumulation of wealth which ignores the needs of the poor, both locally and globally. Churches must not hold back from confronting selfish lifestyles either in their own membership or in the wider population.'

Though not involved in producing the report (*Faithful Cities* was researched over two years by the Commission on Urban Life and Faith, chaired by Baroness Richardson, a Methodist minister), Rowan agreed with its conclusions. At the launch party, he protested against Whitehall's micro-management of regeneration policies, arguing that voluntary groups were spending too much energy on finding new funds to meet the short-term rhythms of government initiatives. The Churches, on the other hand, were stable systems: trustworthy and durable.

Faithful Cities certainly makes the case for robust Christian social action. Church members who tour estates at night with 'street pastor' blazoned on their backs, mentors for disadvantaged children who lag in class, a hostel for former prisoners, a bus that serves as a refuge for prostitutes – these are a few of the enterprises that Christians have set up in urban areas up and down the UK. But there are weaknesses in the report as well, and they map more or less evenly on to Rowan's shortcomings as an economic commentator. Like the Archbishop's Christian Aid lecture, *Faithful Cities* has much to say about the failings of the market economy, and very little about its successes. Moreover, as several of the sharper reviewers pointed out, the report makes the mistake of conflating poverty and inequality. Poverty is the real evil, but it is best alleviated when unemployment is reduced as a result of the dynamism of entrepreneurs and other risk-takers. Sometimes, therefore, inequality is the price paid in vibrant economies for an improvement in the lot of the poor.

Just after midsummer, Rowan issued a momentous, 3,000-word statement to the primates and other bishops warning that the way ahead for Anglicanism lay in a choice between sacrifice and separation. Elaborating on the vision set out in the Windsor Report, he suggested that provinces unwilling to 'limit their local freedoms for the sake of a wider witness' might be granted 'associate' status, as opposed to 'constituent' status, in the Communion. 'Associated Churches' would still be 'bound by historic and perhaps personal links, fed from many of the same sources, but not bound in a single and unrestricted sacramental communion, and not sharing the same constituent structures'. Comparing the relationship with the one between the Church of England and the Methodist Church, the Archbishop said that ' "associated" Churches would not play a direct role in the decision-making of the "constituent" Churches, though they might well be observers'. He then defended ECUSA's critics against the charge of 'blind bigotry against gay people'. The point was that 'no member Church can make significant decisions unilaterally and still expect this to make no difference to how it is regarded in the fellowship'.

Just before the statement was issued, ECUSA appeared to draw back from the prospect of schism when its General Convention backed a motion against the consecration of any bishop 'whose manner of life presents a challenge to the wider Church'. Once again, this compromise offered Rowan and the other powers that be a little more time in which to try to keep Anglicanism's bitterly divided neighbours talking. But the cultural barrier dividing them still looked more like the Berlin Wall than a garden fence.

*　　*　　*

At about this time, the Archbishop hosted a private meeting at Lambeth for a group of Jeffrey John's supporters. Several were friends of Rowan. Their host struck the visitors as 'a very unhappy human being', as one of them put it to me. It was true that he felt buffeted, but negative perceptions of the Archbishop also said much about the disappointment felt by liberals. Life at Lambeth had proved even more arduous than expected, and yet he had always known that the job would be a crown of thorns. As another friend puts it, 'Rowan's world view overall, let alone his view of being Archbishop of Canterbury, might be summed up as "Life's a bitch, but God loves you".'

Self-sacrificial notions aside, what other forces have kept him going? Prayer, of course, has remained one of his bedrocks. So, too, has his family. Jane became a tutor in doctrine at the St Paul's Theological Centre, attached to Holy Trinity, Brompton, and published several more books. Though always popular in Wales, she was even more in her element at Lambeth, partly because she no longer considered it necessary to do things just to please other people. (In Monmouth, on the other hand, she had felt obliged to become patron of the diocesan needlework guild, even though she had never picked up a needle.) And despite her full routine, she continued to be admired for a mixture of calm and sense.

Before she was expecting a child again in the mid-1990s, Rowan said that he did not feel able to be a good parent to a son, because of his aversion to 'masculine' activities such as football. It happened that Pip was developing interests similar to his father's, joining the choir at St Margaret's, Westminster, soon after moving to London. Rhiannon, fourteen at the time of her father's translation to Canterbury, soon took advantage of new opportunities to develop her interest in drama. She performed with the National Youth Theatre, among other groups, before beginning an arts degree at Warwick University in 2006.

Rowan's poise has also remained a source of admiring comment. A typical view comes from Christopher Jones, an adviser to the Archbishops' Council and drafter of some of Rowan's speeches in the House of Lords:

I'm constantly surprised when I meet him to find how resilient he seems, and the way in which the Rowan I know comes bounding out with the quip and the smile and the sense of fun, and the sense of things bubbling up, and I think very wisely he has not allowed himself to be ecclesiastically confined. He's kept a wide range of intellectual interests and has spoken on a huge variety of subjects where he's been interested, and that has helped because it's very important for him to keep his own thinking moving, so that he's not defined by the church problems that he's having to broker all the time. Anybody who didn't have a hinterland away from all that would be destroyed by it.

Writing has naturally dominated this hinterland. Apart from *Tokens of Trust*, the three most important works published during Rowan's early years as Archbishop of Canterbury are *Anglican Identities*,[21] *Why Study the Past?: The Quest for the Historical Church*,[22] and *Grace and Necessity: Reflections on Art and Love*.[23] This quartet of volumes encompasses the gamut of his historical and theological thinking. *Anglican Identities* gives a useful snapshot of its author's thinking about ecclesiology during the pre-Windsor era. Turning the soil of tradition, he begins with a look at some sixteenth-century apologias for the Church of England. Richard Hooker, for example, thought that the ordering of the household of faith required what Rowan terms 'contemplative pragmatism': 'pragmatic' because sin makes the Church more muddled than the tidy-minded are prepared to allow, but 'contemplative' as well, owing to 'the hidden action of God beneath the generally unbroken surface of the world's processes'. Hooker habitually warned his hearers of what an inexact science theology is. As Rowan reminds us, George Herbert gave a similar warning about spiritual experience. In other words, there should be room in the Church for those hanging on by their fingertips, as well as for the firm of faith. And yet Anglicans should not shrink from seeing their weather-beaten Communion as an 'epiphany' of God's glory, not least because the Eucharist is the place where the gap between vision and reality is bridged. Current problems are not overlooked: Rowan grants that Anglicans face 'painfully immediate' questions about what holds them together. For perhaps the last time, though, he disdains the need for tighter controls. This drew a quizzical response from Peter Cornwell, formerly vicar of the University Church in Oxford, and among the mildest of recruits to Roman Catholicism. Reviewing *Anglican Identities* in early 2004, he suggested that 'although Williams repudiates "the necessity of a central executive authority", the pressure of events has moved his Communion in that direction . . . Catholics may be tempted to think that Anglicans will wake up one day to find that they have reinvented the papacy.'[24]

In *Why Study the Past?* (the 2003 Sarum Lectures), the merits and drawbacks of Rowan's arguments in *Anglican Identities* appear transposed into another key. Further stress is laid on the Church's hybrid character: Christ's followers both do and do not accept their Jewish heritage, and their relationship to the world at large is also ambivalent. They are meant to be strangers and pilgrims, citizens of another world. Even when the Church had spread to most corners of the Mediterranean, developed doctrine emerged only after a long and painful recasting of received religious terms. From this Rowan draws a familiar lesson once more – that all theological enquiry is and must remain unfinished business. The book received a keen notice from Eamon Duffy, another distinguished Catholic. But like Cornwell (and, for that matter, respectively harsh and measured Anglican commentators such as Garry Williams and Mike Higton), Duffy was concerned to remind the Archbishop that Christianity provides answers as well as questions:

Tradition [on Rowan Williams's account] can seem a never-
endingly argumentative seminar, constant upheaval without any
point of rest or leverage. Yet if unsettlement is built into the
vocabulary of Christian self-understanding, there is also a venerable Christian vocabulary of solidity, dependability, confidence
in a faith once delivered to the saints, tradition as a rock.[25]

Grace and Necessity is an edited version of the prestigious Clark
Lectures given by the Archbishop in Cambridge in 2005. This
difficult but rewarding book reveals a contrasting side of his
thinking, namely its ambition. Using as a grid the metaphysics of
the French philosopher Jacques Maritain – itself based on the
thought of St Thomas Aquinas – he embarks on a detailed
discussion of Flannery O'Connor, and the draughtsmanship of
David Jones, to ask whether there is an 'unavoidably theological
element' in artistic labour as such. This dauntingly complex area
entails fine but important distinctions between the natural and
supernatural realms. A starting point is furnished by Rowan's
observations about a convergence of emphasis in Thomism and
artistic modernism. At the heart of this overlap stand ideas about
an 'excess' of meaning in the created object. While in the
Thomist view this points towards an awareness of the gratuity of
divine grace, in modernist aesthetics the accent is on the
integrity and autonomy of the artwork.

The year 2005 also saw the reissue of *The Truce of God* in a
revised form. While leaving many of his original reflections on
spirituality and Christian peacemaking unchanged, Rowan
replaced some of his Cold War material with discussion of
the so-called war on terror. This venture was based on a
misplaced confidence that the book's insights remain as relevant
in the post-11 September world as in the Soviet era. On the

contrary, *The Truce of God* is the only book by Rowan not to have stood the test of time. His earlier mistake of being far more critical of his own side than of the West's enemies still appeared wide of the mark, for reasons already broached in our discussion of *Writing in the Dust*. At some points the lack of perspective is very striking. He rightly bemoans the self-righteous rhetoric emerging from the United States under George W. Bush, where many identified the national interest with world rule, and both with the will of God. He is right to judge that the invasion of Iraq was a severe error at best. But it is also surely true that the good-versus-evil mindset anatomised early in *The Truce of God* is displayed even more strongly by Islamic radicals. This simple point is underplayed in Rowan's discourse. So is another consideration germane to the subject: that the British, faced with evidence of multiple jihadist plots since 2005, have on the whole responded with forbearance to those who believe that mass murder is an acceptable response to grievances about government policy.

There are some resonant passages in *The Truce of God*'s second edition, including a paean to the reconciling work of Christians Aware and groups such as Focolare and the Taizé and Sant'Egidio communities. In the end, however, such material serves only to underline the gap between witness literature and comment on the far harsher challenges of politics and international relations. Robert Runcie's reservations about Rowan's book in 1983 still applied two decades on.

*   *   *

When he was on form, Rowan continued to communicate as effectively through talking as through writing. His Alpha supper lecture cited at the start of this book is a good example. It concentrates on the positive case for Christianity, and in passing delivers a blow to crude attacks on faith. Richard Dawkins is perhaps the best known of religion's cultured despisers in the English-speaking world, despite the weaknesses of his case. His best-selling book *The God Delusion*[26] is based on numerous fallacies: not just that the natural sciences provide the only paradigm of warrantable knowledge, but also that God is an item in the universe to be investigated like a physical organism. Since metaphysical claims cannot be measured in a test-tube, the thesis runs, then they must be thrown out altogether. Dawkins has far less to say about the evaluative statements he himself employs willy-nilly.

In short, his arguments can provide a necessary jolt to complacent or unreflective Christians. But his naivety mirrors that of the most superstitious believer. He has not grasped that science achieves its success by the modesty of its ambition, only considering impersonal experience open to potentially endless repetition. Personal experience – let alone spiritual experience – cannot be fitted on to so limited a template.

Several hostile reviewers of *The God Delusion*, including the literary critic Terry Eagleton, have concentrated on Dawkins's theological illiteracy. (Eagleton's notice in the *London Review of Books* famously began by asking readers to 'imagine someone holding forth on biology whose only knowledge of the subject is the *Book of British Birds*, and you have a rough idea of what it feels like to read Richard Dawkins on theology'.) A strong case can certainly be built from this starting point. Dawkins's errors include reading the Bible as a literalistic report, and misinter-preting St Thomas's arguments for the existence of God as foundations for religious belief, rather than as buttresses for convictions reached on other grounds. Rowan, too, has sketched a theological case against Dawkins. During a lecture at Swansea University in 2007, for example, he spoke of the gulf between a Christian understanding of the Creator and the picture presented in *The God Delusion*. But the Archbishop has also seen that the weakest points in Dawkins's argument are philosophical rather than theological, because everyone, theist and atheist alike, has all sorts of convictions that cannot be demonstrated in a laboratory. In an interview published in 2005, for instance, the Archbishop gave short shrift both to Dawkins's overarching assumptions, and to his notion of the selfish 'meme' – the putative mental structure that reproduces itself:

I think that a very respectable sector of the philosophical community would say that reductionism – the mind is no more than physical processes – is actually a philosophically inept way of coming at the issue, because 'no more than physical process' is itself an analysis that presupposes other sorts of process than physical process. And you end up caught in a philosophical trap . . . What fascinates me about the notions of the selfish gene and the selfish 'meme' is that you need metaphors drawn from highly sophisticated intentional accounts of human interaction to describe supposedly physical processes. That ought to give you pause, because it suggests that reductionism collapses on itself. Selfish is a highly loaded, highly sophisticated word. Selfish is a word about motives, not material processes. Selfish is a word that assumes things about purposes, consciousness, and all the rest of it. And you end up with what seems to me an almost comical mythology of little things running around with intentions inside your head or inside your organism. It's what philosophers sometimes call the homunculus problem, the little man who

does things. The selfish gene is bad enough. The selfish meme –
the mental structure that reproduces itself – I can't make any
sense of, philosophically speaking. Come back, A. J. Ayer, I say,
on that point.[27]

Three years later, Rowan enlarged his focus in the following
account of the religious outlook at the start of his major study,
Dostoevsky: Language, Faith and Fiction:

The current rash of books hostile to religious faith will one day
be an interesting subject for some sociological analysis. They
consistently suggest a view of religion which, if taken seriously,
would also evacuate a number of other human systems of
meaning, including quite a lot of what we unreflectively think
of as science. That is, they treat religious belief almost as a solitary
aberration in a field of human rationality; a set of groundless
beliefs about matters of fact, resting on – at best – faulty and weak
argumentation. What they normally fail to do is to attend to
what it is religious people actually do and say – and also to attend
to the general question of how systems of meaning or 'world-
views' work . . .

All of which is to say that no system of perceiving and
receiving the world can fail to depend on imagination, the
capacity to see and speak into and out of a world that defies any
final settlement as to how it shall be described. The most would-
be reductive account of reality still reaches for metaphor, still
depends on words that have been learned and that have been
used elsewhere. So it should not be too difficult to see that a map
of the intellectual world that presents it as a struggle between
rival pictures, well-founded and ill-founded ways of describing
things, literal and fanciful perspectives or even natural and

supernatural vision, is a poor one . . . that threatens to devour itself in the long run, if the search is for the absolutely well-founded and unadorned. How shall we move the cultural discussion on from a situation in which religious perspectives are simply assumed to be bad descriptions of what can be better talked about in simpler terms?

This will involve the discipline of following through exactly what it is that the language of a particular religious tradition allows its believers to see – that is, what its imaginative resources are. When believers are engaged (as they routinely are, despite what may seem to be assumed by the critics of faith) in society and politics and the arts in ways that are recognizable to non-believers, how are their perceptions actually and specifically moulded by the [resources] of their tradition? . . .

Characteristically this repertoire of resources – in any religious tradition – is chaotically varied, not just a matter of a few leading ideas or doctrines. It includes the visual and the aural . . . It includes formative practices, rites, which leave their semantic traces in unexpected settings. And it includes the legacy of others who have engaged in the same ways, at various levels of sophistication. The forming of a corporate imagination is something that continues to be the more or less daily business of religious believers; and it needs to be acknowledged that this is a process immeasurably more sophisticated than the repetitive dogmatism that is so widely assumed to be the sole concern of those who employ religious language.[28]

Away from his soap box, Dawkins has shown a more equable side. In 2006, he and his wife Lalla Ward, the actress whose roles have included Dr Who's assistant, accepted an invitation to a party at Lambeth Palace. Pip Williams is a devoted fan of the Time Lord, and during this encounter all the talk was TARDIS-related. That was fortunate for *The God Delusion*'s author. Victory in the is-religion-credible? contest already belonged to Williams Snr.

9

Bushfires

Bishop Stephen Sykes once gave a crisp account of why he feels both attracted and repelled by Anglicanism.[1] On the positive side, he listed four chief strengths: a 'quiet and confident Catholicism', an openness to a range of spiritual traditions, the exercise of authority with consent, and a developing baptismal ecclesiology. His dislikes included 'the triviality and superficiality into which our eclectic openness can fall', 'the proneness of Anglicanism to fashionable causes' and 'the all-consuming ruthlessness of the campaigners, for whom politics is all'.

The time after Rowan's statement in June 2006 demonstrated that the last of Sykes's *bêtes noires* was growing more baneful still. Liberals tended to oppose the Covenant idea in principle, seeing it as a betrayal of Anglican capaciousness, and a further sign of the Archbishop's apparent shift to the theological Right. In a sermon touching on Rowan's letter, Marilyn McCord Adams argued that 'Challenge and Hope' had failed to distinguish properly between unity and truth, instead positing unity 'or, rather, unified judgement . . . as a criterion of truth'. The Bible, she argued, 'tells of how status-quo conservatism, which complacently settles into its accustomed values and lifestyles, is also risky. Where systematic evils are concerned, waiting upon one another runs the greater chance of betraying the gospel of God.'[2]

Speaking for an equally significant body of opinion, Andrew Goddard, an Evangelical moral theologian, later opposed the opposers in an article justifying the Covenant:

> It is clear . . . that much of the most vehement opposition to the covenant comes from those most determined to lead Anglicanism in an increasingly liberal direction theologically and morally. They oppose any idea of covenant because they do not wish to be accountable to the wider Communion or to develop means to enable us to keep in step with one another . . . The covenant process . . . offers the hope of being able . . . to express biblical and credal faith and to develop the structures of a distinctive global Anglicanism . . . [3]

Yet any idea that most conservatives would be pacified by Rowan's initiative was misplaced. Within a few days, the Nigerian House of Bishops had dismissed the Archbishop of Canterbury's notion of a two-tier membership as 'brilliant as the heartbeat of a leader who wants to preserve the unity of the Church by accommodating every shred of opinion no matter how unbiblical, all because we want to make everyone feel at home'. [4] Also from Nigeria came word that the Global South and Council of Anglican Churches in Africa would hold their own alternative to the Lambeth Conference two years later, unless 'the apostles of revisionist agenda repent and retrace their steps'. A communiqué from Nigeria's Episcopal Synod regretted 'the inability of the see of Canterbury to prevent further impairment of the unity of the Church', and suggested that moral justification for the Lambeth Conference was doubtful, because bishops in ECUSA, Canada and some parts of Britain had 'abandoned the biblical faith of our fathers'.

But by expressing themselves in this way, the Nigerians had failed to see a major implication of Rowan's letter: that the Archbishop of Canterbury does not (and cannot) run the Communion. To less subjective observers, the document entailed a pragmatic acknowledgement that the big choices now lay elsewhere – chiefly in Africa and the United States.

Away from these respective poles of the Anglican Communion, the portents were equally unpropitious. Archbishop Peter Jensen of Sydney held a press conference to announce that the Anglican Communion had now split: 'To use an analogy, partners have separated, although they have not divorced.' According to Jensen, Rowan's statement was late recognition of an irreconcilable split caused by Gene Robinson's consecration. And in the United States, the recent election of the Bishop of Nevada, Katharine Jefferts Schori, to succeed Frank Griswold as Presiding Bishop prompted six ECUSA dioceses to request alternative primatial oversight. Representatives of the dissenting sees – San Joaquin (based in Fresno, California), Fort Worth (Texas), Pittsburgh, Springfield (Illinois), South Carolina and Central Florida – objected to Jefferts Schori both because of her voting record on the sexuality issue, and because of her first sermon to her Church's General Convention, with its reference to Jesus as Mother. A further sign of the deepening alliance between hardliners emerged when Martyn Minns, rector of Truro Episcopal Church in Fairfax, Virginia, was elected as an America-based missionary bishop for the Church of Nigeria. The move was described by the Bishop of Virginia, Peter Lee, as 'an affront to the traditional, orthodox understanding of Anglican provincial autonomy'.

In the meantime, Rowan shifted his gaze back onto the world at large. He spoke forcefully on the airwaves[5] against Israel's invasion of Lebanon, and renewed his call for peace in an article for the *Observer*.[6] He repeated many earlier pleas for prison reform in a speech on penal policy at Worcester Cathedral, in the process showing his aversion to private-sector solutions by questioning the government's willingness to franchise the prison service to private companies. And he completed a fence-mending exercise with the Jewish community by confirming that Israel's two chief rabbis, Shlomo Amar and Yonah Metzger, would come to London a few weeks later to sign a framework for dialogue with Anglicanism. (The encounter had been due to take place in May, but was postponed after the Archbishop's disagreement with Jonathan Sacks.)

Especially important to Rowan personally was his two-week visit to China in mid-October. This was probably not a moment for high-wire heroics. Undiplomatic language from church leaders can easily result in even greater persecution for Chinese Christians. The Archbishop's message of tolerance and openness was nevertheless easy to decipher. China was emerging as a senior partner in the fellowship of nations, and had the potential to do much good, he told an audience of scholars in Nanjing, all of whom had visited the UK on a British government scheme. 'Yours is a society which will have messages to give to the rest of the world,' he said, 'but I hope, too, that it is a society willing to receive and to hear what the rest of the world has to say – and that process begins in experiences like yours.'

He preached to a congregation of more than 1,000 in Shanghai, toured the city's cathedral – designed by Gilbert Scott in 1869 and handed back to China's official (government-controlled) Church by the municipal authority in 2004. He gave a substantial address, 'What is a University?', at Wohan, and had meetings with senior politicians, NGO representatives and business leaders. Like other people accustomed to seeing the world's wealth concentrated (with very ambiguous consequences) in North America and Europe, Rowan was impressed by both the economic and the spiritual vibrancy that he found. He drew a link between these two phenomena at the end of the trip. There are perhaps a hundred million Christians in China, roughly half of whom belong to the unofficial or underground Churches, which face persecution for not submitting to state control. Rowan was criticised in some quarters for not giving enough public support to underground Christians. But before returning to England, he revealed[7] that he had made representations on behalf of half a dozen Christians, from both the official and unofficial Churches, at very senior levels of the Chinese government. He singled out one case, that of Pastor Chai, who had been arrested for illicitly trading Bibles.

The Archbishop also explained why he had not been able to meet underground Christians formally: doing so would have placed them at risk. But he had met them informally. And he also spoke warmly of the official Churches (official and unofficial Christians often co-exist without antagonism, and even co-operate with one another): 'We are content to work with a Church which we see to be lively and active and capable of taking initiatives here . . . We are a long way past the Cultural Revolution: we're a long way past the situation where there was a systematic attempt to block out or extirpate religion,' he told a press conference. Afterwards, preaching at Chaoyang Church in Beijing, he said that people outside China should not seek to 'impose' their conservative or liberal models of Christianity on the country. 'We are encouraged to see a Church that is trying to find its own way forward honestly – find a language that really belongs in this place.'

At the same time, Britain had become consumed by debate over the legitimacy of the full veil worn by some Muslim women, and seen either as a badge of identity, or as betokening a rejection of Western culture. Rowan's instincts were with diversity rather than French-style uniformity, and he said so in a wry article for *The Times* which made front-page news.[8] The proverbial visitor from Mars, he wrote, 'might have imagined that the greatest immediate threat to British society was religious war, fomented by "faith schools", cheered on by thousands of veiled women and the Bishops' Benches in the House of Lords'. Commentators were solemnly asking 'if it were not time for Britain to become a properly secular society'. At this stage, his words drew almost universal praise, especially as the context included a government suggestion that faith schools generally be forced to take more pupils with other kinds of religious background or none. The idea was quickly abandoned after an effective counter-attack led by the Catholic hierarchy.

*   *   *

In November, the first full encounter between the Archbishop and Pope Benedict took place. There was also a silly but tellingly influential news story about Rowan's alleged unsuitability for the Church's top office. I noted at the start of this book that much of the media coverage at this time centred not on events in Rome, but on the right of a British Airways employee, Nadia Eweida, to wear a crucifix around her neck at work. Her case was taken up by John Sentamu, recently translated from Birmingham to York, and already feted in the press as the energetic, confident outsider capable of getting the Christian message across to the man or woman in the street. The unfavourable comparison drawn between the two archbishops was not based on anything that Rowan had said. But this fuss followed a larger commotion in which his strengths and difficulties – not all of them weaknesses – as a public speaker were highlighted as rarely before. Speaking to the *Catholic Herald*[9] on the eve of his departure for Italy, he granted that, in principle, the Church of England might one day reverse its decision to ordain women as priests.

Strictly speaking, this statement was true. The Church was in a process of reception: it had given traditionalists a legal standing through the 1993 Act of Synod, which recognised what came to be termed 'two integrities' on the issue. But Rowan made clear that he remained a firm supporter of women's ordination, and that 'practically' he did not see how the Church's position could be changed. Yet this did not stop the *Herald* and the *Daily Telegraph* from running headlines suggesting that Rowan had reopened the debate, and that the Church might rethink its position.

Some religious affairs correspondents rightly brushed this claim aside. But its publication was due not only to mischief-making, but to a sense that the Archbishop had form as an equivocator. Sometimes, a media grilling is partly a test of an interviewee's willingness to wear a mask or act a role. If Rowan made a mistake, then, it lay in treating his interviewer as an adult, and not foreseeing the manner in which his words would be twisted.

There was fury at Lambeth Palace. A statement said that Dr Williams had dismissed as 'wilfully misleading' reports that he was doubtful about women's ordination, or thought that the move had been 'wrong', or that a revisiting of the question was likely, necessary or desirable. He then made up for any earlier verbal clumsiness with a polished performance in Italy. Far fuller than in 2003, his schedule included visits to St John Lateran (Rome's Cathedral), to the Catacombs and to the Sant'Egidio community, as well as a ceremony commemorating recent martyrdoms in the Melanesian Brotherhood, and ecumenical Vespers with Cormac Murphy-O'Connor in the Cardinal's titular church, Santa Maria sopra Minerva.

At Sant'Anselmo, the liturgical institute, Rowan spoke on 'Benedict and the Future of Europe', describing modern work (exaggeratedly to some ears) as a 'twenty-four-hour business' that 'follows no daily or even weekly rhythms', but is 'sporadically interrupted' when employees become 'infantilised by a vast industry that purports to guess our wants before we ask'. At the Pontifical Academy of Social Sciences, housed in the shadow of St Peter's, he defended the legitimacy of 'public' religion in an address, 'Secularism, Faith and Freedom'.

By the admission of Vatican officials, the centrepiece of the visit was a success. A rare honour had been extended to the visitors: the central door of St Peter's was opened for them on their way into the Basilica. The Archbishop prayed at the tombs of John Paul II, John Paul I, Paul VI and John XXIII before receiving a tour of the Sistine Chapel from Cardinal Kasper. When he at last came face to face with Peter's latest successor, his face evinced unsuppressed delight. The two men spoke in private for longer than planned before reporters and others were invited back into Benedict's private library to witness the formal speeches. The company included Jane Williams, wearing a small black veil in accordance with protocol, and Pip, who was introduced to the Pope along with the Lambeth Palace staff and a group of Anglican bishops.

Part of the Pope's public message to the Archbishop was chastening. He spoke of 'serious obstacles to ecumenical progress' posed by liberal attitudes to sexual morality, and by the prospect of women bishops in the Church of England. But he also underlined the 'reconciliation and friendship' between Anglicans and Roman Catholics which had evolved over the past forty years, and confirmed that the work of ARCIC would be furthered. The chemistry remained good over lunch, during which Rowan was asked about the fruits of women's ministry in the Church of England before the conversation became more abstract. Pope and Archbishop have much in common theologically, despite their differences over questions of church order and certain ethical issues. Both share a classical, sacramental perspective shaped by mid-twentieth-century French and German thinkers; both are steeped in Augustine. Not for the first time, Rowan reflected on how much he has in common with conservative Christians; but the urge to draw closer to Rome would probably have been there in any case. He is naturally aware that the Eastern Mediterranean formed the Church's first geographical centre, and that when Rome rose in importance, the pattern of ecclesiastical authority was a two-centred ellipse, rather than a circle. In their optimistic moments, ecumenical pioneers such as Henry Chadwick hoped Rome might come to acknowledge Anglicanism as another ellipse stretching westwards. Chadwick lived to be disappointed, and was right to feel that the Vatican was at least as responsible as the Anglican Communion for erecting road blocks to unity. But the urge to cut across confessional barriers lives on, and explains Rowan's cautious response to the campaign for women bishops in England.

At home, media absorption in the Eweida case had been sharpened by the disclosure that British Airways permits its female Muslim employees to wear headscarves. Richard Chartres, the Bishop of London, expressed a widely held view in describing the case as 'very important and symbolic'. The 'historic majority faith' was being treated 'with a greater measure of disrespect than others', he said. The *Daily Mail* voiced several complaints about the Archbishop of Canterbury's apparent silence on the matter, but when asked about it during his press conference in Rome, Rowan gave a punchy answer revealing that consultations had begun on a possible disinvestment in BA shares. Later that day, faced with losing the Church of England's £10 million stake, the airline hastily announced a review of its dress code. 'It is just perhaps worth noting with some irony that among the duty-free items for sale [at British airports] are some crosses,' Rowan commented.

With regard to Christian symbols, then, there was no division between England's two Anglican primates. But Sentamu went further, questioning the behaviour of a Muslim woman who had refused to remove her veil in court. The *Mail* was enthralled, summing up its view in the standfirst to its profile of the Archbishop of York: 'As the Church stands accused of PC conformity and weak leadership, meet one man brave enough to challenge the "chattering classes" and their contempt for Britain's Christian values . . .'[10] This was always going to be easier for York than for Canterbury, as we have noted. But although Rowan's position did not match the easy binaries favoured by the press, it was certainly different from Sentamu's in important respects. For example, he was and remains wary about any suggestion that greater public deference should be paid to Christianity than to other faiths. And historians looking into the background of his sharia law lecture fifteen months afterwards could do worse than to read his 'Secularism, Faith and Freedom' lecture. It was vital that religious convictions, whether Muslim or Christian, be accommodated in the public square, he urged. 'Faith is the root of freedom, and programmatic secular-ism cannot deliver anything comparable.' He conceded that Muslims were divided over how strong their allegiance to non-Muslim societies should be, but still insisted that Islam was by no means as unlike Christianity as was often thought. The ranks of those who disagree with this assessment are enormous. Rowan, however, stands by it. His Vatican lecture also throws light on his more conservative interventions – notably in January 2007, when he and Sentamu both backed an attempt by the Catholic Church in England and Wales to gain exemption from a law requiring agencies to consider gay couples as adoptive parents.

Two developments early in the new year served to crystallise Rowan's church-related difficulties. First, he was attacked by Bishop Paul Marshall of Bethlehem, Pennsylvania, who de-scribed relations between the Archbishop of Canterbury and the Episcopal Church as 'distant, confused and multiply triangu-lated'.[11] Though well-intentioned, Marshall said, Rowan was spending more time talking to Bishop Duncan than to 'our entire House of Bishops'. Meanwhile, the Episcopal Church was following the Archbishop's 'own carefully thought-out teach-ings on sexuality, teaching that he only last year dismissed as a sin of his academic youth'.[12] Marshall and other Episcopalians were observing the 'withdrawal of a human who was friend, teacher and colleague to many in this Church, with no notice that either his opinions or commitment were in flux'.

The fire-breathers of the Right were more scornful still. The greatest piece of unpleasantness from this period derived from an indictment of Rowan's allegedly heterodox beliefs produced by an ultra-conservative Illinois-based group, the Society for the Propagation of Reformed Evangelical Anglican Doctrine.[13] Long, stodgily written and one-sided, this document is little more than a piece of contumely. The Archbishop is represented as a wolf in sheep's clothing whose apparent moderation is to be discounted by such factors as his friendship with senior bishops in the Episcopal Church and his willingness to republish 'The Body's Grace'.[14] Homosexuality is thus once more the presenting issue, but the discussion again recalls that of other hostile critics such as Garry Williams, in claiming that the Archbishop has a highly subjective view of Christian doctrine as a whole. At times the argument becomes farcical; for example, when it is claimed that 'Williams worked for many years before becoming Archbishop of Canterbury to replace the Anglican Faith with a different kind of faith which adhered to the sovereign authority of man's reason, intelligence and experience, and promotes a new moral code . . .'.

Questions about power are never far from the surface: for instance, the document expresses anger over Rowan's decision in 2005 to appoint a liberal, Archbishop Peter Carnley of Perth, as chairman of the panel of reference to consider applications from dissenting congregations for alternative episcopal oversight. If the indictment has any value, it lies in the assiduity with which Rowan's many pro-gay comments are enumerated. These nuggets include a record of an interview that the then Archbishop of Wales gave to Anglican Media Sydney in May 2002, in which he defended his having ordained a priest in a gay relationship as follows: 'I am not convinced that a homosexual has to be celibate in every imaginable circumstance. But if that were the case, I would also want to be sure that their attitude to their sexual habits is a responsible, prayerful and theologically informed one.'

*　　*　　*

These volleys preceded the year's Primates' Meeting, held in Tanzania. Some observers, calculating that the event would resemble the Dromantine débâcle, fell to writing the script before events had unfolded. This assumption was perhaps understandable. The primates were holed up in a heavily guarded wing of the White Sands Hotel, in a coastal resort fifteen miles north of Dar es Salaam, and the press office of the official headquarters was inside the security ring designed to keep journalists out. Next door, in the Beachcomber Hotel, primates from the Global South had arrived four days beforehand to plan their strategy. One of their number, when challenged by Jonathan Petre of the *Daily Telegraph*, boasted: 'This isn't an alternative headquarters. It *is* the headquarters.'

The Global South group were accompanied by advisers and lobbyists from England and the United States, including Martyn Minns of the Convocation of Anglicans in North America (CANA) and Chris Sugden. Led by Peter Akinola, they pressed for the solution demanded in a communiqué issued from Kigali in September 2006: a separate Anglican jurisdiction in the United States, in the shape of a new province, which would include both CANA and another conservative group, the Anglican Mission in America.

Things didn't quite conform to plan. Akinola, not Rowan, was outmanoeuvred over the days that followed. The final communiqué presented the House of Bishops of the Episcopal Church of the United States with an ultimatum to clarify its position on same-sex blessings by 30 September. More significantly, the primates signed up to a proposed 'pastoral scheme' to provide oversight for conservative parishes in the US. Interventions from overseas provinces would be expected to stop.

The pastoral scheme would include a 'Primatial Vicar', a suggestion previously advanced by Katharine Jefferts Schori. On the Sunday, all the primates bar Akinola took part in a Eucharist at Zanzibar Cathedral, even though six refused to share communion with the Presiding Bishop of ECUSA. Behind the scenes, Rowan showed the fibre he had been accused of lacking at other moments.

Rowan then codified his position in a letter to the primates at the beginning of March. He acknowledged that the Tanzania meeting had been 'far from an easy few days', but maintained that it was marked by honest conversation and a direct reckoning with the Communion's problems. He stressed his view that ECUSA – lately restyled as The Episcopal Church or TEC – should act on the proposals 'with all seriousness and despatch'. 'Once a sufficiently strong scheme is in place within the Episcopal Church,' he said, 'then this should be sufficient for all dissenting congregations and dioceses to find their home within it.' He affirmed the 'shared conviction' that the Windsor Report pointed the right way ahead; that the Covenant was 'the clearest way for our mutual trust and interdependent life to be renewed in the long term'; and that Lambeth 1.10 was the 'standard of teaching on matters of sexual morality for the Communion'. While acknowledging that the primates could offer the Episcopal Church only advice and suggestions, he stressed that 'We cannot wait for another General Convention [due in 2009] for further clarification.' A readiness by the leadership of the Episcopal Church 'to live by that same formal standard of teaching on these matters which applies elsewhere in the Communion is perhaps the first and most important step in the way forward'.

The Americans were unimpressed. At a meeting in mid-

March, they rejected the proposals for alternative oversight made at the Tanzania meeting, and asked for an urgent meeting with the Archbishop of Canterbury and the Primates' Standing Committee. They argued that the 2006 General Convention had 'struggled mightily' to reckon with the Windsor Report, and spoke of the suffering caused by violations of their provincial boundary. Yielding to the primates' demands before the next General Convention would compromise the Episcopal Church's autonomy and violate its founding principles, they averred.

The Archbishop did not at first reply to the request for a meeting; when at length he announced that he would see the American bishops in September, many thought that the long time frame gave proof of standoffishness. Rowan sought to soften the ill-feeling with a conciliatory statement during a two-day visit to Toronto in mid-April. He spoke of the importance of keeping up personal relations and conversations. 'My aim is to try and keep people together around the table as long as possible on this; to understand one another; and to encourage local churches on this side of the Atlantic and elsewhere to ask what they might need to do to keep in that conversation . . .'[15]

To Peter Akinola, the Episcopal Church's decision constituted further provocation. In early May, despite appeals to desist from Rowan and Katharine Jefferts Schori, he went to Virginia to consecrate Martyn Minns as a bishop under CANA auspices. For years, journalists and others in Britain had been crying wolf over the inevitability of schism. Now that it appeared to have happened, most papers ignored the story. Some American journalists gave the Archbishop of Nigeria more of a run for his money. Writing in the *Falls Church News-Press*, for example,

Wayne Bessen used salty language to portray Akinola as a hypocritical busybody far more eager to meddle in other parts of the world than to face up to chronic rates of sexual promiscuity and political corruption in his own country: 'If Akinola were a real leader, he would be at home fighting disease and tyranny, while leading the opposition against an illegal election. Instead of demonstrating such *cojones,* Akinola is leaving his countrymen to fight this battle, while he jets to America to obsess about Bishop Robinson's *cojones.*'[16]

Since invitations to a Lambeth Conference are in the gift of the Archbishop of Canterbury, attention now focused on how hospitable Rowan would be the following year. Hardliners felt that pro-gay liberals in North America should be excluded en masse, but the host decided to adopt the most peaceable approach consistent with his earlier stances. Only three bishops – Gene Robinson, Martyn Minns and Nolbert Kunonga, a heavily criticised associate of the Zimbabwean dictator, Robert Mugabe – were explicitly named as having been dropped from the guest list when an announcement was made in late May.

*   *   *

Rowan might have wished to be off the guest list for Lambeth himself. Talk about his personal Calvary abounded at this time, and although some of it seemed cloying, it was nonetheless obvious that his life remained very arduous indeed. Some friends suggested that his least worst option was to knuckle down until after the Conference, and then to think about retiring soon after. A sense that the Williamses themselves might be considering this option came in late 2006, when Jane told one of my sources that being a bishop had killed her father, and she didn't want her husband to suffer the same fate.

Yet a decision of this kind was always going to hinge on factors other than personal stress. In any case, temporary deliverance was at hand. For two months in the summer of 2007, Rowan went away on a sabbatical that began at Georgetown, the Jesuit-run university in Washington, DC. He originally planned to be there for all of June and July. In the event, after press rumblings about the length of his absence, he decided to spend half of his leave in Canterbury instead. The decision enabled him to conduct Pip's confirmation service, among other duties. August, as usual, was a holiday month, which meant that he had over twelve weeks' liberty in all. Freedom did not equal rest. On the contrary, he applied himself to a labour as gruelling as anything he had yet undertaken: the writing of *Dostoevsky: Language, Faith and Fiction*.[17] This 100,000-word essay was published twelve months later.

Though modestly disclaiming specialist credentials, Rowan is certainly well placed to offer guidance on the great Russian's status as a 'religious' writer. He maintains that in *The Brothers Karamazov*, Dostoevsky's most important work addressing Christian themes, the novelist is not offering his readers a set of arguments about the existence or non-existence of God, but a picture of 'what faith and the lack of it will *look* like in the political and social world of his day'.[18] Rowan points out that during the twentieth century, Dostoevsky was regularly seen as a spokesman for anguished agnosticism: readers whose minds had been formed in a post-religious climate assumed that the 'irresolution' of his narratives was proof of the author's own lack of conviction, 'whatever his professions of faith in his public and private writing'. This secularist reading of *The*

Brothers Karamazov presupposes that a central figure such as Ivan expresses a single point of view, when his opinions change repeatedly; and that his parable of the Grand Inquisitor (a central passage in the narrative) 'is a definitive and unironic statement, both within the novel and in terms of Dostoevsky's whole narrative strategy'.[19] Far from reflecting a deeply divided authorial mind, Rowan suggests, the text 'consciously writes out the to and fro of dialogue, always alerting us to the dangers of staying with or believing uncritically what we have just heard'.[20]

His discussion develops in dialogue with William Hamilton, who airbrushed Dostoevsky's faith from the picture, and others whose interpretations Rowan finds more palatable, including Mikhail Bakhtin, theologians such as Nicolas Berdyaev and Karl Barth, and, among contemporary anglophone commentators, Stewart Sutherland. It will be evident from this brief digest that Rowan's conclusion about *The Brothers Karamazov* recalls his reading of Eliot's strategy in *Four Quartets*. Dostoevsky's novels are not explicit works of advocacy. Instead, they ask us, in effect,

> whether we can imagine a human community of language and feeling in which, even if we were incapable of fully realizing it, we knew what was due to each other, whether we could imagine living in the consciousness of a solidity or depth in each other that no amount of failure, suffering or desolation could eradicate.[21]

On this basis it could be argued that Dostoevsky observes the world with 'appalled compassion' – the quality that the Archbishop has ascribed to Shakespeare. Rowan also sees a musical correlate for this attitude in the work of Bach (notwithstanding the composer's status as 'an immensely prosaic, harassed figure', scribbling his compositions in the interstices of 101 daily chores) and other religious composers such as William Byrd. In June 2008, when he appeared on *Private Passions*, the Radio 3 music-and-discussion programme hosted by Michael Berkeley, Rowan chose the final chorus of the *St Matthew Passion* as an example of the limits to which musical expression can go, and remarked that Bach had 'the freedom to look, to feel without protection, and still to sense that there is something sayable on the far side'. His other choices were Bach's Concerto for Oboe and Strings, John Dowland's *Lachrimae* Pavane, Byrd's 'Christ Rising Again from the Dead', Mozart's *The Magic Flute*, Britten's *The Burning Fiery Furnace* and, for light relief, Schumann's Piano Concerto and a Welsh folk song, 'The Pure Bird'.

The broadcast gave him a chance to read a passage from one of his recently written poems, in which the Passion narrative is imagined as a sea voyage during a long, wakeful night, and the final chorus of Bach's oratorio, *Wir setzen uns mit Tränen nieder* (We Sit Down and Weep), provides a chance to reflect after a long journey:

Back to the headland fogs, exhausted
with new grief, old treacheries, the view without
    prospect,
rain falling in a slow afternoon, between light
and dark, no questions any more; the long grey
leaving of the day that never reaches night; the
    turning
water that will never carry us to the pole of sleep.

373

White nights; wir setzen uns in some welcoming
   chair
to wait. Scored down the sky, the neighing
of a car alarm, night's horses running sluggishly,
and then the unquiet of the muffled room as it bobs
on a frustrated tide that never breathes out, never
jolts into the wooden warmth of dock.

Wood, pulsing unevenly with a tired surge
as the fire fades; five o'clock cloud and damp,
clogging the throat. Slowly the line is drawn
again, tight between sea and sky, though not
where we remember, settled after the night's
fast-running sweats. With the dawn, sleep soft.

This deeply felt passage comes from 'Matthäuspassion: Sea Pictures', one of several religious poems in *Headwaters*,[22] his 2008 collection. Another, 'Resurrection: Borgo San Sepolcro',[23] was written at speed after a visit to the Tuscan town where Piero della Francesca's great painting of Christ emerging from the tomb is exhibited:

Today it is time. Warm enough, finally,
to ease the lids apart, the wax lips of a breaking bud
defeated by the steady push, hour after hour,
opening to show wet and dark, a tongue exploring,
an eye shrinking against the dawn. Light
like a fishing line draws its catch straight up,
then slackens for a second. The flat foot drops,
the shoulders sag. Here is the world again, well-known,
the dawn greeted in snoring dreams of a familiar

winter everyone prefers. So the black eyes
fixed half-open, start to search, ravenous,
imperative, they look for pits, for hollows where
their flood can be decanted, look
for rooms ready for commandeering, ready
to be defeated by the push, the green implacable
rising. So he pauses, gathering the strength
in his flat foot, as the perspective buckles under him,
and the dreamers lean dangerously inwards. Contained,
exhausted, hungry, death running off his limbs like
   drops
from a shower, gathering himself. We wait,
paralysed as if in dreams, for his spring.

Headwaters contains further translations – this time from the Welsh of D. Gwenallt Jones and the Russian of Inna Lisnianskaya (a poet born between the wars in what is now Azerbaijan, and sometimes likened to Anna Akhmatova) – and a set of sonnets offering riffs on Shakespeare plays. 'Macbeth'[24] vividly realises the sleepless worlds of the murderer and his wife, whose baby has died soon after birth:

The muscles twitch, the skin crawls, all night long:
try again. Try to sleep, try to discover
the last orgasm that will take you into quiet,
the muffling is the itching mind. And each
new thrust will only coil and hone the nerves,
the lockjawed fluttering wakefulness. Be innocent
he says, of the knowledge, dearest chuck, withdrawing
slowly into an empty nursery. He sees her
playing with the dead child. She must be fed

with silences, tilts of the head, averted eyes.
Between them, through the itchy darkness,
move the unspoken things. As they drive desperately
at knifepoint into each other, they will never say
what each sees in the empty room over the other's
  shoulder.

Perhaps Rowan's most valuable statement of his poetic vision
comes in the Preface he wrote to a book about the Incredible
String Band. (The invitation came in early 2003, soon after he
included one of the group's tracks in his *Desert Island Discs*
selections.) This brief essay sets out what he sees as poetry's
fourfold function. It is meant to take the reader into the realm of
myth – 'the stories that give points of reference for plotting your
way in the inner and outer world'. It is meant for celebration –
'to clothe ordinary experience with extraordinary words so that
we see the radiance in the ordinary, whether it's in landscape or
in love or whatever'. It is meant for satire – 'to give us a sideways
glance on familiar ways of talking or of behaving or exercising
power, so that we're not bewitched by what looks obvious and
wants us to think it's obvious'. And fourth, it is meant for lament
– 'to give us ways of looking at our losses and our failures that
save us from despair and apathy'.[25]

The Archbishop lauds the Incredible String Band's songs for
corresponding 'with astonishing completeness' to this definition.
Celebration and lament are the common coin of rock music,
he observes, but few groups move successfully outside these
registers:

for a lot of us growing up in the late Sixties and early Seventies,
there was a gap in the heart where [the] very traditional bardic,

376

even shamanic, sense of poetry was looking for expression; and the ISB did just that. Forget the clichés about psychedelic and hallucinogenic vagueness: this was work of extraordinary emotional clarity and metaphorical rigour – an unusual combination.

He goes on to marvel at the wealth of allusion – to Sufism, Celtic myth, biblical and Gnostic symbols – deployed by the band, and 'a versatility in musical idiom worthy of Lennon and McCartney at their best'.

Undernoticed elsewhere, his conclusion is worth quoting in full for what it unveils about the religious artist as a young man:

> For those of us who fell in love with the ISB, there was a feeling of breathing the air of a very expansive imagination indeed. It was all right to be enchanted – but not bewitched (see above) – by colossal and antique symbols; all right at the same time to be thinking about the experiences of 'ordinary' first loves and betrayals; and all right to find the earnest nonsense of real hallucinogenic maunderings funny. There was no one quite like them; we liked to think it was a very grown-up taste, but that makes it sound too serious . . . I'd have to say . . . that it was simply a discovery of poetry; and as such – risking the embarrassment that so regularly goes with my particular vocation – I'd also have to say that it was a discovery of the holy; not the solemn, not the saintly, but the holy, which makes you silent and sometimes makes you laugh and which above all makes the landscape different once and for all.[26]

This interlude gives a snapshot of the way Rowan's artistic projects have enabled him to blossom outside the torture chamber of church politics. The impression was cemented in mid-July 2008, three days before the start of the Lambeth Conference, when he found the time to celebrate the launch of *Headwaters*, and read several of his recently written poems, during a small party at the Reform Club in London. He looked at ease and contented in the company of friends.

* * *

The Archbishop's only public act during his month at George-town was to grant an interview to *Time* magazine.[27] His comments provided a useful apologia for his policies. Early on, he was asked whether it was not unchristian to exclude some bishops from Lambeth 2008, and he replied that 'exclusion is not particularly a Gospel idea'. Nevertheless, he added,

> The election and ordination of Gene Robinson was an event which many in the Communion had warned would deepen our divisions. Similarly, with Martyn Minns, there had been warnings that [his missionary assignment in the US] looked like a kind of aggression against another Anglican province. I felt we would run the risk of their attendance becoming the subject matter of the conference . . .

The Archbishop was then asked to defend what many in the Episcopal Church had viewed as his tough demands in Tanzania. 'It was seen as interference and colonialism,' he conceded.

> I was a bit taken aback because I didn't see it as the primates trying to dictate terms, but to say, look, here is a scheme which we think you could work with. But I've occasionally thought – rather mischievously – that the issue could be described in terms of a good American slogan: No taxation without representation. That

378

is, in some parts of the world, the decisions of the Episcopal Church are taken to be decisions that the local Anglican Church owns and agrees to, and the local Church can suffer in reputation or worse because of that.

Time: Can you give us an example?

RW: In Egypt there have been denunciations of all Christian churches from the Friday pulpits for sanctioning same-sex relationships.

Time: Isn't Scripture straightforward on homosexuality?

RW: It's impossible to get from Scripture anything straightforwardly positive about same-sex relationships. So if there were any other way of approaching it, you'd have to go back to the first principle of human relationships. Those theologians who've defended same-sex relationships from the Christian point of view in recent decades have said you've got to look at whether a same-sex relationship is capable of something at the level of mutual self-giving that a marriage ought to exemplify. And then ask, Is that what Scripture is talking about? That's the area of dispute.

Time: You yourself once thought it possible that same-sex relationships might be legitimate in God's eyes.

RW: Yes, I argued that in ['The Body's Grace']. I still think that the points I made there and the questions I raised were worth making as part of an ongoing discussion. *I'm not recanting* [my italics]. But those were ideas put forward as part of a theological discussion. I'm now in a position where I'm bound to say the teaching of the Church is this, the consensus is this. We have not changed our minds corporately. It's not for me to exploit my position to push a change.

Time: One gay activist said bitterly that he hoped you liked your newfound friends, but it strikes me that you don't have many. Your position seems very sad and lonely.

379

RW: It feels burdensome, of course. And making decisions that will lose you friends, compromise people's perception of your integrity – that's very hard. On the other hand, that is only a part of the reality. First and foremost, I'm a priest and a bishop, and what I have to do is to celebrate sacraments, to pray, to try to convey the reality of God. I don't spend all my days in self-pity.

Time: Do you see it as the taking up of a cross?

RW: Well, of course. And anybody who expects to go through a Christian life without a cross is deluding themselves . . .

Time: The Western world is struggling to come to terms with Islam. Where should we start?

RW: We – Christians, Westerners, whatever – perceive the Muslim world as large, aggressive, successful, expanding. Muslims in the UK see themselves as small, vulnerable, under attack, suspected by everybody. When you have something like the Muhammad cartoons in the Danish papers, ask yourself what it feels like if you're a member of an economically depressed, rather isolated Muslim community, in a majority non-Muslim environment.

Time: When you return from study leave, you'll focus once more on the problems within Anglicanism. Some people have already decided to stay away from the Lambeth Conference and possibly begin a process of division.

RW: I don't particularly want to be – I won't say blackmailed, but *pressured*, by either extreme on this. I think they'd lose by not coming. I think they need to talk to each other and listen to each other without prejudice.

Time: Are you optimistic?

RW: I'm hopeful, not optimistic.

*   *   *

As Rowan laboured on his literary projects in Georgetown, firm news emerged that Rwanda's bishops would be boycotting the Lambeth Conference, and that some conservatives were planning an alternative episcopal gathering several weeks beforehand – the idea that evolved into the Global Anglican Future Conference (GAFCON) in Jerusalem. Many of the refuseniks cited the welcome that would be given to the North American bishops at Lambeth 2008 as a ground for non-participation; statements from the Global South group suggested that Rowan's willingness even to meet Episcopal Church leaders in New Orleans was itself a mark of bad faith.

This display of brinkmanship led to a rebuke from John Sentamu, who warned hardliners that they would be effectively expelling themselves from the Communion if they acted on their threats to spurn Rowan's invitation.[28] Though the Archbishop of York was mistaken – a quarter of the world's Anglican bishops went to Jerusalem rather than Canterbury – his interview bolstered the sense that conservative ringleaders had again overreached themselves. This impression was further corroborated when Ephraim Radner, a founder of the Anglican Communion Network in the United States, resigned from the group on 31 July in protest against Robert Duncan's latest onslaught against Rowan. Duncan had criticised the Archbishop for a perceived lack of leadership, and declared the see of Canterbury and the Lambeth Conference to be 'lost'.[29] A figure of considerable substance, Professor Radner is a senior fellow of the Anglican Communion Institute, and a member of the Covenant Design Group. He described Duncan's comments as 'dangerously precipitate and unfair', adding that the Bishop was 'astonishingly self-confident and autonomously prophetic in a mode not unlike the baleful claims to visionary authority of those who have long misled the Episcopal Church'. In declaring two of the Instruments of Communion to be lost, Duncan had in effect cancelled out all four, Radner contended. 'Bishop Duncan has, in the end, decided to start a new Church. He may call it "Anglican" if he wishes, though I do not recognize the name in these kinds of actions that break communion rather than build it.'[30]

At the same time came a sign that some – maybe much – of the delirium was synthetic. The evidence emerged when a pastoral letter, apparently written by Peter Akinola to his flock in Abuja, was shown to have been recast by Martyn Minns. The letter[31] included a suggestion that the Archbishop of Canterbury's status as a focus of unity was 'highly questionable', and referred to a 'moment of decision' for the Communion, which was on the 'brink of destruction'. Computer tracking software indicated that the letter was extensively revised over a four-day period by Minns; further amendments had been made by Chris Sugden. Pat Ashworth, the respected journalist who broke the story in the *Church Times*, was later accused by Nigerian church sources of being 'insulting and racist'. The matter, she retorted, had

> nothing to do with race but everything to do with language and politics, in a climate where 'decision' is now drip-fed into every missive. Brainwash us often enough with news that the Anglican Communion is on the brink of destruction, and we will all believe it: that is, until proof comes along that schism really is being orchestrated by a knot of people dedicated to keeping their supporters on message.
>
> 'Forced to choose', 'moment of decision', 'brink of destruction', 'the gravity of this moment', are phrases designed to turn a

drama into a crisis, as US conservatives, with help from English friends, seek to sabotage [the] Lambeth Conference.[32]

Despite the ill-feeling generated by Rowan's apparent reluctance to meet the American bishops sooner, his presence at their September gathering in New Orleans was a relative success. The Episcopal Church confirmed a moratorium on the appointment of non-celibate homosexuals, reiterated a ban on formal blessings for gay couples, and provided the outlines of a scheme for alternative episcopal oversight for dissentient parishes. Their statement, 'A Response to Questions and Concerns Raised by our Anglican Communion Partners', was the bishops' formal reply to the demands made by the primates at Dar es Salaam in February. The primates had given the US bishops until 30 September to concede three points or face possible penalties. This had been widely thought to be an ultimatum. But Rowan, in New Orleans for the first two days of the bishops' colloquy, denied this, saying that 'it would be a mistake to see the three or four proposals from Dar es Salaam as questions that need to be answered strictly with no room for manoeuvre at all'.

His comments had a calming effect, since the 'Response' was itself more conciliatory than many had predicted. At a press conference after its publication, Katharine Jefferts Schori said: 'We have reaffirmed our firm desire to remain as full members of the Anglican Communion.' The statement was almost unanimous, and conservatives had been involved in its drafting. The bishops nevertheless deplored the recent consecrations in America carried out by overseas primates.

Conservative hardliners remained unyielding: their chief complaint sprang from the bishops' refusal to countenance alternative episcopal oversight from abroad. They maintained

that this would 'compromise the authority of our own primates
and place the autonomy of the Episcopal Church at risk'. The
passage on same-sex blessings in the bishops' statement also tilted
in a more liberal direction. It suggested that these might
continue informally, as was known to be the case already in
some dioceses. After pointing out that no rite existed, and that
the majority of bishops did not allow them, the statement went
on: 'We do note that in May 2003 the primates said we have a
pastoral duty "to respond with love and understanding to people
of all sexual orientations".' They added: '[It] is necessary to
maintain a breadth of private response to situations of individual
pastoral care.'

Among other things, Rowan told the New Orleans meeting
that the Lambeth Conference would not be postponed, despite a
request for delay from Peter Akinola. 'I don't think we deal with
our conflicts by just disposing of them,' he said. The suggestion
of a cooling-off period had also come from church sources
outside Nigeria, but he was not persuaded. 'I'm not sure we
could ever define what an adequate cooling-off period would
look like . . . I don't want the next few years to be spent in a lot
of continuing anxiety about when or whether there will be a
Lambeth when there are other things we might be thinking
about.'[33] When asked by a reporter: 'Why not just let the
Anglican Communion split?' Rowan said: 'It would be rather an
admission of defeat if we said we were quite incapable of
working together on the issues that divide us. I have to say,
God forbid. But the importance of it is that the need we have for
each other is very deep – that came across very deeply in much
of the discussion.' Assessing the Archbishop's performance,
Charles Jenkins, Bishop of Louisiana, said that 'everyone was
nervous, and because of that it started off a little rocky. When he

moved beyond his nervousness, and was really able to be Rowan, it got good.'[34]

*   *   *

The international dimension of the Archbisop's role then gave him a further chance to escape from Communion politics. At the end of September he visited Armenia, Syria and Lebanon. He met the Syrian President, Bashar Assad, and the Catholicos of the Armenian Orthodox Church, Karekin II, in his monastery at Etchmiadzin, near Yerevan. While in the Armenian capital, he visited the Genocide Memorial at Tsitsernakaberd. The trip spurred him to issue a sharp put-down to Western politicians contemplating further military adventures around the Middle East. In a BBC interview,[35] he warned that 'we do hear in some quarters about action against Syria or against Iran. I can't really understand what planet such persons are living on when you see the conditions that are already there. The region is still a tinderbox . . . Further deliberate destabilization in this region is terrible folly, terrible folly.' Military action would be 'criminal, ignorant and potentially murderous . . .'. And he emphasised that Christians in Muslim countries were being linked to Western-led conflicts, and ordered to leave their homes. The Archbishop had been told what he termed 'hair-raising' stories of ethnic cleansing in Iraq from nearly 300 Iraqi refugees in the Syrian Orthodox monastery at Ma'aret Sednaya, near Damascus. 'We heard of the firebombing of houses and shops,' he said. 'We heard of abductions and murders.'

The following month, the interview he gave to *Emel*,[36] the Muslim lifestyle magazine, yielded a racy headline in the *Sunday Times*: 'US is "Worst" Imperialist: Archbishop'.[37] What he said was that American foreign policy, which appeared to be focused more on accumulating influence and control than territory, was not working. He described this as the worst of all worlds:

> It is one thing to take over a territory and then pour energy and resources into administering it and normalizing it. Rightly or wrongly, that's what the British Empire did – in India, for example. It is another thing to go in on the assumption that a quick burst of violent action will somehow clear the decks, and that you can move on, and other people will put things back together – Iraq, for example.

He believed the answer in Iraq to be 'a generous and intelligent programme of aid directed to the societies that have been ravaged; a check on the economic exploitation of defeated territories; a demilitarization of their presence. All these things would help.'

In November, tremors from the ecclesiological rumblings in the US were felt in England, when three bishops – Michael Nazir-Ali of Rochester, Peter Forster of Chester and John Hind of Chichester – said that they backed Robert Duncan, who was now facing the threat of disciplinary action from Katharine Jefferts Schori. And Greg Venables, Primate of the Southern Cone, announced that he would be offering a home to traditionalist dioceses wishing to secede from the Episcopal Church.

Rowan decided to write an Advent letter to the world's Anglican bishops, reflecting on recent events and looking forward to the Lambeth Conference. Though cloudy in the eyes of some commentators – and not enough to prevent the GAFCON organisers from pressing ahead with plans for their alternative meeting, details of which were unveiled shortly afterwards – the letter generated a positive response in many quarters, and helped ensure that four-fifths of those invited to Lambeth 2008 accepted.

It expressed the Archbishop's conviction that schism was not unavoidable. He granted that there was no consensus among the primates about the adequacy of the New Orleans statement from the American House of Bishops, but warned that the Communion would be 'seriously wounded and diminished' if it fractured any further. On the Bible's place in the debate, he wrote:

> We recognise one another in one fellowship when we see one another 'standing under' the word of Scripture. Because of this recognition, we are able to consult and reflect together on the interpretation of Scripture and to learn in that process.
>
> Understanding the Bible is not a private process or something to be undertaken in isolation by one part of the family. Radical change in the way we read cannot be determined by one group or tradition alone . . .

He condemned 'the adoption of parishes in distant provinces or the ordination of ministers for distant provinces', and reaffirmed the normative status of Lambeth 1.10. On the consecration of Gene Robinson and the 'implicit sanction' given to same-sex blessings, he found it unsurprising that some had reacted by questioning whether the Episcopal Church belonged to the same family. Acknowledging the politics of the situation to be 'diverse and complicated', he judged that dioceses and bishops at odds with the Episcopal Church's prevailing view 'cannot be regarded as deficient in recognisable faithfulness to the common deposit and the common language and practice of the Communion'.

He also suggested that the exact interpretation of the New
Orleans statement was 'disputable', identified 'a serious gap
between what the Episcopal Church understands and what
others assume as to what constitutes a liturgical provision in
the name of the Church at large', and voiced concern about the
'spiralling disputes before the secular courts'. He also asked why
the US bishops should have apparently bound themselves to
future direction from their General Convention, and insisted
that accepting an invitation to Lambeth 2008 'must be taken as
implying willingness to work with' the Windsor process and
development of a Covenant.

Early in the new year, he hosted a press conference raising the
curtain on Lambeth 2008. His performance was robust. To those
who had declined his invitation, he said: 'I recognize their
absolute right to choose in good faith and in conscience whether
or not they can be there. The invitation is on the table.
Naturally, I would be delighted to see more rather than fewer
bishops there. That's their choice, but the door is open.'

There was a positive message to conservatives in the inclusion
of the Archbishop of the Indian Ocean, Ian Ernest, on the panel
at the press conference: he spoke for the Design Group that had
planned the conference agenda. Ernest had recently taken part in
the African consecration of 'missionary bishops' for the United
States, and also signed the letter calling for a postponement of the
Conference. On reflection, he said, the path of dialogue had
struck him as the wiser option. Tom Wright also sought to
counter the impression that 'the GAFCON movement' had a
monopoly on biblical orthodoxy. The Bishop of Durham
suggested that some bishops who wanted to attend the Conference were 'under primatial pressure not to do so, and to go to
GAFCON instead'.

The agenda for Lambeth 2008 was unveiled during the press conference. It looked uncontentious. Rowan disclosed that the gathering would have two aims: strengthening the sense of a shared Anglican identity, and helping to equip bishops for the role they increasingly had as leaders in mission. The Conference would not be a law-making body, because it had never had such a remit. There would be a few plenary sessions and some resolutions, though not on the scale of Lambeth 1998. A typical day would begin with a Eucharist, followed by breakfast, Bible study in eight-strong clusters of bishops, coffee, meetings in forty-eight-strong *indaba* groups (a SiZulu word meaning an important get-together), lunch, free time, self-selected sessions, evening prayer, an evening meal, and fringe events. The bishops would arrive in Canterbury on 16 July, and spend the first three days in retreat. The opening celebration would take place in the cathedral on Sunday 20 July; there would be daily themes to reflect on for much of the following fortnight.

As the curtain was being raised on the Conference, Jane Williams and Margaret Sentamu introduced the programme for the bishops' spouses – 600 or so wives and a sprinkling of husbands. 'Some of you may think of the spouses' conference as basically Jam and Jerusalem, "more tea, vicar", or mitre-making and flower-arranging,' Jane said. The truth would be otherwise. Margaret Sentamu said that in Africa, bishops' wives were often seen as mothers of their dioceses. The programme would therefore include training in management, microfinance, mission, IT and different forms of ministry. Fair trade, slavery and climate change would also be on the menu.

*   *   *

To a public largely unconcerned about church infighting, Rowan's sharia law lecture seemed by far his most momentous – and incendiary – contribution to public life. For a time, his arguments were buried by an eruption of anger and scorn, both at home and abroad. Now that the lava has cooled, it is easier to see his comments in perspective. He gave the address, 'Civil and Religious Law in England: A Religious Perspective', in London on 7 February. It was originally scheduled to take place in the Inner Temple, but the organisers transferred the venue to the Great Hall of the Royal Courts of Justice when about a thousand people applied for tickets. A useful digest of Rowan's thesis was given by one of his more sympathetic critics, the journalist David Aaronovitch, in an article published the following week:

> There are lots of religious people in Britain who look to religious precepts in their solving of domestic and contractual problems, and in directing their behaviour. This is 'unavoidable'. Some of these solutions are recognised in English and Scottish law, and some of them aren't. Where they aren't, we run the danger that people will both feel and be marginalised.
>
> Not only that, but with a non-hierarchical religion, such as Islam, we risk this marginalised legal process being controlled at a local level by 'primitivists' and not by wise authorities: a bit like, say, the bishops of the Church of England. If we handle this right, we could have sensible Sharia courts with legal standing, and if we handle it wrong we could have a lot of bongo-brains exercising real power, but outside the law. And we don't like that.[38]

In other words, the roots of any legal system lie in communities, and the moral, spiritual and cultural values they adhere to.

Sometimes the values of one group may conflict with those of another. National law must arbitrate, and trump ancillary codes, but it should not overlook the foundations of these codes – a point acknowledged through the leeway already granted to some groups in carefully defined circumstances. Attention must now be given to sharia, and a case could be made for giving Muslims greater jurisdiction, albeit of a supplementary form.

So much for the general picture. Since many who excoriated these ideas also accused Rowan of imprecision and obscurity, it is instructive to record his own choice of words. He looked at some misconceptions about the nature and claims of sharia, including the fact that even in predominantly Muslim states, there is some recognition of the Muslim's dual identity as citizen and believer. 'Sharia is not intrinsically to do with any demand for Muslim dominance over non-Muslims,' he argued. Many Muslim jurists recognised 'a degree of political plurality' as consistent with Muslim integrity. He thus inferred that problems arose

> not only when there is an assumption on the religious side that membership of the community (belonging to the *umma* or the Church or whatever) is the only significant category, so that participation in other kinds of socio-political arrangement is a kind of betrayal. It also occurs when secular government assumes a monopoly in terms of defining public and political identity.

He went on to examine three objections to claims that the law of the land should take account of religious identity. The first was that it might leave 'legal process (including ordinary disciplinary process within organizations) at the mercy of what might be called vexatious appeals to religious scruple'. The risk of such appeals suggested that there needed to be a 'recognized authority acting for a religious group' to help determine 'the relative seriousness of conscience-related claims'. This would need to hold as much for Muslims as for other religious groups.

The second objection was that recognition of supplementary jurisdiction in some areas, especially family law, could have the effect of reinforcing 'retrograde elements' in the life of minority communities, 'with particularly serious consequences for the role and liberties of women'. Accepting this, he warned that if any kind of plural jurisdiction were recognised, 'it would presumably have to be under the rubric that no "supplementary" jurisdiction could have the power to deny access to the rights granted to other citizens [regardless of faith affiliation], or to punish its members for claiming those rights'. He quoted the Jewish legal theorist Ayelet Shachar, who has argued that pluralist societies need to 'work to overcome the ultimatum of "either your culture or your rights"'.

In response to the third objection – that the law is the law – the Archbishop examined prevailing assumptions about what was settled definitively by the Enlightenment: 'Its claim to override traditional forms of governance and custom by looking towards a universal tribunal was entirely intelligible against the background of despotism.' Nevertheless, he argued,

> this set of considerations alone is not adequate to deal with the realities of complex societies: it is not enough to say that citizenship as an abstract form of equal access and equal accountability is either the basis or the entirety of social identity and personal motivation . . . Societies that are in fact ethnically, culturally and religiously diverse are societies in which identity is formed . . . by different modes and contexts of belonging,

'multiple affiliation' . . . This means that we have to think a little harder about the role and rule of law in a plural society of overlapping identities . . . the rule of law is thus not the enshrining of priority for the universal/abstract dimension of social existence but the establishing of a space accessible to everyone in which it is possible to affirm and defend a commitment to human dignity.

At the moment, Rowan maintained,

one of the most frequently noted problems in the law in this area is the reluctance of a dominant rights-based philosophy to acknowledge the liberty of conscientious opting-out from collaboration in procedures or practices that are in tension with the demands of particular religious groups: the assumption, in rather misleading shorthand, that if a right or liberty is granted there is a corresponding duty upon every individual to 'activate' this whenever called upon.

He had an alternative proposal: that where it was possible to recognise religious conviction and discipline without interfering with, or blocking access to, the liberties guaranteed by wider society, due consideration should be given to doing so:

It would be a pity if the immense advances in the recognition of human rights led, because of a misconception about legal universality, to a situation where a person was defined primarily as the possessor of a set of abstract liberties and the law's function was accordingly seen as nothing but the securing of those liberties irrespective of the custom and conscience of those groups which concretely compose a plural modern society.

In relation to aspects of sharia, and following a model sketched by Shachar, he said that

> it might be possible to think in terms of what Shachar calls 'transformative accommodation': a scheme in which individuals retain the liberty to choose the jurisdiction under which they will seek to resolve *certain carefully specified* matters, so that [in Shachar's words] 'power-holders are forced to compete for the loyalty of their shared constituents'. This may include aspects of marital law, the regulation of financial transactions and authorized structures of mediation and conflict resolution – the main areas that have been in question where supplementary jurisdictions have been tried, with native American communities in Canada as well as with religious groups like Islamic minority communities in certain contexts.

What prompted the Archbishop to say these things? Three factors, especially, are worth emphasising:

1 He was reacting against the aggressive promotion of a *laïque* view of the state, where religion is seen as a private matter rather than a major form of communal affiliation across national borders. In this context, Islamic identity arouses suspicion as Catholic identity once did.

2 During the lecture, he made it clear that he was discussing sharia in the wider context of the status and role of all faith communities in relation to the *laïque* view. The background here included not only the row over Catholic adoption agencies' policy towards gay couples, but also the rejection in 2004 of Rocco Buttiglione (a Catholic who supports official church teaching on sexual morality) as Silvio Berlusconi's nominee to be an EU Commissioner.

3 The lecture strongly reflects Rowan's status as a communitarian who fears that an assortment of 'atomic' or private individuals is not able to generate the altruistic motives required for a decent society. In this he is simultaneously on the Right and the Left, which confused people who had thought of him principally as a liberal.

At an indirect level, he was also probably wanting to qualify the line recently taken by Michael Nazir-Ali, whose claim that parts of Britain were no-go areas for non-Muslims had led to threats against his life. (Nazir-Ali was judged courageous by some, and injudicious by others. It was certainly unfortunate that he failed to back up his claims with detailed evidence.)

A core reason for the mauling that Rowan received can be summed up very simply. Both campaigners and large numbers of people without an axe to grind pointed out that Muslim women might be subject both to overt and covert coercion, so that the recognition of customary practice might in the event stop them from exercising their right to go to law in a secular court. Rowan also cited the conscientious right of a Catholic doctor not to perform an abortion as a principle that could be broadened. Aaronovitch spoke for the doubters:

'It is difficult to see,' said the Archbishop, 'quite why the principle cannot be extended in other areas.' Well, no it isn't, actually. These 'rights of conscience' have unmentioned corollaries: the gay couple denied a chance of adoption and the woman who – if surrounded by Catholic doctors – may not get the treatment to which she is entitled. *It is only if such exemptions are rare that they can be at all tolerable* [my italics]. The implication of the Archbishop's speech is that he wants them to be less rare.[39]

In a bid to pre-empt negative publicity, Rowan gave an interview to Radio 4's *The World at One* programme several hours before the lecture, in which he agreed with his questioner's suggestion that the implementation of some aspects of sharia law in Britain was 'inevitable'. This was mistaken on two counts. By talking to the media before and not after the lecture, he lost a chance to nip any misunderstandings of his arguments in the bud. It would have been smarter to arrange an evening interview before the following day's papers went to press. He also fell into a familiar trap by allowing words to be put into his mouth. The words 'sharia' and 'inevitable' were the only ones heard by many listeners; an unprecedented number complained to the BBC about what the Archbishop had said.

Some influential voices were raised in Rowan's support. Sympathetic statements emerged from Gordon Brown, the Muslim Council of Great Britain and the Cambridge-based Centre for the Study of Muslim–Jewish relations, among other sources. More generally, the coverage was savage. The *Sun*'s headline, 'WHAT A BURKHA: Archbishop wants Muslim Law in UK',[40] proved emblematic of the tabloids' response; though more nuanced in their coverage, the broadsheets were also sharply critical for the most part. George Carey wrote articles attacking his predecessor for the *Sunday Telegraph* and the *News of the World*. More worryingly, there was alarm and distress in other parts of the Communion. Bishop Ben Kwashi of Jos, in northern Nigeria, expressed shock and disappointment. His view was echoed by church leaders in several countries with large Muslim populations.

There were other explanations for the strength of the reaction. Since the British press tends to like simplicity and soundbites, a subtle message is liable to be distorted or pilloried as opaque, woolly, academic, arrogant, naive, out of touch. There were the different shades of church conservative who saw in the lecture a golden opportunity to get at the Archbishop, as well as to vent their own dislike of complexity. In another camp stood those who had long felt prevented from expressing their intense dislike for some aspects of Islam (especially the aggressive tone of a militant minority) on pain of being dubbed racist by the forces of political correctness. These people now had the perfect liberal cause – equality before the law – to vent their feelings, and many secular Muslims sympathised.

The deepest problem with the lecture centred on the question of 'supplementary jurisdiction' – that is, using sharia law to supplement the common law, especially in areas affecting the family. A senior Jewish barrister whom I consulted expressed sympathy for the sentiment behind the Archbishop's arguments, but shared the wider worry about some of their practical implications:

> Dr Williams says that sharia law is not monolithic but open to different interpretations. I can well understand this, since I am familiar with both fundamentalist and liberal interpretations of Judaism. But I don't think that this answers the question, given that the British courts and government have no say in whether the Islamic authorities in the UK will adopt a liberal or a hardline attitude. If the Sharia Council took a primitivist approach, it would be little comfort to a Muslim woman to be told that the interpretation of sharia in Malaysia is less misogynistic.

In this light, Rowan's comment that the West does not have a monopoly on justice was right, but irrelevant. The point is that a pluralistic legal system will never work, since the result is inevitably chaos. It would be like saying that cars should drive on the right and lorries on the left. Any society has to have a single system of law which applies equally to everyone. 'The common law has always been adaptable,' my source maintained.

> It will continue to find solutions to new problems by applying old principles in a new way. This will include issues raised by sharia law – for example, the wearing of burqas. It will be a good thing to have experts in Muslim law who are always experts in English law, in order to assist in that process. The approach of the common law should be Benthamite, i.e. allowing minorities to do what they want, provided that they don't interfere unduly with the rest of society and don't take away the rights of their own weaker members.

There is room for applying another system of law if it is with the consent of both parties, he added. This is what happens whenever two parties agree to submit to arbitration, whether it be two Orthodox Jews referring their dispute to a Beth Din, or two property developers deferring to a surveyor. 'However, there has to be a limited right of appeal to the courts, if the arbitrator exceeds his powers or gets it wrong; and the courts should be particularly astute in cases where there is social or economic inequality between the parties to ensure that the weaker one has genuinely consented to the matter being referred to arbitration.'

Non-expert reaction tended to focus on the perceived ills of multiculturalism: it was becoming common to hear that a well-intentioned experiment had been carried too far in Britain. Rowan's appeal to the experience of Canadian Indians was telling in this context. A large degree of the antagonism towards native peoples in Canada has been fuelled precisely by supplementary laws and privileges (many dating from Victoria's reign) in a parallel legal jurisdiction operating across the Indian reservations. 'Parallel legal systems seem to hasten ghettoization,' one of my correspondents urged. 'Overall, Dr Williams's message is so lacking in clarity of expression that it is lost and easily parodied for readers of the tabloids. His lecture takes us on an intellectual bus journey with no indicator at the front as to the ultimate destination.'

Rowan's reaction to the furore was initially one of hurt silence – it took several days for a clarification to appear on his website – during which the fires of hostile comment grew hotter still. Shriller members of the General Synod called for his resignation. 'He's a good man, a godly man, but he's not a leader and he should go,' announced Alison Ruoff, a laywoman representing the London diocese.

But anyone who supposed that Rowan himself thought of stepping down at this time was misjudging both the man and the media – even though Paddy Power, the Irish bookmaker, opened a book on his successor, citing John Sentamu as the 2:1 favourite to take over at Lambeth. The pie-chuckers of Fleet Street quickly moved on to other targets. And the General Synod, which by coincidence was meeting the following week for its February sessions, chiefly provided a rallying point for the Archbishop, who used his presidential address to speak up for himself. There was a long standing ovation before he had even spoken: he looked pleased and then – as the applause went on for a full minute – rather embarrassed.

His speech began with a quote from Ronald Knox: 'The prevailing attitude . . . was one of heavy disagreement with a number of things which the [speaker] had not said.' He then apologised for any 'unclarity' in the lecture and radio interview, but strongly defended the right of a Church of England pastor to address 'issues around the perceived concerns of other religious communities, and to try and bring them into better public focus'. The lecture had posed the question whether English law could accommodate some aspects of Islamic law, but not if it removed any rights enjoyed by people as citizens of the UK:

> We are not talking about parallel jurisdictions; and I tried to make clear that there could be no 'blank cheques' in this regard, in particular as regards some of the sensitive questions about the status and liberties of women. The law of the land still guarantees for all the basic components of human dignity.
>
> So, the question remains whether certain additional choices could and should be made available under the law of the United Kingdom for resolving disputes and regulating transactions. It would be analogous to what is already possible in terms of the legal recognition of certain kinds of financial transaction under Islamic regulation (including special provision around mortgage arrangements). And it would create a helpful interaction between the courts and the practice of Muslim legal scholars in this country.
>
> If – and please note that word – this were thought to be a useful direction in which to move, there would be plenty of work still to be done, with the greatest care, on what would and would not be possible . . .

A subtle shift was apparent here. As well as insisting that he had been misinterpreted, then offering a qualified apology for his own role in this, Rowan was also distancing himself from other parts of the lecture by softening his language.

Lambeth Palace insiders were divided about the episode. One told a friend *sotto voce* that the Archbishop had been working on his text almost until the last minute, and did not give his staff enough time to digest it. Another who did read the lecture beforehand felt at once that it was unnecessary, as well as ill-advised. Despite all the howls of horror directed against him, Rowan himself has no regrets about the enterprise, an attitude that has prompted some to raise further questions about his tactical grasp. The lecture clearly demonstrated his cleverness. What he did not demonstrate, though, was a capacity to see how his words would be received. The presentational aspect was crisply summed up by Paul Vallely:[41]

Diligent website watchers [on 7 February] could see very early . . . that 'Archbishop says sharia is unavoidable in UK' was going rapidly nuclear, as this crudeness of response was transmitted, and magnified, with increasing volatility by this new communications technology.

It seems that there were no diligent website watchers at Lambeth. Or if there were, and they pointed out to the Archbishop how seriously awry things were going, he failed to hear the electronic alarm bells. He would be a fool if he made the same mistake next time. And there will be a next time, make no mistake. Welcome to the world of the new media.

Not long afterwards, a radio documentary[42] presented by another journalist, Quentin Letts, on the office of Archbishop of Canterbury provided a chance to take a longer view. The wisest contribution came from Douglas Hurd. Among other things, he said that the Archbishop had got into difficulty because he was not a politician. He talked like a scholar. Arguably, he should have had someone at his elbow with more worldly wisdom than himself. But it would spoil him were everything he said to be wrapped up in spin-doctor's language. He couldn't tiptoe around on safe ground all the time. Above all, Hurd reminded listeners, Jesus himself would not have got a very good write-up in the British tabloids, either.

IO

Positive Capability

Bishops stayed away in considerable numbers from the first Lambeth Conference. In February 1867 the Archbishop of Canterbury, Charles Longley, issued an invitation to the whole Anglican episcopate to attend. Seventy-six bishops did so. One hundred and fifty-one were invited. Some were prevented by distance or infirmity or both. Australia and India were represented by a single bishop each. But quite a number stayed away on principle. The Archbishop of York refused to attend, as did every other bishop in his province, except Chester. The Bishop of Peterborough likewise refused. The venerable Bishop of St Davids, Connop Thirlwall, was minded to decline since he thought the conference would inevitably seek to modify the constitution and government of the Church of England. He was fearful that bishops from the United States and the colonies would outvote those at home. The Bishop of London, Archibald Campbell Tait, was equally anxious about the authority of such a gathering. He sought an assurance from the Archbishop that the limits of the competence of the conference should be specified carefully beforehand. Hence Archbishop Longley stated in his letter of invitation that *'such a meeting as is proposed would not be competent to make declarations or lay down definitions on points of doctrine'* . . .

In 1867 there was one Anglican . . . who received no invitation: John William Colenso [Bishop of Natal]. Colenso's speeches, sermons and theological writings moved beyond what was then considered orthodox. He questioned the historical reliability and accuracy of the Old Testament and was a champion of indigenous African culture, all of which may suggest he was a man before his time.

Thus writes Graham James, Bishop of Norwich and formerly chaplain to Robert Runcie, in a recent essay on Anglican polity.[1] The piece deserves a wider audience. Among other strengths, it mines the work of scholars such as W. M. Jacob,[2] Owen Chadwick,[3] R. T. Davidson[4] and Alan Stephenson.[5]

James makes clear that the Lambeth Conference was not a synod or a council, but an invitation to confer. All the same, Lambeth prelates have sometimes had a decisive impact on the mind of the Communion worldwide. In 1930, for example, the bishops recognised that there was a morally serious case for approving contraception, and passed a motion favouring birth control by 193 votes to 67. Some members of the minority felt that the vote was deeply mistaken. The Bishop of Bloemfontein left in protest, and the Bishop of Exeter said that contraception was tantamount to infanticide. The bonds of affection and the unity of the Communion were tested, James observes. But overall, '[t]he temper of the times . . . was neither to unchurch minority opinion nor to confuse the boundaries of orthodox faith with divisions over the moral questions of the day'.

Nineteenth-century ecclesiastical history sheds light on the present in other ways. Popular images of the mid-Victorian Church as a calm, self-confident institution are wide of the mark. The 1850s had seen the publication of *Essays and Reviews*, a scholarly collection questioning the reality of eternal hellfire, among other doctrines. Half the clergy in the Church of England signed a petition of protest against what struck them as a fundamental challenge to Christian belief. Among senior clerics, there was also considerable uncertainty about whether Anglicanism's international growth should be reflected in new patterns of governance. Three questions in particular claimed the attention of bishops at the first Lambeth Conference. Should all bishops in the British colonies take an oath of canonical obedience to the Archbishop of Canterbury? Should there be any appeal against the decisions of bishops or synods in the colonial Churches to any authority at home, and, if so, what? And third, what seems the best guarantee for maintaining unity of doctrine and discipline between the scattered branches of the Communion?

James draws an important lesson:

> Uncertainty about authority, an episcopal scandal with all the consequent fall-out, unease about the signs of the times, a deep instinct that this worldwide Communion of Churches needed some international forum to ensure unity in doctrine and discipline – the reason for a Lambeth Conference in 1867 seems a mirror image of the presenting issues in 2008.

He adds that during the General Synod's York meeting in 2007, influential figures argued that the Anglican Communion had never before faced the circumstances that required a novel provision such as the Covenant. 'It seems gravely mistaken to assume Anglicanism has not travelled this way before,' James warns. 'The rails of the Anglican train seem to have been set on much the same uncertain track for a century and a half. That it has not arrived at any final destination may simply be due to the very provisionality of the Anglican tradition.'

The essay puts forward a connected argument: that although Lambeth Conferences have produced a substantial body of recommendations and reports, the bishops have frequently failed to debate and disseminate them in their respective provinces. As a result, many senior clerics have not appreciated how doctrine develops, and Christian practices change, in relation to the surrounding culture and new learning. 'A concentration on isolated resolutions makes the matter worse,' James argues. 'Demands that Resolution 1.10 . . . should be automatically treated as authoritative throughout the Communion have proved unconvincing because of the inattention paid to the other hundred or so resolutions from the same Conference, let alone all those from earlier Conferences.'

He points out that resolutions on homosexuality – now almost forgotten – were also passed in 1978 and 1988. The resolution of 1988 was different in both form and content from the tough message of a decade later, even though 'firmly located within historic Christian teaching'. It ran as follows:

This Conference
1 Reaffirms the statement of the Lambeth Conference of 1978 on homosexuality, recognising the continuing need in the next decade for 'deep and dispassionate study of the question of homosexuality, which would take seriously both the teaching of Scripture and the results of scientific and medical research'.
2 Urges such study and reflection to take account of biological, genetic and psychological research being undertaken by other

agencies, and the socio-cultural factors that lead to the different attitudes in the provinces of our Communion.

3 Calls each province to reassess, in the light of such study and because of our concern for human rights, its care for and attitude towards persons of homosexual orientation.

James's conclusion is that

[t]here is no one likely to replace the Archbishop of Canterbury as the legitimate convenor of a worldwide Anglican conference of bishops. We are fortunate that our present Archbishop is little tempted to coerce or compel but maintains a strong commitment to the value of the invitation to confer. Like Archbishop Longley in 1867, it would be wise not to be disturbed by episcopal refuseniks. Perhaps most of all, however, the bishops who gather for Lambeth in 2008 need fresh induction into their own history and tradition. It is a teaching tradition which gains authority by dissemination in the Communion as a whole and by being reworked every decade. In 1867 a tradition was established through conferring rather than governing which gave life and shape to a worldwide Communion of episcopal churches. It has not yet completed its work.

The praise for Rowan Williams in this passage is genuine. But one implication of the Bishop of Norwich's words is that the Archbishop could have done more to face down the hard-knuckled biblicists. Another, though, is that there is no point in insisting on the strict limits of your power and then expecting others to do what you tell them. In this respect, his performance during the General Synod's crucial vote on women bishops in July 2008 was instructive.

The preceding four months had seen further unsung successes for Rowan. In April he gave a second address (this time at Westminster Abbey) rebutting the views of Richard Dawkins. In May, while in Rome for the international Building Bridges seminar uniting Christians and Muslims, he had further very cordial conversations with Pope Benedict. He gave a stimulating lecture at the London School of Economics knitting together Christian and Wittgensteinian insights to address the subject of the individual's relation to society, and received belated backing for his sharia law lecture from the Lord Chief Justice, Lord Phillips, who described it as profound, and much of the press reaction as misconceived. Then came a tragedy. His old friend Christopher Morgan, a former religious affairs correspondent of the *Sunday Times*, took his own life by throwing himself under a train. He had been suffering from depression for many months, but few suspected that he would commit suicide. Rowan's shock and dismay were intensified by the knowledge that Chris had put a strain on their friendship. For a time, his career had depended on writing stories that Lambeth Palace did not want to see published. The Archbishop nonetheless gave the eulogy at the funeral, held in Llandaff Cathedral near midsummer.

GAFCON met in late June, without the fireworks predicted in some quarters. There were three basic elements in the message put out at the climax of the gathering: the designation of GAFCON as an ongoing fellowship, a fourteen-point 'Jerusalem Declaration' described as the basis for the fellowship, and the formation of a new Primates' Council. Talk of a schism was discounted. GAFCON had now evolved into a network within the Anglican Churches. The Declaration was doctrinal. While not mentioning gay sexuality directly, it described heterosexual marriage as the proper place for physical intimacy. The Primates' Council constituted the most substantial innovation. It would arbitrate over who qualified to belong to the fellowship, and its members claimed the authority to 'authenticate' confessing Anglican jurisdictions, among them various breakaway Anglican groups. On the subject of Rowan's office, the communiqué stated that '[w]hile acknowledging the status of Canterbury as an historic see, we do not accept that Anglican identity is determined necessarily through recognition by the Archbishop of Canterbury'.

A *Church Times* editorial[6] expressed guarded support for the thinking behind the GAFCON movement:

> The reason why GAFCON happened, above all else, is that conservative Anglicans felt that they were not respected in the Communion – not only they, but their Lord. The worst thing that can happen now is that the movement, and its conclusions, are dismissed out of hand by the rest of the Communion. GAFCON Christians expect to be vilified as homophobic. They say they are not. There should be plenty of evidence soon one way or the other.

The response from Rowan himself was more critical. He described GAFCON's vision for the future of the Communion as 'problematic in all sorts of ways', and warned the movement to consider the 'risks entailed' in their proposals. In a detailed statement, he said that the tenets of orthodoxy spelt out in the Jerusalem Declaration 'will be acceptable to and shared by the vast majority of Anglicans in every province'. But he rejected the idea of the Primates' Council.

A Primates' Council which consists only of a self-selected group from among the Primates of the Communion will not pass the test of legitimacy for all in the Communion. And any claim to be free to operate across provincial boundaries is fraught with difficulties, both theological and practical – theological because of our historic commitments to mutual recognition of ministries in the Communion, practical because of the obvious strain of responsibly exercising episcopal or primatial authority across enormous geographical and cultural divides.

He went on to question by what authority the GAFCON primates might be deemed legitimate members of any new Council, and how effective discipline could be maintained 'in a situation of overlapping and competing jurisdictions'. It was wrong, the Archbishop added, to assume that those outside the GAFCON network were 'simply proclaiming another gospel'. He warned against precipitate impulses, and quoted words of St Paul in 1 Corinthians 11:33: 'Wait for one another.'

This was the first of several strong statements made by the Archbishop during what was probably the most critical month of his career. It was followed by an extempore sermon during the General Synod's July sessions. This text gave a good illustration of his habit – a blend of principle and pragmatism – of looking to the spiritual kernel behind political disputes:

In the middle of all our discussions at synod, where would Jesus be? Jesus is going to be with those who feel the waterlessness of their position [a reference to the 'waterless pit' of Zechariah 9:11]: with those traditionalists feeling the Church is slipping away from them, the landmarks have shifted, and they don't know how what they've taught and heard . . . can be life-giving for tomorrow.

He'll be with those in a very different part of the landscape who feel that things are closing in, that their position is under threat, that their liberties are being taken away by those anxious and eager to enforce new ideologies in the name of Christ. He would be with those who feel that their liberty of questioning is under threat, he would be with the gay clergy, who wonder what their future is in a Church so anxious and tormented about this issue . . . Into this darkness comes Jesus to release us in our prison and make us, as the Prophet says, 'Prisoners of hope'.

These words were admired across the spectrum. But this very warmth served to underline one of Rowan's biggest problems as Archbishop of Canterbury, at least until the Lambeth Conference: his difficulty in capitalising on the esteem in which he is held, and translating it into broad alliances. This was exemplified in the synod's failure to take the very strong hints he gave in the women-bishops debate on providing safeguards for traditionalists. In his contribution to a lengthy discussion, the Archbishop sought to balance conservative and reformist opinion. He said that the Church was in the 'unhappy, illogical and untheological' position of having women priests who could not become bishops. He wanted their gifts to be released into a fuller episcopal ministry, and could not see much cause for delay.

He was opposed to any scheme that 'structurally humiliated' women in the episcopate, but equally unhappy with systems that sidelined traditionalists. Both groups were driven by a sense of obedience to Scripture. If Anglican identity was to be preserved, he wanted to see more, not less, security for those who disagreed with women bishops. Whatever the results, he concluded, 'we are going to find ourselves in a deeply changed Church of England'.

A majority of the synod wanted something more clear-cut. While rejecting a single-clause measure, they voted for a statutory code of practice to be drawn up over the months that followed and considered formally in February 2009. The code is expected to mark the end of the provisions made for traditionalist opponents of women priests in the 1993 Act of Synod: it is likely to involve the voluntary delegation of certain episcopal functions by diocesan bishops to so-called complementary bishops.

Before leaving York, Rowan offered a prognosis for the Lambeth Conference, and the broader prospects for church unity.[7] He insisted that despite the Jerusalem Declaration, the Anglican Communion would continue in some form, albeit weakened:

> I am not looking to one great thunderclap of breakage. There will be fractures – there are fractures already, and some of them will get more difficult – but I would hope that the Lambeth Conference will be an occasion where people get their motivation back a little bit – in terms of this mutual responsibility, and crucially, what we have to offer together to the world in terms of mission.

Talk of early retirement was brushed aside: 'This happens to be the job I have been called to do at this particular time; so I try and do that. There are lots of sayings of the Desert Fathers about people wanting the vocation they thought they could do, and getting the vocation God wanted them to do instead.'[8] And he (correctly) pinpointed the 'biggest misconception' about himself as being that 'I am incapable of talking to the person in the pew'. On the contrary, grassroots encounters were what kept him going, especially as '90 per cent' of his public speaking came from unscripted talks to laypeople. 'Actually,' he added, 'people are movingly loyal and generous. When somebody hands me a little card from a rural parish in Lincolnshire or Cumbria that just says "Hi. Lots of prayers," it is not a thankless job. I am supported by that extraordinary generosity.'[9]

From the evidence of events in Canterbury, his overview was reliable. A smooth run was by no means a foregone conclusion, even without the GAFCON bishops in attendance. Most conferences have hinged on the personality and skills of the serving archbishop: this was especially true of Lambeth 2008. Credit for its success therefore belongs chiefly to Rowan himself. The reasons for this are readily itemised. In retrospect, it seems clear that the three-day retreat at the start of proceedings was a masterstroke. Rowan's talks, based on the 'I am' sayings of Jesus in John's Gospel, focused on personal discipleship and apostolic ministry. As often in the past, he operated like a theological picture-restorer, rooting what he said about modern life in Scripture and tradition. Here was a teacher and pastor to the whole Communion, able to address people of varying cultural backgrounds.

The setting seemed intimate – many bishops spoke of feeling addressed personally, as in much good preaching. This impression probably derived from a trick of perspective. The Archbishop's message was in some ways quite impersonal, deliberately transcending more workaday content. The three days of the retreat (17, 18 and 19 July) set the tone. As one bishop, not an uncritical fan of Rowan, put it to me: 'His luminous intelligence and godliness were clear from the start.' The remark draws us back to a paradox previously identified by some of the Archbishop's Monmouth colleagues – that although genuinely committed to categories such as brokerage and conversation, he is also a loner endowed with the self-confidence that accompanies a willingness to shoulder a very large individual burden.

Before the retreat began, he told the bishops of his prayer for the Conference – 'not that after two weeks we will find a solution to all our problems but [that] we shall . . . find the trust in God and one another that will give us the energy to change in the way God wants us to change'. Referring to the absentees, he said that he respected their decision not to attend,

> but together we need in prayer to acknowledge the wound that that makes in our fellowship and to acknowledge also, as I must do myself, that we still have to . . . mend relations that have been hurt. I hope that in these weeks we shall daily be remembering those who are not with us, upholding them in our prayers, in our respect and love.

Another source of the Conference's success lay in the decision – contradicting earlier statements, and irritating to some conservatives – to avoid resolutions. Splits were thereby avoided; at the same time, bishops reported that they had felt freer to speak openly. The *indaba* groups were mixed, theologically as well as geographically, and the fruit of their deliberations was passed (via minutes produced by rapporteurs) into the 'hearings' that took place every afternoon. The results of the hearings were in turn fed to the Windsor Continuation Group and the Covenant Design Group – the two bodies charged with shaping the Communion's future course. Another positive signal was given out during the first week, when the bishops were bused to London in their cassocks for a march down Whitehall in support of the Millennium Development Goals on tackling Third World poverty. The demonstrators then converged on the Lambeth Palace Gardens, where they were addressed by the Prime Minister, among others.

For most of the Conference, the *indaba* conversations focused on the work and mission of a bishop. In the final week, attention turned to the hot potatoes: sex and ecclesiology. One bishop told me of his scepticism about how the assembly could produce a solid conclusion in the absence of clearer protocols, especially as deep disagreements over scriptural interpretation were never far from the surface. 'But perhaps the desire for firm results is a reflection of the Western mindset,' he added. 'On second thoughts, I was glad the process was honoured.'

The formal result of all the talking was the so-called Reflections document, which passed through several drafts as the Conference went on. 'Many of us have discovered more fully why we need one another and the joy of being committed to one another,' it states. 'At a time when many in our global society are seeking just the sort of international community that we already have, we would be foolish to let such a gift fall apart.'[10] The Archbishop endorsed a call from the Windsor Continuation Group for moratoriums on gay consecrations, same-sex partnership blessings, and interventions across provincial boundaries. If these were not accepted, he said at the final press conference, 'then, to say the least, we are no further forward'.

Plans for a Covenant survived the Conference, though some doubts were recorded in the Reflections document. It was announced that the Covenant Design Group would give further thought to the bishops' comments, and discuss provincial reactions, at a meeting in April 2009. A further draft would then be presented to the Anglican Consultative Council at its meeting in

Jamaica in May. During his sermon at the final Eucharist of the Conference, Rowan said that the Covenant had 'the potential to make us more of a Church, more of a "Catholic" Church . . . That we wanted to move in such a direction would, in itself, be a weighty message. But it might even be a prophetic one.'

Conservatives and liberals seemed divided among themselves over the manner in which the Conference had unfolded. The Archbishop of Hong Kong, Paul Kwong, said that everyone had been heard with respect. 'Now we are asking . . . people to stop defending what they do as right, and stop accusing other parties of what they do as wrong. Instead, we must come together and say: "What sacrifice, what concession, can you make for the sake of the integrity of the Communion?"' But the Bishop of Louisiana, Charles Jackson, was among several figures to express doubts about the notion of sacrifice. 'There is a big difference between making a sacrifice for others and asking others to make a sacrifice,' he said. 'It is a moral dilemma.'

The Bishop of New Westminster, Michael Ingham, whose diocese was the first to vote for same-sex blessings, said that it must 'consider deeply' its response to the Conference. While he had found the *indaba* groups 'a great success', he criticised the Windsor Continuation Group for 'rigidity and a lack of wisdom . . . The primary mindset of the Windsor Group is conformity or expulsion. As yet, they display no capacity for creating space, only for taking it away.'

Phillip Aspinall, Archbishop of Adelaide and one of Rowan's most important allies among the primates, said that he expected some provinces to have difficulties with the Covenant 'because, at the heart of Anglicanism, is the notion of autonomy, self-rule. And so provinces will guard that very jealously. It will only be as a result of deep and careful reflection that they agree to self-limit in order to protect something which is equally valuable, and that is our Communion.'

Bishop Katharine Jefferts Schori said that many people had come to Lambeth 'in fear and trembling, expecting either a distasteful encounter between those of vastly different opinions, or the cold shoulder from those who disagree'. The overwhelming reality had been just the opposite, she suggested. 'We have prayed, cried, learned and laughed together, and discovered something deeper about the body of Christ. We know more of the deeply faithful ministry of those in vastly different contexts, and we have heard repeatedly of the life-and-death matters confronting vast swaths of the Communion.' On the other hand, eleven primates of the Global South, all present throughout the Conference, put out a more critical statement. This group – from the Indian Ocean, Burundi, Congo, South East Asia, Burma, Tanzania, Sudan, West Africa, Jerusalem and South India – supported the Covenant plan, but added: 'We deeply regret that during the Conference proceedings substantial theological voices outside of the Western world have not been present in the evening plenary sessions . . . We are concerned with the continuing patronising attitude of the West towards the rest of the Churches worldwide.'

GAFCON issued a short statement saying that its Primates' Council would produce a considered reaction to the Conference at the end of August. One of the principal boycotters, Archbishop Peter Jensen, said: 'Our absence focused minds on the problems within the Communion and spoke louder than our presence would have. However, the issues which have caused such division are still before us and require decisive action so that the mission of the Church will not be further impaired.' Canon

Kenneth Kearon, Secretary-General of the Communion, announced that he would write personally to every bishop not present at the Conference, in an effort to keep them involved in future discussion.

*　　*　　*

Rowan himself showed enormous stamina during these days. There was no time for him to participate fully in the *indaba* process, because he was putting the finishing touches on most of his speeches, as well as hosting many meals – some in the Old Palace, others in a private dining room on the university campus – for smaller groups of bishops. At times the strain showed. He looked especially tired halfway through the Conference, but rallied towards the end.

The second and third of his three presidential addresses stand out. The second centred on a call that both wings of the Church resist a tendency to cling 'to one dimension' of the truth, and instead acknowledge a need for 'a bit more of a structure in our international affairs', and a clearer sense of what would and would not be 'a grave and lasting' divisive course of action by a local church. While the current focus was on sexual ethics, he suggested that it could just as well be pressure for a new baptismal formula, or the abandonment of formal reference to the Nicene Creed in a local church's formulations, or lay presidency at the Eucharist, or the regular use of non-scriptural or even non-Christian material in liturgy.

Some had voiced unhappiness about the alleged legalism implied by having a Covenant. 'But we should be clear that *good* law is about guaranteeing consistence [*sic*] and fairness in a community; and also that in a community like the Anglican family, it can only work when there is free acceptance. Properly understood, a covenant is an expression of mutual *generosity* . . .' The first half of the Conference had been designed to help the bishops establish 'what the other person or group really means and really needs . . . so that when we *do* address divisive issues, we have created enough of a community for an intelligent generosity to be born'. It was by no means a full agreement, he acknowledged, 'but it will, I hope, have strengthened the sense that we have at least a common language, born out of the conviction that Jesus Christ remains the one unique centre'.

Then came a summary of what he hoped Western liberals and conservatives from the Global South might have got, or were beginning to get, from the previous days' reflections. It entailed another fluent piece of theological ventriloquism, bearing out Rowan's reputation as a harmoniser of opposing interests and tribal antipathies:

So first, what might the traditional believer hope others have heard? 'What we seek to do in our context is faithfully to pass on what you have passed on to us – Holy Scripture, apostolic ministry, sacramental discipline. But what are we to think when all these things seem to be questioned and even overturned? We want to be pastorally caring to all, to be "inclusive", as you might say. We want to welcome everyone. Yet the gospel and the faith you passed on to us tell us that some kinds of behaviour and relationship are not blessed by God. Our love and our welcome are unreal if we don't truthfully let others know what has shaped and directed our lives – so along with welcome, we must still challenge people to change their ways. We don't see why welcoming the gay or lesbian person *must* mean blessing what they do in the Church's name or accepting them for ordination, whatever their lifestyle. We seek to love them – and, all right, we don't always make a good job of it: but we can't just say that there is nothing to challenge. Isn't it like the dilemma of the early Church – welcoming soldiers, yet seeking to get them to lay down their arms? . . .

'We've taken a risk in coming [to the Conference], because many who feel like us feel we've betrayed them just by meeting you. But we value our Communion, we want to understand you and we want *you* to understand us. Can you find some way of being generous that helps us believe you are about us and about the common language and belief of the Church? Can you – in plain words – step back and let us think and pray about these things without giving us the impression that the debate is over and we've lost and that doesn't matter to you?'

The Archbishop then imagined a liberal riposte to this, drawn from a perceived need 'to bring Jesus alive' in contemporary culture:

'Trying to speak the language of the culture and relate honestly to where people really are doesn't have to be a betrayal of Scripture and tradition. We know we're pushing the boundaries – but don't some Christians always have to do that? Doesn't the Bible itself suggest that?

'We are often hurt, angry and bewildered at the way many others in the Communion see us and treat us these days – as if we were spiritual lepers or traitors to every aspect of Christian belief. We know that no one is the best judge in their own case, but we see in our church life at least some marks of the Spirit's gifts. And part of that is acknowledging the gifts we've seen in gay and lesbian believers. They will certainly be likely to feel that the restraint you ask for is a betrayal. Please try to see why this is such a dilemma for many of us. You may not see it, but [gay people are] still at risk in our society, still vulnerable to murderous violence. And we have to say to some of you that we long for you to speak up for *your* gay and lesbian neighbours in situations where they are subject to appalling discrimination. There have been Lambeth Resolutions about that too, remember.

'A lot of the time, we feel we're being made scapegoats. Other provinces have acute moral and disciplinary problems, or else they more or less successfully refuse to admit the realities in their midst. But those of us who have faced the complex issues around gay relationships in what we feel to be an open and prayerful way are stigmatised and demonised . . .

'We want to be generous, and we are hurt that some throw back in our faces both the experiences and the resources we long to share. Can you try and see us as fellow-believers struggling to proclaim the same Christ, and to be patient with us?'

For the first speaker, then, the cost of generosity would involve the risk of being accused of compromise; for the second, the accusation of 'sacrificing the needs of an oppressed group for the sake of a false or delusional unity'. But if both were able 'to hear and to respond generously', then the result might be 'something more like a conversation of equals – even something more like a Church'.

His final address on Sunday 3 August suggested he felt that the message had been taken to heart by most of the bishops. In the first place, he described the Conference as a time when everyone had taken responsibility for everyone else. People had been loyal to the process devised, he said, even when they had had serious difficulties and objections to it; and in so doing they had been loyal to one another. The commitment had been shown not only in people's 'steady' involvement in the work of the groups, but also in their reluctance to step outside the Conference, gather in small groups for meals away from the campus, and look for a platform or an audience elsewhere. Not that the bishops had overlooked theological principle in the interests of papering over the cracks. Citing various historical precedents, Rowan argued that 'every association of Christian individuals and groups makes some sort of "covenant" for the sake of mutual recognition, mutual gratitude and mutual learning'. This was the background against which church divisions should be handled. A fellow Christian might believe that they have 'profound fresh insight'. They might seek to persuade others of it. A healthy Church should give space for such exchanges. 'But the Christian with the new insight can't claim straightaway that *this* is now what the Church of God believes or intends; and it quite rightly takes a long time before any novelty can begin to find a way into the public liturgy, even if it has been widely agreed.' Herein lay the rationale behind appeals for moratoriums, including a moratorium on extra-provincial interventions. Such moves often implied that '*nothing* within a province, no provision made or pastoral care offered, can be recognisably and adequately Christian'; and this was a claim 'not lightly to be made by any Christian community regarding any other without grave breach of charity'.

In conclusion, he granted that there were still 'many questions' to be answered about the shape of the Covenant. Further spadework would be undertaken before the Primates' and ACC meetings in early 2009. 'We may not have put an end to all our problems – but the pieces are on the board. And in the months ahead it will be important to invite those absent from Lambeth to be involved in these next stages.'

British press reaction to the Conference was broadly positive, even though several correspondents complained of being treated with undue suspicion.[11] Yet peace, such as it is, in the Communion remains fragile. Bishop Scott-Joynt of Winchester, who has tried the Archbishop's patience more than once, thought that the decision to avoid resolutions on the basis of their potential divisiveness had had the effect of 'legitimising, in the life of the Conference and by implication in the Communion, the whole range of convictions about same-sex relationships'. Scott-Joynt continued to advocate a 'negotiated orderly separation' as the 'best and most fruitful way forward'.[12]

A rude reminder of the problems the Archbishop still faces came a few days after the bishops had dispersed, when *The Times*[13] published details of a pro-gay sentiment voiced by Rowan in correspondence written in 2000 and 2001 to Deborah Pitt, an Evangelical laywoman. The revelation was not substantially new. Its significance did not reside in any apparent novelty, despite the protestations of conservatives who cited it as evidence for the inevitability of schism, and liberals who saw in it a sign of the Archbishop's alleged *mauvaise foi*. The chief interest of the story lay in what it revealed about the determination of some Evangelicals to blacken Rowan's name. The correspondence had been sent to various religious affairs correspondents just as they were departing for Canterbury. As it happened, then, Rowan was fortunate. If the letters had been published a fortnight earlier, the Conference might have been sabotaged.

When the news broke, the Archbishop's colleagues rallied to his defence. George Cassidy, Bishop of Southwell and Nottingham, described the story as 'an old thing', which 'looked piqueish' because Lambeth 2008 had witnessed greater than expected levels of harmony. 'Rowan played a blinder at the Conference, showing masterful leadership in a non-pejorative and non-belligerent way. It was very subtle.'[14]

*   *   *

Lambeth Conferences now always feature a group photo of the bishops in their Convocation robes, with the Archbishop of Canterbury at the centre. It is appropriate to end by cropping the picture – and not just because this book is a biography. The future direction of Anglicanism remains difficult to predict with confidence, but the nature of Anglicanism's leader is not. In 2005, he received an honorary Doctorate of Civil Law from Oxford University, one of many similar awards. The tribute read out at the ceremony was well judged. Composed by Richard Jenkyns, this text is a polished piece of Latin (*Vanitas vanitatum, dixit Ecclesiastes, omnia vanitas; et biblia sacra aliis etiam locis monent fallacem et caducam esse huius mundi gloriam . . .*). The English translation runs as follows:

> Vanity of vanities, saith the Preacher, all is vanity; and in various places the Bible warns us that the glory of this world is deceitful and transitory. And yet the office of bishop has a certain splendour about it, so that the traditional *nolo episcopari* used once to seem somewhat insincere. But these days a prelate's life is less gracious and more burdensome, and so that man is especially to be praised who has the chance to spend his life in the shady groves of academe, and yet consents to undertake the business of administering the Church. Moreover, the Archbishop of Canterbury has to unite opposites: he holds the first place among the Queen's ministers in the order of precedence, and yet is required to despise worldly success; he is most exalted and most lowly, the shepherd of the shepherds, the servant of the servants of God.

We are indeed fortunate that at a time when the Church faces difficult challenges, we have a guide and governor who exhibits so many and various virtues. His writings embrace both divinity and human life, since as well as producing profound and penetrating theological studies he has written poems of subtle and delicate feeling. The Latin word *vates* means both bard and seer; he merits that label, since he writes about God with a poetic imagination, while his verse finds the spirit of God in people and places. 'Behold the great priest': he has the mind of a theologian, a saintly smile, the eye of a poet, and the beard of a prophet. He knows that an honorary doctorate is to be reckoned of small worth and to be classed with that vanity of which Ecclesiastes wrote; he asks not for our praise but for our prayers. Yet it is right and proper that we should bestow such honours as are in our power on a good and wise man; and so it is with sincere warmth that we offer him this pledge of our affection and symbol of our hope . . .

Nothing here is untrue; some of it is prophetic. Yet I suspect Jenkyns's words might have been more sharply angled had they been composed a few years later. An updated verdict would need to take account of suffering and courage in abundance. Further insight comes from one of the Archbishop's favourite poets. Rowan Williams has not endured public disgrace and imprisonment, of course, but there is still a parallel to be drawn between his qualities and situation and those of Oscar Wilde, as assessed by W. H. Auden: 'He had a private, even secret generosity to match the public generosity, the copiousness of his achievement. An enviable gift, then, though not always an enviable life – unless we say that in some cases the gift is indeed the life, and that the suffering is all part of the gift.'

Notes

Introduction

1 Rowan Williams, 'The Body's Grace' (LGCM, Oxford House, Derbyshire Street, London E2 6HG, 1989; reissued in 2003). The text of the lecture has also appeared on a variety of websites.

2 Peter Cornwell, *The Times Literary Supplement* (*TLS*), 22 June 2007.

3 Peter Akinola, 'Why I Object to Homosexuality', *Church Times* (*CT*), 4 July 2003.

4 David L. Edwards, obituary of Robert Runcie, *CT*, 14 July 2000.

5 Rowan Williams, *Independent on Sunday*, 5 April 1992.

6 Richard Harries, profile of Rowan Williams, *Observer*, 8 April 2007.

7 Oliver O'Donovan, in Rupert Shortt (ed.), *God's Advocates: Christian Thinkers in Conversation* (Darton, Longman and Todd (DLT), 2005), p. 268.

8 Rowan Williams, *Tokens of Trust: An Introduction to Christian Belief* (Canterbury Press, 2007).

9 Roger Scruton, *Gentle Regrets: Thoughts from a Life* (Continuum, 2005).

10 ibid., pp. 226–7.

11 *Alpha News*, November 2004–February 2005, pp. 20–1 (see also www.alpha.org).

12 Rowan Williams, *Christ on Trial: How the Gospel Unsettles Our Judgement* (Fount, 2000).
13 Harries, profile in *Observer*.
14 ibid.

1 Semper Sursum

1 Cynwil Williams, *Yr Archesgob Rowan Williams* (Gwasg Pantycelyn, 2006).
2 ibid., p. 26.
3 See, for example, David Martin, *On Secularization: Towards a Revised General Theory* (Ashgate, 2005).
4 *The Archbishop of Canterbury*, ITV, 17 June 2005.
5 Samuel Taylor Coleridge, *The Friend* (Princeton University Press, 1969), p. 524.
6 Rowan Williams, in Mick Gordon and Chris Wilkinson (eds), *Conversations on Religion* (Continuum, 2008), pp. 27–8.
7 Williams, *Yr Archesgob Rowan Williams*, p. 41.
8 ibid., pp. 40–1.
9 Rowan Williams, 'Menace and Atonement', *RSL – The Royal Society of Literature Magazine* (January 2004).
10 ibid.
11 Williams, *Conversations on Religion*, p. 28.
12 John A. T. Robinson, *Honest to God* (SCM Press, 1962).
13 A. R. Vidler (ed.), *Soundings: Essays Concerning Christian Understanding* (Cambridge University Press, 1963).
14 Rowan Williams, in an interview with the author in March 2007.
15 Rowan Williams, 'God the Son', a lecture given to a Church Union audience in Bristol. It formed part of a series delivered between 1997 and 2002 on the Trinity, atonement theory and several major spiritual writers. Recordings of the addresses may

be obtained from Adrian Jay Productions, 1 Mendip Cottages, Smithams Hill, East Harptree, Bristol BS40 6BZ.

16 Rowan Williams, in a lecture to theology students in Cambridge, 2 March 2002.

17 Shortt, *God's Advocates*, especially Chapters 1, 10 and 14.

18 Tom Wright, in conversation with the author, March 2007.

19 Iris Murdoch, *The Sovereignty of Good* (Routledge & Kegan Paul, 1970), p. 80.

2 Tradition and the Individual Talent

1 Theo Hobson, 'An Eye for the Other', *The Tablet*, 25 August 2007.

2 Blair's unfamiliarity with aspects of his tradition emerged when I interviewed the newly elected Labour Party leader for a *CT* profile in 1994. I asked whether he was an Anglo-Catholic. He replied, 'No, I'm Church of England.'

3 'The Spirit of the Age to Come', *Sobornost*, summer 1974, pp. 613–26.

4 'The Theology of Personhood: A Study of the Thought of Christos Yannaras', *Sobornost*, winter 1972, pp. 415–30.

5 'Eric Gill', *Sobornost*, winter–spring 1977–8, pp. 261–9.

6 Rowan Williams, 'Art: Taking Time and Making Sense', in T. Devonshire-Jones (ed.), *Images of Christ: Religious Iconography in Twentieth-Century British Art* (exhibition catalogue) (St Matthew's, Northampton, Centenary Art Committee, 1993), pp. 25–7.

7 ibid.

8 Samuel Wells, in Shortt (ed.), *God's Advocates*, p. 180.

9 Rowan Williams, *CT* interview, 6 December 2002.

10 See Chapter 9, 'The Ecclesiastical Tradition'. The thesis is available to readers at the Bodleian Library in Oxford.

11 D. E. Nineham, *Saint Mark* (Pelican, 1963), p. 235.

12 Solrunn Nes, *The Uncreated Light* (Eerdmans, 2007); Preface by David Bentley Hart.

13 ibid.

14 Rowan Williams, in conversation with Lesley Chamberlain, *Prospect* magazine (May 2007).

15 Kenneth Leech's initiative and its fruits are traced on websites such as www.anglocatholicsocialism.org.

16 His more questionable comments include a claim on the eve of the 2001 general election that 'the greater part of the world's population lives in a downward spiral of poverty'.

17 David Martin, in an interview with the author.

18 *The Gemini Poets* (Gemini Press, Cambridge, 1972); *Gemini Twin* (Gemini Press, Oxford, 1974); *Gemini 3* (Occasional Impressions, Huddersfield, 1987).

19 The lectures are currently unpublished.

20 *Ad Tuendam Fidem* ('For the Defence of the Faith'), Pope John Paul II's 1998 Apostolic Letter. This document was drafted by the then Cardinal Joseph Ratzinger.

21 Williams, 'Menace and Atonement'.

22 ibid.

23 Nicholas Boyle, *TLS*, 5 April 2007.

24 Rowan Williams, *The Wound of Knowledge* (DLT, 1979).

25 Michael Ramsey, *Theology*, January 1981, p. 52.

26 Rupert Shortt, *Rowan Williams: An Introduction* (DLT, 2003), pp. 91–102.

27 Williams, *The Wound of Knowledge*, p. 5.

28 ibid., p. 11.

29 Mike Higton, *Difficult Gospel: The Theology of Rowan Williams* (SCM Press, 2004), pp. 35–6.

30 Williams, *The Wound of Knowledge*, p. 72.

31 ibid., p. 87.

32 The lecture is currently unpublished.

3   Where All the Ladders Led

1 John Hick (ed.), *The Myth of God Incarnate* (SCM Press, 1977).

2 Shortt, *God's Advocates*, p. 17.

3 Stephen Sykes (ed.), *Karl Barth: Studies in his Theological Method* (Oxford University Press, 1979).

4 Hans Urs von Balthasar, *The Glory of the Lord*, *Theo-Drama* and *Theo-Logic*. An English–language edition of the trilogy was published in instalments by the Ignatius Press between 1990 and 2005.

5 Edward T. Oakes SJ, *TLS*, 13 April 2001.

6 Gerald Priestland, *The Case Against God* (Fount, 1984).

7 ibid., p. 110.

8 ibid., p. 111.

9 Rowan Williams, 'Religious Realism: On Not Quite Agreeing with Don Cupitt', reprinted in Mike Higton (ed.), *Wrestling with Angels: Conversations in Modern Theology* (SCM Press, 2008), pp. 228–54.

10 Don Cupitt, *Taking Leave of God* (SCM Press, 1980).

11 Rowan Williams, 'Interiority, Interiorization', in Alan Richardson and John Bowden (eds), *A New Dictionary of Christian Theology* (SCM Press, 1983), p. 304.

12 Rowan Williams, *Resurrection: Interpreting the Easter Gospel* (DLT, 1982).

13 J. L. Houlden, review of *Resurrection* in *Theology*, November 1982, pp. 452–3.

14 Donald MacKinnon, review of *Resurrection* in the *Scottish Journal of Theology*, 1983, p. 131.

15 Kenneth Leech and Rowan Williams (eds), *Essays Catholic and Radical* (Bowerdean, 1983).

16 G. K. Chesterton, *St Thomas Aquinas* (Hodder & Stoughton, 1933), p. 24.

17 References to the report are drawn from the *CT* digest, carried on 19 October 1979.

18 A further example of Rowan Williams's theological discussion of homosexuality comes in 'Knowing Myself in Christ', in Timothy Bradshaw (ed.), *The Way Forward? Christian Voices on Homosexuality and the Church* (Hodder & Stoughton, 1997). See also 'Is there a Christian Sexual Ethic?' in Rowan Williams, *Open to Judgement: Sermons and Addresses* (DLT, 1994).

19 N. T. Wright, *The New Testament and the People of God* (SPCK, 1992). This book forms the first instalment of a multi-volume series, 'Christian Origins and the Question of God'.

20 Rowan Williams, *Arius: Heresy and Tradition* (DLT, 1987). A core argument of this book is that Arius was more influenced than previously thought by strands in contemporary Neoplatonism. This caused the arch-heretic to criticise aspects of what Williams terms the 'middle-Platonic consensus' among Christian theologians. This (the thesis goes) coloured Arius's views about issues such as the relationship between ultimate reality and the created order, and the status of the human intellect.

21 Rowan Williams, 'A Theological Response to AIDS', in *AIDS: A Diocesan Response* (Oxford Diocesan Board for Social Responsibility, 1987).

22 *CT*, 20 May 1988.

23 Rowan Williams, Introduction to *Speaking Love's Name: Homosexuality: Some Catholic and Socialist Reflections* (The Jubilee Group, 1988).

24 ibid.

25 Williams, 'The Body's Grace', p. 5.

26 ibid., p. 8.

27 Rowan Williams, 'Postmodern Theology and the Judgment of the World', in Frederic B. Burnham (ed.), *Postmodern Theology: Christian Faith in a Pluralist World* (Harper & Row, 1989).

28 ibid., p. 93.

29 Rowan Williams, 'Affirming Tradition', in *Affirming Catholicism* (a pamphlet published by the Affirming Catholicism movement in 1990), p. 2.

30 See for example, Rowan Williams, 'Between Politics and Meta-physics: Reflections in the wake of Gillian Rose', *Modern Theology*, January 1995.
31 Rowan Williams, *Teresa of Avila* (reissued by Continuum, 2000).

4 Fox and Hedgehog

1 Rowan Williams, 'Butler's *Western Mysticism*: Towards an Assessment', *The Downside Review* (July 1984).
2 Rowan Williams, in an interview with Charles Moore, *Daily Telegraph*, 12 February 2003.
3 All quotations relating to St Teresa of Avila and Meister Eckhart are drawn from the Church Union lecture series in Bristol (see above).
4 ibid.
5 Thomas Merton, *Conjectures of a Guilty Bystander* (Doubleday, 1966), p. 156.
6 Williams, *Tokens of Trust*, p. 33.
7 ibid., p. 33.
8 ibid., p. 33.
9 ibid., p. 35.
10 ibid., p. 35.
11 ibid., p. 41.
12 ibid., p. 44.
13 ibid., p. 44.
14 ibid., p. 57.
15 ibid., p. 66.
16 ibid., p. 68.
17 ibid., pp. 86–8.
18 ibid., p. 92.
19 Williams, 'The Holy Spirit' (Bristol Church Union lecture); see also Shortt, *Rowan Williams: An Introduction*, pp. 86–90.

20 Williams, *Tokens of Trust*, p. 116.

21 ibid., p. 122.

22 ibid., pp. 124–5.

23 Garry Williams, *The Theology of Rowan Williams* (The Latimer Trust, 2002), p. 23.

24 Williams, *Open to Judgement*, p. 145.

25 Williams, *Tokens of Trust*, pp. 106–10.

26 Lucy Beckett, *TLS*, 24 August 2007.

27 Theo Hobson, *Anarchy, Church and Utopia: Rowan Williams on Church* (DLT, 2005).

28 David Martin, *CT*, 27 May 2005.

29 ibid.

30 *An Archbishop Like This*, broadcast on Advent Sunday, 2002.

31 Rowan Williams, *The Truce of God* (Fount, 1983). (A revised version of the book was published by Canterbury Press in 2005.)

32 ibid., p. 16.

33 ibid., p. 17.

34 ibid., pp. 18–19.

35 ibid., p. 19.

36 O'Donovan, *God's Advocates*, pp. 262–3.

37 ibid., p. 263.

38 Stephen Sykes, *Power and Christian Theology* (Continuum, 2006).

39 Oliver O'Donovan, 'Rowan Williams: The New Archbishop of Canterbury. A Symposium', *Pro Ecclesia*, vol. XII, no. 1.

40 O'Donovan, *God's Advocates*, p. 262.

41 Williams, *The Truce of God*, p. 30.

42 ibid., p. 32.

43 ibid., p. 50.

44 ibid., pp. 118–19.

5   The Newport Years

1 Bob Jackson, 'Church Decline and Growth in the Diocese of Monmouth', a report for the diocesan conference, 15 May 2004.

2 See, for example, Owen Chadwick, *Michael Ramsey: A Life* (Oxford University Press (OUP), 1991), p. 80. Chadwick quotes the definition of episcopal ministry given by Ramsey at his first diocesan conference as Bishop of Durham.

3 Rowan Williams, in *Cambridge* (the magazine of the Cambridge Society), January 2005.

4 See www.lambethconference.org/1998/news.

5 'A Pastoral Statement to Lesbian and Gay Anglicans from some Member Bishops of the Lambeth Conference'; see www.whosoever.org, the online magazine for gay, lesbian, bisexual and transgendered Christians.

6 Rowan Williams, 'Our Differences Need Not Destroy Us', *The Tablet*, 8 April 2000.

7 Rowan Williams, 'No Life, here – No Joy, Terror or Tears', *CT*, 17 July 1998.

8 Fred Burnham's recollections are drawn from a video he made giving a minute-by-minute account of his experiences on 11 September 2001. I am grateful to him for supplying me with a copy.

9 Rowan Williams, *CT*, 14 September 2001.

10 See, for example, Oliver O'Donovan, *God's Advocates*, p. 268.

11 Rowan Williams, *Writing in the Dust: Reflections on 11th September and its Aftermath* (Hodder & Stoughton, 2001).

12 ibid., p. 25.

13 Peter Mullen's comments were reported by Andrew Brown in his round-up of religious affairs coverage, *CT*, 26 July 2002.

14 Rowan Williams, *Open to Judgement: Sermons and Addresses* (DLT, 1994).

15 Rowan Williams (ed.), *Sergii Bulgakov: Towards a Russian Political Theology* (T. & T. Clark, 1999).

16 Rowan Williams, *Lost Icons: Reflections on Cultural Bereavement* (T. & T. Clark, 2000).

17 Rowan Williams, *On Christian Theology* (Blackwell, 2000).

18 Geoffrey Rowell, Kenneth Stevenson and Rowan Williams (eds), *Love's Redeeming Work* (OUP, 2000).

19 The lecture can be read in an online archive, www.hayfestival.co.uk.

20 Williams, *On Christian Theology*, pp. xiii–xvi.

21 Rowan Williams, *After Silent Centuries* (Perpetua Press, 1994).

22 Rowan Williams, *Remembering Jerusalem* (Perpetua Press, 2001).

23 Rowan Williams, *The Poems of Rowan Williams* (Perpetua Press, 2002).

24 John Greening, *TLS*, 19 and 26 December 2003.

6 On the Front Line

1 George Carey, *Know the Truth: A Memoir* (HarperCollins, 2004), p. 439.

2 David L. Edwards, 'Now Make the Job Fit the Man', *CT*, 17 May 2002.

3 *The Tablet*, 13 April 2002.

4 *Daily Mail*, 24 July 2002.

5 *CT*, 26 July 2002.

6 Damian Thompson, 'Fighting Primates', *Spectator*, 3 August 2002.

7 I am grateful to Professor O'Donovan for supplying me with the letter, and to Dr Williams for permission to reproduce it.

8 *CT*, 16 August 2002.

9 Alister McGrath, 'The Writings of Rowan Uncovered', *Church of England Newspaper* (*CEN*), 8 August 2002.

10 Francis Bridger and Christina Rees, 'Evangelicalism and a Lesson in Seismology', *CT*, 8 November 2002.

11 An extract from the address, headlined 'Why I Believe in the Bible', was carried in the *CT* of 18 October 2002.

12 ibid.

13 Rowan Williams, 'Defending the Unborn Human', *The Times*, 24 July 2002.

14 Unless otherwise indicated, texts of all the Archbishop's speeches and lectures referred to in this book are available on his website (www.archbishopofcanterbury.org.uk) and catalogued chronologically.

15 Matthew Parris, 'For God's Sake, Archbishop, this isn't the State we're in', *The Times*, 21 December 2002.

16 Ferdinand Mount, 'Tony and the Turbulent Priest Get Serious', *The Sunday Times*, 29 December 2002.

17 *Guardian*, 25 September 2002.

18 Rowan Williams, 'Neighbours from Hell – Does it Have to be Like This?', *CT*, 12 April 2002.

19 Rowan Williams, *CT*, 6 December 2002.

20 Rowan Williams, Preface to Duncan Dormor, Jack McDonald and Jeremy Caddick (eds), *Anglicanism: The Answer to Modernity* (Continuum, 2003).

21 *CT*, 6 December 2002.

22 Williams, Preface to *Anglicanism: The Answer to Modernity*.

23 *CT*, 21 February 2003.

24 For the full text, see www.archbishopofcanterbury.org.uk.

25 Andrew Brown, *CT*, 7 March 2003.

26 Stephen Bates, *A Church at War: Anglicans and Homosexuality* (Hodder & Stoughton, 2005), p. 197.

27 The first edition of Bates's book was published by I. B. Tauris in 2004. It was reissued in an expanded form the following year.

28 John S. Peart-Binns, *A Heart in my Head: A Biography of Richard Harries* (Continuum, 2007), Chapter 19.

29 Jeffrey John, *Permanent, Faithful, Stable: Christian Same-Sex Relationships* (Affirming Catholicism, 2000).

30 Peart–Binns, *A Heart in my Head*, p. 208.

31 *CT*, 27 June 2003.

32 ibid.

33 Bates, *A Church at War*, p. 219.

34 Paul Vallely, *CT*, 11 July 2003.

35 O'Donovan, 'Rowan Williams: The New Archbishop of Canterbury. A Symposium'.

7   The Windsor Way

1 *The Virginia Report* (Morehouse, 1999), p. 40.

2 Rowan Williams, General Synod Presidential Address, 14 July 2003.

3 Libby Purves, *The Times*, 15 July 2003.

4 *Guardian*, 15 July 2003.

5 *CT*, 19 September 2003.

6 *New Directions*, Autumn 2003.

7 For a brief discussion of the lecture, see Shortt, *Rowan Williams: An Introduction*, pp. 63–4.

8 See, for example, John Cornwell, *The Pope in Winter: The Dark Face of John Paul II's Papacy* (Viking, 2004), p. 267.

9 *New Directions*, Autumn 2003.

10 *CT*, 24 October 2003.

11 The Commission's members were the Most Revd Robin Eames, Primate of All Ireland, chairman; Canon Alyson Barnett-Cowan, Director of Faith, Worship and Ministry, Anglican Church of Canada; the Rt Revd David Beetge, Dean of the Church of the Province of Southern Africa; Professor Norman Doe, Director of the Centre for Law and Religion, Cardiff University, Wales; the Rt Revd Mark Dyer, Director of Spiritual Formation, Virginia Theological Seminary, USA; the Most Revd Drexel Gomez,

Primate of the West Indies; the Most Revd Josiah Iduwo-Fearon, Archbishop of Kaduna, Nigeria; the Revd Dorothy Lau, Director of the Hong Kong Sheng Kung Hui Welfare Council; Anne McGavin, Advocate, formerly Legal Adviser to the College of Bishops of the Scottish Episcopal Church (resigned for personal reasons after first meeting); the Most Revd Bernard Malango, Primate of Central Africa; Dr Esther Mombo, Academic Dean of St Paul's United Theological Seminary, Limuru, Kenya; the Most Revd Barry Morgan, Primate of Wales; Chancellor Rubie Nottage, Chancellor of the West Indies; the Rt Revd John Paterson, Bishop of Auckland, New Zealand, and Chairman of the Anglican Consultative Council (ACC); Dr Jenny Te Paa, Principal of St John's College, Auckland, New Zealand; the Rt Revd James Terom, Moderator of the Church of North India; the Rt Revd Tom Wright, Bishop of Durham. Secretary: Canon Gregory Cameron, Director of Anglican Communion Affairs and Studies, Anglican Communion Office. Legal consultant: Canon John Rees, Legal Adviser to the ACC.

12 *CT*, 24 October 2003.

13 *Today*, BBC Radio 4, 17 October 2003.

14 Andrew Brown, *CT*, 19/26 December 2003.

15 *CT*, 24 October 2003.

16 See Rowan Williams, 'No Life Here – No Joy, Terror or Tears' (*CT*, 17 July 1998). The essay was a comprehensive rebuttal of Spong's revisionist approach to the creeds.

17 Gene Robinson, interview, *CT*, 2 May 2008.

18 Rowan Williams, *The Dwelling of the Light: Praying with Icons of Christ* (Canterbury Press, 2003).

19 Rowan Williams, *Ponder these Things* (Canterbury Press, 2002).

20 This is the view of Professor Robin Cormack of the Courtauld Institute in London, who feels that the Archbishop sometimes interprets icons in an undifferentiated way, 'like treating Roman and Greek sculpture as essentially the same thing'.

21 Rowan Williams, *Silence and Honey Cakes: The Wisdom of the Desert* (Lion, 2003).

22 *CT*, 5 March 2004.

23 Rowan Williams, *Guardian*, 10 March 2004.

24 Rowan Williams, *Daily Telegraph*, 17 March 2004. The paper carried an edited transcript of his debate with Philip Pullman.

25 Rowan Williams, *The Times*, 26 May 2004.

26 ibid.

27 ibid.

28 Rowan Williams, *Observer*, 11 July 2004.

29 *CT*, 15 October 2004.

30 *CT*, 22 October 2004.

31 Tom Wright, 'Face to Faith', *Guardian*, 23 October 2004.

32 Marilyn McCord Adams, 'How to Quench the Spirit', *CT*, 29 October 2004.

33 Rowan Williams, *Sunday Telegraph*, 2 January 2005.

34 ibid.

35 Bates, *A Church at War*, p. 287.

36 *CT*, 4 March 2005.

37 Bates, *A Church at War*, p. 291.

38 Robinson, *CT*, 2 May 2008.

39 *CT*, 4 February 2005.

40 David Martin, review of Philip Jenkins, *The New Faces of Christianity: Believing the Bible in the Global South* (OUP, 2006), *CT*, 23 February 2007.

8   Multiple Echo

1 Peter Sedgwick, in conversation with the author.

2 Rowan Williams, in *Cathedral*, an eight-part ITV series. The programmes were produced by Peter Williams Television.

3 Rowan Williams, *Sunday Times*, 19 March 2005.

4 Rowan Williams, in conversation with the author, May 2005.

5 Andrew Brown, *CT*, 24 June 2005.

6 Peter Akinola's remarks were reported in the *Sunday Times*, 31 July 2005.

7 ibid.

8 Giles Fraser, *CT*, 5 August 2005.

9 *CT*, 4 November 2005.

10 *CT*, 25 November 2005.

11 ibid.

12 ibid.

13 *CT*, 10 February 2006.

14 *CT*, 17 February 2006.

15 Andrew Brown, *CT*, 10 March 2006.

16 *Guardian*, 21 March 2006.

17 ibid.

18 ibid.

19 ibid.

20 *Faithful Cities: A Call for Celebration, Vision and Justice* (Methodist Publishing House and Church House Publishing, 2006).

21 Rowan Williams, *Anglican Identities* (DLT, 2004).

22 Rowan Williams, *Why Study the Past?: The Quest for the Historical Church* (DLT, 2005).

23 Rowan Williams, *Grace and Necessity: Reflections on Art and Love* (Continuum, 2005).

24 Peter Cornwell, *TLS*, 9 July 2004.

25 Eamon Duffy, *TLS*, 5 August 2005.

26 Richard Dawkins, *The God Delusion* (Bantam Press, 2006).

27 Williams, in *God's Advocates*, pp. 6–7.

28 Rowan Williams, Series Introduction to *Dostoevsky: Language, Faith and Fiction* (Continuum, 2008).

9 Bushfires

1 Stephen Sykes, in Marsha L. Dutton and Patrick Terrell Gray (eds), *One Lord, One Faith, One Baptism: Studies in Christian Ecclesiality and Ecumenism in Honor of J. Robert Wright* (Eerdmans, 2006).

2 Marilyn McCord Adams, preaching at Christ Church Cathedral, Oxford. An abridged version of the sermon appeared in the *CT*, 14 July 2006.

3 Andrew Goddard, *CEN*, 29 June 2007.

4 *CT*, 7 July 2006.

5 Rowan Williams, *Today*, BBC Radio 4, 20 July 2006.

6 Rowan Williams, *Observer*, 6 August 2006.

7 *CT*, 27 October 2006.

8 Rowan Williams, *The Times*, 27 October 2006.

9 *Catholic Herald*, 17 November 2006; *Daily Telegraph*, 16 November 2006.

10 *Daily Mail*, 17 November 2006.

11 *CT*, 19 January 2007.

12 Bishop Marshall was referring to an interview the Archbishop had given in August 2006 to the Dutch Christian daily newspaper, *Nederlands Dagblad*. Challenged about his views on sexuality, he said that he did not necessarily stand by everything he had ever said and written before becoming Archbishop of Canterbury.

13 This text is entitled 'Rowan Williams and Scripture' and can be read online at www.anglicanspread.org.

14 The essay was republished in Eugene F. Rogers (ed.), *Theology and Sexuality: Classic and Contemporary Readings* (Blackwell, 2001).

15 *CT*, 20 April 2007.

16 See Andrew Brown, *CT*, 11 May 2007.

17 Williams, *Dostoevsky: Language, Faith and Fiction*, Introduction.

18 ibid.

19 ibid.

20 ibid.

21 ibid.

22 Rowan Williams, *Headwaters* (Perpetua Press, 2008), pp. 23–5.

23 ibid., p. 26.

24 ibid., p. 59.

25 Rowan Williams, Preface to Adrian Whittaker (ed.), *Be Glad: An Incredible String Band Compendium* (Helter Skelter Publishing, 2003).

26 ibid.

27 *Time*, 18 June 2007.

28 *Daily Telegraph*, 23 July 2007.

29 *CT*, 3 August 2007.

30 ibid.

31 *CT*, 24 August 2007.

32 *CT*, 7 September 2007.

33 *CT*, 28 September 2007.

34 ibid.

35 *The World Tonight*, BBC Radio 4, 5 October 2007.

36 *Emel*, November 2007.

37 *Sunday Times*, 25 November 2007.

38 David Aaronovitch, *The Times*, 12 February 2008.

39 ibid.

40 *Sun*, 8 February 2008.

41 Paul Vallely, *CT*, 15 February 2008.

42 *What is the Point of the Archbishop of Canterbury?*, BBC Radio 4, 11 March 2008.

10   Positive Capability

1 Graham James, 'Resolving to Confer and Conferring to Resolve: The Anglican Way', in Kenneth Stevenson (ed.), *A Fallible Church* (DLT, 2008).

2 W. M. Jacob, *The Making of the Anglican Church Worldwide* (SPCK, 1997).

3 Owen Chadwick, *The Victorian Church Volume 2* (A. & C. Black, 1972).

4 R. T. Davidson (ed.), *The Lambeth Conferences of 1867, 1878, 1888* (SPCK, 1889).

5 Alan Stephenson, *The First Lambeth Conference, 1867* (SPCK, 1967), and *Anglicanism and the Lambeth Conferences* (SPCK, 1978).

6 *CT*, 4 July 2006.

7 Rowan Williams, *CT*, 11 July 2008.

8 ibid.

9 ibid.

10 See the Lambeth Conference website, www.lambethconference.org.

11 See, for example, Martin Beckford, *CEN*, 8 August 2008 and Pat Ashworth, *CT*, 8 August 2008.

12 *CT*, 15 August 2008.

13 *The Times*, 7 August 2008.

14 *CT*, 15 August 2008.

Picture Acknowledgements

© Ian Davies Photography: 5 above. Philip Hollis/*Daily Telegraph*: 15 above. Getty Images: 9 below, 11 above, 14 above. PA Photos: 9, 10, 11 below, 12 above, 13, 14 below, 16 above. Reuters/Antony Njuguna: 12 below. Jim Rosenthal: 15 below.

All other photos courtesy of Rowan Williams.

Every reasonable effort has been made to contact the copyright holders, but if there are any errors or omissions, Hodder & Stoughton will be pleased to insert the appropriate acknowledgement in any subsequent printing of this publication.

Index